Culture in the Anteroom

Culture in the Anteroom

The Legacies of
Siegfried Kracauer

Edited by
Gerd Gemünden
Johannes von Moltke

THE UNIVERSITY OF MICHIGAN PRESS • ANN ARBOR

Published in the United States of America by
The University of Michigan Press
Manufactured in the United States of America
⊚ Printed on acid-free paper

2015   2014   2013   2012   4   3   2   1

A CIP catalog record for this book is available from the British Library.

Library of Congress Cataloging-in-Publication Data

Culture in the anteroom : the legacies of Siegfried Kracauer / edited
   by Gerd Gemünden, Johannes von Moltke.
      p. cm.
   Includes index.
      ISBN 978-0-472-07167-8 (cloth : alk. paper) — ISBN 978-0-472-
   05167-0 (pbk. : alk. paper) — ISBN 978-0-472-02815-3 (e-book)
      1. Kracauer, Siegfried, 1889–1966—Criticism and interpretation.
   2. Kracauer, Siegfried, 1889–1966—Philosophy.   I. Gemünden, Gerd, 1959–
   II. Von Moltke, Johannes, 1966–
   PT2621.R135Z585   2012
   834'.912—dc23   2011045479

In memoriam
Miriam Bratu Hansen

Contents

Acknowledgments

Many of the essays gathered in this volume were first presented at the 2008 conference "Looking After Siegfried Kracauer" at Dartmouth College, which laid the foundation for *Culture in the Anteroom*. We are grateful to the many individuals and institutions that made this event possible. These include, foremost, the Leslie Center for the Humanities, its director Adrian Randolph and its chief administrator Isabel Weatherdon; the German Academic Exchange Service (DAAD); the Max Kade Foundation in New York City; the Consulate General of the Federal Republic of Germany at Boston; the John Sloan Dickey Center for International Understanding; Provost Barry Scherr; the Ted and Helen Geisel Third Century Professorship in the Humanities; and the Dartmouth Professorship in German Language and its holder, Bruce Duncan.

At the University of Michigan Press, we are indebted to our editor, Tom Dwyer, who supported the project from its first stages onward, and to Alexa Ducsay who led the manuscript expertly and efficiently through production. At Michigan, we also had the assistance of Marc-Niclas Heckner, currently a doctoral student in German and Screen Arts & Cultures; we are grateful for his diligent help in preparing the manuscript.

Like all Kracauer scholarship, work on this collection has benefited enormously from the expertly maintained collection of his *Nachlass* at the German Literary Archive in Marbach; we are grateful to its director and staff for their assistance with research questions and illustrations. We would like to use this opportunity also to thank Susan Bibeau in Humanities Resources at Dartmouth for her layout work, as well as Karola Gramann, who curated the Asta Nielsen program that accompanied the conference. Nia Perivolaropoulou graciously made time for a stimulating conversation over coffee in Paris about the past and present French reception of Kracauer.

In our introduction, we make a case for both the canonicity and the contemporaneity of Kracauer's cultural critique; if this argument has any plausibility today, it is thanks to the tireless work of Miriam Hansen. Well before the rediscovery of Kracauer's Weimar work in the wake of his centennial, Hansen consistently championed Kracauer's writings as theorizations of modernity, of cinema's public sphere, and as contributions to Critical Theory; her research on the "Marseille Notebooks" single-handedly shifted the ossified debates on *Theory of Film* onto a new, historical ground that brought into view the book's lasting relevance and its contemporaneity. At the time of this writing, Miriam's late work *Cinema and Experience* is still forthcoming, a poignant temporal suspension in which we recollect her forceful presence, her sharp wit, her meticulous attention to nuance, and her capacious vision of cinema's role in modernity as much as of its shifting functions alongside various new media today.

At the conference where this volume originated, we all benefited from this presence and wit: consistently engaged in every discussion, Miriam would raise the speakers' contributions to a higher level through her probing questions that could be gentle and forceful at once, a model of constructive, erudite critique that future scholars of Kracauer, the Frankfurt School, Cinema and Media Studies, and in the humanities at large can only hope to emulate. We dedicate this volume to Miriam's memory.

Introduction

Kracauer's Legacies

Gerd Gemünden and Johannes von Moltke

Sometimes that which is buried under an imposing either-or may shine forth from a casual aperçu written in the margin of a close-up.[1]

Kracauer's Cultural Critique

In one of many grant applications composed in exile—this one dated 14 October 1942 and addressed to the Guggenheim Foundation—Siegfried Kracauer proposed to write the "History of German Film" that would later become *From Caligari to Hitler*. In this proposal, he lays out a methodological commitment to "seemingly unimportant details" that will be familiar to readers of Kracauer's works—from his Weimar essays on mass culture through his final, posthumous book on historiography. Perhaps because of the demands of grant writing, this formulation of that commitment is particularly succinct in laying out the importance of "little things" and their relationship to "history's moving forces" for the humanities at large. Characteristically, Kracauer develops this broad claim by way of a seemingly remote reference—in this case, to farming and engineering—as if to model the very practice he is advocating.

> Both the farmer and the engineer know something about the importance of seemingly unimportant details. Many small factors, they know, must work together to ripen the corn or to make a complicated machine function. Their experience teaches them to distrust the pretensions of pure ideas while at the same time they find in little things more than just little things. Such an outlook proves helpful, too, in the field of human-

ities, where any survey interested solely in the display of ideas runs the risk of missing the ideas' very significance. . . . To focus directly upon ideas is at any rate a sure means never to grasp them. But it may well happen that a close scrutiny of some minor event of the kind favored on the screen allows one secretly to watch history's moving forces in full action. Ideas manifest themselves rather in by-ways, in unobtrusive facts. And in examining these facts, it is often as though one looked through a narrow window at strange scenes that, outdoors, would be entirely invisible.[2]

This passage is richly evocative of many assumptions and motifs that guide Kracauer's thinking through its various phases from the early Weimar years through his success as a cultural critic with the *Frankfurter Zeitung* in the 1920s and early 1930s, to his exile in France (1933–41) and then in America, where, during the last quarter century of his life, he would write his major books on film and history: *From Caligari to Hitler: A Psychological History of the German Film* (1947), *Theory of Film: The Redemption of Physical Reality* (1960), and *History: The Last Things Before the Last* (1969, published posthumously). The brief methodological sketch hints at Kracauer's dialectical interest in "unobtrusive facts" *and* in "history's moving forces"; his phenomenological approach to the "many small factors [that] make a complicated machine function;" the emphasis on the epistemological power of vision, on "*watch*[*ing*] history's moving forces" on screen and finding a perspective—if not a medium (film)—from which to perceive the otherwise invisible. In that perspective, we might even find a resonance of the extraterritorial position that Kracauer defined as the rightful place of the cultural critic. Like the exile he himself became after 1933, and like the historian whose ideal vantage point Kracauer would locate in an exilic "near vacuum of extra-territoriality,"[3] here we find the critic peering "through a narrow window at strange scenes" of which he is not part, but that he is privileged to see—whereas those who populate those same scenes "outdoors" see nothing.[4]

In addition to these motifs, however, the cited passage also enacts a structural paradigm of Kracauer's thinking: his tendency to work through oppositions such as that between "little things" and "pure ideas" by keeping them in motion, "in a fluid state," as he would put it: how else to resolve the apparent oxymoron of "find[ing] in little things more than just little things" or seeing what is invisible?[5] This commitment to conceptual fluidity is in evidence from an early essay that sides with "those who wait," through the give-and-take between formative and realistic "tendencies" of photography, between cinema's powers to "record" and "reveal," all the way to the methodological reflections at the close of *History* regarding "top-down" and "bottom-up" modes of inquiry and the relationship between the general and the particular. Fueling these various struggles to keep binary alternatives in suspension, we submit, is the underlying methodological commitment to a unique form of *cultural critique,* for which Kracauer gradually has been gaining posthumous recognition.

We deploy the notion of cultural critique here as distinct, on the one hand, from cultural criticism, which would exhaust itself in the attentive treatment of individual objects; and on the other hand, from cultural theory, which would join philosophy in its construction of overarching concepts for defining the very notion of culture itself. Rather we understand cultural critique after Kracauer to occupy a middle ground—what he would call an "intermediary area"—between these two poles, which it subsumes in turn. Constantly attuned to the twin demands of criticism and theory, Kracauer's work blends the kind of "practical criticism" enabled by experience with a "theoretical criticism" enabled by synoptic perspectives and the power of abstraction.[6] The essays in this volume combine to explicate this approach and chart paths for exploring its uses across the many disciplines that Kracauer's work intersects—from architecture to film studies, from literature to museum studies, from journalism to ethnography, from sociology to anthropology, from the history of art to media studies, from photography to the digital turn.

Looking back at Kracauer's development, one might be tempted to say that criticism and theory battled for primacy in his work, trading places in the hierarchy of his pursuits as his life circumstances changed. On the one hand, we have his massive corpus of film and cultural criticism for the *Frankfurter Zeitung* during the 1920s, for the *Basler National-Zeitung* during the 1930s, and for the "little magazines" of the New York intellectual scene in the 1940s and 1950s; cultural criticism in this sense was a job at first, then a vocation as his reputation as an editor grew during the late Weimar Republic, and then again a way to make ends meet in exile. On the other hand, there are the magisterial tomes: first, an attempt to define the relatively new discipline of sociology, then his two most famous books devoted to film: *From Caligari to Hitler* mapped the idea of Weimar's decline onto its films, while *Theory of Film* places the emphasis squarely on the "idea" of cinema, offering a theory that insists on the medium's ability to "record and reveal physical reality."[7] *History,* the final book, would again seem to fall squarely on the side of theory in that it explicitly undertakes to write, not a history, but a historiographical intervention, a theory of history. Together, these would appear to mark rather clearly the place of "pure ideas" in Kracauer's oeuvre, his intention to make a theoretical contribution alongside his production as a critic.

But a closer look reveals the complex relationships between theory and criticism in Kracauer's work. In many ways, that relationship is implicit throughout—one need only think of the theoretical import of a piece of criticism such as the article "The Mass Ornament," or note to what degree both of the film books, for all their teleological and normative thrust as exemplars of (classical) film theory, are really sustained works of criticism and would perhaps be read more profitably as such. It is hardly surprising, then, that the relationship between criticism and theory, between the "close-up" of close reading and the "long shot" of generalizing interpretation, becomes the object of sustained reflection toward the end of his life. In the final chapter of *History: The Last Things Before the Last*, Kracauer revisits almost verbatim the concerns he laid out for the Guggenheim Foundation some two decades earlier. Building on the book's founding analogy between photographic media and historiography, or between "camera reality" and "historical reality," Kracauer outlines here the importance of "thinking *through* things, not above them."[8] This means that he does tend to endorse a "bottom-up" approach to historiography, much as he approvingly notes the farmer's attention to detail as an "outlook [that] proves helpful . . . in the field of humanities" at large. Simultaneously, however, Kracauer will insist on what he calls a "'side-by-side' principle"—a conceptual approach that refuses to reify either the concrete detail or the overarching abstraction but focuses on a realm in between. In the filmic terms that he preferred, we might say that, as opposed to the isolated, decontextualized detail of the close-up and the omniscient, bird's-eye perspective of the long shot, Kracauer proposes to investigate the medium shot. Not coincidentally, this is a shot scale generally measured by reference to the human figure: for Kracauer, the human—or, as he puts it in the introduction to *History*, the humane—is the measure of all things; even if it is often precisely the "things" themselves, the world of material objects, that furnish the material of Kracauer's analyses—from urban spaces to film sets, from everyday objects to the thinglike geometry of the Tiller Girls. In the medium shot, the privileged epistemological scale of Kracauer as a visual thinker, these objects lead a particular form of existence: neither immediately present to unreflective perception as in the close-up nor minimized to the point of insignificance as in the long shot, like the objects of Kracauer's cultural critique more generally they need to be *read*. For Kracauer, this means not to decode them by reference to some overarching cultural or semiotic code, but to restore to them their ambiguity—a concept that is as central to Kracauer's realism as it is to that of his French contemporary, André Bazin.

In the "intermediary area" of the medium shot, "ambiguity is of the essence," writes Kracauer. This is not to advocate a relativist stance on cultural production but to resist the abstraction of top-down theorizing as much as the myopia of decontextualized "readings" in the vein of New Criticism. Throughout his work, Kracauer developed notions of historical and cultural study that proceed from the particular and the "hitherto unnamed"—from the "terra incognita in the hollows between the lands we know." He dubbed this approach "anteroom thinking" to distinguish it from the deductive, top-down theorizing that proceeds from systematic certainties (an intellectual practice that, as Heide Schlüpmann argues in her contribution to this volume, underscores Kracauer's proximity to feminism). From his early Weimar years through the decades of his French and American exile, Kracauer modeled this form of cultural critique as a way of illuminating even the most ephemeral surface appearances and probing some of the most intractable constellations of modernity.

Kracauer's Canonicity

To recover the relevance of Kracauer's work necessarily involves reconstructing its reception; indeed, the present volume aims to intervene in the latter's trajectory by redirecting some of the paths along which Kracauer has habitually been read, as well as opening up new avenues for exploration. Our aim, in keeping with the arguments advanced both explicitly and by implication in the contributions that follow, is to pursue two lines of inquiry that seem incompatible only at first glance. On the one hand, we wish to *historicize* Kracauer's work and its reception by placing it in context, reconsidering the logics of its (selective) canonization as well as recovering some of the overlooked aspects of his wide-ranging contributions. On the other hand, in keeping with our claim that Kracauer's cultural critique retains its relevance for the present, we want to insist on the *contemporaneity* of his work, its potential for invigorating ongoing debates in the humanities—from questions about posthumanist ethics or the "digital turn" to the place of interdisciplinary work. To open up these vistas, however, requires that we first account for the reception of Kracauer's work to date, which has tended to follow a somewhat limited double track by pegging Kracauer either to the history of the Frankfurt School of Critical Theory or to the trajectory of so-called classical theory—whether sociological or realist—within film studies.

Although the film-theoretical reception of Kracauer arguably predates a broader appreciation of his work in relation to its roots in the intellectual culture of the Weimar Republic and the Frankfurt School, the link to thinkers such as Theodor W. Adorno, Walter Benjamin, and others certainly precedes Kracauer's contributions to film studies in terms of his own intellectual biography. In the Anglo-American context, those links were first highlighted by a conference, exhibition, and journal publication at Columbia University on the occasion of Kracauer's hundredth birthday,[9] and they have since been explored in numerous venues—ranging from Miriam Hansen's enormously important work on Kracauer in the context of "the other Frankfurt School" through the publication of Kracauer's correspondence with Benjamin and, most recently, Adorno.[10] These contributions have established a crucial intellectual context for understanding Kracauer's work; but at the same time, they have tended to place Kracauer in the large shadow cast by Adorno and Benjamin.

Though he was never a member of the Institut für Sozialforschung itself,[11] Kracauer's interactions with some of the leading figures of the group were numerous and significant enough to warrant including him in their intellectual orbit: he befriended and mentored the young Adorno, with whom he would entertain a lifelong correspondence; he shared the experience of French exile as well as many conversations with Benjamin, whose essays he had championed at the *Frankfurter Zeitung* and who had returned the favor with a glowing review of Kracauer's *Die Angestellten* (*The Salaried Masses*, 1930). The two men would spend Benjamin's last days in Marseille together before the latter committed suicide and Kracauer managed to escape to the United States via Lisbon, as Benjamin had also hoped to do. While Kracauer's relations with Max Horkheimer, the head of the institute during its exile in New York and California, appear to have been cordial at best, he was able during his U.S. years to rely heavily on the help of Leo Löwenthal, another Frankfurt School affiliate.[12]

In this context, however, Kracauer has tended to appear as a somewhat marginal figure, whose contributions would seem never to have matched those of Adorno in philosophical authority (not to mention sheer volume) or of Walter Benjamin in stylistic brilliance and aphoristic acuity. Nor would Kracauer, the inveterate interdisciplinarian whose only university affiliation came late in life as a participant in the Columbia University Seminars, ever find his niche alongside bona fide sociologists such as Löwenthal, political theorists such as Herbert Marcuse, philosophers such as Ernst Bloch, or psychoanalytic thinkers such as Erich Fromm. And while the personal bonds among these men remained strong (if not untested), exchanges about their work could be testy to the point of hurtfulness.

The debates around Kracauer's book on Jacques Offenbach provide a case in point.[13] Composing the book in the dire circumstances of his exile in Paris, Kracauer hoped—and succeeded—to reach a wider French and international audience through a book with commercial potential; it was simultaneously published in German, English, and French editions in 1937. Yet the subject matter baffled many critics at the time, not least since Kracauer himself had provided a scathing critique of the genre in his 1930 essay "The Biography as an Art Form of the New Bourgeoisie."[14] Both Adorno and Benjamin severely criticized the book in their correspondence, Benjamin expressing his disbelief regarding Kracauer's radical change of heart vis-à-vis the biography, and Adorno taking Kracauer to task for what he perceived as crass commercialism: "It is so completely bad that it may easily become a bestseller."[15] Yet on closer inspection we can read Kracauer's *Gesellschaftsbiographie* as a biography of a society that entertains remarkable parallels to the one that drove Kracauer into exile. Subtly infused with the autobiographical dimension that Christian Rogowski also detects in his novels, *Offenbach* is both a personal account of the artist/intellectual in exile and of Kracauer's generation of German Jews; it forms part of an impressive canon of literary biographies written by German exile writers that include the likes of Lion Feuchtwanger, Stefan Zweig, Bruno Frank, Ludwig Marcuse, Bertolt Brecht, and Heinrich Mann.

Just as he did not hold back in his critique of Kracauer's *Offenbach*, Adorno massively edited an article on Nazi propaganda that the *Zeitschrift für Sozialforschung* had commissioned from Kracauer. Given the extent of the alterations, the latter withdrew the article from consideration, not without first having accused Adorno of plagiarizing his work.[16] Whether as a result of such controversies and profound disagreements or for other reasons, much of the literature on the Frankfurt School continues to ignore Kracauer's work or subsume it under paradigms that fail to do it justice.[17] Consequently, as cultural studies and any number of attendant disciplines witnessed the rise of Benjamin to critic extraordinaire in the 1990s, Kracauer's work, while clearly germane to the central questions about modernity, history, and visual and popular culture, languished in relative obscurity.[18]

If the circumstances of Kracauer's affiliation with the Frankfurt School have prejudiced the reception of Kracauer's work, so did other contexts—most prominently the development of Anglo-American film studies. Kracauer's seminal contributions here coincided precisely (albeit in ways yet to be charted more carefully) with the institutionalization of film studies in the United States, but the two books on film achieved their classical status at some cost. Although both *From Caligari to Hitler* and *Theory of Film* remain staples of film theory reading lists, routinely assigned together with the work of André Bazin as representing the realist tradition of "classical" film theory, that very label makes the books—and the other theories it subsumes, for that matter—appear quaint and dated, safely contained in an earlier era that so-called contemporary film theory helped us supersede. While this state of affairs may be changing with the current revaluation of classical film theory (more on this below), the reception of Kracauer's two film books clearly illustrates the limiting effects of the disciplinary discourses in which they became enmeshed.

In this country, Kracauer is still best known for his history of Weimar cinema, *From Caligari to Hitler,* in which he attempts to make sense of Hitler's rise to power from a postwar perspective. Kracauer here advances a sustained argument about the relationship between film and the collective "psychological dispositions" of a nation. Not only do the films produced in Germany between 1918 and 1933 provide insights into German mentalities during the Weimar Republic, Kracauer claims, they also clearly "presage" the rise of Hitler at its close. The book has been faulted by readers in film studies for crafting an overly teleological narrative with the exile's benefit of hindsight; for basing its historical argument on a narrow selection of prestigious films at the expense of the popular fare that constituted the bulk of Weimar cinema;[19] and for positing an essential German character, to be psychoanalyzed by reviewing the films of the era.[20] In his work on Weimar cinema and its afterlife, Thomas Elsaesser has chronicled these critiques, framing them in terms of Kracauer's exile situation. Rereading *From Caligari to Hitler* alongside Lotte Eisner's *The Haunted Screen,* Elsaesser argues that these postwar books on Weimar cinema addressed audiences in the United States and France in ways that also reflected the critics' indebtedness to their respective host countries and the gratitude for the patronage they had enjoyed—in Kracauer's case particularly to Iris Barry at the Museum of Modern Art (MoMA). The perspective Kracauer offered on pre-

Nazi Germany, Elsaesser claims, thus "favored discourses and perspectives on [its] subject that necessarily occluded other, equally well-founded film-historical approaches and film-aesthetic evaluations, or at any rate . . . made these others more difficult to articulate."[21]

While such a historicization is in keeping with the project we wish to advance with this volume, it should not replace the direct engagement with the substance of the criticisms that have been leveled against Kracauer's *Caligari.* For all of these, indeed, merit another look on their own terms. Thus, the argument regarding Kracauer's national essentialism overlooks his explicit claims to the contrary in the introduction to *Caligari,* the consistent historicization of all "psychological" findings throughout the book, and the class-specific focus on the petty bourgeoisie, which had already been the object of Kracauer's important study of white-collar workers, *The Salaried Masses.* The former two critiques of *Caligari* carry more weight, but they need to be reevaluated in view of Kracauer's earlier work as film critic, now readily available in toto as part of Kracauer's collected works.[22] As the original articles in the *Frankfurter Zeitung* make clear, Kracauer harbored the same mistrust of the direction German film was taking during the 1920s as he would in retrospect; and the breadth of his reviewing activities in Germany clearly attests to his familiarity with a far broader cross-section of Weimar-era film culture than what ultimately found its way into *From Caligari to Hitler*—a selection that was after all constrained by the holdings of the film library at the MoMA in New York during the 1940s.

Just as a reading of *Caligari* benefits from stepping outside of the canonic sequence of classical texts in film theory and keeping a focus on the continuities from Kracauer's feuilleton work of the 1920s, so does a reading of *Theory of Film.* Within film studies, the book has been indicted for everything from its Teutonic pedantry to its normative ontology and its philosophically misguided notions of medium-specificity.[23] Often unfamiliar with the premises of Kracauer's phenomenological approach, reviewers and scholars have criticized what they perceive as Kracauer's naive realism; accordingly, a recent introductory text justifiably describes *Theory of Film* as the "whipping boy" of 1970s film theory and its antiveristic "rage."[24] This tendency has been reversed, however, by Miriam Hansen's crucial work on *Theory of Film,* which not only traces the book's long gestation from Kracauer's "Marseille Notebooks" through its publication in 1960, thereby reinserting the history *of* the book and recovering the repressed historical dimension *in* the book. This work has also allowed Hansen to situate *Theory of Film* in relation to the concerns of film and cultural studies in the ostensibly postphotographic, digital present. She reads Kracauer as a theorist of nonnarrative forms in ways that resonate with work on early cinema (Gunning) and the movement image (Deleuze); in contrast to earlier attacks on Kracauer's realism, she recovers from *Theory of Film* an anticlassical impetus that anticipates precisely the ideological critique of classical cinema's ostensible transparency; she notes the subterranean links between Kracauer's emphasis on the embodied nature of spectatorship ("with skin and hair") and more recent interest on the part of film scholars in the relationship between body, genre, and affect; and she invites us to reflect on the "chances of alienation" that emanate from new media as much as from the cinema of Kracauer's time.[25]

Hansen's historicization, in other words, restores to Kracauer's *Theory of Film* its historical and dialectical underpinnings, even as it shows how and why both of these became muted in the conception, and reinforced in the reception, of the book. A number of essays in the present volume—Hansen's own among them—contribute to this project of rewiring the reception of Kracauer, so to speak, by tapping into alternative trajectories. Although Kracauer liked to invoke the notion of "extra-territoriality" for himself, this project at times involves insisting on the territorial situatedness of Kracauer's work—whether by locating his essays from the 1940s in the context of postwar American journalism, as Noah Isenberg suggests; by reading *Theory of Film* in dialogue with the contemporary contributions of the New York Intellectuals, as Johannes von Moltke does; or by retracing the vagaries of Kracauer's reception in Germany upon the belated translation and publication of works such as *Caligari* and *Theory of Film* in his native tongue, as Eric Rentschler proposes.

Thus, Noah Isenberg highlights Kracauer's analytical acumen and his positionality as an "extraterritorial" critic in New York in the wake of World War II. Scrutinizing Kracauer's writings for American journals and magazines upon his arrival in New York in 1941, Isenberg attends to the specific arguments that Kracauer advances in these pieces, to his principal theoretical motifs, and even to the style of his writing; on this basis he contends that we may detect continuities with his earlier writings, and particularly with the elaboration of *From Caligari to Hitler* in what appear to be occasional pieces, commissioned by the "little magazines" of the day, and written by a freelance writer seeking to sustain himself financially in exile. Johannes von Moltke likewise emphasizes the historically specific location of Kracauer in American exile, advocating a reading of Kracauer's works from this period that would situate him at the hub of a transatlantic exchange between the Frankfurt School and the New York Intellectuals. Although recent work has shown that exchange to have been rather limited as far as the major representatives of these two groups were concerned,[26] von Moltke takes some marginalia by Robert Warshow on Kracauer's manuscript for *Theory of Film* as the starting point for exploring the rich intellectual give-and-take between the exile and his host community. Even if that exchange may have been limited in terms of actual face-to-face conversations, von Moltke argues that the implications for our reading of a book like *Theory of Film*, let alone the more occasional pieces that Isenberg analyzes, are substantial.

Where Isenberg and von Moltke attend to the American context, Eric Rentschler traces the widely influential, though still underresearched, impact Kracauer's "classic" books made during the 1960s and 1970s in the Federal Republic of Germany. In stark contrast to Anglo-American film studies, West German critics such as Enno Patalas, Wilfried Berghahn, and others associated with Germany's most important postwar film journal, *Filmkritik*, explicitly cited *Caligari* as the role model for their own version of film criticism that, at least for a while, favored a study of social content over that of aesthetic form. In contrast, during the 1970s critics like Michael Rutschky, and filmmakers ranging from Wim Wenders to Herbert Achternbusch, latched on to Kracauer's understanding of realism as a redemption of physical reality; like von Moltke, Rentschler highlights the importance of Kracauer's notion of experience, showing how it allowed the New German filmmakers to formulate their own aesthetic agenda, or helped Rutschky to give voice to a leftist subjectivity of the post-1968 era. Yet as Rentschler concludes, while these efforts did much to shed a limelight on texts that had been relegated to the status of dust-covered classics, their own idiosyncratic and highly selective reading of Kracauer make them examples of productive misreadings rather than interpretations that rise to the level of complexity of Kracauer's own work.

If some of Kracauer's theorizing of film has avoided being subsumed under the "classical," this is largely due to the work of Heide Schlüpmann, who has consistently sought to activate his insights in relation to the periods that preceded the classical, that is, early film theory, as well as to the various strands labeled "contemporary" film theory, whether semiotic, psychoanalytic, or feminist.[27] In an intriguing argument that seeks to claim Kracauer's writings on film for the latter in particular, Schlüpmann turns her attention to certain lacunae in Kracauer's two famous film books. If we consider his almost complete disinterest in issues such as gender divisions and the emancipation of women, his disregard for the role of actresses, or the relative absence of feelings and emotions in his writings, Schlüpmann asks, how can we still think of Kracauer's as an ally to 1970s German and American feminist film criticism? In reading Kracauer from the margins—a strategy that he himself was so fond of—we discover numerous revealing points of intersection, be it his brief but insightful discussion of Asta Nielsen, his use of psychoanalysis as a critique of authoritarian structures, or his "un-masculine" way of thinking that subverts the male-dominated discourse of the sciences and humanities during his day.

Kracauer's Contemporaneity

To claim the relevance of Kracauer's cultural critique for the present, as we do with this volume, it is not enough to address and contextualize the past misreadings and selective canonizations of his major works; rather, we would also insist on the contemporary resonance of Kracauer's contributions. Already in 1994, Dana Polan had expressed the "hope that Kracauer will become an obligatory and productive reference" in cultural studies and contemporary criticism;[28] with the intervening work, especially on the nine-volume critical edition of Kracauer's work by Inka Mülder-Bach and Ingrid Belke, this hope has certainly begun to be realized. If, in 2000, Gertrud Koch could still write that "the reception of Kracauer . . . stands on unsteady feet, to the extent that it stands at all,"[29] a decade later, there are ample signs of renewed interest in Kracauer, both in Germany and abroad, particularly in the Francophone world.[30] The present volume aims to contribute to these developments by highlighting Kracauer's relevance in two areas of pressing concern to the humanities today: first, as several contributors demonstrate, current trends in visual culture, and particularly the ongoing transition from photographic to digital regimes, can benefit from a return to the sophisticated models of "visual thinking" (Arnheim) that Kracauer developed during his lifetime. While the impact of this contribution is perhaps most directly relevant within the discipline of film studies, Kracauer's work also stands to gain renewed recognition, second, for the way it crosses disciplinary boundaries. As the humanities have turned increasingly toward interdisciplinary work since the 1990s, Kracauer's forays into the fields of architecture, film, literature, sociology, historiography, and the arts, among others, provide a model of cultural analysis that bridges disciplinary divides. Individual contributions to this volume, but especially the picture that emerges from the essays taken together, confirm Kracauer's contemporaneity as a visual thinker for interdisciplinary work in the humanities as we come to terms with the digital age.

If Kracauer's books on film richly reward rereading from any number of perspectives, as Isenberg, von Moltke, and Rentschler suggest, we are inclined to see this as part of a larger trend toward the recovery of "classical" film theory and its relevance for the humanities. There is mounting evidence that cinema studies is prepared to take on the task of historicizing not only itself as a discipline but also the ostensibly outdated contributions to film theory from the first half of the twentieth century as it revisits the work of Hugo Münsterberg, Rudolf Arnheim, Bela Balazs, and André Bazin.[31] This resurgence of interest takes place, significantly, amid the most profound technological shift in visual culture since the invention of cinema at the end of the nineteenth century. As film takes on an increasingly "virtual" life in the digital age, it stands to reason that we should want to return to those texts that most decisively located the specificity of what preceded the digital—namely, the indexical nature of the photographic.[32] Doing so allows us to distinguish moments of continuity and change amid rhetorical assertions of rupture and revolution. For not only do many of the conventions that photography and cinema helped to establish persist—even if only as icons or metaphors—in the digital age (think only of the electronic shutter sound on a digital camera or the "tools" provided by Photoshop), but some of the formal devices and stylistic notions most closely associated with the photographic also appear alive and well even after its purported demise at the hands of the digital. Among these, the features of "realism" arguably deserve pride of place; rather than dismiss as outdated the discussions of realism in classical film theory, then, we may want to revisit those discussions from a contemporary perspective.

Kracauer famously contributed some of the seminal arguments to these discussions with essays such as "On Photography" (1927) and, of course, his *Theory of Film*. Accordingly, the renewed interest in the work of Siegfried Kracauer may in some respects be attributed to precisely the kind of historicizing attention we are witnessing elsewhere in film and media studies.[33] A number of contributions in this volume build on and contribute to this reevaluation, confronting head-on the misguided assumption that theories of the photographic have nothing more to tell us in the digital age. Thus, Kracauer's lifelong concern with the photographic media plays a role in virtually all of the essays assembled here, but it is the explicit object of two interventions in particular, both of which mount convincing—if differently angled—cases for the continuing relevance of Kracauer's work in our ostensibly postphotographic, digital present.

Miriam Hansen offers a careful rereading of Kracauer's seminal essay "On Photography" from 1927. In the process, she both restores to this essay its rich historical referentiality and mounts a compelling case for reconsidering Kracauer's concern with indexicality, with the "having-been-there" of photographic presence, from the perspective of the digital image. Not only does Hansen read the photography essay against a lapsarian discourse of modernity, but she also uses that essay to reconstruct a different genealogy to *Theory of Film* than the one (itself generally lapsarian) that routinely pits the book's opening sections against the ostensibly richer earlier essay.

In his consideration of photography and the photographic, Lutz Koepnick, too, offers a spirited defense of Kracauer against the claims that his later writings in particular subscribed to a "naive" realism. Emphasizing his profoundly dialectical view of photography as a medium that straddles nature *and* history, Koepnick like Hansen activates Kracauer's insights for the digital age. Whereas some critics would write off Kracauer's work as contributing to a classical, realist film theory whose interest has become merely historical and cut off from our digital present, Kracauer's writings on photography help to point out some of the profound *continuities* that still bind us to the photographic age: his views on photography as a medium that casts an alienated glance at alienated existence, his emphasis on the materiality of the photographic medium and of its representations, Koepnick suggests, hold with equal force today as they did at the time they were formulated in Germany and the United States.

If these contributions make a case for Kracauer's relevance to the specific disciplinary concerns of film and art history (even as they alert us to the broader impact of the digital turn and how we conceptualize its effects), others highlight the significance of Kracauer's radical interdisciplinarity. While his highly eclectic style and his open disregard for entrenched academic disciplines resulted in the fact that his work on architecture, sociology, philosophy, and history has hardly been read in these respective disciplines, there is now mounting evidence that Kracauer is beginning to have an impact across the humanities conceived as an interdisciplinary project. The present volume wishes to contribute to this trend by bringing together scholarship from across the disciplines in which Kracauer himself

Fig. 1. Siegfried Kracauer around 1920. Deutsches Literaturarchiv Marbach.

worked. Exploring a wide array of Kracauer's writings, the authors gathered here concern themselves not only, as already discussed, with film, photography, and the digital turn; but also with current discussions about early twentieth-century experiments in abstraction and photomontage (particularly at the Bauhaus); the history of radio as well as new media; urban studies and architecture; literature and anthropology; and museum and exhibition culture.

A number of these concerns remain linked, across disciplinary divides, by the emphasis on the visual, as if to underscore Kracauer's relevance to the various configurations of "visual culture" as it is discussed today. As Adorno had written in a well-known, if ambivalent, tribute on the occasion of his friend's seventy-fifth birthday, Kracauer "thinks with an eye that is astonished almost to helplessness but then suddenly flashes into illumination."[34] This emphasis on vision—what Arnheim would label, in a different context, "visual thinking" and what Adorno calls the "primacy of the optical"[35]— provides a thread across Elizabeth Otto's concern with Kracauer's art criticism, Claire Zimmerman's reading of his architectural work, and Kerstin Barndt's reconstruction of his thinking about the medium of exhibition.

As Otto points out, Kracauer's art criticism—like other aspects of his work—has consistently been overlooked by critics. Otto traces Kracauer's writing on art and art exhibits during the 1920s, ranging from his review of a 1920s exhibit of German Expressionism through his better-known writings on photography (which go well beyond the famous 1927 essay "On Photography") and on photomontages of avant-garde artists to the use of light in installations as well as advertisement. While acknowledging the eclecticism in his approach, Otto argues that Kracauer's intention of making "Verknüpfungen" (connections), or what Benjamin famously described as ragpicking, provides a consistent approach that bridges Kracauer's otherwise significantly shifting interest in, and position vis-à-vis, contemporary artistic movements. Claire Zimmerman likewise considers less-studied aspects of Kracauer's work, particularly his dissertation on architectural metalwork, "The Development of the Art of Forging in Berlin." Zimmerman traces the transition of Kracauer's fascination with ornamental architectural surface as evidenced in the dissertation to very different forms of cultural surfaces in his Weimar essays, arguing that the larger shift from the nineteenth to the twentieth century is central to Kracauer's early writings but has largely escaped critics.[36] Thus where others describe Kracauer as firmly rooted in Weimar modernity, Zimmerman shows that his formal training as architect transcended the narrowing disciplinary confines that architectural culture would take on after World War I, allowing him to already then explore conditions of physical experience and collectivity that would become lifelong concerns. In light of today's fascination with (Weimar) surface culture, Kracauer's earliest published writings become newly important through Zimmerman's readings.[37]

Taking an approach to visual culture that is informed by work in museum studies, Kerstin Barndt reminds us that Kracauer's cultural critique also addressed the burgeoning medium of exhibition during the Weimar years, and that this critique went well beyond the walls of the art museum as an institution. Reviewing a number of exhibitions that captured the social and aesthetic imagination of his contemporaries, Kracauer honed his critical vocabulary to discuss the architectural, spatial, and social forms of Weimar modernity. What appears to have attracted Kracauer's interest in these events was their intermediary and intermedial position: exemplars of an exhibition culture informed by the tradition of world's fairs, they brought together avant-garde strategies and mass cultural dimensions and staged historically specific *Raumbilder* (spatial images) that can also be traced across other media such as film and dance. Providing a synoptic account of Kracauer's intermittent but consistent return to thinking about exhibitions, Barndt shows how a medium that prominently shaped Weimar modernity figures centrally within the coordinates of Kracauer's critical apparatus. Reading Kracauer's contributions alongside Walter Benjamin's simultaneous and influential work on exhibitions, Barndt reconstructs a media theory of exhibition that not only has historical specificity but whose distinct conceptualization of museological temporalities also harbors important insights for museum studies today.

The visual was not Kracauer's only culturally alert sense. However well-trained his eyes may have been, it appears that his ears were equally well attuned to the sound waves of contemporary culture. Moreover, the two senses are, for Kracauer, intimately related. Theodore F. Rippey supplies a highly innovative account of Kracauer's interest in sound (which includes screams, noise, the use of headphones and loud speakers, etc.), proposing that Kracauer's understanding of what we hear sheds a light on the interconnected problems of perception, reading, and subjectivity. Rippey traces Kracauer's fascination with sound from early feuilletonistic texts such as "Boredom" (1924) and "Screams in the Street" (1930) through "The Mass Ornament" (1927) and his celebration of René Clair's early sound films all the way to *Theory of Film*, a trajectory that, according to the author, reflects fundamental changes in the articulation of human subjectivity from an integral self to an increasingly porous subject that is at once a mass component and an active processor of image flows and textual surfaces. Since sound can go where vision often cannot follow, Rippey concludes, approaches to Kracauer that focus exclusively on the visual are always subject to being caught off-guard by sound.

Other contributions follow Kracauer's work from the visual and the aural to the imaginative and the conceptual, tracking his contributions to literature, philosophy, and anthropology. Thus, although Kracauer has played a significant role in literary theory and criticism (especially thanks to his analysis of New Objectivity), his own contributions as a literary author have largely been overlooked.[38] In their contributions, Christian Rogowski and Andreas Huyssen each focus on Kracauer as a literary author in his own right, tracing his work at two opposite ends of the genre spectrum. Thus, Rogowski focuses on the autobiographical components of Kracauer's novels, showing how in *Ginster* (1928) and *Georg* (1934), Kracauer constructs a self that is both related to and at odds with his life experience. Arguing that the novels are auto-biographical in a literal sense, Rogowski traces how they attempt to rewrite the story of Kracauer's life from his own perspective in order to combat an identity assigned to him by others. Rogowski's insightful interpretation highlights in particular the subtle narrative gestures that at once hint at and disavow the Jewish aspects of German-Jewish identity.

Andreas Huyssen, by contrast, focuses on the short form of Kracauer's scattered urban miniatures, collected in the 1960s under the title *Straßen in Berlin und anderswo*. Huyssen compares Kracauer's texts with those of Benjamin's *Einbahnstraße* as distinct contributions to a mode of modernist feuilleton writing in the Baudelairean tradition. The modernist miniature emerged as an experimental literary space to test new metropolitan perceptions in the context of the breakdown of boundaries between the visual and verbal arts and the rise of new technological image media. Benjamin's miniatures are related to the baroque medium of the emblem, which combined language and image, while Kracauer's texts are discussed in relation to the snapshot photograph. Neither writer supplements his texts with images, but both first published these short prose pieces in the feuilletons of urban papers before collecting them into book format.

Like many of Kracauer's writings, the urban miniatures challenge clear generic categories, appearing first as occasional pieces in a daily newspaper and then (much later) in an anthology that claims a generic status in its own right, shedding new light on the *Städtebilder* as a literary form. Indeed, most texts that Kracauer writes shade into other forms as well, straddling the border between literature and philosophy. The latter pursuit becomes clearest, perhaps, in Kracauer's final, posthumously published book on historiography, which outlines a philosophy of history that operates in the "anteroom" to philosophy proper. In her reading of this book, Christina Gerhardt situates it in comparison to the late work of Adorno, whom Kracauer had mentored in the early years of their friendship. In constant epistolary (and occasionally personal) contact during the 1960s, both men were working in their own ways on notions of (natural) history—a concept that is central to both *Negative Dialectics* and Kracauer's posthumous *History*. It is, as Gerhardt shows, an object of occasionally intense disagreement between the two as they work out the place of freedom and the human in relation to nature and the sciences.

This concern with the specificity of the human is also one that Sabine Biebl picks up in her contribution, as she rereads Kracauer's writings with a view to their anthropological assumptions about the nature of man. Juxtaposing his works from the Weimar years with the notebooks on film that Kracauer compiled toward the end of his French exile in Marseille, Biebl traces an arc that leads us from early, emphatic universalisms through the rather more carefully historicized notions of "man" in the late Weimar years (particularly in *The Salaried Masses*), and that apparently reverses itself as Kracauer begins to prioritize the material world of objects over the anthropological subject when he begins working toward a sustained theory of film. In an intriguing exploration of Kracauer's feuilleton article on the reconstruction of Berlin's "Lindenpassage" alongside the Marseille notebooks that he would compose a decade later, Biebl notes the continuities of this emphasis on the material world even as the central figure of the *Passant* moving through space becomes replaced by the stationary spectator of moving images in the theater.

Drehli Robnik surveys Kracauer's most influential writings on film and their relation to philosophy to situate them not only alongside contemporaneous efforts by Benjamin and Adorno but also more recent writings by Giorgio Agamben, Stanley Cavell, Jacques Rancière, and Gilles Deleuze, as well as the work of film scholars coming out of the tradition of the Frankfurt School such as Miriam Hansen, Gertrud Koch, and Heide Schlüpmann, who have not only provided extensive criticism of Kracauer but explicitly claimed him for a film theory indebted to feminism and Critical Theory. Like several other contributors to this volume, Robnik takes issue with facile misreadings of *Caligari* and *Theory of Film* while also highlighting the continuities, rather than the ruptures, between Kracauer's work of the 1920s and that of his New York period. In particular, he criticizes Adorno's double-edged homage to Kracauer, "The Curious Realist," for its dismissal of Kracauer's alleged naïveté, underscoring instead the latter's proximity to the sophisticated media theories of Deleuze and Rancière.

Finally, in a panoramic essay that considers Kracauer's entire career trajectory, Inka Mülder-Bach focuses on the oft-cited motif of extraterritoriality and Kracauer's embrace of the perspective of the outsider. Taking her cue from his first English-language essay from May 1942, she argues that this notion was not simply a reaction to the experience of his exile in France and the United States but served as a cognitive concept that he developed throughout the 1920s and put to the test upon his arrival in New York. Building on Edmund Husserl's phenomenology, his teacher Georg Simmel's notion of the stranger, and his own earlier essay, "Those Who Wait," Kracauer advocates a bracketing or suspension of judgment in which the foreigner seeks to make strange what seems close at hand. Mülder-Bach reads this ethnographic stance in direct opposition to the radical avant-garde of the interwar years and its commitment to an "armored subject" bent on innovation, provocation, and intervention. Nor did Kracauer's approach align in any straightforward way with the diagnoses provided by his closest friends in the Frankfurt School, as Mülder-Bach argues; rather, she makes a case for rereading even the unsystematic feuilleton writings of the 1920s as a form of cultural critique that remains very much Kracauer's own—and is still in need of further attention for what it might have to offer for the present.

In 1943, the Guggenheim Foundation awarded Kracauer the grant for which he had applied the previous year. The resulting study, which appeared in 1947 under the title *From Caligari to Hitler: A Psychological History of the German Film*, became his best-known book. But with that renown came the inevitable reduction of Kracauer's painstaking work to what was quickly codified, for better or for worse, as Kracauer's unique "method"— his historical and psychoanalytic approach, and his ostensible top-down sociology of a national cinema. In this process, which set in with the book's contemporary reception and has persisted through the institutionalization and development of film studies as a discipline, much of the nuance of the approach Kracauer had outlined in his proposal by reference to farming and engineering has been elided: the focus on seemingly unimportant aesthetic detail, the keen eye for a phenomenology of the everyday, of "byways" and "unobtrusive facts," the perspective that looks at films as if through a narrow window revealing "strange scenes that, outdoors, would be entirely invisible." For Kracauer, work on film was always a means of making broader sociological and philosophical arguments about the culture of modernity. Especially in this country, Kracauer never fully persuaded his critics that for him film "was never anything but a means of making certain sociological and philosophical points."[39] *Culture in the Anteroom* aims to recover the nuance of Kracauer's arguments and make them available for current debates in the humanities, as he had originally intended. It is our hope that the contributions collected here will demonstrate that Kracauer's work still harbors untapped resources for understanding, analyzing, and theorizing culture today.

NOTES

1. Siegfried Kracauer, *History: The Last Things Before the Last* (Princeton, NJ: Markus Wiener, 1969), 216.

2. *Siegfried Kracauer—Erwin Panofsky: Briefwechsel 1941–1966*, ed. Volker Breidecker (Berlin: Akademie Verlag, 1996), 16.

3. *History*, 83.

4. Aside from the locus classicus for such figures of thought in the "Mass Ornament" essay, consider for example the claim, in Kracauer's essay on Simmel, that "the core of mankind's essence is accessible through even the smallest side door." "Georg Simmel," in Kracauer, *The Mass Ornament: Weimar Essays*, trans. and ed. Thomas Y. Levin (Cambridge: Harvard University Press, 1995), 225–57; here 237.

5. See *History*, 8–15; the formulation comes in the portrait of Erasmus that anchors the introduction to his posthumous book on history, but that can also be read as a thinly veiled self-portrait of Kracauer's own "fear of all that is definitely fixed," his interest in how "the humane" may be located in the interstices of any given era rather than in its outwardly defining movements. Kracauer the exile who constantly had to work for recognition likely also projected himself into the ways in which "Erasmus remained largely invisible" (*History*, 12).

6. On this opposition, see Andrew DuBois, "Close Reading: An Introduction," in *Close Reading: The Reader*, ed. Frank Lentricchia and Andrew Dubois (Durham: Duke University Press, 2003), 18.

7. *Theory of Film: The Redemption of Physical Reality* (New York: Oxford University Press, 1960), 28.

8. *History*, 192; emphasis in the original.

9. See the special issue on Siegfried Kracauer, *New German Critique* 54 (1991).

10. Miriam Hansen, "'With Skin and Hair': Kracauer's Theory of Film, Marseille 1940," *Cultural Critique* 19, no. 3 (1993): 437–69; Hansen, *Cinema and Experience: Siegfried Kracauer, Walter Benjamin, and Theodor W. Adorno* (Berkeley: University of California Press, 2011); Gerhard Richter, *Thought-Images: Frankfurt School Writers' Reflections from Damaged Life* (Stanford: Stanford University Press, 2007); Walter Benjamin, *Briefe an Siegfried Kracauer. Mit vier Briefen von Siegfried Kracauer an Walter Benjamin*, ed. Theodor W. Adorno Archiv (Marbach: Deutsche Schillergesellschaft, 1987); Theodor W. Adorno and Siegfried Kracauer, *Der Riß der Welt geht auch durch mich: Briefwechsel 1923–1966*, ed. Wolfgang Schopf (Frankfurt am Main: Suhrkamp, 2008). On the latter, see Johannes von Moltke, "Teddie and Friedel: Theodor W. Adorno, Siegfried Kracauer and the Erotics of Friendship," in *Criticism* 51, no. 4 (Fall 2009), 683–94. Other recent editions of Kracauer's

correspondence include Helmut Asper, ed., *Nachrichten aus Hollywood, New York und anderswo: Der Briefwechsel Eugen und Marlise Schüfftans mit Siegfried und Lili Kracauer* (Trier: Wissenschaftlicher Verlag, 2003); Peter-Erwin Jansen and Christian Schmidt, eds., *In steter Freundschaft: Leo Löwenthal—Siegfried Kracauer, Briefwechsel 1921–1966* (Springe: Zu Klampen, 2003); and Erich Auerbach and Siegfried Kracauer, "Neun Briefe 1951–1957," in Karlheinz Barck and Martin Treml, eds., *Erich Auerbach: Geschichte und Aktualität eines europäischen Philologen* (Berlin: Kadmos, 2007), 483–88.

11. Kracauer's wife, Lili Ehrenreich, by contrast, had served in an official—albeit clerical—function at the institute during the 1920s.

12. See Leo Löwenthal, "As I Remember Friedel," *New German Critique*, special issue on Siegfried Kracauer, 54 (1991): 5–17.

13. Siegfried Kracauer, *Jacques Offenbach und das Paris seiner Zeit* (Amsterdam: Allert de Lange, 1937), now available in *Werke* 8.

14. Siegfried Kracauer, "The Biography as an Art Form of the New Bourgeoisie," in *The Mass Ornament*, trans. and ed. Thomas Y. Levin (Cambridge: Harvard University Press, 1996), 101–6.

15. *Adorno-Benjamin: Briefwechsel 1928–1940*, ed. Henri Lonitz (Frankfurt am Main: Suhrkamp, 1994), 241. Benjamin wrote in response: "He has composed a text which only a few years ago would not have found a harsher critic than himself," ibid., 242. Adorno's harshest critique to Kracauer himself came in the form of a letter, dated 13 May 1937 in Adorno / Kracauer, *Briefwechsel*, 352–59. Ernst Bloch, another of Kracauer's close friends, chided Kracauer for having written on a composer without actually addressing his compositions: "It's a unique book in its genre—as if someone were to write about Michelangelo without mentioning that he was a painter and sculptor. And yet that is what Kracauer did." Ernst Bloch, "Der eigentümliche Glücksfall: Über *Jacques Offenbach* von Siegfried Kracauer," *Text und Kritik* 68 (1980): 73–75; here 75. (The piece is based on a 1976 conversation between Karsten Witte and Ernst and Karola Bloch.)

16. See letters exchanged in May 1938 between Kracauer and Adorno in Adorno / Kracauer, *Briefwechsel*, 381–402.

17. Thus, although he receives mention in passing, Kracauer is not considered important enough to merit an entry into the index for Thomas Wheatland's *The Frankfurt School in Exile* (Minneapolis: University of Minnesota Press, 2009); and even though Gerhard Richter devotes a chapter to Kracauer in *Thought-Images: Frankfurt School Writers' Reflections from Damaged Life* (Stanford: Stanford University Press, 2007), he considers Kracauer within the concept of the "Denkbild," which owes more to Adorno and Benjamin. Dagmar Barnouw, by contrast, takes the other—and equally inadequate—extreme position by dismissing as "single-minded fictions" the philosophical contributions of the Frankfurt School's principal members and insisting on Kracauer's absolute difference from the latter. See Dagmar Barnouw, *Critical Realism: History, Photography, and the Work of Siegfried Kracauer* (Baltimore: Johns Hopkins University Press, 1994), 4.

The important exceptions to these trends remain the work of Martin Jay (*Permanent Exiles: Essays on the Intellectual Migration from Germany to America* [New York: Columbia University Press, 1986]) and, again, of Miriam Hansen (see above).

In a recent essay, Christian Sieg has elaborated the significant differences between the Frankfurt School and Kracauer, emphasizing the proximity of Kracauer's notion of ethnography to Clifford Geertz and Pierre Bourdieu. See Christian Sieg, "Beyond Realism: Siegfried Kracauer and the Ornaments of the Ordinary," *New German Critique* 109 (2010): 99–118. See also Gérard Raulet's differentiating account of Frankfurt School thinkers, along with Husserl and Simmel, "Verfallenheit ans Objekt: Zur Auseinandersetzung über eine Grundfigur des Denkens bei Adorno, Benjamin, Bloch und Kracauer," in Frank Gruner and Dorothee Kimmich, eds., *Denken durch die Dinge: Siegfried Kracauer im Kontext* (Munich: Fink, 2009), 119–34.

18. In a gesture that is revealing of the cultural capital that Kracauer and Benjamin command in today's Germany, the city of Berlin, where Kracauer resided from 1930 to 1933, recently named a square in his honor. Marking the spot where he lived during his sojourn as the Berlin editor of the *Frankfurter Zeitung*, this modest and inconspicuous street corner is just a stone's throw from the luscious and elegant Benjamin-Promenaden.

19. See Christian Rogowski, "From Ernst Lubitsch to Joe May: Challenging Kracauer's Demonology with Weimar Popular Film," in Randall Halle and Margaret McCarthy, eds., *Light Motives: German Popular Film in Perspective* (Detroit: Wayne State University Press, 2003), 1–23.

20. Barry Salt, "From *Caligari* to Who?" *Sight and Sound* 48, no. 2 (1979): 119–23.

21. Thomas Elsaesser, *Weimar Cinema and After: Germany's Historical Imaginary* (London: Routledge, 2000), 21–22.

22. *Werke*, vol. 6.

23. The charge of pedantry, and the implied conclusion that we had best dismiss out of hand the entirety of Kracauer's theoretical project, was launched early on in Pauline Kael's acerbic attack. It survives, albeit in muted form, in even the most well-meaning contributions aimed at rehabilitating *Theory of Film*, as in Miriam Hansen's comments on the "pretense of academic systematicity" and Kracauer's "grandfatherly and assimilationist diction," which make of the book a somewhat "painful caricature of the German scholarly mind in exile." Cf. Pauline Kael, "Is There a Cure for Film Criticism," in *Sight and Sound* (1962); Miriam Hansen, "With Skin and Hair," 438–39. For other critiques of *Theory of Film*, see Noel Carroll, "Kracauer's Theory of Film," in *Engaging the Moving Image* (New Haven: Yale University Press, 2003), 281–302; Dudley Andrew, *The Major Film Theories: An Introduction* (Oxford: Oxford University Press, 1976), 106–33.

24. Robert Stam, *Film Theory: An Introduction* (Oxford: Blackwell, 2000), 77. Though originally directed more at Bazin than at Kracauer, the critique of ontological realism was launched by the *Cahiers du Cinéma* in a decidedly oedipal and hardly veiled attack on the theoretical views of Bazin, one of the journal's founders: In a widely reprinted programmatic essay, the editors hold that "the classic theory of cinema that the camera is an impartial instrument which grasps, or rather is impregnated by, the world in its 'concrete reality' is an eminently reactionary one. What the camera in fact registers is the vague, unformulated, untheorized, unthought-out world of the dominant ideology" (Jean-Louis Comolli and Jean Nar-

boni, "Cinema / Ideology / Criticism," in Bill Nichols, ed., *Movies and Methods*, vol. 1 [Berkeley: University of California Press, 1976], 25). The critique was soon joined by semiotic theories that insisted on the multiple mediations of the cinematic image as opposed to its putative transparency.

25. Hansen, "Introduction," *Theory of Film*, vii–xlv; and "With Skin and Hair" (different emphases here); see also Hansen's essay in this volume.

26. See Wheatland, *The Frankfurt School in Exile*.

27. See Heide Schlüpmann, *The Uncanny Gaze: The Drama of Early Cinema* (Chicago: University of Illinois Press, 2010), a partial translation of her *Unheimlichkeit des Blicks: Das Drama des frühen deutschen Kinos* (Basel: Stroemfeld, 1990); and *Ein Detektiv des Kinos: Studien zu Siegfried Kracauers Filmtheorie* (Basel: Stroemfeld, 1998).

28. Dana Polan, "Enzo Traverso, 'Siegfried Kracauer: itinéraire d'un intellectual nomade,'" in Andreas Volk, ed., *Siegfried Kracauer: Zum Werk des Romanciers, Feuilletonisten, Architekten, Filmwissenschaftlers und Soziologen* (Zurich: Seismo, 1996), 299; translation ours.

29. Gertrud Koch, *Siegfried Kracauer: An Introduction*, trans. Jeremy Gaines (Princeton: Princeton University Press, 2000), 3.

30. See among others Momme Brodersen, *Siegfried Kracauer* (Reinbek: Rowohlt, 2001); Nia Perivolaropoulou and Philippe Despoix, *Culture de masse et modernité: Siegfried Kracauer sociologue, critique, écrivain* (Paris: Éditions de la maison de l'homme, 2001); Helmut Stadler, *Siegfried Kracauer: Das journalistische Werk in der "Frankfurter Zeitung," 1921–1933* (Würzburg: Königshausen und Neumann, 2003); Jacques Lohourou Digbeu-Badlor, *Siegfried Kracauer et les grands débats intellectuels de son temps* (Stuttgart: Akademischer Verlag, 2005); Henrik Reeh, *Ornaments of the Metropolis: Siegfried Kracauer and Modern Urban Culture* (Cambridge: MIT Press, 2005); Christine Holste, ed., *Siegfried Kracauers Blick: Anstöße zu einer Ethnographie des Städtischen* (Hamburg: Philo, 2006); a special issue of *New Formations* 61 (Summer 2007); Tara Forest, *The Politics of Imagination: Benjamin, Kracauer, Kluge* (Bielefeld: Transcript, 2007); Philippe Despoix and Peter Schöttler, eds., *Siegfried Kracauer: Penseur de l'histoire* (Paris: Éditions de la maison de l'homme, 2008); Georg Steinmeyer, *Siegfried Kracauer als Denker des Pluralismus: Eine Annäherung im Spiegel Hannah Arendts* (Berlin: Lukas Verlag, 2008); Frank Grunert and Dorothee Kimmich, *Denken durch die Dinge: Siegfried Kracauer im Kontext* (Munich: Fink, 2009); Johannes von Moltke and Kristy Rawson, eds., *Siegfried Kracauer's American Writings: Essays on Film and Popular Culture* (Berkeley: University of California Press, forthcoming May 2012).

31. For a spirited renewal of some of classical film theory's central tenets, see Dudley Andrew, *What Cinema Is!* (Oxford: Wiley-Blackwell, 2010). Both Alan Langdale's (English) and Jörg Schweinitz's (German) editions of Münsterberg's seminal *Photoplay* usefully contextualized the latter with shorter, film-related publications by Münsterberg along with detailed appraisals of the theorist's background and impact; see also Eric Ames, "The Image of Culture—Or, What Münsterberg Saw in the Movies" in: Lynne Tatlock and Matt Erlin, eds., *German Culture in Nineteenth-Century America: Reception, Adaptation, Transformation* (Rochester: Camden House, 2005), 21–41. Erica Carter recently prepared a meticulous English lan-

guage edition of Béla Balázs, *Early Film Theory: Visible Man* and *The Spirit of Film*, transl. Rodney Livingstone (New York: Berghahn, 2010). It is perhaps not accidental that the 2008 Kracauer conference at Dartmouth College, at which some of the essays here collected were first presented, roughly coincided with a double conference on Bazin at the Université Paris Diderot and Yale, and one on Rudolf Arnheim at Harvard. See Dudley Andrew and Hervé Joubert-Laurencin, eds. *Opening Bazin: Postwar Film Theory and Its Afterlife* (Oxford: Oxford University Press, 2011) and Scott Higgins, ed. *Arnheim for Film and Media Studies* (New York: Routledge, 2011).

32. See David N. Rodowick, *The Virtual Life of Film* (Cambridge: Harvard University Press, 2007). On indexicality, see the special issue of *Differences* 18, no. 1 (Spring 2007), "Indexicality: Trace and Sign."

33. Both *Theory of Film* and *From Caligari to Hitler* have been reissued with extensive new critical introductions by Hansen and Leonardo Quaresima, respectively, which contextualize the publication history of the two volumes and grapple with their difficult reception histories.

34. Theodor W. Adorno, "The Curious Realist: On Siegfried Kracauer," in *New German Critique* 54, "Special Issue on Siegfried Kracauer" (Fall 1991): 163.

35. Rudolf Arnheim, *Visual Thinking* (Berkeley: University of California Press, 1969); Adorno, "The Curious Realist," 163.

36. Zimmerman's work is closest to Henrik Reeh's *Ornaments of the Metropolis*, but unlike Reeh, who focuses exclusively on the ornament, Zimmerman studies the concept of the surface and its use in both nineteenth-century and early twentieth-century discourses of art history, architecture, and craftsmanship.

37. On this topic, see Janet Ward, *Weimar Surfaces: Urban Visual Culture in 1920s Germany* (Berkeley: University of California Press, 2001); and John Allen, "The Cultural Spaces of Siegfried Kracauer: The Many Surfaces of Berlin," *New Formations* 61 (2007): 20–33.

38. See Kerstin Barndt, *Sentiment und Sachlichkeit: Der Roman der neuen Frau in der Weimarer Republik* (Cologne: Böhlau, 2003); and Helmuth Lethen *Cool Conduct: The Culture of Distance in Weimar Germany*, trans. Don Reneau (Berkeley: University of California Press, 2002). For work on Kracauer's novels, see Jörg Lau, "'Ginsterismus': Komik und Ichlosigkeit: Über filmische Komik in Siegfried Kracauers erstem Roman *Ginster*," in Volk, *Siegfried Kracauer*, 13–42. Notably, Kracauer's two novels have not been translated into English, but there exist various translations of *Ginster* in French (*Genêt*, 1933), Italian (*Ginster—Scritto da lui stesso*, 1984), and Japanese (*Ginsuta*, 1985).

39. Kracauer in a letter to Wolfgang Weyrauch, 4 June 1962. Cited in Belke and Renz, eds., *Siegfried Kracauer 1889–1966*.

Patterns of Reception

This Pen for Hire

Siegfried Kracauer as American Cultural Critic

Noah Isenberg

Over the span of a decade, from roughly 1941 to 1951—or from the moment that the former editor and lead critic of Weimar Germany's *Frankfurter Zeitung* first managed to relocate himself from Vichy France to New York City to the time that his writing became more exclusively focused on his *Theory of Film* (and on his posthumously published *History: The Last Things Before the Last*)—Siegfried Kracauer contributed some two dozen freelance essays and reviews to the American popular press. He wrote literary and film criticism for such magazines as the *Nation*, the *New Republic*, *Commentary*, and *Harper's;* he contributed pieces to the *New York Times*, the *Saturday Review of Literature*, and the *Kenyon Review;* and he published a few longer, more scholarly articles for *Social Research*, the flagship journal of the New School for Social Research (then still appropriately known as the University in Exile) and for *Public Opinion Quarterly*. The first half of Kracauer's extended stint as an American freelancer overlapped with the writing of his famous study of Weimar cinema, *From Caligari to Hitler*—and there are some obvious links in subject and method—but the diversity of assignments was such that Kracauer did not always have the leeway or the authority to treat subjects of his own choosing. The predicament of the freelancer, fending off heavy-handed editorial input while staying in good standing with magazines and assigning editors and trying to eke out a living in a competitive marketplace, prompted the exiled Kracauer to take on a variety of assignments that came his way.

In what follows I shall examine Kracauer's work as American freelancer within the context of his career trajectory, recognizing various links to his past, present, and future undertakings, while also placing the work within the larger context of German-Jewish exile. There has often been a ten-

dency in Kracauer scholarship to see each phase of his career, and his man-
ifold pursuits, in a separate light. As Gertrud Koch has noted in her tren-
chant analysis, "Kracauer exists either as a film theorist or as a distant relative of the Frankfurt School, either as a journalist or as a philosopher,
either as an essay-writer or as a novelist."[1] (Kracauer himself demonstrated
considerable awareness of this problem, suggesting late in life that he
should *not* be viewed merely as "a film man" but as a "philosopher of culture, or also a sociologist, and as a poet.")[2] His work as a freelancer gives us
the chance to reevaluate Kracauer for the polymath that he was. My remarks are based largely on the body of writing that Kracauer published in
the American popular press, in magazines and newspapers with a wider
readership, though I will also draw on some of his spirited contributions
made during the same period to trade and academic publications.

At the time of his departure, in spring 1941, on one of the last ships to
leave the port of Lisbon bound for New York harbor, Kracauer expressed a
profound awareness of the predicament he faced as an exile in his early
fifties, needing to start all over again. In a letter to his friend Theodor W.
Adorno, written just days before he boarded the SS *Nyassa*, he lamented,
"It's terrible to arrive like us—after eight years of an existence that doesn't
deserve the name. I have grown older. . . . Now comes the final station, the
last opportunity, which I can't squander or else it's all over."[3] The stakes of
the freelancer were unusually high. Not long after arriving in the United
States, Kracauer landed his first assignment for an American publication, a
short film review of Walt Disney's *Dumbo*. Commissioned by the *Nation*
magazine, and published in early November 1941, the one-page review af-
forded him the chance to demonstrate his firm grasp of Hollywood film
practices (of those put into operation by Walt Disney, in particular) and to
weigh in on the new cartoon introduced by Disney at this otherwise inaus-
picious moment in time. As the Europe that he had narrowly escaped became further engulfed by the fascist storm, Kracauer was free to focus his
attention on "a flying baby elephant."[4] Of course, there is nothing terribly
unusual about Weimar-era-trained intellectuals ruminating on Disney (we
have, among many examples, Walter Benjamin's poignant reflections on
Mickey Mouse from the early 1930s),[5] and after taking us back through the
early cartoons, Kracauer points to Disney for a larger critique of camera
reality. "One could wish," he writes, "that Disney would stop animating
fairy tales into conventional everyday life, and, proceeding like Chaplin,
develop everyday life into fairy tales through his cartoons. As to the methods of representation, he might be able, after the example of the great

painters, to transform *both* real and imaginary objects in his art and thus bring it to a new level."[6] As he would go on to formulate it many years later, Kracauer is here already concerned with a kind of "redemption of physical reality" that film—in this case, a cartoon—ostensibly possesses.

During his first years in America, in his numerous assignments of cultural criticism, Kracauer frequently directed his gaze at Hollywood. Two pieces in particular, both from May 1942, stand out in this vein: in the pages of *Social Research*, he filed a short review of Leo Rosten's *Hollywood, The Movie Colony—The Movie Makers*, a generally positive evaluation of Rosten's effort to debunk the "Hollywood Legend";[7] and in the industry trade publication, *National Board of Review Magazine*, he quickly adopted the collective pronoun in "Why France Liked Our Films," his survey of A-list Hollywood pictures (directed by Raoul Walsh, Frank Capra, Howard Hawks, William Wyler, and others) that were warmly received by French intellectuals on the other side of the Atlantic.[8] For different reasons, which I will attempt to enumerate below, both pieces warrant deeper consideration.

The Rosten review begins with an expression of gratitude to the American sponsors of his study—the Carnegie Corporation and the Rockefeller Foundation, the latter of which was then underwriting Kracauer's own film research at the Museum of Modern Art; Kracauer seizes the opportunity, in other words, to note the profound difference between working conditions in the United States and Europe.[9] In the same review, Kracauer goes on to lavish upon Rosten, a *New Yorker* short-story writer and future Hollywood screenwriter who later attained fame for his best-selling *Joys of Yiddish* (1968), the kind of praise he may well have wished for himself and for his own work as a film historian. Of Rosten he writes, "he combines the faculty of immediate observation with a far-reaching sociological background, a vivid concern for each specimen of this peculiar human fauna with an ability, if necessary, to keep a distance, the talents of a writer with the capacity of a scholar—gifts that are seldom found together."[10] As a veteran of the cultural pages, the acclaimed feuilleton section of the *Frankfurter Zeitung*, Kracauer knew to rate such gifts. He remarks further in his analysis, "[Rosten's] point of view is near enough to let him discriminate and characterize the multifold traits of the movie world, and at the same time is sufficiently remote to free him from the fetters of intimacy and permit him to look at Hollywood as a whole."[11] Without the full frontal assault of Budd Schulberg's *What Makes Sammy Run* (published the same year as Rosten's book), Rosten nonetheless sees Hollywood as the "quintessence of *nouveau riche*." In Kracauer's estimation, the end result of Rosten's book is "a reliable topography of Hollywood's psychic structure." If *Hollywood* in this formulation were to be replaced with *Weimar Germany*, it might approximate what Kracauer was himself seeking to offer in *From Caligari to Hitler*, which would later be fittingly tagged in his *Harper's* author bio as "a study of the German mind as expressed in German films between the wars."[12] Finally, he notes, "[Rosten] explains the optimism that movie-makers exhibit as their cloak for a deep-rooted anxiety, for the subconscious conviction that luck cannot last and that catastrophe may come at any moment," a remark that almost seems to have slipped out of his *Caligari* file.[13]

In "Why France Liked Our Films," what is significant is not merely Kracauer's discussion of recent Hollywood movies (*Mr. Deeds Goes to Town, The Bowery, Nothing Sacred,* among others) in terms of their European reception—as in his later essay, "Hollywood's Terror Films," faint traces of the French notion of film noir, not yet formally established, lurk between the lines—but also the very subtle ways in which he positions himself, in writing the piece as a newly arrived refugee in his adopted homeland, addressing "our" films (just a few years later, in his essay in *Harper's*, "Those Movies with a Message," he even speaks of "our way of life").[14] Elaborating upon the position that he now occupies, he remarks, "There is only one short moment in which the European observer can judge the validity of the image of American life he had received in European theatres: the moment of his arrival in this country. As a newcomer, he is still entirely connected with the Old World and thus can compare his fresh impressions on American soil with the pictures in his mind."[15] Kracauer points, however, to a deeper paradox of American assimilation and the bearing it has upon his work as a critic: "As soon as the former European acquires an opinion of American reality, he loses the possibility of using it to confirm or reject his old impressions." He recalls his "marvelous first meeting with life in America" while entering New York harbor and passing "such old acquaintances as the Statue of Liberty, Ellis Island and the sky-line." Or, as he puts it somewhat further, "the strange feeling of having already seen all this began to grow upon me," a feeling, so it seems, like Yogi Berra's proverbial "déjà vu all over again." Here Kracauer anticipates the entire premise of Woody Allen's *Purple Rose of Cairo* (1985): "To the passionate movie-goer it was like a dream: either he had suddenly been transplanted onto the screen or the screen itself had come into three-dimensional existence." Noting his recent transformation in America, Kracauer ends the essay by admitting, "It is no longer a European observer who is making these observations."[16]

Yet Kracauer's state of in-betweenness may not have been merely a product of his migration to the United States. As early as 1923, in a letter addressed to Leo Lowenthal and Theodor Adorno, Kracauer had sardonically adopted a phrase from Georg Lukács, giving his whereabouts as "the headquarters of the transcendental homeless."[17] Among the key concerns that followed Kracauer throughout his career, the idea of homelessness, of exile or lack of center—what he later termed "extraterritoriality"—figured prominently in his intellectual orbit. Certainly much of this was professionally related, as Kracauer never seemed to fit into the rigidly defined boundaries of the vocations he pursued; he was unable to find a place for himself in the academy, and his role in journalism, even with the extended stint at the *Frankfurter Zeitung*, was often more of a temporary or freelance nature. But there was also, as Martin Jay has pointed out in his essay on Kracauer's "Extraterritorial Life," a personal dimension to his sense of marginality: Kracauer not only had a highly noticeable speech impediment, which prevented him from occupying certain "stable" public positions, such as teaching, but he also possessed other unusual traits (Adorno invoked the term *extraterritorial* to explain how Kracauer looked) that set him apart from his peers.[18]

While Kracauer may have thought of himself differently in America, the methods of his analysis did not necessarily change as dramatically as did his sense of national identity. As he wrote in 1932 concerning the task of the film critic, "His mission is to unveil the social images and ideologies hidden in mainstream films and through this unveiling to undermine the influence of the films themselves wherever necessary."[19] A major focus of Kracauer's early writings in America, beyond the field of Hollywood film productions, was the German newsreel and propaganda films (perhaps most famously, in 1942, he published his Rockefeller Foundation–sponsored report, "Propaganda and the Nazi War Film," with the Museum of Modern Art and, soon after, contributed a related article, "The Conquest of Europe on the Screen," to *Social Research*).[20] Aimed at a larger audience, in 1944, Kracauer published "The Hitler Image" in the *New Republic*, a brief essay in which he dissected the rhapsodic, highly choreographed depictions of Hitler in Nazi newsreel footage. He examines how these films tend to "assign the traits of a savior to Hitler;" how, in certain instances, as if following each cue in Goebbels's script for him, Hitler "behaves exactly like a popular movie star." In turn, Kracauer uncovers the masks that Hitler wears: "savior as genius," "lord of hosts," man of the people, guarantor of "victory of German arms," and healer in chief.[21] Kracauer offers close sequence analysis, intricately laid out, combined with a touch of trademark American journalistic panache. "He enters a room full of severely wounded soldiers," writes Kracauer, "and as he strides from bed to bed, his raised arm seems to exorcise all infirmities, while cripples and invalids look at him with an excitement that implies their faith in his thaumaturgical faculties." Then, shifting attention from the visual to the audio track, he tacks on: "'They live to see the proudest day of their lives,' the commentary modestly adds."[22]

Today Kracauer's reputation may rest on his writings on German cinema, both pre- and post-Hitler, but arguably his best-known essay from this period, one of the few essays that has elicited critical attention over the years, is "Hollywood's Terror Films," published in *Commentary* in August 1946.[23] It offers a kind of proto-noir meditation (on Alfred Hitchcock's *Shadow of a Doubt*, Robert Siodmak's *Spiral Staircase*, and Billy Wilder's *Lost Weekend*, among others)—indeed, Kracauer lived in France when its film critics were beginning to envision the term *film noir*. As Edward Dimendberg has suggested, "Kracauer describes all of the principal textual, thematic, and narrative traits identified with the film noir cycle: shadowy *mise-en-scène*, postwar anxiety, and narratives of crime, sadism, and transgressive sexuality."[24] In addition, the piece shares, in terms of approach, remarkable affinities with Kracauer's other work, in particular, *From Caligari to Hitler*. Kracauer contends, among other things, that the "tide in Hollywood has turned toward sick souls and fancy psychiatrists" (Kracauer would go on to write a separate piece for *Commentary*, "Psychiatry for Everything and Everybody," on Hollywood's boom in psychological films).[25] As he remarks further, in "Hollywood's Terror Films," "movies not only cater to popular demands; they also reflect popular tendencies and inclinations."[26] Indeed, this thorny issue lay at the heart of his study of German film between the wars—where Kracauer famously argued, "It was all as it had been on the screen. The dark premonitions of a final doom were also fulfilled."[27]

Kracauer's work-for-hire in the mid-1940s, for *Commentary* and other magazines, was not something he would necessarily have chosen for himself, had there been other options. As he wrote to his friend the cinematographer Eugen Schüfftan, whom he met aboard the SS *Nyassa*, asking about prospects in Southern California: "What I don't want at any price is to live again as a freelance writer, as I already got my fill of that in Paris. Please make a little propaganda for me in Hollywood."[28] In a similar vein, in the correspondence addressing the publication of his article on "Hollywood's Terror Films," we are able to glean additional insight into some of the difficulties experienced by the transplanted critic. As Kracauer writes to his editor Clement Greenberg, in a letter of 25 July 1946, "I left you yesterday with a heavy heart. I had to rush over your version and could not grasp it and discuss it with you as fully as I would have liked to. I wish you would give me a chance to go over your rewritten article more thoroughly."[29] According to Kracauer, Greenberg, who was twenty years his junior and had already established himself in the vanguard of American art criticism, had deployed very little tact or judgment when editing his manuscript. In the same letter, he asks of Greenberg, "Why not send me a copy to my vacation address? You would really put me at ease. . . . Being a writer yourself, you will doubtless understand my feelings." Then, however, realizing that his wishes might come across as an unwelcome intrusion, he adds, almost sheepishly, "Of course, on the other hand, I do not wish to make things difficult for you. Therefore, if you cannot send me the copy for some reason, we will simply have to live with it as it is. (What about galley proofs, in this case?)"[30]

Two days later, Kracauer writes to his friend Barbara Deming, whose *Partisan Review* essay "The Artlessness of Walt Disney" he cites in his piece, "I had a nasty experience: the editor of *Commentary* has completely rewritten my article on sadism: it has become flat, explicit, and vulgar in style. I was tempted to withdraw the piece, but the thought of having to try again to sell it, frightened me so much that I agreed after having made a few hasty changes."[31] When reading the two versions of the text, the typescript and the printed article, back to back, the changes to which Kracauer alludes may seem rather small today: a matter of style ("vulgar" in Kracauer's eyes), a massaging of the text here and there by a native speaker and writer of English known for his own refined sense of style. The only major substantive change is the reworking of his conclusion and the inclusion of a paragraph on French existentialism. Yet, as his letter to Barbara Deming attests, Kracauer was loath to retract the essay, given the difficulty of "selling" it elsewhere and perhaps given the import of appearing in the relatively high-profile, distinguished pages of *Commentary* magazine.[32]

To be sure, this was the early *Commentary*, established just a year earlier by the American Jewish Committee (AJC), a much more left-leaning (less stridently Zionist) and more culturally progressive magazine than the arch conservative *Commentary* under Norman Podhoretz during the 1970s (and of course today). In other words, it had not yet become the magazine that would be so caustically mocked by Woody Allen's Alvie Singer in *Annie Hall* (1977), who forecasts the ultimate merger between Irving Howe's leftist journal *Dissent* and Podhoretz's *Commentary* to form *Dissentary*. In his writings for *Commentary*, Kracauer does on occasion—whether under pressure from the editors, from the AJC, or completely on his own volition—take up more overtly Jewish matters. In his review of a biography of Ada Isaacs Menken, for example, he presents the life of the nineteenth-century actress, a trailblazing figure who set the stage for such later actresses as Sarah Bernhardt, as an occasion to discuss the historical development of Jewish acculturation (in a context that is at once American and European). "Released from the ghetto one or two generations earlier," he writes, "the Jews strove to assert themselves in a world of mounting industrialism which favored the expression of their long-suppressed energies. This might well account for the intensity with which they developed inner potentialities or seized upon fortuitous chances. But the world into which they emerged proved a sort of vacuum, a place outside the boundaries of fixed values and venerable traditions. As much as they tried to assimilate, they went astray in it, losing foothold, confidence, and discernment."[33] Was Kracauer commenting here on Menken's or on his own biography? Was this not an oblique reference to a kind of extraterritoriality? Unlike many of his German-born friends and colleagues (e.g., Horkheimer and Adorno), who returned to Germany after the war, Kracauer chose to remain in the United States, accepting a fate that he would later describe somewhat ruefully in *History: The Last Things Before the Last*. "I am thinking of the exile," he writes, "who as an adult person has been forced to leave his country or has left it on his own free will . . . and the odds are that he will never fully belong to the community to which he now in a way belongs. . . . Where then does he live? In the near-vacuum of extra-territoriality, [a] no-man's land."[34]

Overall, Kracauer's work as an American book critic covered a vast amount of ground. For example, he reviewed English translations of Sartre, speeches by Albert Schweitzer, the writings of Eisenstein, and a biography of Chaplin.[35] Some subjects, like the biography of Menken, were admittedly a bit closer to home. In a short review of Richard Plant's novel *The Dragon in the Forest*, published in the *New Republic* in March 1949, Kracauer outs himself as a German exile. Like Kracauer, Plant, who many years later would publish *The Pink Triangle*, his pioneering study of homosexual persecution during the Third Reich, had grown up in Frankfurt am Main and landed in New York during the war. His novel is set in pre-Hitler Germany and takes place in Kracauer's former native city. "I can vouch for the book's respect for reality," Kracauer writes; "its local color is authentic;

important characters appear under their own names and some of those who do not are easily identifiable."[36] And as he later puts it, "the fiction it contains does not overshadow the veracity." The book's greatest merit, then, is "[Plant's] awareness of something as evasive as the mental climate of those years. He does not try to define it; nor does he play the prophet in retrospect. It arises out of the array of facts, related unobtrusively, which together convey the impression."[37] In fictional format, Plant's intimation of a "climate of doom" does not lie far from what Kracauer himself had set out to convey in *From Caligari to Hitler*. Yet in Kracauer's case, some of the early reviewers of his *Caligari* book were concerned about his playing "the prophet in retrospect" and employing a strategy, as Eric Bentley famously called it, of a "refugee's revenge."[38]

During the late 1940s, Kracauer turned his eye toward his former home, writing such review pieces as "Re-education Program for the Reich" (in the *New York Times*) and "The Teutonic Mind" (in the *New Republic*), both of which focused on the Herculean task of establishing a postwar democracy.[39] In one of his final essays from the period, "The Decent German," published in *Commentary*, Kracauer uses his critique of a postwar German film from the Soviet zone, *Ehe im Schatten* (*Marriage in the Shadows*, 1947) as an opportunity to reflect, from the vantage point of a German-Jewish refugee, on the state of de-Nazification. After making a point of noting the duplicitous way in which the film casts "Jewish emigrants almost in the role of deserters," Kracauer levels his blanket indictment: "What is wrong with the majority of Germans is the way they conceive of authority, of the role of reason, of the interrelation between culture and civilization. Any effective mobilization of German decency must depend on a change in habits of thought that are centuries old" (habits, of course, that Kracauer addresses with unremitting force in *From Caligari to Hitler*).[40] He ends the piece on a similarly gloomy note: "Our correspondents in Germany report an ever-increasing rehabilitation of former Nazis and a mounting wave of anti-Semitism. One fears that the decent Germans of today may again let the evil grow without penetrating and resisting it, and may again be caught in the maelstrom with nothing left intact but their precious decency."[41]

During the period in which Kracauer wrote his American freelance criticism, he continued to grapple with the unusual conditions of his existence, as a man who no longer felt a sense of belonging to his former home but who was also not entirely at home in America or, more specifically, in the world of American letters. In his summation of Kracauer's critical

ON THE HORIZON

The Decent German: Film Portrait

SIEGFRIED KRACAUER

WITHIN the last few month, several German postwar films have come to us from the Soviet zone of occupation. One of these, *Marriage in the Shadows*, though not precisely a work of art, at least represents a serious attempt at self-scrutiny. It is, moreover, a film essentially German in technique and outlook; though it was made under Russian auspices, there is no significant evidence of Russian influence to be found in it. It offers, therefore, certain indications of the present state of the German mentality.

This is all the more useful because current reports from Germany, concerned with day-to-day politics rather than deeper currents, do not give a coherent picture of what is going on in the minds of the Germans. On the one hand, they very optimistically speak of a turn to the better, with democratic thought gaining strength; on the other, they record facts which give about the reverse impression,—all too often, apparently, objective estimates are watered down by wishful thinking and moral preachment.

To be sure, the psychological meaning of a film is not always to be found on its sur-

face. Hollywood films, for instance, have been criticized for misleading people abroad into believing that America is a paradise for gangsters, a country where money means everything and acts of unbridled violence alternate with scenes effusively sentimental. These films, it has been remarked, distort American life. No doubt they do, if they are taken at face value. Yet there is a sense in which Hollywood films—the films of all nations, for that matter—reflect a deeper reality: often they reveal less obvious motivations and behavior patterns which in one way or another do correspond to actually existing mass tendencies. In an earlier article in COMMENTARY ("Hollywood's Terror Films," August 1946), the writer tried to show that those screen pageants of horror and sadism which flourished immediately after the war had a distinct bearing on the mental climate of the time. Similarly, it is not difficult, at least in retrospect, to realize that there was a close relation between such a film as Capra's *Mr. Deeds Goes to Town* and the era of the New Deal. Or, to take a more recent example, the Italian film *Paisan*, a blend of political inertia and stirring humanity, clearly reveals its origin in the psychological climate of a nation that has seen many ideas come and go, invariably entailing war and misery, and is now suspicious of all ideas and all politics.

COVERING the period from 1933 to 1945, *Marriage in the Shadows* tells the story, said to be based on real-life events, of a popular Berlin actor and his Jewish wife, herself a prominent actress. The story begins with her enforced retreat from the stage, drags on in an atmosphere of gloom and ever-growing despair, and ends with the actor poisoning himself and his wife to spare her the horrors of imminent deportation. But this is only the nucleus of a plot which clearly aims at driving home the impact of Nazi

---

ON THE HORIZON, devoted to comment on cultural and social events and trends, presents this month an analysis by Siegfried Kracauer of a postwar German film, *Marriage in the Shadows*, which reveals disturbing facts about the present state of the German mind; and a report by HEINZ POLITZER on the interaction of American, East European, and Israeli culture in New York's Yiddish Theater. Dr. Kracauer is the author of *From Caligari to Hitler*, a psychological history of the German cinema. Dr. Politzer, now teaching at Bryn Mawr, has been a frequent contributor to these pages; his article is translated by F. C. Golffing.

74

Fig. 1. First page of Kracauer's review of *Ehe im Schatten* (Germany, 1947, dir. Kurt Maetzig) for *Commentary* magazine, January 1949.

legacy, the eminent art historian Meyer Shapiro, who had been instrumental in assisting Kracauer's flight from Vichy France to America, poignantly remarked, "[Kracauer] should become better known, not only because of his actual gifts as a writer and as a man with important interests in sociology and theory and philosophy . . . but also [because] he's an example of the type of nonacademic man who is saturated with the standards of German scholarship without belonging to one of the professions."[42] Nonbelonging, in Shapiro's assessment, was a considerable asset to Kracauer—his lack of permanent affiliation, let alone permanent residence, a critical factor in the agility of his intellect and his multidisciplinary writing. At a time when scholarly disciplines continue to remain relatively rigid in definition and unimaginative in approach, when the academy only rarely interacts with the public at large, and when an unconventional career path such as that of Kracauer no longer seems viable, the import of his work—and, more generally, the act of looking after Kracauer—has not lost any of its urgency.

NOTES

1. Gertrud Koch, *Siegfried Kracauer: An Introduction*, trans. Jeremy Gaines (Princeton: Princeton University Press), 3.

2. Siegfried Kracauer, letter to Wolfgang Weyrauch, 4 June 1962. Quoted in *Siegfried Kracauer: 1889–1966*, ed. Ingrid Belke and Irina Renz, *Marbacher Magazin* 47 (1988): 118.

3. Siegfried Kracauer, letter to Theodor W. Adorno , 28 March 1941. Quoted in Belke and Renz, 100.

4. Siegfried Kracauer, "Dumbo," *The Nation*, 8 November 1941, 463.

5. Walter Benjamin, "Mickey Mouse," *The Work of Art in the Age of Its Technological Reproducibility, and Other Writings on Media*, ed. Michael W. Jennings, Brigid Doherty, and Thomas Y. Levin (Cambridge: Harvard University Press, 2008), 276.

6. Kracauer, "Dumbo," 463.

7. Siegfried Kracauer, review of *Hollywood, The Movie Colony—The Movie Makers*, by Leo Rosten, *Social Research* 9, no. 2 (May 1942): 282–83.

8. Siegfried Kracauer, "Why France Liked Our Films," *National Board of Review Magazine* 17, no. 5 (May 1942): 15–19.

9. It is worth underscoring the extent to which Kracauer benefited from the largesse of American grant agencies—apart from the Rockefeller aid, he garnered support from the Guggenheim and Bollingen Foundations—and together with fellow refugees Hermann Broch and Erich Kahler, he forcefully defended the work of such foundations in print. On the significance of the letter by Broch, Kahler, and Kracauer, defending the Bollingen Foundation in the *Saturday Review*, see William McGuire, *Bollingen: An Adventure in Collecting the Past* (Princeton: Princeton University Press, 1982), 214.

10. Kracauer, review of *Hollywood*, 282.

11. Ibid.

12. See Siegfried Kracauer, "Those Movies with a Message," *Harper's Magazine* 196 (June 1948): 567.

13. Kracauer, review of *Hollywood*, 283.

14. Kracauer, "Those Movies with a Message," 571.

15. Kracauer, "Why France Liked Our Films," 19.

16. Ibid.

17. Cited in Leo Lowenthal, "As I Remember Friedel," *New German Critique* 54 (Fall 1991): 12.

18. Martin Jay, "The Extraterritorial Life of Siegfried Kracauer," *Permanent Exiles: Essays on the Intellectual Migration from Germany to America* (New York: Columbia University Press, 1986), 153.

19. Siegfried Kracauer, "The Task of the Film Critic," in *The Weimar Republic Sourcebook*, ed. Anton Kaes, Martin Jay, and Edward Dimendberg (Berkeley: University of California Press, 1995), 635.

20. See Siegfried Kracauer, "The Conquest of Europe on the Screen: The Nazi Newsreel, 1939–40," *Social Research* 10, no. 3 (September 1943): 337–57. The larger study is appended to his *From Caligari to Hitler: A Psychological History of the German Film*, revised and expanded edition, ed. Leonardo Quaresima (1947; Princeton: Princeton University Press, 2004), 275–307.

21. Siegfried Kracauer, "The Hitler Image," *New Republic* 110, no. 1 (1944): 22.

22. Ibid.

23. Siegfried Kracauer, "Hollywood's Terror Films: Do They Reflect an American State of Mind?" *Commentary* 2, no. 2 (August 1946): 132–36.

24. Edward Dimendberg, "Down These Seen Streets A Man Must Go: Siegfried Kracauer's 'Hollywood Terror Films' and the Spatiality of Film Noir," *New German Critique* 89 (Spring–Summer 2003): 124.

25. Kracauer, "Hollywood's Terror Films," 133. See also Kracauer, "Psychiatry for Everything and Everybody," *Commentary* 5, no. 3 (March 1948): 222–28.

26. Kracauer, "Hollywood's Terror Films," 135.

27. Kracauer, *From Caligari to Hitler*, 272.

28. Siegfried Kracauer, letter to Eugen Schüfftan, 28 April 1946. Quoted in *Nachrichten aus Hollywood, New York und anderswo: Der Briefwechsel Eugen und Marlise Schüfftans mit Siegfried und Lili Kracauer*, ed. Helmut G. Asper (Trier: Wissenschaftlicher Verlag, 2003), 66.

29. Siegfried Kracauer, letter to Clement Greenberg, 25 July 1946. Quoted in Inka Mülder-Bach, ed., *Kleine Schriften zum Film*, vol. 6.3 of Siegfried Kracauer, *Werke* (Frankfurt am Main: Suhrkamp, 2004), 485.

30. Ibid.

31. Ibid.

32. On the general lack of compatibility between the so-called New York Intellectuals and their Frankfurt-born counterparts, see Mark Krupnick, "Criticism as an Institution," *Crisis of Modernity: Recent Critical Theories of Culture and Society in the United States and West Germany*, ed. Günter H. Lenz and Kurt L. Shell (Boulder: Westview, 1986), 156–76.

33. Siegfried Kracauer, "A Lady of Valor," *Commentary* 4, no. 4 (October 1947): 395.

34. Siegfried Kracauer, *History: The Last Things Before the Last* (Princeton: Markus Wiener, 1995), 83–84. Cited in Koch, *Siegfried Kracauer*, 114.

35. See Siegfried Kracauer, "Consciousness, Free and Spontaneous," review of *The Psychology of Imagination*, by Jean-Paul Sartre, *Saturday Review of Literature* 31, no. 26 (26 June 1948): 22–23; review of *Goethe: Two Addresses*, by Albert Schweitzer, *Saturday Review of Literature* 31, no. 27 (3 July 1948): 9; "The Russian Director," review of *Film Form*, by Sergei M. Eisenstein, *New Republic* 121, no. 13 (26 September 1949): 22–23; and "Portrait in Film," review of *Chaplin: Last of the Clowns*, by Parker Tyler, *New Republic* (26 July 1948): 24–26.

36. Siegfried Kracauer, "Climate of Doom," review of *The Dragon in the Forest*, by Richard Plant, *New Republic* 120, no. 10 (7 March 1949): 24.

37. Kracauer, "Climate of Doom," 25.

38. Eric Bentley, "The Cinema: Its Art and Techniques," *New York Times Book Review*, 18 May 1947. See also Quaresima's editor's introduction, "Rereading Kracauer," in *From Caligari to Hitler*, esp. xl–xlii.

39. See Siegfried Kracauer, "Re-education Program for the Reich," *New York Times*, 4 January 1948; "The Teutonic Mind," *New Republic* 18, no. 8 (23 February 1948): 23–24.

40. Siegfried Kracauer, "The Decent German: Film Portrait," *Commentary* 7, no. 1 (January 1949): 77.

41. Ibid.

42. Cited in Mark M. Anderson, "Siegfried Kracauer and Meyer Schapiro: A Friendship," *New German Critique* 54 (Fall 1991): 19–20.

Manhattan Crossroads

Theory of Film between the Frankfurt School and the New York Intellectuals

Johannes von Moltke

Eine entscheidende theoretische Arbeit über den Film ist von der allergrößten Bedeutung und zwar im höchst belasteten, keineswegs bloß dem üblichen soziologischen Sinn, weil hier die tiefsten Schichten der Veränderung des Erfahrens, bis in die Wahrnehmung hinein, sich niedergeschlagen haben.

—Theodor W. Adorno,
Letter to Siegfried Kracauer 17 October 1950[1]

When Siegfried Kracauer's long-projected book on film aesthetics finally saw the light of day as *Theory of Film* in 1960, Kracauer's fellow émigré Rudolf Arnheim reviewed it as "probably the most intelligent book ever written on the subject of film."[2] This was an auspicious beginning for a book whose publication coincided with the institutionalization of Film Studies in the United States.[3] Recognized for its "lofty purpose and scholarly appeal," *Theory of Film* seemed predestined to occupy a central place in discussions among the cinematologists of the day (where Kracauer was a card-carrying member) and in curricula of cinema studies departments to come.[4]

And there it long remained, respectfully referenced as it acquired patina on its academic pedestal as an exemplar of "classical film theory." That label makes the book—and the other theories it subsumes, for that matter—appear quaint and dated, safely contained in an earlier era that so-called contemporary film theory helped us supersede. According to the progressivist assumptions underlying such thinking, *Theory of Film* can now appear to students as a labored contribution to an earlier set of debates at best, and a pedantic, theoretical aberration at worst.[5] In sum, it has acquired what Max Frisch, speaking of Brecht, once called "the resounding ineffectiveness of a classic."[6]

To counter this ossifying tendency, it is no use simply to tout the contemporary relevance of the classic in question and proclaim that the lessons it contains are as fresh as they ever were; to do so would be to marry a misguided presentism with the assertion of the classic's timelessness, which is to say: to avoid historical reflection, including on the intervening history of canonization itself. The following remarks aim, by contrast, at restoring to *Theory of Film* some of the historical frameworks and discussions that have fallen by the wayside over the course of its reception. Specifically, given Kracauer's emigration to the United States in 1941, as well as the fact that he would spend the rest of his life as a naturalized U.S. citizen in New York, I propose to consider that city's vibrant intellectual scene as a crucial horizon for his work on the film book.[7] Wishing to contribute to the historicization of classical film theory, and of Kracauer's book in particular, I propose to resituate *Theory of Film* geographically and trace its travels from Frankfurt and Marseille to Manhattan—that is, from Kracauer's intellectual roots in Critical Theory and the preparatory work he undertook in French exile, to what he saw as his "last station" in the United States.[8]

Miriam Hansen has charted the first part of this journey in her important work on the Marseille Notebooks.[9] My emphasis here, consequently, will be on the American context, and on situating Kracauer and his work among the "New York Intellectuals"—a group of thinkers who dominated the cultural discourse during the quarter century Kracauer spent in the city, but whose relationship with the exiled members of the Frankfurt School is only just beginning to be explored; to date, Kracauer's position in this constellation of Frankfurt and New York has been overlooked almost entirely.[10] And yet, rereading Kracauer's books as well as his variegated smaller publications in this context allows us not only to place his work historically but also to reconstruct the contours of a fascinating "Manhattan Transfer"—a transatlantic exchange among two of the most influential schools of thought at midcentury. With both the Frankfurt School and the New York Intellectuals, Kracauer shared the fundamental commitment to cultural critique as a tool for debunking received ideas, conventional wisdom, and reigning ideologies. Indeed, given the limited and often abortive exchanges that transpired between the main representatives of these two schools,[11] one is tempted to see in Kracauer the missing link between the Frankfurt School and the New York Intellectuals. On the margins of both

Fig. 1. Siegfried Kracauer on vacation in Stamford, Connecticut,
around 1950. Deutsches Literaturarchiv Marbach.

movements, Kracauer was able to forge compelling insights into the cultural phenomena of his day from a transatlantic perspective that combined
his deep affinities with Critical Theory (and the critical theorists he had
mentored) with a commitment to grasping his American surroundings. His
writings permit us to rethink the relationship between the New York and
the Frankfurt Intellectuals not simply in terms of missed opportunities;

they also provide an occasion for developing the theoretical sight lines that emerge if we place these two intellectual traditions, usually associated with two separate sides of the Atlantic, within the perspective offered by Kracauer's work in exile.

Although this constitutes a larger project than the present article permits,[12] we may gauge its relevance by isolating and investigating one central conceptual strand from the fabric of this intellectual exchange: the question of experience.[13] It plays a key role in the elaboration of Critical Theory by members of the Frankfurt School,[14] but it also receives extensive treatment in New York circles[15]—particularly, I will suggest, at the hands of the critic Robert Warshow.

The concept of experience of course has a long and complex history—one that Martin Jay has chronicled in his magisterial *Songs of Experience*.[16] Even if we leave aside the conservative tradition and focus exclusively on what might be called the progressive modulations of the notion of experience, we are confronted with a recurring struggle over its proper *place:* is it, as thinkers from the French existentialists to Raymond Williams up through the present resurgence of phenomenology might claim, the wellspring of proper theorizing? Or is it, as Terry Eagleton posited in an attack on Williams, his erstwhile teacher, the "proper home of ideology," false consciousness, the very opposite of understanding? With Warshow on one side, and his friends Walter Benjamin and Theodor W. Adorno on the other, I suggest, Kracauer would have felt acutely the pull of these two competing claims and their weighty intellectual genealogies.

Amalgamating these two backgrounds, Kracauer assigns the concept a central role in his *Theory of Film*, which concludes with a section on "Experience and Its Material." Here, he illustrates the importance of the concrete with a conspicuously localized example: whereas the grid of Manhattan's streets is a well-known fact, he argues, "this fact becomes concrete only if we realize, for instance, that all the cross streets end in the nothingness of the blank sky."[17] For abstract knowledge to gain traction in a world increasingly dominated by scientific paradigms, Kracauer suggests, it needs to be grounded in experience. *Theory of Film*, of course, is devoted to defining cinema as the medium through which such experience might be restored to modernity—"redeemed," as Kracauer puts it in the subtitle of the book. This claim, like the book itself, "becomes concrete" only if we realize that it was composed at the crossroads of Frankfurt and New York, the fruit of a transatlantic intellectual history yet to be explored.

Robert Warshow and the New York Intellectuals' Critique of Experience

> We mean by abstract: really not thinking through experience. What is the subject of our thought? Experience! Nothing Else!
>
> —Hannah Arendt[18]

To reread *Theory of Film* from such a transatlantic perspective is to reconsider who Kracauer's interlocutors were for this project. Judging by the references in the published book, some of these were temporally and/or geographically remote.[19] But other interlocutors were closer, as the surviving manuscripts reveal. A "tentative outline" records critical comments not only by Adorno (then still in California) and Arnheim, who was teaching at Sarah Lawrence College in nearby Yonkers, but also by a third reader who appears in the margins of the document: Robert Warshow, then editor of the influential New York journal *Commentary* and a frequent contributor to *Partisan Review* and *The Nation*, where Kracauer had also managed to place some articles.[20] Warshow was a brilliant critic who died too young, perhaps, to be remembered as a major contributor to the debates of the times. But Thomas Jeffers considers him in retrospect as "surely the archetypal *Commentary* writer"—an assessment readily confirmed by the posthumous anthology of Warshow's writings.[21] To the degree that editing and publishing in journals such as *Commentary* or *Partisan Review* conferred membership status among the group, Warshow was representative not merely of an influential form of writing but of the New York Intellectuals as a whole.[22]

Kracauer's interventions during his New York years communicate closely with Warshow's work, whether through editorial comment or through explicit reference.[23] The two men had been in contact with respect to various articles that Kracauer proposed to *Commentary*, and they even appear to have competed for space to write on film in the pages of *Partisan Review*.[24] As both their published and unpublished writings of the time indicate, the two men shared an intense interest in the cultural landscape of their day, which—unlike some of their more unabashedly Europhile and avant-garde-minded colleagues (take Clement Greenberg, for example)—they found to be mapped most clearly in the movies. From Chaplin to Italian Neorealism, Kracauer and Warshow reviewed the same films and books on the cinema. Even if, as in the case of Rossellini, they may have reached slightly different conclusions, their forms of cultural critique not only converged on the same objects but also shared a number of theoretical concepts.[25] Notions of realism and alienation figured centrally

Fig. 2. *Partisan Review* issues from 1947, including preprint of the "Caligari" chapter from Kracauer's forthcoming book, *From Caligari to Hitler*. Photograph by Johannes von Moltke.

among these, but in retrospect, it is the question of experience that constituted the starting point for Warshow's work and the conceptual telos of *Theory of Film*.

As I will suggest below, experience is for Warshow a category less thoroughly theorized, perhaps, than it is in Kracauer's writings, which owe a debt also to Critical Theory; but it is significant to note, at the outset, that this is where Warshow, like Kracauer, locates the specific cultural value of the movies as well as of his approach: the "fundamental *fact* of the movies," he contends after an explicit acknowledgment of his debt to Kracauer, is not only "a fact at once aesthetic and sociological, but also something more. This is the actual immediate experience of seeing and responding to the movies as most of us see them and respond to them."[26] As opposed to high-minded art criticism on the one hand and sociological generalizations on the other, Warshow advocates an approach to movies and popular culture that begins with the critic's own response, with the experience of reading, looking, or watching, and with the explicit "acknowledgment of [the critic's] own relation to the object he criticizes."[27]

From this premise, Warshow develops a critique of contemporary culture and its effects on experience that, in a vocabulary slightly different from Warshow's own, we might label a critique of reification. His essays indict cultural practices, from publishing to the movies, for the obfuscation of authentic needs and the abstraction of human relations in received ideas, opinions, and ideologies that subjects mistake, in turn, for their own experience. By the same token, all of Warshow's essays implicitly call for forms of cultural practice and criticism that might rekindle genuine modes of "actual, immediate experience." Whether writing about the Rosenbergs' shocking alienation from their own experience in prison ("almost nothing really belonged to them, not even their own experience") or of the way in which the *New Yorker* deals with experience "not by trying to understand it but by prescribing the attitude to be adopted toward it," Warshow indicts middlebrow culture across the political spectrum for estranging midcentury Americans from their lived reality.[28] In its place, Warshow argues, they receive preformulated "ideas," sociological theories, or misguided pretensions to art—a tendency exacerbated by (film) critics who fail to see the experiential qualities of the movies behind ready-made categories drawn from sociology or misplaced aesthetic formalism. Warshow sums up this state of affairs in a grant proposal to the Guggenheim Foundation for a project with which he proposed to break through these false alternatives: "The sociological critic says to us, in effect: It is not *I* who goes to the movies; it is the audience. The aesthetic critic says: It is not the *movies* I go to see; it is art."[29] By contrast, the form of critique that Warshow advocates would begin, as I have suggested, with the centrality of *both* subject ("I") and object ("the movies") as they encounter one another in the medium of experience. Unfortunately, Warshow's untimely death meant that the proposal to fashion—and theorize—a new form of film criticism remained just that, a grant proposal. From the posthumous anthology of his writings, however (for which the proposal now serves as a preface), the contours of Warshow's approach are readily apparent—much as they would have been to a discerning reader of the "little magazines" at the time the essays were originally published. We should count Kracauer among those readers.

Warshow himself formulated his fundamental question at the close of an important essay for *Commentary* in 1947. Having surveyed the Communist legacy of the 1930s that defined his cohort, as well as the pressures exerted on that legacy by both Stalinism in the Soviet Union and the rise of middlebrow culture in the United States, Warshow concluded by asking, "How shall we regain the use of our experience in the world of mass culture?"[30] Kracauer's *Theory of Film*, I propose, takes up this same question, modulated through his long-standing engagement with the work of his friends Theodor Adorno and Walter Benjamin; as if in answer to Warshow's query, the book formulates a theory of film as a medium of experience, and of realism as its style.

Theory of Film and the Dialectics of Experience

> The medium of his thought was experience.
> —Theodor W. Adorno[31]

The centrality of experience as a notion in *Theory of Film* has long been recognized, most clearly by Hansen who argues that "what *Theory of Film* can offer us today is not a theory of film in general, but a theory of a particular type of film experience, and of cinema as the aesthetic matrix of a particular historical experience."[32] Nor is Kracauer's concept of realism ontological or referential, as critics are fond of repeating; it, too, is fundamentally experiential.[33] In the photographic medium of film and in the stylistic commitment to realism, Kracauer sees the promise of breaking through the reification of everyday life by confronting viewers with the estranged fragments of their existence and allowing them to recoup these fragments in the medium of experience. Film, according to Kracauer's underlying argument, at once estranges us from our ingrained habits of (alienated) perception and models a form of experience that overcomes alienation in the act of spectatorship.[34]

Besides forming the *basso continuo* of *Theory of Film*, "the momentous issue of the significance of the film experience"[35] is raised quite explicitly in various places throughout the book, from the preface's anecdotal recollection of his first film experience and its lasting impact, to the crucial chapter on the spectator. But the keystone in Kracauer's discussion of the cinema's experiential dimension remains the final chapter, "Film in Our Time."

Even though it appears simply as an epilogue in the book, Kracauer considered it as the "masterkey to all that precedes it."[36] As is well known to
readers (and critics) of *Theory of Film*, Kracauer's argument here turns on
the claim that the world of modernity—the postwar, post-Holocaust, post-
Stalinist, nuclear age—is one governed by "abstraction." Somewhat pre-
dictably, Kracauer proposes that film provides a "remedy" for abstractness
in the form of "experience of things in their concreteness."[37] What is un-
available to experience in everyday life, where experience itself has come
under threat, film facilitates: by gravitating toward the unstaged, the fortuitous, and the "flow of life," the cinema allows the modern subject to reconnect to forms of experience that redeem transience and indeterminacy
in the face of reification. In view of the scripted forms of experience promulgated, according to Warshow, by middlebrow culture, it is no accident
that Kracauer's theory—like that of his contemporary André Bazin, who
reached similar conclusions working independently in France—ultimately
amounts to a defense of ambiguity: it is his way of locating the resistance of
experience to reification.[38]

As should be clear from the discussion above, such a conclusion also
resonates locally with the forms of cultural critique launched by New York
Intellectuals such as Robert Warshow. For like Warshow, Kracauer essentially formulates a *critique* of experience. That is to say, both authors diag-
nose the waning of experience in contemporary culture and at the same
time seek to rescue genuine forms of experience—whether "immediate"
(Warshow) or cinematic and "concrete" (Kracauer)—as a resource against
the alienating forces of modernity that they variously define as abstraction,
reification, ideology. The fact that both authors locate that resource at least
partly within the realm of mass culture (as distinct from both the "ooze" of
middlebrow culture and the pretensions of high art) sets them apart, I will
suggest, from their contemporaries in both the New York and the Frankfurt School circles. Before locating the significance of this specific contribution in its historical context, however, we must attend to an important
distinction between Warshow's and Kracauer's notions of experience,
which will provide further contours to their form of cultural critique—including its potential *limits*.

Such limits become clear if we consider the apparent tendency to construct experience in strict opposition to ideology as an unmediated, subjective act. For Warshow's central question—how shall we regain the use of
our experience in the world of mass culture?—only makes sense if we as-

sume that experience is still available for the having. Warshow posits emphatically that there is such a thing as "immediate experience" whose bearer is the autonomous subject; though middlebrow culture poses a severe threat to that subject's ability to own its experience, a critic such as Warshow would claim that the latter can be recovered through robust cultural critique. For all the power of Warshow's prose on this issue, however, he never quite seems to consider the possibility that experience, rather than being immediate, is of necessity a multiply mediated relationship between subject and object—one in which the two sides are not transparent to one another and remain in certain respects incommensurable.[39] This aspect had been formulated forcefully by Kracauer's interlocutors from the other side of the Atlantic, particularly by Walter Benjamin and Theodor W. Adorno.[40]

To the degree that he simply posits experience and the concrete as the opposite of abstraction, Kracauer would seem to share Warshow's premise. Throughout his writings, from the Weimar years onward, Kracauer had placed great emphasis on the particular sui generis; as he puts it in the final chapter of *Theory of Film*, "there is no substitute for the direct perception of the concrete achievement of a thing in its actuality. We want concrete fact with a high light thrown on what is relevant to its preciousness."[41] Such an assertion appears to echo Warshow's insistence on "immediate experience" and is thus open to the same criticism: it suggests the possibility of wholly unmediated perception and cognition—a claim all the more troubling for the fact that it occurs at the heart of a theory of film *as a medium* of experience. In this sense, it is understandable that Adorno, for one, would fault Kracauer for failing to attend to the dialectical mediations of the concept. Of his friend, the "curious realist," Adorno wrote, "Dialectical thought never suited his temperament. He contented himself with the precise specification of the particular for use as an example of general matters."[42] To the extent that Kracauer shares Warshow's emphatic, subject-centered notion of experience, Adorno would appear to be justified in claiming that Kracauer fails to see how the particular is determined by the general, the concrete is the sum of abstractions. The central thesis about the redemption of physical reality would necessarily falter, in the critical eyes of Kracauer's closest friends in the Frankfurt School, on its undialectical assertion of the primacy of sense data and subjective experience. Adorno put it this way in a well-known article, "The Essay as Form," which resonates strongly with the importance of the essay as a (journalistic) form for the New York Intellectuals:

> The relation to experience . . . is a relation to all of history; merely in-
> dividual experience, in which consciousness begins with what is nearest
> to it, is itself mediated by the all-encompassing experience of historical
> humanity; the claim that social-historical contents are nevertheless sup-
> posed to be only indirectly important compared with the immediate life
> of the individual is a simple self-delusion of an individualistic society
> and ideology.[43]

In this view, championing any "immediate experience," as Warshow did
and Adorno accused Kracauer of doing, would merely duplicate rather
than critique the underlying ideology of quasi individuality.

But we should remain attentive to the considerable nuance with which
Kracauer constructs his argument. Kracauer's roots in the Frankfurt
School, while muted in exile and modified through his work in New York,
anchor the conceptualization of experience in *Theory of Film*, where it retains its dialectical valence. Redemption, after all, is not equivalent to a
nostalgic return; for all his attention to the concrete experience, Kracauer
is loath to hypostasize it in the face of its counterparts in abstraction and
fragmentation, much in the same way he will refuse to dissolve the tension
between the transcendental and the immanent in his posthumous *History*.[44]
Theory of Film hardly offers a return to unfettered individualism or even to
any preexisting forms of experience at all; rather, it *inaugurates* a specific
kind of experience that places subject and object, the individual and society
in dialectical tension. This is the implication of Kracauer's somewhat enigmatic claim that "we are free to experience [the material world] because we
are fragmentized": modernity, and film as its quintessential medium, produce the antidote to the alienation or "abstraction" of which they themselves are symptoms. A "fragmentized" subject is not autonomous with respect to the material world it experiences; it is as much an effect of
historical shifts in that world—including its shifting media landscape—as it
is a receptive membrane that registers such shifts.

What is true of Kracauer's notion of experience also holds for his notion of the "concrete" as the object of experience. Whereas one might be
inclined to understand concretion as the positive term in opposition to the
prevailing "abstractness," Kracauer significantly refuses to equate the concrete with empirical sense data. Nor is the abstract simply immaterial. Abstraction, Kracauer specifies in *Theory of Film*, "refers us to physical phenomena, while at the same time luring us away from their *qualities*. Hence

the urgency of grasping precisely these *given and yet ungiven* phenomena in their concreteness."[45] What looks like an equivocation—how can a concrete phenomenon be "given and yet ungiven"?—can now be explained as a dialectical image. In a line of thinking that reaches from Marx to Brecht and Benjamin, the concrete only has explanatory power as "a synthesis of determinations" that begins, not with sense data, but with abstract determinations that lead "to the reproduction of the concrete."[46] Given as the physical reality of Kracauer's title, phenomena yet remain "ungiven"—that is, abstract and uncomprehended—until they reach the spectator as a concrete synthesis of determinations in the medium of film. Consequently, the cinematic concrete is for Kracauer not an ontological fact but an experiential one that relies, precisely, on mediation.

In the epilogue to *Theory of Film*, Kracauer exemplifies his own method by a reference to Alfred North Whitehead. To understand the workings of a factory, Whitehead suggests, it is not sufficient to deal "merely in terms of economic abstractions"; what we want to train is "the habit of apprehending such an organism in its completeness."[47] Kracauer quotes this passage approvingly but goes on to note that "perhaps the term 'completeness' is not quite adequate. In experiencing an object, we not only broaden our knowledge of its diverse qualities but in a manner of speaking incorporate it into us so that we grasp its being and its dynamics from within—a sort of blood transfusion, as it were."[48] The organicist vocabulary here is intriguing for what it suggests about the phenomenology of the film experience, but it can be deceiving in that it once again suggests a form of immediacy where Kracauer is in fact attempting to work out a series of complicated mediations. For what is at stake in this image of introjection and blood transfusion are again the relations between subject and object, the concrete and the abstract: film has the power to mediate between these poles; it is able to represent (rather than simply reproduce) reality—the diverse qualities of the object, its abstract dynamics as much as its sensible surface appearance—as a concrete perceptual object for the spectator, who in turn experiences that object as a synthesis of determinations. In this reading of *Theory of Film*, the medium's appointed task to record and reveal is itself a dialectical one. For merely to record would be to reproduce the false concrete, just as unmediated revelation would yield a false abstraction. The "redemption of physical reality" depends precisely on this dialectics of recording and revealing, of concretion and abstraction, of the given and yet ungiven.

Conclusion: Mass Culture, Cinema, and Experience

If Kracauer's elaboration of the relationship between film and experience was ultimately more nuanced than Warshow's, this may have had to do partly with the more occasional style of the latter's articles compared to Kracauer's long-gestating, magisterial book on film aesthetics; and one can only wonder how the dialogue might have developed had Warshow lived to work out his proposed book for the Guggenheim grant and see the publication of *Theory of Film*. For it seems likely that, for all their differences, the two men would have found themselves aligned in the cultural climate of their day on the side of those few intellectuals willing to take quite seriously the promises of popular culture. Where the leading lights of the Frankfurt School passed summary judgment on the culture industry and its systematic annihilation of experience, and New York Intellectuals like Clement Greenberg ruled out as kitsch whatever did not live up to their avant-garde standards, Warshow and Kracauer let themselves be guided by a profound cinephilia that helped them illuminate the utopian and redemptive qualities of the movies.[49] The two authors shared the diagnosis of the reification of experience—whether at the hands of ideology and opinion-mongering, as Warshow claimed, or as the fallout of scientific progress and some more generalized notion of abstraction. Similarly, both critics harbored a belief that one could reconnect to this lost experience and gather up its shards within popular culture and at the movies. The route to this redemption, for Warshow as for Kracauer, was film, and realism in particular—whether in the form of the gangster film or the Western, the found story or the episode, or in the figures of actors like Gary Cooper or Gregory Peck who "are in themselves, as material objects, 'realistic,' seeming to bear in their bodies and their faces mortality, limitation, the knowledge of good and evil."[50]

As such formulations of the aesthetic power of stardom would suggest, Warshow was considerably less worried about the blurred boundaries between high and low culture than some of his fellow New Yorkers. Emphasizing the "actual, immediate experience of seeing and responding to the movies as most of us see them and respond to them," Warshow advocated—and practiced—a phenomenology of popular culture that shares a number of features with Kracauer's work from the Weimar years through *Theory of Film*. Mass culture, Warshow ventured, was a central facet of contemporary existence, to be treated by the critic as "the screen through which we see reality and the mirror in which we see ourselves."[51] Like Kracauer, Warshow read the surface manifestations of cultural life—from *Krazy Kat* to the *New Yorker* to the figure of the Gangster in Hollywood film, from his son's obsession with horror comics to his father's postmortem physiognomy—for their social meanings. "In some way," Warshow admitted in a programmatic (under)statement, "I take all that nonsense seriously"—especially the "nonsense" that was cinema.[52]

For Kracauer, too, no object was too low or abject to be worthy of his attention—in numerous texts and through his posthumous *History*, he would reiterate his attention to "overlooked" modes of being and the interstices of culture as one of his central methodological tenets. To be sure, Kracauer brought the devotion to the movies with him to exile from his years as a film critic in Germany. But in his commitment to working out an experiential aesthetics of the cinema, he was closer, perhaps, to his New York contemporaries than to his friends from Frankfurt, and to Adorno in particular, who continued to champion the cause of an autonomous art. It seems significant in this respect that *Theory of Film* at every turn argues decidedly against nobilitating film as a traditional art form, making a claim instead for film's power to revise the very notion of what constitutes the cultural category of art in the first place. Given the role of film as a mass medium, that category would include the popular by definition, a thesis explicitly ruled out in Adorno's and Horkheimer's theorizations of the culture industry.

Even after the publication of *Theory of Film*, it would still take Adorno half a decade to grudgingly admit that Kracauer's was "the most plausible theory of film technique."[53] But when he did so, Adorno alighted on the importance of experience at the heart of cinema, arguing that the aesthetics of film must "base itself on a subjective mode of experience which film resembles and which constitutes its artistic character."[54] By placing the notion of experience at the heart of cinema, Adorno revealed himself to be a careful reader of his friend's work in exile, though to this reading we should now add the intellectual context in which Kracauer had formulated his film aesthetics. To situate *Theory of Film* at the crossroads of Frankfurt and New York, where Kracauer made his home in exile, is to recover not only its historical richness but also its dialectical underpinnings and the centrality of the notion of experience, which the emphasis on ontology and medium-specificity in classical film theory has served to obfuscate.

NOTES

1. "A decisive theoretical work on film is of the greatest importance—and I mean this in the emphatic sense, not just in the habitual sociological sense: for it is here that we can register the deepest layers of a shift in experience that reaches all the way into perception." Theodor W. Adorno and Siegfried Kracauer, *"Der Riß der Welt geht auch durch mich"*: *Briefwechsel 1923–1966*, ed. Wolfgang Schopf (Frankfurt am Main: Suhrkamp, 2008), 453. Unless otherwise noted, all translations are my own.

2. Rudolf Arnheim, "Melancholy Unshaped," in *Journal of Aesthetics and Art Criticism* 21, no. 3 (Spring 1963): 291–97, here 291. It should be noted that Arnheim goes on to qualify this assessment, faulting Kracauer's emphasis on realism for its logical ambiguity (292) and pointing out several "aesthetic problems" on which *Theory of Film* falters (293).

3. See Stephen Groening, "Appendix: Timeline for a History of Anglophone Film Culture and Film Studies," in Lee Grieveson and Haidee Wasson, eds., *Inventing Film Studies* (Durham: Duke University Press, 2008). With the fiftieth anniversary of the society's founding, a number of scholars have turned their attention to the history of the discipline; in addition to the essays collected in Grieveson and Wasson, see Dana Polan, *Scenes of Instruction: The Beginnings of the US Study of Film* (Berkeley: University of California Press, 2008); Peter Decherney, *Hollywood and the Culture Elite: How the Movies Became American* (New York: Columbia University Press, 2006); as well as the section "In Focus: SCMS at Fifty" in *Cinema Journal* 49, no. 1 (Fall 2009): 128–76.

4. In April 1960, the recently founded Society of Cinematologists convened its first national meeting at New York University, just downtown from Kracauer's Upper West Side apartment; the society, whose council proudly counted Kracauer as "one of its most eminent members," would begin publication of its scholarly journal by 1961. As *Cinema Journal* noted upon Kracauer's death, Kracauer "responded to the challenge of film scholarship before there was group organization or governmental support, and his pioneering work stands as an inspiration for those who came after him" (*Cinema Journal* 6 [1966–67]: 32). The Society of Cinematologists was the precursor to the Society for Cinema Studies, recently renamed Society for Cinema and Media Studies (SCMS); on its history, see Lee Grieveson, "Discipline and Publish: The Birth of Cinematology," in *Cinema Journal* 49, no. 1 (Fall 2009): 168–75.

5. For the reception of *Theory of Film*, see the editors' Introduction, above, and Eric Rentschler's contribution to this volume.

6. The German phrase is *durchschlagende Wirkungslosigkeit eines Klassikers.* Max Frisch, *Öffentlichkeit als Partner* (Frankfurt am Main: Suhrkamp, 1967), 73.

7. Miriam Hansen points in a similar direction with her suggestion that "it might be productive to think of *Theory of Film* as contemporaneous with the magazine *Film Culture* and developments in independent film production and distribution; . . . with Susan Sontag's essay 'Against Interpretation,' Miles Davis's *Kind of Blue*, Lawrence Ferlinghetti's *A Coney Island of the Mind*." Miriam Hansen, introduction to *Theory of Film: The Redemption of Physical Reality*, by Siegfried Kracauer (Princeton: Princeton University Press, 1997), ix.

8. Letter to Theodor W. Adorno, 28 March 1941, in Adorno / Kracauer, *Der Riß der Welt*, 427.

9. See Miriam Hansen, "With Skin and Hair: Kracauer's Theory of Film, Marseille 1940," in *Critical Inquiry* 19, no. 3 (Spring 1993): 437–69; also Hansen, introduction.

10. None of the three recent studies of Critical Theory in Exile touches on Kracauer's role or on the question of film, both of which I consider central to the transatlantic construction of Critical Theory. See David Jenemann, *Adorno in America* (Minneapolis: University of Minnesota Press, 2007); Thomas Wheatland, *The Frankfurt School in Exile* (Minneapolis: University of Minnesota Press, 2009); Eva Maria Ziege, *Antisemitismus und Gesellschaftstheorie: Die Frankfurter Schule im amerikanischen Exil* (Frankfurt: Suhrkamp, 2009). The substantial scholarship on the New York Intellectuals, by contrast, barely touches on the Frankfurt School at all, let alone on Kracauer's presence and work in New York. For more on Kracauer's work in the United States, see Isenberg in this volume.

11. See Wheatland, *The Frankfurt School in Exile*.

12. For some further aspects of this exchange, see Johannes von Moltke and Kristy Rawson, "Affinities: Siegfried Kracauer's American Writings," in *Affinities: Siegfried Kracauer's American Writings: Essays on Film and Popular Culture* (University of California Press, forthcoming May 2011). See also Noah Isenberg's contribution in this volume.

13. Not coincidentally, then, the notion of experience also becomes central to the reception of Kracauer's work in West Germany in subsequent decades, as Eric Rentschler demonstrates in his contribution to this volume.

14. The diagnosis of a "withering of experience" certainly constitutes one of the central premises of Critical Theory, from Benjamin's lament on the decline of storytelling through Adorno's *Minima Moralia;* numerous commentators have picked up on this notion that "the experience of the loss of experience is one of the oldest motifs of Critical Theory" (Detlev Claussen, *Theodor W. Adorno: One Last Genius,* trans. Rodney Livingstone [Cambridge: Harvard University Press, 2008], 7). Cf. among others, Martin Jay, "Lamenting the Crisis of Experience: Benjamin and Adorno," chap. 8 of *Songs of Experience;* Miriam Hansen, "Benjamin, Cinema, and Experience: 'The Blue Flower in the Land of Technology,'" *New German Critique* 40 (Winter 1987): 179–224; Howard Caygill, *Walter Benjamin: The Colour of Experience* (London: Routledge, 1998).

15. The centrality of "experience" for the New York Intellectuals has escaped the scholarly accounts to date but should be apparent from Warshow's writings (as detailed below), from seminal essays such as Philip Rahv's "The Cult of Experience in American Writing," *Partisan Review* 1940, from the pages of *Commentary* and its attempt to understand and shape the Jewish experience of the war and postwar years, or from the various "Forums" conducted during the 1940s and 1950s by *Partisan Review* on the shifting experience of the American intellectual and political landscape.

16. Martin Jay, *Songs of Experience: Modern American and European Variations on a Universal Theme* (Berkeley: University of California Press, 2006).

17. *Theory of Film*, 297. This formulation derives almost verbatim from Kra-

cauer's moving account of his own first experience of the United States during his entry into New York Harbor aboard the steamship that had carried him and his wife to safety from Lissabon in 1941. Siegfried Kracauer, "Why France Liked Our Films," *National Board of Review Magazine* 17, no. 5 (May 1942): 15–19.

18. Melvin Hill, ed., *Hannah Arendt: The Recovery of the Political World* (New York: St. Martin's, 1972), 308.

19. Temporally remote references would include those to Béla Balázs or literature on film from the Weimar era, as well as French references that presumably constitute traces of the notes Kracauer took in Marseille; other references, however, testify to Kracauer's up-to-date engagement with French discussions on cinema, including the budding movement of *filmologie*. On the tenuous relations between Kracauer and the *filmologie* movement, see Leonardo Quaresima's insightful article, "De faux amis: Kracauer et la filmologie," in *Cinémas* 19, no. 2–3: 333–58.

20. See "Nachbemerkung und editorische Notiz," in Siegfried Kracauer, *Theorie des Films: Die Errettung der äußeren Wirklichkeit*, vol. 3 of *Werke*, ed. Inka Mülder-Bach with Sabine Biebl (Frankfurt: Suhrkamp, 2005). My thanks to Miriam Hansen for sharing details of her archival work on this question.

21. Thomas L. Jeffers, "What They Talked About When They Talked About Literature: *Commentary* in Its First Three Decades," in Murray Friedman, ed., *Commentary in American Life* (Philadelphia: Temple University Press, 2005), 121. Warshow's writings are collected in *The Immediate Experience: Movies, Comics, Theatre, and Other Aspects of Popular Culture* (Cambridge: Harvard University Press, 2011), originally published in 1962.

22. The New York Intellectuals have been the object of numerous studies. Especially from the mid-1980s on, there was a decade of steady publications on the group, initiated by Alexander Bloom, *Prodigal Sons: The New York Intellectuals and Their World* (Oxford: Oxford University Press, 1986), and Terry A. Cooney, *The Rise of the New York Intellectuals: Partisan Review and Its Circle* (Madison: University of Wisconsin Press, 1986); followed by Alan Wald, *The New York Intellectuals: The Rise and Decline of the Anti-Stalinist Left from the 1930s to the 1980s* (Chapel Hill: University of North Carolina Press, 1987), and Neil Jumonville, *Critical Crossings: The New York Intellectuals in Postwar America* (Berkeley: University of California Press, 1991); later publications had the benefit of being able to build on these texts and offer new perspectives, such as Hugh Wilford's institutional investigation, *The New York Intellectuals: From Vanguard to Institution* (Manchester: Manchester University Press, 1995), and Harvey M. Teres's thought-provoking, revisionist account *Renewing the Left: Politics, Imagination, and the New York Intellectuals* (Oxford: Oxford University Press, 1996).

23. Cf. Warshow's 1948 review of *Paisan* in *The Immediate Experience*, 221–29, which references Kracauer's thoughts on the film; though Kracauer did write a full-fledged review of the film, this was never published (perhaps because of the placement of Warshow's piece in *Partisan Review*?); presumably, Warshow was referring to Kracauer's praise for Rosselini's film at the close of an article entitled "Those Movies with a Message," *Harper's Magazine*, June 1948, 567–72.

24. Cf. letter from Philipp Rahv, editor, *Partisan Review*, from 24 March 1948: "Dear Dr. Kracauer, We do like this piece quite a bit, but it appears impossible to

use it in view of the fact that another film chronicle by Warshow is scheduled for the May issue and we cannot print more than one film piece in any given issue. If, in a few weeks, you have not placed this review elsewhere, do let me know and we will take the matter up again." Kracauer Nachlass, Marbach.

25. Both authors clearly considered Rossellini's *Paisa* a signature event in the history of cinema (Kracauer calls it "one of the greatest films ever made") but disagreed on the sentimentality of the film. See note 20, above.

26. Warshow, *The Immediate Experience*, xl. In his overview of different approaches to the cinema, Warshow lists Kracauer—the author not yet of *Theory of Film* but of *From Caligari to Hitler*—as an "excellent example" of sociological criticism; ibid., xxxix.

27. Ibid., xl.

28. Ibid., 46, 75.

29. Ibid., xli.

30. "The Legacy of the 30s," in ibid., 18.

31. Theodor W. Adorno, "The Curious Realist: On Siegfried Kracauer," *New German Critique* 54 (Fall 1991): 162.

32. Hansen, introduction, x. Also, see again Rentschler's contribution to this volume.

33. See Miriam Hansen's contribution to this volume.

34. See especially Kracauer, "The Spectator," chap. 9 of *Theory of Film*.

35. Ibid., 172.

36. Letter to Barbara Deming, 16 November 1960 (KN Marbach).

37. Ibid., 296.

38. *Theory of Film*'s term for ambiguity is "the indeterminate," but he will elaborate this emphasis in defining the "intermediary area" of film, culture, and history in his final book, where "ambiguity is of the essence." On this point, see the editors' Introduction, this volume. Bazin famously opined that "depth of focus reintroduced ambiguity into the structure of the image." Like Kracauer and Warshow, he found this promise enacted most compellingly by the Italian neorealist films, which were able, in his estimation, "to give back to the cinema a sense of the ambiguity of reality." André Bazin, *What Is Cinema*, vol. 1, trans. Hugh Gray (Berkeley: University of California Press, 2004), 28, 37.

39. Adorno would define the attention to incommensurability as "Kracauer's central theme." Adorno, "The Curious Realist," 163.

40. See Jay, *Songs of Experience*, chap. 8.

41. Kracauer, *Theory of Film*, 296.

42. Adorno, "The Curious Realist," 164.

43. Theodor W. Adorno, "The Essay as Form," trans. Bob Hullot-Kentor and Fredric Will, *New German Critique* 32 (Spring–Summer, 1984): 151–71; 158.

44. Siegfried Kracauer, *History: The Last Things Before the Last* (New York: Oxford University Press, 1969), 201. As if repaying Adorno's critique in kind, Kracauer makes this argument explicitly contra Adorno, with whom he discussed these issues during a long conversation in the early 1960s. See Martin Jay, "Notes on a Troubled Friendship" and "Gespräch mit Teddie" in *Werke*, as well as Christina Gerhardt's contribution to this volume.

45. Kracauer, *Theory of Film*, 298. Emphasis added.

46. Marx and Engels, *Collected Works*, vol. 28 (New York: International Publishers, 1986), 36.

47. Kracauer, *Theory of Film*, 297.

48. Ibid.

49. For an argument about Kracauer and cinephilia, see Christian Keathley, *Cinephilia and History, or The Wind in the Trees* (Bloomington: Indiana University Press, 2006), chap. 5.

50. Warshow, *The Immediate Experience*, 120.

51. Ibid., 9.

52. Ibid., xlii.

53. Theodor W. Adorno, "Transparencies on Film," in *New German Critique* 24–25 (Autumn–Winter 1981–82): 199–205; 200.

54. Ibid., 201.

Kracauer, Spectatorship, and the Seventies

Eric Rentschler

During the 1970s Siegfried Kracauer's work on film had a strong resonance in the Federal Republic of Germany (FRG); indeed, it exercised a marked influence on the decade's film culture. A central notion from his *Theory of Film* (1960), "hunger for life," became the impetus for the most compelling depiction of leftist subjectivity in the post-1968 epoch, Michael Rutschky's as yet untranslated monograph, *Erfahrungshunger: Ein Essay über die siebziger Jahre* (1980).[1] In Anglo-American circles, by comparison, Kracauer barely figured in the seminal exchanges of the so-called Screen Studies Era. At best *Theory of Film* gained scholarly attention as a belated contribution to classical film theory. In the main, however, Kracauer functioned either as a convenient straw man for eschewers of a naive realism (even more so than André Bazin)[2] or, as the author of *From Caligari to Hitler*, an easy target for opponents of a reductive sociological film historiography.

How are we to understand this disparity of reception? One might simply write off the enthusiasm for Kracauer in the FRG as an anomaly or an anachronism, a function of the underdeveloped state of discourse about film in postwar Germany, where well into the 1980s most sustained discussion about the medium took place in journalistic venues.[3] (The situation was altogether different in France where film theory entertained a fruitful interaction with avant-garde production, where film discourse resonated within an elaborate network of ciné-clubs and maintained an integral presence in intellectual life and cultural activity.) Through the 1970s academic film studies remained virtually nonexistent on West German campuses; likewise, there was a conspicuous lack of significant film theorizing.[4] To be sure, one might be tempted to surmise that this surprising regard for Kracauer came from the New Left with its penchant for ideological criticism, especially when we bear in mind the renewed significance of the Frankfurt School's media theory during the student movement. As stated, though, it was *Theory of Film*, and not the exemplar of symptomatic analysis, *From Caligari to Hitler,* which would play the more significant role in the FRG during the seventies.

In the following I would like to suggest why Kracauer appealed so vividly to post-1968 sensibilities in the Federal Republic and to elaborate how *Theory of Film*, in this specific national and temporal context, came to take on meanings unknown to and unappreciated by Anglo-American film theorists.

Nonsynchronicities

In North American film studies, until the mid-1980s, Kracauer had a generally contested and largely diminished status; it would be fair to say that his work was far more often referred to than relied on. In fact, with the exception of the translation of "Das Ornament der Masse" in the spring 1975 issue of *New German Critique,*[5] knowledge of his writings on film derived chiefly from the two lengthy studies that bore the marks of exile and, as books, reflected organizational frameworks much different from Kracauer's essayistic and journalistic entries of the twenties and thirties.[6] *From Caligari to Hitler,*[7] in the age of the New Film History, of sophisticated notions of cinema's constitution by complex constellations of institutional, social, and aesthetic forces,[8] seemed hopelessly insufficient and, in some minds, even spurious in its attempt to demonstrate how a national cinema mirrors and prefigures a national destiny. The films of the Weimar Republic, at least the ones selected by Kracauer, become a preview of coming fascist attractions. The book, claimed the positivist Barry Salt, not mincing his words in the least, "is a strong runner in two crowded competitions: for the most worthless work of 'cultural criticism' ever written, and for the worst piece of film history."[9] Even though commentators regularly rejected the volume's premises and faulted both its essentialism and its teleology, *From Caligari to Hitler* would figure strongly in refining notions of the historical determinants of a national cinema, for instance, in the work of Philip Rosen, Patrice Petro, and Thomas Elsaesser.[10] For all its faults, argues Elsaesser, the study constitutes "the most thorough attempt at outlining the historical determinants of a body of films whose common denominator is neither author nor genre but a historical period."[11]

Theory of Film, to put it mildly, did not fare as well. It received rejection from a host of commentators, ranging from scathing castigations by film critics like Pauline Kael to less invective but equally dismissive appraisals by scholars such as Peter Harcourt, Richard Corliss, Andrew Tudor, Dudley Andrew, and, more recently, Noel Carroll and Malcolm Turvey.[12] Kracauer came under attack for his painstaking (and, in numerous minds, pedantic) insistence on film's calling as a reflector and redeemer of a poorly defined, indeed amorphous reality. With its overwhelming drive for system and its bland universalism, *Theory of Film* appeared to be monomaniacal, willful, and at times risible;[13] the author's fanatic stress on mimesis, according to Tudor, "shows us some of the strange places to which the realist aesthetic can lead."[14] For Carroll, the study may well appear to have a clear structure, but its argument, upon closer examination, proves to be muddled and confusing. In fact, "the book as a whole has a very ad hoc flavor to it."[15] In a sarcastic and dismissive play on Kracauer's valorization of the incidental and the inanimate, Kael quipped, "How can you build an *aesthetic* on *accident*—on the *ripple of the leaves?*"[16] West German respondents of the seventies, as we shall see, would do exactly that.

Kracauer's Postwar Courses in Time

The history of discourse about cinema in the FRG, one might argue, has to a great extent depended on which of Kracauer's two film books was privileged. If *From Caligari to Hitler* influenced much writing about film from the late fifties through the late sixties, it would be *Theory of Film* that had the stronger impact in the next decade. The most noteworthy West German film journals of the sixties (*Filmkritik, Film,* and *Filmstudio*) consciously deferred to and sought to continue Kracauer's critical project, that is, to illuminate the ideological contents and social meanings of contemporary film production.[17] Although commentators paid lip service to the importance of formal concerns, their actual critical praxis remained exceedingly content-bound, so much so that Kracauer, in an otherwise supportive letter of March 1956 to the editors of *film 56*, a forerunner of *Filmkritik*, suggested that these young writers would do well to expand their focus: "I believe that this sociological approach to film production is most necessary; nonetheless, I would be happier if in the future you would be more systematic about seeking out what is socially and politically false in the aesthetic realm as well. At present it seems to me as if you are being too one-sided in your emphasis on manifest content."[18]

Enno Patalas's and Wilfried Berghahn's programmatic essay of 1961,

"Gibt es eine linke Kritik?" encapsulates Kracauer's impetus; the authors cite *From Caligari to Hitler* as *Filmkritik*'s decisive role model. Contrasting an old school of culinary film appreciation (e.g., Günter Groll, Karl Korn, and Friedrich Luft) with a progressive new criticism, the editors of *Filmkritik* privileged an approach more interested in social content than aesthetic form, even if they considered form to be a part of the content. The critic should seek to comprehend the audience and its wishes, especially because the spectator had heretofore remained underappreciated. The new criticism "searches for unspecific, latent messages," "reveals the predilections of the director," "hopes for a socially responsible film," "pays attention to production-related concerns," and "criticizes the society that produces certain films."[19] Patalas would nuance this initiative in his "Plädoyer für eine ästhetische Linke" of July 1966. There he called for a film criticism that is more sensitive to structures and processes, that does not allow an emphasis on ideological inscriptions to obscure a work's formal dimensions. Sociological criticism, he maintains, should understand "aesthetic operations as social activities" and "activate aesthetic behavior."[20] The problem with Kracauer's symptomatic approach, argued Helmut Färber in the April 1967 number of *Filmkritik*, was that it concentrated on the *Zeitgeist* of a film without adequately comprehending its *Geist*.[21] Frieda Grafe's essay of 1970, "Doktor Caligari against Doktor Kracauer," represents, as the polemic title suggests, a further challenge to the realistic-sociological school of film criticism in West Germany.[22]

The split on the editorial board of *Filmkritik* between political leftists and aesthetic leftists ultimately would lead to a showdown and the subsequent resignation of the political wing in the spring of 1969.[23] Looking through the pages of the journal, one finds a marked shift of paradigms, a new penchant for ardent effusions that focus on the subjective dimension of the experience in the dark, a descriptive rather than prescriptive impetus, a preference for fragmentary observations and aphoristic willfulness, a tendency to deny the whole of a film and appreciate its privileged parts, and, in keeping with Susan Sontag's exemplary essay of 1964, a turn "against interpretation" because it stifles rather than enhances aesthetic response.[24]

The new editorial collective of *Filmkritik* distanced itself from the ideological emphases of *From Caligari to Hitler;* critics like Wim Wenders, Gerhard Theuring, Klaus Bädekerl, Wolf-Eckart Bühler, and Siegfried Schober were referred to as *Sensibilisten*.[25] As exponents of a private and personal relationship to the film experience,[26] they discovered dimensions of meaning in *Theory of Film* that surely had not been appreciated by the book's initial commentators.[27] Indeed, what Kracauer articulated as well as catalyzed was a unique mode of cinephilia. When the study's German translation had arrived in 1964,[28] reviewers had been surprised that it had so little in common with the Weimar essays that had been reissued in 1963 under the title *Das Ornament der Masse*.[29] Where, reviewers wondered, was the critique of distraction and the Culture Industry? Why was there not a single mention of Adorno or *Dialectic of Enlightenment*? Why would such an otherwise incisive social critic insist on divesting objects of their historical status and shrouding them in an undialectical, whimsical, and even mystical idealism? As Helmut Lethen observed, *Theory of Film* seemed to provide little intellectual sustenance for readers of the mid-1960s with progressive agendas.[30]

The appropriation of Kracauer by the Munich sensibilists was decidedly selective. They drew on bits and pieces of *Theory of Film*; the whole of the work and its overarching realist argument were never at issue. In that regard, their response fell in line with Miriam Hansen's later claim that Kracauer had written not a comprehensive theory of film but rather "a theory of a particular kind of film experience."[31] Wim Wenders, inspired by this idiosyncratic cinephilia, repeatedly finds himself thunderstruck by images that bring him closer to the concrete world. Kracauer, writes Wenders, "spoke of film as the 'redemption of physically reality,' meaning the tenderness that cinema can show towards reality. Westerns have often brought out this tenderness in a dreamily beautiful and quiet way. . . . In their images they spread out a surface that was nothing else but what you could see."[32] Tenderness, I would note, is not a word that Kracauer uses. Rather he speaks of a restraint that allows images to maintain their integrity and not be forced into a narrative corset. "There are moments in films," Wenders notes in June 1970, "that are suddenly so unexpectedly direct and overwhelmingly concrete that you hold your breath or sit up straight or put your hand on your mouth." He goes on to provide an inventory of privileged moments from a variety of films, strikingly concrete images from selected features, shots when an initial perception gives way to a play of affect: "Suddenly there's nothing more to describe, something's become all too clear and leapt out of the picture, become a feeling, a memory. . . . For a moment the film was a smell, a taste in the mouth, a tingle in the hands, a draught felt through a wet shirt, a children's book that you haven't seen since you were five years old, a blink of the eye."[33]

Or take, to use a final example, Wenders's 1969 notice on the experimental film *Kelek*. The review begins, "A film by Werner Nekes and by

everyone who has seen it so far," linking the film on the screen to the spectator's mental screen. He praises the work whose subject is seeing itself.
The film is self-apparent and utterly direct, so much so that "film critics
will lose their jobs. They won't need to go to the cinema anymore. All that
will be left for them to do is go for strolls in the park, look at their toes, or
at manhole covers as they walk along, have it off, and when they turn into
suburban streets, slowly open and shut their eyes." *Kelek*, claims Wenders,
"works on only one level, the level of seeing." It is, in that regard, "an in-
credibly physical affair." The piece ends with a quote from *Theory of Film*:
"All this means that films cling to the surface of things. . . . Perhaps the way
today leads from, and through, the corporeal to the subjective?"[34]

These rhapsodic sensibilists with their fetishistic embrace of haptic details and random objects by and large remained on the margins of intellectual discussion during the late sixties. As one might imagine, they came
under frequent attack for their candid displays of personal preference and
their unabashed willingness to give voice to what they saw and felt in the
dark. In the June 1968 issue of *Film*, Klaus Kreimeier assailed the sensibilists as denizens of "a murky realm with an increasingly complicated and
increasingly dead-ended subjectivity." They may call themselves noncon-
formists, but they are in truth reactionaries; they claim to be in touch with
images and things, but in fact they are out of touch with reality.[35] To fixate
on films as unique experiences, according to the sensibilists' detractors, was
to take things out of context. "The internalizing and totalizing of individual films," wrote Heinz Ungureit in May 1969, divests them of their social
determinations. All that remains is "the solitary film, the solitary image,
the solitary director."[36]

Stop Making Sense

In the wake of the failed student revolt of 1967 and 1968, even leftist commentators in West Germany would come to suspect that discourses that
ruled out the subjective factor and the power of feelings might well be the
function of authoritarian personalities. Unlike the student activists who
promulgated conceptual frameworks that could account for social reality in
its totality, the sensibilists favored single moments and a selective attention,
aiming to escape theoretical cubbyholes that for them remained abstract
constructions devoid of experiential immediacy. They went to the movies to
see and not to cerebrate, to discover the visual presence of the physical

world far away from words and the dimension of verbal meanings. Like Kracauer's eccentric spectator of *Theory of Film*, what they sought in cinema was "perception, experience, contemplation—not interpretation."[37]

Michael Rutschky's *Erfahrungshunger* explicitly acknowledged Kracauer's pertinence for a larger understanding of intellectual life in the FRG after 1968. Describing the widespread disaffection that attended the demise of the student movement, Rutschky saw a collective shift from a will to enact theoretical constructs to a desire to remain undefined by social mechanisms. The melancholy resulting from the collapse of a leftist public sphere brought a retreat into a lonely subjectivism. If anything, this new sensibility (*Neue Innerlichkeit* or *Neue Subjektivität*) was out of touch with everything and everyone. The cinema, in this context, provided a welcome refuge from a threatening material world, where objects, otherwise functionalized and commodified, gained new immediacy and tangibility, where one, in general, could breathe more easily. In the dark, one experiences a dreamlike fascination while enjoying the intensity of isolated images: the corporeal world comes alive, freed from the conditioning forces that structure the everyday, liberated from the discursive frameworks that bind certain signs to particular associations, redeemed in that it comes to be felt and experienced in all its sensual richness. In the cinema the world stops making sense and in that way takes on new meanings, meanings Kracauer elaborates in his *Theory of Film*.[38]

The most crucial notion that Rutschky took from *Theory of Film* derived from Kracauer's comments on spectatorship, especially the emphasis on a disenganged specularity, a response that seeks sensuality (*Sinnlichkeit*) rather than sense (*Sinn*), a gaze more concerned with haptic stimulation and tactile frisson than conceptual understanding. In chapter 9 of his book, Kracauer refers to Hugo von Hofmannsthal's essay of 1921, "The Substitute for Dreams,"[39] a piece describing the working class's escape to the cinema and its search there for a fuller life, "life in its inexhaustibility which the cinema offers to masses in want of it."[40] Denizens of modernity are out of touch with the "breathing world" around them, "that stream of things and events which . . . would render . . . existence more exciting and significant."[41]

Common to von Hofmannsthal, Kracauer, and the New Subjectivity of the seventies, according to Rutschky, was an all-consuming hunger for experience, the recognition that the world in modernity has become impossibly abstract and complex, beyond all synthesis and simplification. Cinema affords compensations not found otherwise; there one can fill one's shrinking self with images of life as such. "Material existence, as it manifests itself in film, launches the moviegoer into unending pursuits"[42] that go in two directions, into the image or away from it. On the one hand, we have self-abandonment; on the other, self-absorption. In this way films catalyze two types of dreaming, one that brings the spectator into the image in a contemplative embrace; another whose sights and sounds fuel the spectator's imagination, spurring associations and stimulating the memory.

Kracauer's mobile spectator either moves into the image or away from it, losing itself in the diegesis or using the flow of images as a catalyst for its own reveries. The choice between radical identification and willful free association in fact corresponded to the preferred subject effects of the two dominant paradigms in New German films of the seventies. On the one hand, we have filmmakers who allowed viewers a contemplative immersion in the image, directors whose mise-en-scène privileged the long take and called on the spectator to inhabit and explore the frame space. Obvious examples in this vein are Wenders, Herzog, Straub/Huillet, Thome, Achternbusch, and Schroeter. On the other hand, there were those directors whose montage-driven films sought to spark spectators' memories and spur their imaginations, filmmakers like Kluge, Sander, Reitz, and Syberberg. Here the single shot enjoys a less privileged status; instead the stress lies on chains of images, a collagelike construction, a notion of film as a marketplace of competing discourses where the spectator is free to pick and choose as he or she will and create his or her own *Zusammenhang*. Film narratives are not simply limited to captivating us by dint of their suspense, discomfort, and danger. They promote other responses as well: waiting, wandering, hanging out, killing time, being silly.

West German appropriators thus discovered meanings in *Theory of Film* altogether at odds with the impatient responses it received in Anglo-American circles. As Rutschky puts it, "We found in the details many single observations whose incisiveness would not become clear until the seventies."[43] Again, people drew on bits and pieces of the book and did not consider the whole—and it had been precisely the study's perceived claim to being systematic that would consternate so many American respondents. Clearly, reception history has much to tell us about film theory, about the historical status of certain texts in particular national and temporal constellations, that is, within concrete expectation horizons. *Theory of Film* valorizes a mode of spectatorship far more dynamic than Anglo-American critics, until quite recently, had been willing to allow, a mode which for that reason had a remarkable resonance among many West German spectators in the 1970s.

Postcards from Poona

The afterlife of sensibilism is a curious tale. This discourse of evocative description and passionate appreciation came to dominate the reconstituted new *Filmkritik* through the 1970s and into the 1980s. Its authors, in the words of Olaf Möller, "rarely used purely evaluative words for films by those they loved, esteemed and honoured. Instead a scene is described for pages on end, very carefully, with each word scrupulously weighed up against its implications, its resonance, its role in the logic and the poetry of the sentence and the text."[44]

Creating essayistic webs and intertextual networks, by turns elegant and exhilarating, authors found unique routes of access to privileged filmmakers, directors who above all do not impose a worldview on their spectators, people like Straub, Rossellini, Renoir, Ford, Grémillon, and Ophüls, among others. These directors do not, as Möller puts it, "hit you on the head with their visions, leave you lying paralysed, ready for a serious brainwash; rather, they approach the world, describe it."[45] In the process, to be sure, the journal all but took leave of contemporary films and current events; its readership dwindled radically until publication finally ceased in 1984. To this day, nonetheless, many cinephiles hold the whimsical and epiphanous pages of the new *Filmkritik* in high esteem as a rich haven of impetus and inspiration.

Sensibilism would take a different course elsewhere in the FRG and have a more lasting (and problematic) impact on a host of regional and urban program guides read by a large young alternative culture. This so-called open form of writing found its acme in the periodical *Filme* that programmatically espoused a descriptive form of highly personalized appreciation and became well known for its aphoristic accounts of experiences in the dark.[46] As one of the journal's editors, Norbert Jochum, put it, "For me a review is not so much a matter of how a critic interprets a given film, but rather what he has seen. . . . Film criticism doesn't mean writing down what I know, but rather expressing one's thoughts about a film; this is a process that does not necessarily lead to a conclusion that explains everything."[47] Coeditor Norbert Grob insisted that single moments are much more important than films as a whole. Analysis, he maintained, destroys the aesthetic power of a film. A film critic is not a judge but rather an observer and, in that capacity, a stand-in for other viewers. As a critic, Grob simply wants to write about what he sees and feels when he watches a film. In this way writing becomes the means by which he articulates his experience as a spectator.[48]

Over time, this subjectivism would in some quarters assume manneristic contours and narcissistic extremes. Its practitioners would go on to occupy influential positions at such mainstream news organs as *Die Zeit*, the *Süddeutsche Zeitung*, and the *Frankfurter Allgemeine*. The initial cinephilia with its heightened sensitivity to cinema's play of signs and its remarkable meaning potential would give way to an anti-intellectual hedonism that, as in a review by Claudius Seidl, celebrated filmgoing as a thought-free experience: "Let's just forget art! Let's forget all the clever palaver and socially critical relevance. Instead let us go into ourselves and consider what really is important to us about the cinema! Right: it is feelings, that is to say, our own. And these have nothing to do with whether a film is particularly intellectual or whether a script corresponds to reality. They only attach themselves to moments on the screen which allow us to confront our own dreams. *Tequila Sunrise* is full of such moments."[49]

This dandyistic indulgence, as Karsten Witte complained, foregrounds the reviewer's emotional constitution and affective predilection.[50] Such lyrical flights of fancy resemble postcards from Poona, quipped Joe Hembus in response to a particularly ripe example of the so-called open writing from the pages of *Filme*: "That this scene contains nothing beyond itself: and itself before it came into being: and, in this way, refers to nothing beyond itself, and yet refers to all kinds of things: so that all kinds of things become possible."[51] We are, to be sure, not far from the kind of feuilletonistic preciousness and pretentiousness that the editors of *Filmkritik* once so ardently eschewed.

Rutschky's *Erfahrungshunger* and the Munich sensibilists returned to *Theory of Film* and found thoughts that resonated strongly; their responses, to be sure, employed an insistent jargon of authenticity decidedly out of keeping with Kracauer's work.[52] The radical solipsism that came in their wake, the onanistic proclivity of critics like Seidl and journals like *Filme*, would be a far cry from the poignant search for concreteness that Kracauer had in mind, the whimsical cinephilia that embraced random encounters and celebrated fleeting images that reenchanted reality and made the viewer, at least for moments, feel at home in—and in touch with—the world. Revisiting the West German reception of Kracauer's monograph allows us, I would suggest, a provocative preview of coming attractions as we partake of recent scholarship that provides a fuller appreciation of Kracauer's redemptive resolve and his insight into the invigorating potential of the cinematic experience. *Theory of Film*, Vivian Sobchack argues, "located the uniqueness of cinema in the medium's essential ability to stimulate us physiologically and sensually; thus he understands the spectator as a 'corporeal-material being,' a 'human being with skin and hair.'"[53] The once so maligned and misunderstood monograph has come to serve much more productive purposes within film studies, as new publications, for instance, by Sobchack, Helmut Lethen, Miriam Hansen, Heide Schlüpmann, and Christian Keathley convincingly demonstrate, contributions that in a variety of ways help us, at long last, to fathom the book's historical dimensions as well as its utopian designs.[54]

NOTES

1. Michael Rutschky, *Erfahrungshunger: Ein Essay über die siebziger Jahre* (Frankfurt am Main: Fischer, 1982). The initial edition of the book appeared in 1980 and was published in Cologne by Kiepenheuer und Witsch.

2. The book, in fact, was seen as either out of time or behind the times. Surely none of its early reviewers considered it, as Miriam Hansen later would, within wider intertextual constellations. It might be productive, Hansen argues, to think of the volume "as contemporaneous with the magazine *Film Culture* and developments in independent film production and distribution; with existentialism in philosophy and life-style, minimalism in art and music; with Susan Sontag's essay 'Against Interpretation,' Miles Davis's *Kind of Blue*, Lawrence Ferlinghetti's *A Coney Island of the Mind*, and movies such as *Shadows* and *The Hustler*." See Hansen's introduction to the most recent edition of *Theory of Film* (Princeton: Princeton University Press, 1997), ix. A notable exception to the otherwise lackluster initial reception granted to *Theory of Film* is Rudolf Arnheim's appreciative review, "Melancholy Unshaped," reprinted in Rudolf Arnheim, *Toward a Psychology of Art* (Berkeley: University of California Press, 1966), 181–91. Arnheim goes so far as to characterize the study as "probably the most intelligent book ever written on the subject of the film" (181).

3. For two useful surveys of West German film criticism of the postwar era, see Ulrich von Thüna, "Filmzeitschriften der fünfziger Jahre," in *Zwischen Gestern und Morgen: Westdeutscher Nachkriegsfilm 1946–1962*, ed. Hans-Peter Reichmann and Rudolf Worschech (Frankfurt am Main: Deutsches Filmmuseum, 1989), 248–62; and Joachim Paech, "Filmwissenschaft, Filmtheorie und Filmkritik in Westdeutschland 1960–1980. Das alte (Klage-)Lied," in *Abschied von Gestern: Bundes-*

deutscher Film der sechziger und siebziger Jahre, ed. Hans-Peter Reichmann and Rudolf Worschech (Frankfurt am Main: Deutsches Filmmuseum, 1991), 212–23.

4. See Walter Schmieding's scathing assessment in *Kunst oder Kasse: Der Ärger mit dem deutschen Film* (Hamburg: Rütten und Loening, 1961), 16: "There is no department of film studies in [West] Germany, no scholarly literature, no scholarly research, no academy where young directors, cinematographers, scriptwriters, and dramaturgs might study." See also Helmut Färber, "Diskussion: Zum Selbstverständnis der *Filmkritik*," *Filmkritik* 11, no. 4 (April 1967): 228. According to Färber, there is no theoretical basis for film criticism in West Germany. Universities may occasionally offer film courses, but no serious research on film comes from academic quarters. Notable exceptions to the rule included Walter Hagemann and the Münster Institut für Publizistik; the Deutsche Gesellschaft der Filmwissenschaft, established in 1953, and its periodical, *Beiträge zur Filmforschung*. Noteworthy as well was the Hamburger Gesellschaft für Filmkunde and its annual publication, *Hamburger Filmgespräche*.

5. The essay appeared with Karsten Witte's insightful "Introduction to Siegfried Kracauer's 'The Mass Ornament,'" trans. Barbara Correll and Jack Zipes, *New German Critique* 5 (Spring 1975): 59–66.

6. Any informed assessment of Kracauer, Inka Mülder-Bach incisively argued in the mid-1980s, requires a familiarity with his feuilletons of the 1920s and 1930s. See her important monograph, *Siegfried Kracauer—Grenzgänger zwischen Theorie und Literatur: Seine frühen Schriften 1913–1933* (Stuttgart: Metzler, 1985), 16.

7. Siegfried Kracauer, *From Caligari to Hitler: A Psychological History of German Film* (Princeton: Princeton University Press, 1947).

8. See Thomas Elsaesser, "The New Film History," *Sight and Sound* 55, no. 4 (Autumn 1986): 246–51.

9. Barry Salt, "From Caligari to Who?" *Sight and Sound* 48, no. 2 (Spring 1979): 122. For an equally disparaging assessment of the book, see Martin Sopocy, "Re-examining Kracauer's *From Caligari to Hitler*," *Griffithiana* 40–42 (October 1991): 61–73.

10. See Philip Rosen, "History, Textuality, Nation: Kracauer, Burch, and Some Problems in the Study of National Cinemas," *Iris* 2, no. 2 (1984): 69–84; Patrice Petro, "From Lukács to Kracauer and Beyond: Social Film Histories and the German Cinema," *Cinema Journal* 22, no. 3 (1983): 47–67; Thomas Elsaesser, "Film History and Visual Pleasure: Weimar Cinema," in *Cinema Histories, Cinema Practices*, ed. Patricia Mellencamp and Philip Rosen (Frederick, MD: University Publications of America, 1984), 47–84. For an updated assessment, see Thomas Elsaesser, "Weimar Cinema, Mobile Selves, and Anxious Males: Kracauer and Eisner Revisited," in *Expressionist Film—New Perspectives*, ed. Dietrich Scheunemann (Rochester: Camden House, 2003), 33–71.

11. Elsaesser, "Film History and Visual Pleasure," 59.

12. See Pauline Kael, "Is There a Cure for Film Criticism? Or: Some Unhappy Thoughts on Siegfried Kracauer's *Nature [sic] of Film*," *Sight and Sound* 31, no. 2 (Spring 1962): 56–64; reprinted in Pauline Kael, *I Lost It at the Movies: Film Writings, 1954–1965* (New York: Boyars, 2002), 269–92; Peter Harcourt, "What Indeed, Is Cinema?" *Cinema Journal* 6, no. 1 (Fall 1968): 22–28; Richard Corliss,

"The Limitations of Kracauer's Reality," *Cinema Journal* 10, no. 1 (Fall 1970): 15–22; Andrew Tudor, "Aesthetics of Realism: Bazin and Kracauer," in *Theories of Film* (New York: Viking, 1973), 77–115; Dudley Andrew, "Siegfried Kracauer," in *The Major Film Theories* (New York: Oxford University Press, 1976), 106–33; Noël Carroll, "Kracauer's *Theory of Film*," in *Defining Cinema*, ed. Peter Lehmann (New Brunswick: Rutgers University Press, 1997), 111–31; and Malcolm Turvey, *Doubting Vision: Film and the Revelationist Tradition* (Oxford: Oxford University Press, 2008), esp. 41–48.

13. Kael includes Kracauer "in the great, lunatic tradition." See "Is There a Cure for Film Criticism?" 271.

14. Tudor, *Theories of Film*, 79.

15. Carroll, "Kracauer's *Theory of Film*," 111.

16. Kael, "Is There a Cure for Film Criticism?" 272.

17. "Briefly stated," Kracauer wrote in a programmatic essay of 1932, "the film critic of note is conceivable only as a social critic. His mission is to unveil the social images and ideologies hidden in mainstream films and through this unveiling to undermine the influence of the films themselves wherever possible." See Siegfried Kracauer, "Über die Aufgabe des Filmkritikers," in *Kleine Schriften zum Film 1932–1961*, vol. 6.3 of *Werke*, ed. Inka Mülder-Bach (Frankfurt am Main: Suhrkamp, 2004), 63.

18. *film 56* 3 (March 1956): 155. All translations from German, unless otherwise noted, are the author's.

19. Enno Patalas and Wilfried Berghahn, "Gibt es eine linke Kritik?" *Filmkritik* 5, no. 3 (March 1961): 134.

20. Enno Patalas, "Plädoyer für eine ästhetische Linke: Zum Selbstverständnis der *Filmkritik* II," *Filmkritik* 10, no. 7 (July 1966): 407.

21. Helmut Färber, "Diskussion: Zum Selbstverständnis der *Filmkritik*," *Filmkritik* 11, no. 4 (April 1967): 228.

22. Frieda Grafe, "Doktor Caligari gegen Doktor Kracauer," *Filmkritik* 14, no. 5 (1970): 242–44. The author of *From Caligari to Hitler* claims Grafe was, like the fictional Dr. Caligari, "a victim of books" (244).

23. At the Oberhausen Festival of 1969, the political wing of *Filmkritik*, i.e., the contributors Gregor, Hellwig, Jansen, Kotulla, Ripkens, Stempel, and Ungureit, announced their departure from the journal. For detailed accounts of the rift in the Filmkritik editorial board, see Claudia Lenssen, "Der Streit um die politische und die ästhetische Linke in der Zeitschrift *Filmkritik*: Ein Beitrag zu einer Kontroverse in den sechziger Jahren," in *Die Macht der Filmkritik. Positionen und Kontroversen*, ed. Norbert Grob and Karl Prümm (Frankfurt: edition text + kritik, 1990), 63–78; and Irmbert Schenk, " 'Politische Linke' versus 'Ästhetische Linke.' Zum Richtungsstreit der Zeitschrift *Filmkritik* in den 60er Jahren," in *Filmkritik. Bestandsaufnahmen und Perspektiven*, ed. Irmbert Schenk (Marburg: Schüren, 1998), 43–73.

24. Sontag's "On Interpretation" appeared in German as "Gegen Interpretation," in the German collection of Sontag's writings, *Kunst und Antikunst: 24 literarische Analysen* (Frankfurt am Main: Fischer, 1964). Many West German film critics felt encouraged by Sontag's essay to become subjective and fragmentary,

descriptive rather than prescriptive. See Ulrich Kurowski, "Sieben einzelne Gedanken zu einem Film," *Kirche und Film* 23, no. 1 (January 1970): 3–4.

25. Karsten Witte, "'Die Augen wollen sich nicht zu jeder Zeit schliessen': Die Zeitschrift *Filmkritik* und Junger Deutscher Film 1960–1970," *Medium* 15, no. 11–12 (November–December 1985): 93.

26. See Siegfried Schober, "Kino statt Kritik?" *Filmkritik* 14, no. 1 (January 1970): "Cinema and no more film criticism, a mere compilation of experiences and feelings, no longer any critical reflection and resistance, that's what we seem to have come to, and if we replace criticism with cinema, we now, almost without exception, partake of the images of politics rather than the reality of politics, seldom what is concrete and specific about politics and increasingly the larger and, as such, vague picture" (3). It should be noted, to be sure, that angry letters to the editor as well as a decline in readership confirmed that numerous readers were not happy with *Filmkritik*'s new direction. See Thomas Brandlmeier, "Filmtheorie und Kinokultur. Zeitgeschichte und filmtheoretische Debatten," in *Kino-Fronten: 20 Jahre '68 und das Kino*, ed. Werner Petermann and Ralph Thoms (Munich: Trickster, 1988), 54.

27. Urs Jenny, for instance, lamented that the revered sociological critic of *From Caligari to Hitler* had become the dogmatic—and reactionary—author of *Theory of Film*. See his review, "Gottsched im Kino," *Film* (June 1965): 6.

28. The West German edition of *Theory of Film* appeared as *Theorie des Films: Die Errettung der äußeren Wirklichkeit* (Frankfurt am Main: Suhrkamp, 1964). The book was initially to be published by Rowohlt, but a disagreement between Kracauer and the press put an end to these plans.

29. *Das Ornament der Masse: Essays* (Frankfurt am Main: Suhrkamp, 1963).

30. Helmut Lethen, "Sichtbarkeit: Kracauers Liebeslehre," in *Siegfried Kracauer: Neue Interpretationen*, ed. Michael Kessler and Thomas Y. Levin (Tübingen: Stauffenberg, 1990), 197.

31. Hansen, introduction to *Theory of Film*, x.

32. Wim Wenders, "Vom Traum zum Trauma. Der fürchterliche Western Spiel mir das Lied vom Tod," review of *Once Upon a Time in the West*, *Filmkritik* 13, no. 11 (November 1969): 649. Wenders's film reviews have been collected and are available in English. See *Emotion Pictures: Reflections on the Cinema*, trans. Sean Whiteside and Michael Hofmann (Boston: Faber and Faber, 1989).

33. Wenders, "Van Morrison," *Filmkritik* 14, no. 6 (June 1970): 292.

34. Wenders, review of "*Kelek*," *Filmkritik* 13, no. 2 (1969): 113.

35. Klaus Kreimeier, "Zeit der Flaneure: Der junge deutsche Film und seine Propheten," *Film* (June 1968): 2.

36. Heinz Ungureit, "Kann die Filmkritik noch parieren?" *Kirche und Film* 22, no. 5 (May 1969): 3. One finds a number of similar interventions against *Filmkritik*'s aesthetic turn in the Frankfurt journal *Filmstudio*, many of whose contributors had frequented the lectures of Horkheimer and Adorno.

37. Rutschky, 187.

38. See the section in Rutschky's book entitled "Allegorese des Kinos," 167–93.

39. *Theory of Film*, 167–69. The German title of von Hofmannsthal's essay is "Ersatz für die Träume."

40. Ibid., 168.

41. Ibid., 169. This formulation bears much in common with a sentiment voiced by the Bavarian director Herbert Achternbusch, arguably the most radically willful subjectivist among West German auteurs of the 1970s: "I don't want to think at the cinema. I want to see. I scoff at a kind of cinema that won't let me re-discover my own feelings. I demand a sense of justice back from cinema. To keep myself going cinema was always important to me. Too much has been lost in my dreams." See Herbert Achternbusch, *Die Stunde des Todes* (Frankfurt am Main: Suhrkamp, 1975), 10.

42. *Theory of Film*, 165.

43. Rutschky, 189.

44. Olaf Möller, "Passage along the Shadow-Line: Farocki and Others—Approaching a Certain Filmkritik Style," trans. Roger Hillman and Timothy Mathieson, *Senses of Cinema* 21 (July–August 2002).

45. Ibid.

46. *Filme* (1980–82) was published in Berlin and coedited by Antje Goldau, Norbert Grob, Norbert Jochum, and Jochen Brunow; it ran for thirteen issues.

47. Frank Arnold, "Bekenntnis zur 'offenen Form des Schreibens.' Gespräch mit Norbert Grob und Norbert Jochum über Filme, *Filme* und Filmkritik," *Film-Korrespondenz* 27, no. 2 (10 February 1981): 21.

48. Ibid., 21–22.

49. Claudius Seidl, *Tempo*, March 1989. Quoted in Karsten Witte, "Von der Diskurskonkurrenz zum Diskurskonsens," in *Die Macht der Filmkritik: Positionen und Kontroversen*, ed. Norbert Grob and Karl Prümm (Munich: edition text + kritik, 1990), 165.

50. Ibid., 164.

51. Joe Hembus, *Der deutsche Film kann gar nicht besser sein: Ein Pamphlet von gestern. Eine Abrechnung von heute* (Munich: Rogner und Bernhard, 1981), 176.

52. Cf. Theodor W. Adorno, *The Jargon of Authenticity*, trans. Knut Tarnowski and Frederic Will (London: Routledge, 2003).

53. Vivian Carol Sobchack, *Carnal Thoughts: Embodiment and Moving Image Culture* (Berkeley: University of California Press, 2004), 55.

54. See Helmut Lethen, "Sichtbarkeit: Kracauers Liebeslehre," in *Siegfried Kracauer: Neue Interpretationen*, ed. Michael Kessler and Thomas Y. Levin (Tübingen: Stauffenberg, 1990), 195–228; Miriam Hansen, introduction to *Theory of Film: The Redemption of Physical Reality*, by Siegfried Kracauer (Princeton: Princeton University Press, 1997), vii–xlv, and "'With Skin and Hair': Kracauer's *Theory of Film*, Marseille 1940," *Critical Inquiry* 19, no. 3 (Spring 1993): 437–69; Heide Schlüpmann, *Ein Detektiv des Kinos. Studien zu Siegfried Kracauers Filmtheorie* (Frankfurt am Main: Stroemfeld, 1998); and Christian Keathley, *Cinephilia and History or The Wind in the Trees* (Bloomington: Indiana University Press, 2006), esp. 112–32. See as well the thoughtful appropriations of Kracauer's *Theory of Film* in Hermann Kappelhoff, *Realismus: Das Kino und die Politik des Ästhetischen* (Berlin: Vorwerk 8, 2008), and Drehli Robnik, "Leben als Loch im Medium: Die Vermittlung des Films durch Siegfried Kracauer," *kolik.film* 2 (2004).

Highway Through the Void
The Film Theorist and the Film Actress

Heide Schlüpmann

Concerning Lacunae

In the following essay I would like to present some reflections on Kracauer's writings on film and cinema, the starting point of which is the perception of certain lacunae, particularly noticeable against the backdrop of a history of feminist film theory. The themes of gender relations and women's emancipation, the contribution of actresses to the history of film, and to a certain degree even emotions and feelings, appear in Kracauer's texts on the periphery at most. This in no way means that his texts lack a sensitivity for those critical moments in modern history. In fact he explicitly touches on them here and there. A criticism of this point, which my studies of Kracauer have repeatedly been tempted to make, merges therefore with discoveries about his attitude as a theorist. My concern is to relate that attitude—which is ultimately a political one—to the world he lived in and to the history he experienced because it underscores the significance of Kracauer for present feminist film theory.

Kracauer's history of Weimar cinema, *From Caligari to Hitler*, provides the impetus for my reflections while forcing us back to the Weimar essays, and ahead to *Theory of Film*. I have been repeatedly intrigued by a particular passage in the *Caligari* book. In the midst of the masculine figures of tyrants and rebellious sons, frustrated husbands and degraded employees, attention is given for once to a woman, the actress. The heading of this brief chapter is "The Prostitute and the Adolescent."[1] A lot is brought together in this chapter, including the social situation of the woman who does not fit into the scheme of proletarian or democratic-liberal politics; love as a film topic; the feeling of affection felt by the viewer; and thoughts about the actress Asta Nielsen. However, all of this suddenly ceases to matter with Kracauer's terse assessment that love is devoured by fascism's dream of a new order. The street films of the Weimar era, Kracauer contends—especially those with the motif of "Love on the Street"—have an undercurrent that tends in the direction of fascism; they do not present a liberation of the "German soul" (*Caligari*, 3) from the "crucial dilemma" (*Caligari*, 9) that exists between "tyrannical rule and instinct-governed chaos" (*Caligari*, 107).

In retrospect, Kracauer sees only two films as having imagined emancipation from the authoritarian tendencies of the Germans. *Der Golem* (*The Golem*, 1920) and *Schatten* (*Shadows*, 1923) delineate an "attempt to enthrone reason" that unmasks as a phantom the "torturing alternative of tyranny and chaos" (*Caligari*, 112). It is no surprise that he picks these two films, because as self-reflexive films they also implicitly present film and the cinema as a model of emancipation. In *The Golem*, Rabbi Loew succeeds in having the emperor revoke his call for a pogrom by conjuring up a projection of catastrophes that threaten those in power. In *Shadows*, a juggler employs the play of shadows to lead a small group, who had been caught up in the confusion of their instinctual lives, to see the light of reason. These two examples of Weimar cinema thus also come close to Kracauer's idea of the redemptive potential of film. They offer a bridge between the essays of the 1920s, in which he discovered the importance of cinema, and *Theory of Film*, which he completed in the late 1950s.

Yet if *The Golem* and *Shadows* still stood for models of projection guided by reason, one can now scarcely speak any more of the hope for an audience that would enlighten itself by going to the cinema—a hope still expressed, for example, in Kracauer's "Cult of Distraction" from 1925. Yet with his "Psychological History of the German Film," Kracauer does not fall back on the stance of the scientist, mastering the past with categories and concepts, or even that of the philosopher, instructing those who have fallen or been left behind. His approach remains that of someone who is himself embroiled in history, who wants to grasp reality by assimilating it from within. So perhaps the lacunae I detect in Kracauer's work point to something that eschewed being assimilated.

The Powerless

Siegfried Kracauer's writings nowhere address issues related to women's emancipation, yet they contain a mode of perception akin to that of women. He never denies that his social position is not far removed from theirs. *From Caligari to Hitler* can serve today not least as a document of that proximity. Long before the feminist critique of Hollywood cinema by Laura Mulvey, Mary Ann Doane, and Teresa de Lauretis, Freud's psychoanalysis became a tool for Kracauer to highlight the authoritarian structures that, in his experience, Weimar cinema reproduced. A similar intellectual approach noticeable today corresponds to that of the profession chosen by Kracauer in his day. Kracauer did not move in official university circles, which are characterized by centuries of a male-dominated history of ideas. He was an employee and thus part of a milieu to which, with the onset of modernism, women were increasingly gaining access. Kracauer could encounter women not only in department stores, restaurants, and telephone companies but also in the newspaper world—as journalists (for example, Margarete Susmann at the *Frankfurter Zeitung*) or as photographers for the emerging mass illustrated press. In addition to his intellectual method of enlightenment and his professional stratum, it was ultimately the use of leisure time that brought him into contact with a female audience, which only formed in the modern era, and in the cinema. This latter proximity, however, was decisive in raising explicit doubts about Kracauer's intellectual rank.

The reception of Kracauer's work was, and still is, marked by resistance, ignorance, and helplessness, and was completely unlike the reception of his friends and intellectual kindred spirits Walter Benjamin and Theodor W. Adorno, and even of Ernst Bloch. Adorno's condescending homage, which even in Kracauer's lifetime toyed with his closeness to the "little shop girls," has meanwhile been copiously cited and has surely contributed to the dismissive assessment of the film theorist in the academic context. Yet it merely echoes a general estimation with which people responded to a—correct— sense of Kracauer's proximity to women and to the masses associated with them. The attitude of his thinking and his theory is not male in the strict sense of the implicit rules of the male alliance within the history of ideas and science; the so-called femininity of man, which has been cited in connection with Nietzsche, would certainly also be attributable to Kracauer.

In the face of widespread disdain, efforts to raise Kracauer's status have had recourse to a sublime intellectual tradition into which to place him. Traces of Jewish theology, in particular of Messianism, would seem to have qualified him for inclusion in the ranks of the great thinkers. By comparison, a consideration of the lacunae pertaining to a reflection on women's emancipation draws attention to just how imbued Kracauer's writings were with everyday experience, indeed with the everyday politics of a history of Jewish emancipation in the twentieth century. His outlook on history from the grass roots, the perspective of the ruled for whom modern society once harbored the promise of liberation from servitude, represents a further proximity to the women's movement. In such a light, however, the difference also becomes visible. Victor Klemperer's diaries and autobiographical writings, for example, provide insight into the everyday aspect of pre–First World War Jewish emancipation in all its complex contradictoriness—the Jews' emphatic feeling of belonging to German culture, and finally their wish to belong to the German nation. Kracauer turns up in Klemperer's diaries from the time of the First World War (a point also discussed in Rogowski's contribution to this volume). Like Klemperer, he too was in Munich at the outbreak of war. We learn little about him, though, except for his idealistic desire to be active in the patriotic war. All in all, the First World War paralyzed, if not destroyed, the vitality of the modern emancipation movements. The great horror of this demise becomes clear in Klemperer's writings. For Kracauer, however, unlike for Klemperer, the specter of national culture, of the national state, was finally gone. He expectantly awaited the Weimar Republic, the association with modern democracies. "America" came into view. What can be learned from his film reviews, and even more from his later history of Weimar cinema, is that the only thing left of the libidinous cathexis of the German nation was a sensitivity for its crises, that is, for what was taking place beneath the republican surface.

From Caligari to Hitler not only documented that sensitivity, it also took leave of critical participation in the crisis, a participation no longer possible at the time the book was written. While Expressionist film was gaining fame in the United States and exerting an influence on the film noir of the 1940s, Kracauer's "Psychological History of the German Film" centered on an already lost social process and not on the victor's appropriation of cultural or artistic assets. This did not promote the reception of the book in the United States, as it preserved the grassroots perspective, the viewpoint of the powerless. The history of emancipation in which Kracauer's perception of film was formed had disappeared. After National Socialism and the mass murders, "European Jews" no longer existed. The history of their emancipation could not renew itself, whereas in the 1960s it became possible for a new women's movement to emerge. When Kracauer wrote his *Theory of Film*, he had already bid farewell to a European understanding of freedom anchored in the subjectivity of the bourgeois individual that still informed the developing feminist movements of the 1960s. That in light of this movement's expectations Kracauer's book would contain lacunae is becoming meaningful for feminist thinking today. Today's feminism has come to lack a social movement on the one hand as well, and on the other it is opposed more than ever to the dominant scientific institutions. In this respect, *Theory of Film* strikes a chord.

Dominating Science

The reasons why Kracauer did not work at a university in the 1920s were not just biographical. His decision in favor of employment with the *Frankfurter Zeitung* had to do with his wide-ranging criticism of science, as is well known from his essay "Sociology as a Science." Yet in my view it was not until he was in the United States that he was confronted with the real force of a radicalizing development, the permeation of society by scholarship and technology. The result of that permeation was the "prevailing abstractness,"[2] a phenomenon that had already preoccupied Kracauer in the 1920s, as for example in "The Mass Ornament," where it vied for his attention with the phenomenon of spiritual homelessness. *From Caligari to Hitler* is the first book that adopts the gesture of science, at least to a degree, since Kracauer's task was that of a film historian. It only does this, however, so as to rob abstraction of its omnipotence and to arrive at a depiction of the historical facts in which these are absorbed in their concreteness "from within" (*Theory*, 297).

The films made in the 1920s had been handed down as facts, or as something like remains or fragments of that era; reels in an archive, they survive materially but without an audience. Kracauer did his research in the film archive of the Museum of Modern Art, which means he was still pursuing his work outside an academic institution. At the same time, science had since moved out of its traditional sites so as to dominate the everyday. In the future, film museums, which were only inaugurated in the 1930s, would control access to film history. For once, Kracauer was to remove a piece of German film history from the confines of the museum. In *Theory of Film* he later writes, "But if we want to do away with the prevailing abstractness, we must focus primarily on this material dimension which science has succeeded in disengaging from the rest of the world. For scientific and technological abstractions condition the minds most effectively; and they all refer us to physical phenomena, while at the same time luring us away from their qualities. Hence the urgency of grasping precisely these given and yet ungiven phenomena in their concreteness" (*Theory*, 298).

In the modern art museum, films are archived, registered, ordered, physically preserved—they are "given and yet ungiven." They have a physical existence, yet they are abstracted from a living context. Works that Kracauer had once encountered in the cinema he now found in the museum, "disengaged from the rest of the world." Commissioned to write a history of Weimar cinema, he starts with these physical objects, the film material, which MoMA could place at his disposal. Although the book orders the presentation of these films in chapters, their portrayal is not determined by a sense of order but rather by the intention of putting the films back in a specific context and returning their qualities to them, qualifying them in this literal sense, and not in the sense of art criticism. The aim of penetrating the physical, isolated materiality of the films is to render their soul visible. Kracauer's undertaking is opposed to an aesthetic assessment of the Weimar film—such as that by Lotte Eisner, for example—in which what comes to the fore is the artistic composition based on the technical handling of light and shadow, and the moving camera. The soul that Kracauer tries to present is not something he saw developing out of the technology and materiality of the films, nor is it something that is breathed into them by their creator. That soul, which Kracauer speaks of as something that is collectively created, is the historically and socially situated human, that which is not directed by reason, be it an instrumental or an idealistic one, yet which determines the making of the film. This human-suprahuman moment emerges not from nature, not from a genius, but from society. When the film corpus isolated in the archives is recontextualized within German society, the soul of these films, and with it their quality, can be rendered visible.

Someone like Kracauer was excluded from the German society in which the Weimar masterpieces were produced. He did not emigrate, rather he was forced into exile. The outside from which he looks (back) at the films, therefore, was not just a physical state in the New York archive. In turn, the seemingly value-neutral outside position of the scientist was for him merely the passage to a spiritual outside, whose genesis Kracauer was to find in the films, or which he saw mirrored in them. Initially, they reflected the psychophysical situation of the exile through their presence in the archive, torn from their context. By means of such self-reflection, Kracauer ensures that the scientific, technical gesture of isolation in the archive has no power over his work. If the films as he presents them seem distanced, "objective" as it were, this objectivity reveals a distance that those films always had for a viewer once interested in them as a cinemagoer and critic—while the films in turn had no interest in him. The recontextualization, the discovery of the soul of the films, also reveals his exclusion as a human being, as well as the sociopolitical implosion of that soul. And in this revelation Kracauer ascertained his lost reality.

In *Theory of Film* Kracauer would address the theme of science's abstraction from reality and confront this with film. He speaks of film as a means of enabling people in modern society to ascertain their reality, which is lost due to the influence of science and technology. This ascertainment expresses itself as a dream of a possible reality beyond the prevailing abstractness, dreamt by those living "unreally." In 1926 Margarete Susman wrote that "the only way for woman is a roundabout way," and that the "roundabout way through the world of man [is] the way of the female soul to itself."[3] A proximity between Kracauer and Susman existed not just through his work at the *Frankfurter Zeitung* but also through the influence Georg Simmel had on both of them. If I adopt Susman's contemporary perspective for a moment, then Kracauer took the roundabout way to its very end. This was a path on which the soul could no longer be spoken of in a mystical mode but solely in a scientific, psychoanalytical one. He confronted the language of dehumanization (*Ent-seelung*) with the perception of the physical, in photography, as something broken—the fragmented "foundation of nature"[4] to which science reduces the soul. On the roundabout way through photography, film led Kracauer to the dream of an external reality, a dream that enabled him to evade a (scientific) determination of the soul. The Weimar author-cinema, however, led the dream back to determination.

Dreams

Dreaming is at the very core of Kracauer's thoughts about the spectator in his *Theory of Film*, while his 1926 essay "Cult of Distraction," underscores the enlightening mirror-function that cinema had for the public. Something that was only blindly experienced by the latter in everyday life is "revealed" in the cinema: the fragmentation, the "distraction" of life, the violence of business that permeates work. On the other hand, Kracauer was speaking of the dream at that time with a view to film. The much-remarked end of his essay on photography introduces film as something dreamlike. As he states, film's "game with the pieces of disjointed nature is reminiscent of dreams in which fragments of daily life become jumbled." And further, "This game shows that the valid organization of things remains unknown" ("Mass Ornament," 63). In Kracauer's mind, then, the dream of the film was already a game with the fragments of reality, a game that did not veil destruction or death and thus maintained a certain anxiety for real life. In 1928, Kracauer introduced the dream not as a flight from reality in the transition from photography to film but rather as a departure from unreality.

The cinemas that the film critic Kracauer frequented in Frankfurt, Berlin, and elsewhere in the 1920s showed films of all kinds, of national and international origin, and especially of American provenance. The by-now-canonical Weimar films were only some of what was shown. They were clearly dedicated to dreamworlds, with their visualization of inner states, their staging of the imagined and the nightmarish, and of the "secrets of a soul." They offered cinemagoers not so much distraction as encounters, with potent psychological processes lurking beneath the surface of a democratic order. The vehemence of these unconscious processes was determined by the experience of the First World War, which led, as Kracauer put it, to a spiritual homelessness. While for him cinema offered the possibility of waiting without recourse to ideologies, the film worlds of the Weimar author-cinema could not dissociate themselves from the authoritarian patriarchal order—not even in the face of its loss, for social collapse brought the threat of the disintegration of the male ego. Concern about this ego, as the only remaining shelter, becomes the determining factor. To eschew the actual shattering of the ideology of the individual, films offer refuge in the dream or the nightmare of it. They sometimes do this solely through their aesthetic form, thereby restoring the artist-director. Yet even then, this refuge was not a valid one for Kracauer. *From Caligari to Hitler* clearly indicates that the dreamworlds of the famous Weimar film excluded his kind of dreaming in the cinema. For him, the collapse of the monarchy did not mean the loss of stability in the form of an authority, it meant the collapse of a history of emancipation. And that history had always been about escaping from the social state of physical nonexistence.

The moviegoer Kracauer garners dreaming from the radical disintegration, from the game with fragments. It was in the very explosion of the ego that he saw cinema's promising potential.[5] Kracauer's repeated engagement with the Weimar author-cinema not only allows him to recognize the exclusion of his dreams, his hope for the future, in the imaginary of those films, it also brings to light the way these films ran counter to the potential of cinema itself. The new organization into which the fragments of reality might blend at some point is not available for these films. This is manifest not least in the scenarios, the artificial spaces, which capture an inner world that no longer exists. Whenever Kracauer speaks about dreaming in *From Caligari to Hitler*, he finds it suspicious, for example, that "in dreams opposition to an attitude is often tantamount to its acceptance" (*Caligari*, 162). Wherever a new organization appears in the dream game, that "new order" (*Caligari*, 164) is the approaching order of fascism. One could say that all the dreams go inward, where they thrive on early infancy and the archaic experiences of social power; they devour the soul.

"The Prostitute and the Adolescent"

In this chapter from *Caligari to Hitler*, more than at any other point in the "Psychological History of the German Film," Kracauer engages with the dreaming that films inspire in viewers. The "Tyrantfilms" and the "Instinctfilms" can be read almost as illustrations of Freudian psychoanalysis. They present themselves as reproductions of collective dreams and their stereotypes. In *Dirnentragödie* (*Tragedy of the Street*, 1927) and *Asphalt* (1929), by contrast, something comes into play that stimulates the dreams of the "little shop girls," albeit without corresponding to the stereotypes that Kracauer pointed to in his essay sequence of 1928, "Die kleinen Ladenmädchen gehen ins Kino" ("The Little Shop Girls Go to the Movies"). To this extent, an affinity emerges in the text of 1947, an attitude of expectation is adopted again, as if here the love story was casting off its clichés. But it was only a brief flash. For the escape is not into the openness of the outside world but, as in the street films in general, back into the inner world. In a later reading of Kracauer's book (with which I concur), a lacuna therefore appears: What about women in Weimar society, the female audience in the cinema, and the actress, who also was part of the collective of filmmakers? The "collective mentality" (*Caligari*, 6) that Kracauer subjects to an analysis by means of Freudian theory does not yet include women as a matter of course, even though they gained the right to vote in 1919. For Patrice Petro, this was precisely the reason for a necessary new perspective on Weimar film history, which she provided with *Joyless Streets* (1989).[6] Kracauer's thoughts on *Die freudlose Gasse* (*Joyless Street*, 1925), *Dirnentragödie* (*Tragedy of the Street*), and *Asphalt* link these films primarily with Grune's *Die Straße* (*The Street*, 1923). They are also street films, but with an important difference. While in Grune's film female persons, or nonpersons, belonged in part to the tyrannical home and in part to the chaos outside, prostitutes now point to the "hope of genuine love" (*Caligari*, 159). They seem at least to be a symptom of woman's entrance into the universe of the male collective soul. Kracauer points out that in the new street films of the "stabilized period" (*Caligari*, 131), "the paralysed inner attitude rose to the surface" (*Caligari*, 159). An emotional spark jumps from the film to the viewer; "*Tragedy of the Street* and *Asphalt* radiated a warmth rarely to be found during the stabilized period" (*Caligari*, 159). The warmth that the home had lost is now to be found on the street. And the fact that in these films "the centre of life is the street" motivates Kracauer to a cursory political aside: The street is a "quarter peopled not with proletarians, but with outcasts," and this, the text continues, "indicates that the discontented are far from being socialist-minded. Love in the street stands for ideals averse to Locarno, Weimar, and Moscow" (*Caligari*, 159).

Asta Nielsen is the secret focus of Kracauer's recollections in this chapter. He describes her as having "portrayed the prostitute incomparably" (*Caligari*, 158). Nielsen is said to embody the prostitute "not as a realistic one, but that imaginary figure of an outcast." Nielsen overcame the filmic realism with a self-aware imagination of her own, which did not originate in the male unconscious and did not subject itself to its projections. What is perceptible in these passages is Kracauer's proximity to a political stance that adhered neither to communist nor to liberal or social-democratic ideals. Yet the films seem to him not to achieve a political stance: "But they were able to pierce the cover of neutrality only by manifesting themselves in the form of dreams" (*Caligari*, 159). As already mentioned, in *From Caligari to Hitler* these dreams were all under suspicion. And rightly so. For even where the trauma of the collective male mentality could have been resolved by the appearance of the self-aware woman, this does not happen. Her imagination, out of which the figure of the "outcast" is formed, is monopolized in *Tragedy of the Street* by the unconscious of the rebellious young man—of the new generation. Kracauer writes in connection with *Metropolis*, "Now it can no longer be doubted that the 'new order' . . . is expected to feed upon that love with which Asta Nielsen's prostitute overflows, and to substitute totalitarian discipline for the obsolete mechanical one" (*Caligari*, 164). In the trauma of postwar German society, however, a political aspect of the women's movement perished with that devouring of the actress's self-determined dynamism. And so after underscoring an empathy with the female audience of the time, I return, in contrast to Petro, once again to Kracauer's reading. For it is precisely this loss of a cinema of the 1910s that "grew up" together with its female audience that I see reflected in Kracauer's history of Weimar cinema and its lacunae.

In 1931 Kracauer had written in detail in the *Frankfurter Zeitung* about the scandalous fact that Asta Nielsen was not being given adequate roles and was largely being overlooked by the film industry. His article tried to give the work on her first talkie the veneer of a new beginning, something that he sincerely hoped for. *Unmögliche Liebe* (*Impossible Love*, 1932) then fulfilled all the expectations he had of her acting, although in retrospect the film is also a document of the hopelessness of the political situation, as well as of the actress's situation. In her essay "Verschränkte Erinnerungen," Nia Perivolaropoulou reflects on the importance of the late encounters between Kracauer and Nielsen.[7] In *From Caligari to Hitler* we find only a hint of attention paid to the actress's distinctiveness. All in all, the chapter "The Prostitute and the Adolescent" remains in this sense also a lacuna. Yet through that gap we can look at a history of film other than the psychological history of Weimar cinema, a history of the feature film of the first decade of the twentieth century that Asta Nielsen shaped in decisive ways.[8]

The Actress in History and Theory

To judge by the short chapter on the prehistory of Weimar cinema in *From Caligari to Hitler*, it would seem as if Kracauer had no real appreciation of the history of the films made in Wilhelminian Germany. On the other hand, the book's approach is not one of redeeming a lost cinema process— unless this means the redemption of his own cinemagoing and his activity as a film critic. Instead, the approach is one of (self-) enlightenment and separation, revealing how the Weimar films excluded the liberated and liberating dream of which film is capable thanks to its photographic quality. *From Caligari to Hitler* had to be written so as to be able to theoretically grasp the shape of film history in moments of lost processes. The movement that Asta Nielsen introduced into film became one such moment. As an actress, she had much more to do with the redemption of physical reality than with what the film critic Kracauer saw as the focus of attention during the Weimar era, namely, the loss of spiritual shelter. To this extent, Nielsen seemed untimely in Weimar cinema, not only because her roots were in early cinema but also because she was ahead of her time.

The passage of time, however, had abstracted the process of filmic redemption of physical reality from the actress. Nielsen experienced this personally. Her élan, which is related to Kracauer's impetus, involved taking advantage of the abstraction of technology as a possibility, on the one hand, while on the other not subjecting herself to its power. It originated in the delight in liberation that she experienced in the collapse of paternalism in the early twentieth century. She did not hanker after "spiritual shelter." She was keen to finally discover her reality in the world. In the course of the postwar social depression, however, that delight waned; it was worn down. In Nielsen's films of the late war and early postwar era—*Die Börsenkönigin* (*The Stock-exchange Queen*, 1916), and even more so *Nach dem Gesetz* (*According to Law*, 1919)—it is evident how the actress experienced the disintegration of the women's movement, caught between an identification with power and a regression into a presocial state. She anticipates the disintegration of her own vitality of acting, which is never only a technical dynamism of the body but always a dynamic of the soul as well. Michael Wedel presents Nielsen's struggle against the montage form of Weimar films as her resistance to the fracturing of her acting.[9] Basically, the potential the actress had for redeeming physical reality was already lost after the First World War. *Theory of Film* manifests just this when it focuses primarily on camera technique, recording processes, and film takes.

In *Theory of Film* a lacuna is formed by the actress (with her entourage of emotionalism, love, and emancipation of the gender relations) and also by the actor (with the exception of Chaplin). Gender difference has fallen prey to abstraction in the "Remarks on the Actor" (*Theory*, 93), although it was of considerable importance for the concretization of the possibilities acting showed in film history. Acting succeeds in a go-for-broke game between loss of ego and the expectation of a psychophysical reality that emerged through body techniques. Asta Nielsen played that game. Unlike her male colleagues, she had nothing to lose—but a lot to gain. *From Caligari to Hitler* contains a critique of the genre of the "Instinct Film," which was influenced by Carl Mayer's film scripts. This critique is actually expressed in connection with F. W. Murnau's *Der letzte Mann* (*The Last Laugh*, 1924). This is a moment in criticism that sheds light on the actor and what he allowed to happen to him. After describing what the "freed camera can facilitate," Kracauer states, "However, despite its eagerness for ever-changing aspects, the camera, at home in the dimension of instincts, refrains from penetrating that of consciousness. Conscious acting is not allowed to prevail. The player is the passive subject of the camera" (*Caligari*, 105). Until she was forced to end her film work, Asta Nielsen resisted any such subjection, which was something she was well able to do.

Nielsen's acting, however, pursued the scientific-technical reduction of soul to instinct. Just as the photographic film presents life as such, she isolates sexual life with her body and at the same time contextualizes it by also letting the same body be an object among objects again. This is already apparent in her first film, *Afgrunden* (1910). In the famous gaucho scene, she steps out of love—or at least out of a love that the film up to this point has shown as a psychophysical relationship between a man and a woman that ranges from romanticism to battle of the sexes. She steps out into the loneliness of a body that has been stripped of all meaning and become pure movement and pure gesture. The audience might see this as obscene or as mere expression of drives, but Nielsen's acting is performed as explicit rejection of a visual pleasure sought by an audience that has brought its expectations from theater to film. She becomes an offering to the coldness of the camera. She becomes one with the lens, which turns the movement of her body into a part of reality. No matter how spectacular her bodily contortions might be, they do share our attention with the bucket of the fireman standing in the sets, with the lasso around the dance partner, or with the monotonous beating of the baton of the bandmaster barely visible above the ramp. Thus the arousal of physical desire is suffused with a melancholy that makes the loss of soul beyond individual suffering appear as an outer reality. It is not the drama as mirror of social circumstances but rather the relationship between objects that forms the filmic soul, where the separation of inside and outside is suspended (*aufgehoben*). This soul knows no ego; it surrounds the protagonist with an environment of emotions, feelings, and sensory reactions that depend on the takes of external reality.

Asta Nielsen was close not only to the explicit politics of the women's movement in the 1910s but also to the politics implicit in *Theory of Film*. She assumed that abstraction—not the male person—was the real opponent, promising possibilities while at the same time threatening annihilation because of its power status. By comparison, patriarchal ideology and reality had already become secondary. For Nielsen, an "outcast," love does not take place on the street but instead on film. For film theorist Kracauer, film constituted the escape from the traps of "Lebensphilosophie" (philosophy of life). Like concepts, film isolates life while at the same time contextualizing it in its takes of reality. For Nielsen, film became an escape route from the traps of a love life in which woman is always forced back into patriarchal structures. Her hope for a redemption of humanity has an echo in the final passage of Kracauer's *Theory of Film*. The longing for a reality above and beyond what is socially monopolized and reproduced bound them both, and also bound cinemagoers into a public dispersed worldwide in diversion (and not in global unification).

NOTES

1. Siegfried Kracauer, *From Caligari to Hitler: A Psychological History of German Film* (Princeton: Princeton University Press, 1947), 153–64. Subsequent quotations from this book appear parenthetically with page numbers.
2. Kracauer, *Theory of Film: The Redemption of Physical Reality*, introduction by Miriam Hansen (Princeton: Princeton University Press, 1997), 298. Subsequent quotations from this book appear parenthetically with page numbers.
3. Margarete Susman, "Das Frauenproblem in der gegenwärtigen Welt," in Susman, *Das Nah- und Fernsein des Fremden: Essays und Briefe*, ed. Ingeborg Nordmann (Frankfurt am Main: Jüdischer Verlag im Suhrkampverlag, 1992), 143–67, here 159, 166.
4. Kracauer, "Photography," in *The Mass Ornament: Weimar Essays*, trans. and ed. Thomas Y. Levin (Cambridge: Harvard University Press, 1995), 47–63, here 62.
5. Drehli Robnik emphasizes the political significance of this in his contribution to this volume.
6. Patrice Petro, *Joyless Streets: Women and Melodramatic Representation in Weimar Cinema* (Princeton: Princeton University Press, 1989).
7. Nia Perivolaropoulou, "Verschränkte Erinnerungen," in *Unmögliche Liebe: Asta Nielsen, ihr Kino*, ed. Heide Schlüpmann, Eric De Kuyper, Karola Gramann, Sabine Nessel, and Michael Wedel (Vienna: Filmarchiv Austria, 2009), 220–30.
8. My book *Unheimlichkeit des Blicks: Das Drama des frühen deutschen Kinos* (Frankfurt am Main: Stroemfeld, 1990) is dedicated to this cinema. The first part of this book is now available in English translation in *The Uncanny Gaze: The Drama of Early German Cinema*, trans. Inga Pollmann, foreword by Miriam Hansen (Chicago: University of Illinois Press, 2010).
9. Michael Wedel, in *Unmögliche Liebe*, 110–30.

Looking after Kracauer

Kracauer's Photography Essay
Dot Matrix—General (An-)Archive—Film

Miriam Bratu Hansen

A common reading of Kracauer's 1927 essay "Photography" takes its most important insight to be the opposition between the photographic image and the memory image, including the claim that the proliferation of technologically produced images threatens the very possibility and truth-character of images preserved by memory.[1] Against such a reading, which effectively assimilates Kracauer to a genealogy of media pessimism (from Baudelaire and Proust through Virilio and Baudrillard), I contend that the essay's radical insights lie elsewhere. For Kracauer does not simply puncture the ideologically available assumption that the meaning of photographs is given in their analog, iconic relation to the object depicted; rather, he examines how meanings are constituted at the pragmatic level, in the usage and circulation of photographic images in both domestic and public media practices. Another, equally far-reaching concern of the essay is with the aging and afterlife of photographs, the transformation they undergo over time, especially once they have lost their original reference and presence effect. In the precarious temporality and historicity of photography, its alienation from human intention and control, Kracauer traces a countervailing potential, neither positivistic nor nostalgic, that he believes can be actualized in the medium of film. It is this potential that places photography at the crossroads of modernity: "The turn to photography is the *go-for-broke game* [*Vabanque-Spiel*] of history."[2]

The question of historicity no less concerns the aging and afterlife of this text itself. It takes the by now ritual form of asking whether and how an essay that emphatically seeks to theorize photography in relation to the historical moment—Weimar democracy between economic stabilization and crisis, the larger trajectory of technological capitalist modernity—can speak to a present in which the photographic paradigm, to the extent that it props its claims to authenticity and accuracy onto an indexical (physical or existential) relation with the object depicted (the registration of reflected light on a photochemical surface at a particular point in space and time), seems to have been radically displaced and reframed by digital modes of imaging.[3] Moreover, since the digital is not just another, more current medium, it has challenged traditional concepts of mediality and has made the idea of medium specificity, taken to be central to classical film theory, appear as a high-modernist preoccupation.[4] As I hope to show, Kracauer's essay, much as it responds to a particular stage of media culture, points up issues of technological image production and usage, proliferation and storage that persist, in different forms and infinitely vaster dimensions, in the ostensibly postphotographic age; it likewise complicates key concepts of this debate—such as indexicality—by unfolding them as historically contingent and mutable. Finally, with a view to film theory and, not least, Kracauer's own *Theory of Film* (1960), the photography essay projects a film aesthetics that compels us to rethink the question of cinematic realism.

Like Benjamin's artwork essay, which it prefigures in important ways, Kracauer's photography essay is organized in discrete sections that frame the object of investigation in the manner of different camera positions or separate takes. The protagonists of the resulting theory-film, as it were, are two photographs that the writer introduces by way of juxtaposition: the contemporary image of a film star (caption: "our demonic diva") on the cover of an illustrated journal and the portrait, over six decades old, of an unspecified grandmother, possibly Kracauer's own, cast in the private setting of family viewing. Both images show women twenty-four years old; both images become the respective focus of later sections; and both metamorphose in the course of the essay—until they are united, in the eighth and last section, in the surreal panorama of modernity's "general inventory" or "main archive" (*Hauptarchiv*).

The image of the film star, posing in front of the Hotel Excelsior on the Lido, embodies the present moment ("time: the present")—not just a fashionable cosmopolitan modernity, but also a culture of presence, performance, perfection: "The bangs, the seductive tilt of the head, and the twelve eyelashes right and left—all these details, diligently enumerated by the camera, are in their proper place, a flawless appearance" (*MO*, 47). Kracauer emphasizes the photograph's double status as a material object that can be perceived in its sensory texture and a symbolic representation whose referent is elsewhere. Looking through a magnifying glass, one would see "the grain, the millions of dots that constitute the diva, the waves, and the hotel" (*MO*, 47); at the same time, the image is an "optical sign" (*MO*, 54) whose function it is to evoke the star as a unique, corporeal being. However, the referent that validates the sign in the eyes of the general public is not the star in person but her appearance in another medium: "Everyone recognizes her with delight, since everyone has already seen the original on the screen" (*MO*, 47). Resuming the duodecimal figure of the well-groomed eyelashes, Kracauer goes on to assert the paradoxical effect of the star's mass-mediated individuality with recourse to yet another entertainment intertext, that of the revue: "It is such a good likeness that she cannot be confused with anyone else, even if she is perhaps only one-twelfth of a dozen Tiller Girls."[5] And he concludes the presentation of the star photograph with a deadpan refrain of the beginning of the paragraph: "Dreamily she stands in front of the Hotel Excelsior, which basks in her fame—a being of flesh and blood, our demonic diva, twenty-four years old, on the Lido. The date is September" (*MO*, 47).

As he mounts his case against the ideology of presence and personality connoted by the mass-addressed image, Kracauer's writing already punctures that effect, even before the passage of time will have disintegrated the photograph and relegated it to history's vast central archive. The microscopic look that reveals "the millions of dots that constitute the diva, the waves, and the hotel" evokes the materialist, egalitarian pathos of Kracauer's frequent observation that in film, the actor is nothing but "a thing among things." The abstraction of the image into minimal units—halftone dots, a precursor to pixels[6]—defamiliarizes the resemblance with a particular living being; it also deflates the authority of the indexical bond (in the narrow sense of referring to the photochemical process of inscription) by foregrounding the image's mediation, if not de/composition, at the level of raster reproduction. The image's claim to depicting a singular referent is further undercut by the tongue-in-cheek remark that attributes its recognizability to the slippage between the image of the actual person and her representation in another medium—film—just as the suggestion that the star might be "only one-twelfth of a dozen Tiller Girls" corrodes the aura of her uniqueness.

The photograph of the diva functions as a synecdoche for the emerging mass culture of industrial-capitalist image production that Kracauer saw flourishing in the illustrated journals and weekly newsreels. By 1927, the term *illustrated magazine* was actually becoming something of a misnomer: the main purpose of the photograph, according to publisher Hermann Ullstein, was "no longer to illustrate a written text but to allow events to be seen directly in pictures, to render the world comprehensible through the photograph."[7] In Kracauer's analysis, such ideological investment in photographic representation corresponds to the false concreteness by which the individual image mimics the logic of the commodity form; it goes hand in hand with the massive increase—not simply mass reproduction—of photographic images on an imperial, global scale. "The aim of the illustrated magazines is the complete reproduction of the world accessible to the photographic apparatus" (*MO*, 57–58).[8]

Kracauer sees in the relentless "blizzard" of photographic images a form of social blinding and amnesia, a regime of knowledge production that makes for a structural "indifference" toward the meanings and history of the things depicted.

> Never before has an age known so much about itself, if knowing means having an image of objects that resembles them in a photographic sense. . . . Never before has an age known so little about itself. In the hands of the ruling society, the invention of illustrated magazines is one of the most powerful weapons in the strike [*Streikmittel*] against understanding. (*MO*, 58; *S*, 5.2:93)

Understanding is prevented above all by the contiguous arrangement of the images—"without any gaps." Such an arrangement systematically occludes reflection on things in their relationality (*Zusammenhang*) and history, which would require the work of consciousness. The illustrated magazines, like the weekly newsreels, advance a social imaginary of complete coverage (anticipating later media genres such as twenty-four-hour cable news and online news services), which affords an illusory sense of omniscience and control. The surface coherence of the layout glosses over the randomness of the arrangement, and with it the arbitrariness of the social conditions it assumes and perpetuates; the illustrated magazines offer an image of the world that domesticates otherness, disjunctions, and contradictions. But, Kracauer adds, "it does not have to be this way" (*MO*, 58).

Kracauer's critique of these practices should not be mistaken for a lapsarian complaint that the media of technical reproduction are distorting an ostensibly unmediated reality. Rather, "photographability" has become the condition under which social reality constitutes itself: "the world itself has taken on a 'photographic face'; it can be photographed because it strives to be absorbed into the spatial continuum which yields to snapshots" (*MO*, 59). Here he works toward a medium- and institution-specific account of what Heidegger, a decade later, will call the "age of the world picture"— "world picture" understood not as a picture of the world, "but the world conceived and grasped as picture."[9] From this condition, there is no way back, neither conceptually nor ontologically, to an unmediated state of being that would release us from the obligation to engage contemporary reality precisely where it is most "picture"-driven—which for Kracauer is as much a political as a philosophical and psychotheological concern.[10]

Let me note parenthetically that Kracauer's critique of illustrated magazines was not exactly fashionable at the time. Avant-garde artistic and intellectual circles such as the Berlin group assembled around the magazine *G: Material für elementare Gestaltung* (1923–26), an important platform of German constructivism, and valorized the *Berliner Illustrirte Zeitung* and other mass-marketed journals for their innovative layout, the dynamic integration of photographs, text, and typography.[11] The pedagogic potential of this graphic form inspired not only the layout of *G* and avant-garde journals but also Laszlo Moholy-Nagy's famous book *Malerei, Fotografie, Film* (1925, 1927). And Benjamin, a member of the *G* group, wrote a defense of the *Berliner Illustrirte Zeitung*, "Nichts gegen die 'Illustrirte'" (1925), that praised the journal for its contemporaneity, its "aura of actuality," documentary precision, and conscientious technological reproductions.[12]

If Kracauer remains skeptical toward the illustrated magazines it is for the same reason that he indicts the vernacular style of New Objectivity in his analysis of the Berlin entertainment malls: "Like the denial of old age, it arises from dread of confronting death."[13] Benjamin, too, comments on the juncture of photography and death, as do later writers such as André Bazin, Roland Barthes, Susan Sontag, and Georges Didi-Huberman. For Kracauer, the fact that the world "devours" this image world is a symptom of the fear and denial of death, inextricably linked to German society's refusal to confront the experience of mass death in the lost war. (This refusal is not incompatible with the fascination with disasters, crashes, and catastrophe that Kracauer observes in the media's sensationalist exploitation of violence and death.)[14] "What the photographs by their sheer accumulation attempt to banish is the recollection of death, which is part and parcel of every memory image." Yet, the more the world seeks to immortalize itself qua "photographable present," the less it succeeds: "Seemingly ripped from the clutches of death, in reality it has succumbed to it" (*MO*, 59).

The concept of the "memory image" appears to furnish an epistemological and spiritual counterpoint to photography, especially in its mass proliferation. As an immaterial, unstable, and degenerative image, it belongs to a different order of reality and works on a fundamentally different principle of organization. From the perspective of photographic representation, with its claims to accuracy and fullness, memory is fragmentary, discontinuous, affectively distorted, and exaggerating; from the perspective of memory, however, "photography appears as a jumble that partly consists of garbage" (*MO*, 51). The memory image relates to those traits of a person that resist being rendered in the spatiotemporal dimensions of photographic representation, and which in fragmentary form may survive after death, as the person's actual or proper "*history.*" In a photograph, by contrast, "a person's history is buried as if under a layer of snow" (*MO*, 51).

The opposition between photography and memory image participates in a broader discourse, associated with *Lebensphilosophie*, which sought to reconceptualize perception, time, and memory in response to modernity's alleged reduction of experience to spatiotemporal terms. While Kracauer does not mention Bergson by name, the notion of *durée* resonates in the essay's critique of pretensions to chronological and spatial continuity, as manifested, respectively, in historicism and photography.[15] Likewise, he assumes the Proustian distinction between voluntary and involuntary memory, which Benjamin was to mobilize in his work on Baudelaire. Benjamin links the "increasing atrophy of experience" to the fact that devices like photography and film "extend the range of the *mémoire volontaire.*" But this expansion comes at a cost: "The perpetual readiness of voluntary, discursive memory, encouraged by the technology of reproduction, reduces the imagination's scope for play [*Spielraum*]."[16] Similarly, Kracauer warns that, instead of serving as an aid to memory, "the flood of photos sweeps away the dams of memory. The assault of these collections of images is so powerful that it threatens to destroy the potentially existing awareness of crucial traits" (*MO*, 58).

The problem with this kind of argument is that it casts memory and technological reproduction as antithetical, exclusive terms, rather than analyzing their complex interactions.[17] Moreover, it assumes an economic logic by which the expansion of the photographic (and, for that matter, phonographic) regime inevitably entails the withering away of human capacities of memory, reflection, and imagination. Given the exponential growth of media technologies, this logic cannot but imply a trajectory of cultural decline. It occludes the possibility that film and photography have also enabled new and qualitatively different types of experience—a possibility in which both Kracauer and Benjamin had a great stake.

I take the opposition of photographic and memory image to be only one element in the rhetorical movement of Kracauer's essay, part of a larger, more dialectical argument that turns on the constellation of photography, historical contingency, and film. As we have seen, the corrosive, allegorical gaze that drains the pretension of life and coherent meaning from contemporary media culture—a sensibility germane to Benjamin's treatise on the baroque *Trauerspiel*—is a function of critical reading, beginning with the opening section.[18] Yet, at least as important is the essay's effort to ascribe this effect to the temporality and historicity of the medium itself, performed by the two photographs as material objects. For much as photography and film were becoming complicit with the social denial of death, Kracauer still discerned in them the unprecedented possibility of confronting the subject with contingency and mortality, and of challenging the natural appearance of the prevailing social order.

Kracauer builds up to this turn from his meditation on the portrait of the grandmother, viewed as part of the family archive by the grandchildren. Because of its age, the temporal gap of over sixty years that separates the moment of recording from its reception, the image of the grandmother poses the question of photographic referentiality in a different way from that of the diva. With the death of the "*ur*-image," the connection with the living person may survive for a while by way of oral history but is ultimately loosened, literally defamiliarized, to the point of randomness—"it's any young girl in 1864" (*MO*, 48). Barely remembering the grandmother and the fragmentary stories about her, the children perceive in her photograph only a "mannequin" in an outmoded costume or, rather, a collection of once fashionable accessories—the chignons, the tightly corseted dress— that have outlived their bearer. What makes the grandchildren giggle and at the same time gives them the creeps, Kracauer suggests, is that the photograph amalgamates these remnants with the incongruous assertion of a living presence. It is this "terrible association" that haunts the beholder like a ghostly apparition, and makes him "shudder"; like the early films screened in the "Studio des Ursulines" in Paris, the aged photograph conjures up a disintegrated unity, a reality that is "*unredeemed.*" The configuration of its elements "is so far from necessary that one could just as well imagine a different organization of these elements" (*MO*, 56).

Kracauer relates photography's precarious afterlife to the split-second nature of photographic exposure—that is, he locates the problem precisely in the technologically supported indexical bond traditionally invoked to assert the photograph's accuracy and authority. In the mechanical reduction of time to the moment of its origin, Kracauer observes, the photograph is intrinsically more vulnerable (than, for instance, film) to the subsequent passage of time: "If photography is a *function of the flow of time*, then its substantive meaning will change depending upon whether it belongs to the domain of the present or to some phase of the past" (*MO*, 54; emphasis in the original). While the photograph of the diva maintains a tenuous connection, mediated by film, between the corporeal existence of the original and her still-vacillating memory image, the grandmother's photograph affords no such comfort. In the measure that the photograph ages and outlives its referential context, the objects or persons depicted appear to be shrinking or diminishing in significance—in inverse proportion to memory images that "enlarge themselves into monograms of remembered life." The photograph represents merely the dregs that have "settled from the monogram"; it captures the remnants "that history has discharged" (*MO*, 55). However, in the tension between history and that which history has discarded, photography begins to occupy the intermediary zone that appeals to Kracauer the ragpicker, the intellectual seeking to gather the refuse and debris, the ephemeral, neglected, and marginal, the no longer functional.

Kracauer aligns the temporality of photography with that of fashion and discerns in both a characteristic feature of capitalist modernity—a connection already implicit in the German word for fashion, *Mode*.[19] Like Benjamin, Kracauer is interested in fashion here primarily for its paradoxical imbrication of novelty and accelerated obsolescence, the moment when both photography and fashion, like all outdated commodities, join the ever-faster-growing garbage pile of modern history.[20] While the very old traditional costume, which has lost all contact with the present, may attain "the beauty of a ruin," the recently outmoded dress, pretending to photographic life, appears merely comical (*MO*, 55).

The grandchildren's giggles are a defense against dread, a shocklike, visceral recognition of their own contingency and mortality, of a history that does not include them. In a typical rhetorical gesture, Kracauer switches from the third person to the first, assuming the grandchildren's shudder as his own: "This once clung to us like our skin, and this is the way our property clings to us even today. We are contained in nothing and photography assembles fragments around a nothing" (*MO*, 56). Rather than affording a prosthetic extension into a period not lived by consciousness, the photograph irrupts into the beholder's living present in an unsettling way, signaling his own physical transience along with the instability of the social and economic ground of his existence. In its emphasis on discontinuity and estrangement, this account anticipates Kracauer's later discussions, in *Theory of Film* and his posthumously published *History*, of a passage from Proust in which the narrator, describing a visit to his grandmother after a long absence, actually equates the sudden, terrifying sight of her as a sick, dejected old woman with a photograph; for Kracauer, this passage marks photography as a "product of complete alienation," epitomized by the view of a stranger unclouded by incessant love and memories, but also the vision of the exile who "has ceased to 'belong.'"[21]

Benjamin too, in his "Little History of Photography" (1931), comments on the haunting quality of early photographs—something that remains in them "that cannot be silenced."[22] Likewise, he attributes this haunting quality to the photograph's association with death, as in his evocation of the portrait of the nineteenth-century photographer Dauthendey and his fiancée who was to commit suicide after the birth of their sixth child. But where Benjamin suggests the mystical possibility of a spark that leaps across the gap between the photograph's time and his own, Kracauer stresses irreversible disjuncture and dissociation into dissimilarity. (It is important to note that he is talking less about the physical, chemically based process of decay than about a disintegration of the depicted material elements.) The photograph of the young grandmother-to-be does not return the gaze across generations. For Kracauer, the chilly breeze of the future that makes the beholder shudder conveys not only intimations of his own mortality but also the liberating sense of the passing of a history that is already dead, depriving the bourgeois social order of its appearance of coherence and continuity, necessity and legitimacy.[23]

More than an existential memento mori, the outdated photograph assumes the status of evidence in the historical process (or "trial," as Benjamin will pun).[24] What up to this point in the essay has remained a private, individual encounter emerges as a public and political possibility toward the end of the essay. It is precisely *because* of the medium's negativity—its affinity with contingency, opacity to meaning, and tendency toward disintegration—that Kracauer attributes to photography a decisive role in the historical confrontation between human consciousness and nature. Shifting to the historicophilosophical register, he sees photography assigned to that stage of practical and material life at which an at once liberated and alienated consciousness confronts, as its objectified, seemingly autonomous opposite, "the foundation of nature devoid of meaning" (*MO*, 61). In other words, it is the problematic indexicality at the heart of photographic representation that enables it to function as an index in the sense of deixis, an emblem pointing to—and pointing up—a critical juncture of modernity.[25]

As a category inseparable from history, nature refers both to the historically altered *physis* (including its ostensibly untouched preserves) and to the "second nature" of a society "[secreted by] the capitalist-industrial mode of production"—a social order that "regulates itself according to economic laws of nature" (*MO*, 61).[26] I would stress that in this phase of Kracauer's work his concept of nature, including the bodily and instinctual nature of human beings, has a ferociously pejorative valence, lacking the philosophical solidarity with nature as an object of domination and reification one finds, for instance, in Benjamin and Adorno and, with a different slant, in Kracauer's own *Theory of Film*. As in the essay "The Mass Ornament" (published earlier the same year), nature becomes the allegorical name for any reality that posits itself as given and immutable, a social formation that remains "mute," correlating with a consciousness "unable to see its own material base."

> One can certainly imagine a society that has fallen prey to a mute nature that has no meaning however abstract its silence. The contours of such a society emerge in the illustrated journals. Were it to endure, the emancipation of consciousness would result in the eradication of consciousness; the nature that it failed to penetrate would sit down at the very table that consciousness had abandoned (*MO*, 61).

However, if historically emancipation and reification have gone hand in hand, consciousness is also given an unprecedented opportunity to reoccupy the place at the table with a different agenda: "Less enmeshed in the natural bonds than ever before, it could prove its power in dealing with them." In this alternative, Kracauer pinpoints the significance of the photographic media for the direction of the present, the fate of modernity: "The turn to photography is the *go-for-broke game* of history."

In the eighth and final section of the essay, Kracauer steps up the rhetorical stakes of this gamble to highlight the historical chance that presents itself with photography, an argument that turns into a case for the photographic foundation of film. In a vast panoramic collage, he evokes the image of a "*general inventory*" or "main archive" (*Hauptarchiv*) that assembles the infinite totality of outdated photographs. "For the first time in history, photography brings to light the entire natural cocoon; for the first time, it lends presence to the world of death in its independence from human beings" (*MO*, 62; *S*, 5.2:96). In the dialectics of presence effect and disintegration, the medium-specific negativity of photography comes to define its politically progressive potential, indeed its task "to disclose this previously unexamined *foundation of nature*" (*MO*, 61–62). In the confrontation with "the unabashedly displayed mechanics of industrial society," photography enables consciousness to view "the reflection [*Widerschein*] of the reality that has slipped away from it" (*MO*, 62).

Understood as a general warehousing of nature, photography provides an archive that makes visible, in a sensorily and bodily experienced way, both the fallout of modernity and the possibility of doing it over, of organizing things differently. This archive, however, is anything but easy to access and navigate; it is rather an *an*-archive—a heap of broken images—that lends itself to the task precisely because it lacks any obvious and coherent organizational system.[27] It is closer in spirit to dadaist or surrealist montage (or, for that matter, the essay's epigraph from *Grimms' Fairytales* and Kracauer's 1926 essay "Calico-World").

> Photography shows cities in aerial shots, brings crockets [*Krabben*] and figures from the Gothic cathedrals. All spatial configurations are incorporated into the main archive in unusual overlaps [*Überschneidungen*] that distance them from human proximity. Once the grandmother's costume has lost its relationship to the present, it will no longer be funny; it will be peculiar, like a submarine octopus. One day the diva will lose her demonic quality and her bangs will go the same way as the chignons. This is how the elements crumble since they are not held together. The photographic archive assembles in effigy the last elements of a nature alienated from meaning. (*MO*, 62; *S*, 5.2:96–97)

From a future vantage point that shows the present intermingled with everything else that is past, and the human nonhierarchically cohabitating with the nonhuman, even the illustrated magazines lose their market-driven actuality and coverage effect; their images become as random, fragmentary, and ephemeral as the portraits and snapshots in the family album. Kracauer's photographic *an*-archive evokes Benjamin's image of the backward-flying Angel of History facing the wreckage piled up by a storm from paradise, written at a time when the historical gamble seemed all but lost. Kracauer's vision is not quite as desperate: it still discerns concrete images of disfiguration, assembled in a textual bricolage.

The passage cited reinforces the essay's programmatic subordination of photographic resemblance or iconicity to the idea that photographs do not simply replicate but are themselves part of nature, material objects like the commodities they depict in their configuration of and with the human.[28] This comes across not least in the way that Kracauer's text materializes the photographs of the star and the grandmother as "things"—in the emphatic sense of "thingness" theorized by Heidegger.[29] Like Heidegger's famous jug, the two exemplary images take on an amazing plasticity, tactility, and agency; they spawn and participate in public life, and disclose their meanings through social usage and cultural practices. Unlike the jug, however, which seems to exist—and endure—in an abstract timeless if not mythic space, Kracauer's photo-things are temporal and transient; their very thingness emerges in the dynamics of split-second exposure, commodified presence effect, and archival afterlife. The encounter with aged photographs does not put the beholder in touch with a reality repressed by scientific reason and capitalist appropriation, let alone with nature, but rather with the historical reality of irreducible mediation and alienation.

Kracauer's investment in photographic negativity is fueled by photography's potential to point up the disintegration of traditional and reinvented unities, the arbitrariness of social and cultural arrangements at the level of both the individual image and the protocols of public media. Once the bonds that sustained the memory image are no longer given, the task of artistic and critical practice is "to establish the *provisional status* of all given configurations." Kracauer finds a model of writing that "demolishes natural reality and displaces the fragments against each other" (*MO*, 62; *S*, 5.2:97) in the works of Franz Kafka whose novel *The Castle* he had reviewed enthusiastically a year earlier.[30] If that review reads like a blueprint of Kracauer's early gnostic-modernist theory of film, the photography essay makes this connection explicit. By putting techniques of framing and editing to defamiliarizing effect (associating "parts and segments to create strange figurations"), film has the capacity not only to make evident the "disorder of the detritus reflected in photography" by suspending "every habitual relationship among the elements of nature" but also to "stir up" and reconfigure those elements (*MO*, 62–63; *S*, 5.2:97). Combining photographic contingency with cinematic montage, film can "play" with "the pieces of disjointed nature" in a manner "reminiscent of *dreams*" (*MO*, 63). In other words, it can enlist a logic inspired by the unconscious to mobilize the inert, mortified fragments of photographic nature and associate them to suggest the possibility of a different history.

Although film becomes the overt object of Kracauer's reflections only at the end, the whole essay is central to his emerging film theory, if not conceived from this vantage point.[31] In that sense, it provides the foundation for his later effort, in *Theory of Film*, to ground a "material aesthetics" of the cinema in the photographic basis of film. Whatever cinema's potential for "the redemption of physical reality," Kracauer's advocacy of realism in the later book remains tied to a historical understanding of *physis* and a concept of reality that depends as much on the estranging and metamorphic effects of cinematic representation as on the role of the viewer. As the essay makes sufficiently clear, Kracauer's conception of film's relationship with photography is not grounded in any simple or "naive" referential realism. On the contrary, it turns on the technological medium's capacity to mobilize and play with the reified, unmoored, multiply mediated fragments of the modern *physis*, a historically transformed world that includes the viewer as materially contingent, embodied subject. The concept of realism at stake is therefore less a referential than an experiential one.

Kracauer does not posit the relationship between photography and film in evolutionary terms but seeks to articulate an aesthetic of film in the interstices of the two media. In this intermedial space, film does not "remediate" photography by way of containing it;[32] rather, photography, running alongside and intersecting with film both institutionally and ideologically, provides radical possibilities that film can draw on. To the convergence of film and photography in contemporary capitalist media culture—as prefigured in the cognitive regime that links weekly newsreels and illustrated magazines, and metonymically present in the photograph of the film star—he opposes an alternative configuration of intermedial relations in which the unstable specificity of one medium works to cite and interrogate the other.[33]

Around the time the photography essay was written, the kind of film it envisioned may not have existed, though there are clearly affinities with experimental films of the period (e.g., René Clair, Jean Vigo, Dziga Vertov, and Kinugasa Teinsuke, all of whom Kracauer reviewed). By and large, contemporary commercial cinema had no use for the defamiliarizing and disjunctive aesthetics projected in the essay. With the stabilization of the German film industry and mounting political instability toward the end of the decade, Kracauer's writing on film shifted toward a more immanent critique of ideology that took aim at the films' recycling of outdated bourgeois forms, settings, and values, the gentrification of exhibition practices, and the shaping of a mass-cultural imaginary in collusion with the emerging white-collar class. Increasingly, his critique of these developments was coupled with an evocation of the cinema's forgotten anarchic and materialist beginnings, the promise that the discarded possibilities of film history could yet become decisive for the cinema's future.

In its focus on the present as historic dis/juncture, the photography essay highlights an important dynamic in Kracauer's early work on film and mass culture, which at once dates it and makes it prescient. For its radicalism still participates in the 1920s' break with the "long nineteenth century," a century prolonged by efforts, enhanced by the capitalist entertainment industry, to restore a cultural façade that Kracauer, like the avant-garde artists of his time, strongly believed could not be patched up. Moved by a modernist impulse that made him defend the cinema against the educated bourgeoisie, he found in the technological mass media a sensory-perceptual discourse on a par with the experience of modernity, encompassing its traumatic, pathological effects as well as its transformational, emancipatory possibilities. Accordingly, the essay discerned in technologically and mass-based media institutions like the illustrated journals and cinema the emergence of new forms of publicness (different from the traditional liberal public sphere of the newspaper to whose readers it was addressed) that demanded recognition and critical debate, insisting that they were key to the political future of Weimar modernity.

Beyond its prognostic purchase on the imminent future, the photography essay contains a remarkably acute premonition that the issue was not merely that a discourse equal to the challenges of modernity was *lacking*— a lack to which film and photography supplied a certain answer—but that these same media generated and circulated an exponentially increased abundance of images, a random multiplicity and an indifferent interchangeability and convergence. It thus anticipates a key feature of contemporary media culture, in a changed socioeconomic and geopolitical landscape and new, infinitely more powerful technological forms. The point is not just that Kracauer's disintegration of the star photograph into an abstract grid of halftone dots intuits something of the logic of algorithmic procedures. It is at least as important that his rhetorical magnifying glass discovers a similar logic at another level, in the protocols governing the use of photographs in contemporary media practices; that it draws attention to the historical dynamic of presentism and ephemerality, and thus to aesthetic and political possibilities of reconfiguration.[34]

NOTES

1. See, for instance, Inka Mülder, *Siegfried Kracauer—Grenzgänger zwischen Theorie und Literatur: Seine frühen Schriften 1913–1933* (Stuttgart: Metzler, 1985), 97–102, and Christine Mehring, "Siegfried Kracauer's Theories of Photography: From Weimar to New York," *History of Photography* 21, no. 2 (Summer 1997): 129–36. Benjamin H. D. Buchloh reiterates this emphasis, citing the "Photography" essay as evidence of Kracauer's "extreme media pessimism"; see Buchloh, "Gerhard Richter's Atlas: The Anomic Archive," *October* 88 (Spring 1999): 117–47, esp. 129–34.

2. Kracauer, "Photography," in *The Mass Ornament: Weimar Essays (MO)*, trans., ed., and intro. by Thomas Y. Levin (Cambridge: Harvard University Press, 1995), 61; "Die Photographie," first published in the feuilleton section of *Frankfurter Zeitung (FZ)*, 28 October 1927, rpt. *Aufsätze 1927–1931*, vol. 5.2 of *Schriften (S)*, ed. Inka Mülder-Bach (Frankfurt am Main: Suhrkamp, 1990): 96. In the following, references will be given in the text; an additional reference to the German edition indicates that the translation has been modified.

3. This question is addressed in greater detail by Lutz Koepnick, "In Kracauer's Shadow: Physical Reality and the Digital Afterlife of the Photographic Image," in this volume. For a critique of a narrow adaptation of Charles Sanders Peirce's concept of the index in film theory see Tom Gunning, "What's the Point of an Index? Or Faking Photographs," in *Still Moving: Between Cinema and Photography*, ed. Karen Beckman and Jean Ma (Durham: Duke University Press, 2008), 23–40, and "Moving Away from the Index: Cinema and the Impression of Reality," *differences: A Journal of Feminist Cultural Studies* 18, no. 1 (2007): 29–52. Also see Mary Ann Doane's introduction to this special issue of *differences* as well as her essay "The Indexical and the Concept of Medium Specificity," ibid., 128–52.

4. For a critique of a high-modernist (Greenbergian) notion of medium-specificity, see Rosalind Krauss, *"A Voyage on the North Sea": Art in the Age of the Post-Medium Condition* (London: Thames and Hudson, 1999); also see Ji-Hoon Kim, "The Post-Medium Condition and the Explosion of Cinema," *Screen* 50, no. 1 (Spring 2009): 114–23.

5. Kracauer had repeatedly written on the Tiller Girls from May 1925 on, most notably in his 1926 essay "The Mass Ornament," *MO*, 75–86.

6. The reprographic halftone process reproduces images by means of dots varying in size and spacing. Digital pixels, by contrast, are homogeneous in size and relation to each other; what varies is their color value. Both involve a perceptual shift from discrete to continuous appearance.

7. Hermann Ullstein, *The Rise and Fall of the House Ullstein* (New York: Simon and Schuster, 1943), 85, cited in Mila Ganeva, *Women in Weimar Fashion: Discourses and Displays in German Culture, 1918–1933* (Rochester, NY: Camden House, 2008), 53. Also see Kurt Korff, "Die 'Berliner Illustrirte,'" *Fünfzig Jahre Ullstein 1877–1927* (Berlin: Ullstein, 1927), 297–302.

8. Kracauer expands this argument—in language anticipating Bazin—in his

first analysis of the sound film: "The sound film is so far the final link in the chain of a series of powerful inventions which, with blind certainty and as if guided by a secret will, push toward the complete representation of human reality. This would make it possible, in principle, to wrest the totality of life from its transitoriness and transmit it in the eternity of the image." "Tonbildfilm: Zur Aufführung im Frankfurter Gloria-Palast," *FZ*, 12 October 1928, rpt. Kracauer, *Kleine Schriften zum Film 1921–27*, vol. 6.1 of *Werke (W)*, ed. Inka Mülder-Bach and Ingrid Belke (Frankfurt am Main: Suhrkamp, 2004), 124.

9. Martin Heidegger, "The Age of the World Picture" (1938), in *The Question of Technology and Other Essays*, trans. William Lovitt (New York: Harper and Row, 1977), 129.

10. I borrow the term *psychotheological* from Eric L. Santner, *On the Psychotheology of Everyday Life: Reflections on Freud and Rosenzweig* (Chicago: University of Chicago Press, 2001), which throws into relief remarkable resonances between Franz Rosenzweig and Kracauer's writings of this period.

11. On the G group and German constructivism, see Frederic J. Schwartz, *Blind Spots: Critical Theory and the History of Art in Twentieth-Century Germany* (New Haven: Yale University Press, 2005), 39–62.

12. Walter Benjamin, "Nichts gegen die 'Illustrierte'" (1925), *Gesammelte Schriften*, 4:448–49.

13. Kracauer, *Die Angestellten* (1929, 1930), *The Salaried Masses: Duty and Distraction in Weimar Germany*, trans. Quintin Hoare, intro. Mülder-Bach (London: Verso, 1998), 92.

14. See Kracauer's remarkable review of a newsreel showing the fatal crash of an aviator, which he contrasts with Dziga Vertov's ability, in *Man with a Movie Camera* (1929), to bring death to collective and public consciousness, "Todessturz eines Fliegers," *FZ*, 5 February 1932, *Kleine Schriften zum Film: 1932–1961*, vol. 6.3 of *W*, 14–27.

15. Kracauer refers to Bergson's critique of "measurable, chronological time" in "Tonbildfilm," 124. Also see his critique of the architectural politics of the Berlin Kurfürstendamm as the "embodiment of the empty flow of time" in "Straße ohne Erinnerung" (street without memory), *FZ*, 16 December 1932, *Aufsätze 1932–1965*, vol. 5.3 of *S*, 170. He aligns photography with "historicist thinking" in section 2 of the photography essay, a comparison to which he returns in his posthumously published *History: The Last Things Before the Last* (1969; Princeton: Markus Wiener, 1995), 4, 49–51.

16. Benjamin, "On Some Motifs in Baudelaire" (1940), *1938–1940*, vol. 4 of *Selected Writings* (SW), ed. Howard Eiland and Michael W. Jennings (Cambridge: Harvard University Press, 2003), 316, 337.

17. Phenomenological media theory, for instance, conceives of technologically produced images as "tertiary memory." Defined as "experience that has been recorded and is available to consciousness without ever having been lived by that consciousness," tertiary memory significantly affects the perceptual dynamics of secondary (individual) memory and primary retention. See Mark B. N. Hansen, *New Philosophy for New Media* (Cambridge: MIT Press, 2004), 255.

18. In his review of Benjamin's *Origins of German Tragic Drama* and *One-Way*

Street (both 1928), Kracauer asserts that its "method of dissociating immediately experienced unities," the laying-in-ruins of the seemingly live and organic, "must take on a meaning which, if not revolutionary, is nonetheless explosive when applied to the present" (*MO*, 263).

19. On the affinity of Moderne and Mode, see Jürgen Habermas, *Der philosophische Diskurs der Moderne* (Frankfurt am Main: Suhrkamp, 1985), 18. On the cultural-conservative inscription of the term *fashion*, particularly in opposition to the category of *style*, see Schwartz, *Blind Spots*, chap. 1; also see Ganeva, *Women in Weimar Fashion*.

20. Benjamin's reflections on fashion can be found in *The Arcades Project*, trans. Howard Eiland and Kevin McLaughlin (Cambridge: Harvard University Press, 1999), Konvolut B, 62–81, and his exposés for that project, ibid., 8, 18–19. On the temporality instantiated by fashion, see Peter Osborne, *The Politics of Time: Modernity and the Avant-Garde* (London: Verso, 1995), 134–50.

21. Kracauer, *Theory of Film: The Redemption of Physical Reality* (1960; Princeton: Princeton University Press, 1997), 15, and *History*, 83. On the difference between Kracauer's interpretation of that passage in the former and the latter, see Elena Gualtieri, "The Territory of Photography: Between Modernity and Utopia in Kracauer's Thought," *New Formations* 61 (Summer 2007): 76–89, esp. 84–86.

22. Benjamin, "Little History of Photography" (1931), trans. Edmund Jephcott and Kingsley Shorter, *SW* 2:510.

23. Kracauer elaborates this point in his important review of the 1932 Berlin film and photo show, "An der Grenze des Gestern [On the border of yesterday]: Zur Berliner Film- und Photo-Schau," *FZ*, 12 July 1932, *W*, 6.3: 77, but does so to contrast early with contemporary photography.

24. Benjamin, "The Work of Art in the Age of Its Technological Reproducibility," *SW*, 3:108; 4:258.

25. On the distinction between index as a trace and index as deixis and its implications for cinema, see Doane, "The Indexical." Also see Philip Rosen, *Change Mummified: Cinema, Historicity, Theory* (Minneapolis: University of Minnesota Press, 2001), chap. 8.

26. Kracauer's understanding of nature as "second nature" was indebted to Lukács's *Theory of the Novel* and *History and Class Consciousness*. See Steven Vogel, *Against Nature: The Concept of Nature in Critical Theory* (Albany: State University of New York Press, 1996), 17. The term goes back to Hegel's *Philosophy of Right*, paragraph 151.

27. In that sense, the concept of the archive here is actually more an-archic than both institutional archives and the counterarchival projects of the Weimar period cited by Buchloh ("Gerhard Richter's *Atlas*," esp. 118–34); while ultimately cognitive, its mnemonic function is less didactic (as in Hannah Höch and Aby Warburg) than buried in virtuality. On the problematic of the archive in general, see Jacques Derrida, *Archive Fever: A Freudian Impression* (1995), trans. Eric Prenowitz (Chicago: University of Chicago Press, 1996).

28. A similar argument can be found in André Bazin, "The Ontology of the Photographic Image" (1945), *What Is Cinema?* ed. and trans. Hugh Gray (Berkeley: University of California Press, 1967), esp. 1:14–16.

29. Heidegger, "Das Ding" (1950), *Vorträge und Aufsätze* (Pfullingen: Neske, 1954), 157–75; "The Thing," *Poetry, Language, Thought,* trans. Albert Hofstadter (New York: Harper and Row, 1971), 165–86; 165–66. Heidegger's notion of "the thing" (as opposed to the object [*Gegenstand*] and its idealist corollaries, the subject and representation) appears appropriate here, despite the fact that Heidegger himself would specifically have excluded the technological media from such consideration as the very agents that eradicated all distances and any sense of distance, both farness and nearness, and were thus antithetical to the condition under which things can said to be "thinging" (*dingen*).

30. Kracauer, "Das Schloß: Zu Franz Kafkas Nachlaßroman," *FZ,* 28 November 1926, *Aufsätze 1915–1926,* vol. 5.1 of *S,* 390–93. On the significance of this review for Kracauer's early film theory and its affinity with secular-Jewish literary Gnosticism, see M. Hansen, "Decentric Perspectives: Kracauer's Early Writings on Film and Mass Culture," *New German Critique* 54 (Fall 1991): 56–57.

31. See Heide Schlüpmann, "Phenomenology of Film: On Siegfried Kracauer's Writings of the 1920s," trans. Thomas Y. Levin, *New German Critique* 40 (Winter 1987): 97–114.

32. See Jay David Bolter and Richard Grusin, *Remediation: Understanding New Media* (Cambridge: MIT Press, 2000).

33. We might take this possibility to have found its most inventive realization in more recent artistic practices, for example, the analytic, dissociating, and transformative engagement with film and film history in electronic and digital video, interactive storage modes, and multimedia installations—in work as diverse as that of Ken Jacobs, Douglas Gordon, Zoe Beloff, and Harun Farocki, to mention only a few.

34. On the persistence of some of these issues in digital media and fantasies about them, see Wendy Hui Kyong Chun, "The Enduring Ephemeral, or the Future Is a Memory," *Critical Inquiry* 35 (Autumn 2008): 148–71.

In Kracauer's Shadow

Physical Reality and the Digital Afterlife of the Photographic Image

Lutz Koepnick

A cursory reading of Kracauer's writing on photography, as developed in his 1927 essay and then continued in the opening chapter of his 1960 *Theory of Film*,[1] will in all likelihood situate him as a critic principally unfit to help theorize the digital transformation of the photographic image. Kracauer's reputation remains that of a naive realist,[2] not simply stressing the indexical nature of the photographic process but understanding the technological foundation of the photographic image as a reason to favor documentary uses over formative, artistic, or experimental ones. Though Kracauer's normative privileging of the transitory and contingent may be seen as in accord with certain avant-garde sensibilities,[3] his definition of photography as a means to "record and reveal physical reality"[4] is condemned either for abandoning the political stakes of his earlier work or for endorsing a helplessly modernist theory of medium specificity. Neither of these assessments helps to bring Kracauer's work into a productive conversation with more current writing about the digital image. As a champion of the material world, a common assumption, Kracauer has nothing to offer for conceptualizing how the digital image replaces the real with the simulated, the indexical with binary code.

It is the principal aim of this essay to argue against such arguments and thus explore the ongoing actuality of Kracauer's theory of photography. Whereas naive readings of Kracauer's work advance reasons to consider his work as incompatible with the digital turn, I contend that a more thorough understanding of Kracauer's writing—an understanding stressing the overarching historico-philosophical trajectories of his thought—must come to very different conclusions. Kracauer's work, I submit, invites us to emphasize decisive continuities between chemically and electronically based modes of photography and to understand the recent prominence of the pixel as part of a much larger and ambivalent process of rationalization and disenchantment. The central relay station of my argument in this effort is Kracauer's notion of "nature," used in his work not only to describe the material world in front of the camera, but also to designate the material base of the photographic medium. Though the concept of "nature" has not fared well in critical theory during the last decades, I see this dual and, in fact, reciprocal use of the term in Kracauer's work as the foundation for his continued relevance.

Two assumptions are of critical importance for this argument. The first is that Kracauer's Weimar writings on photography and his American ones are not as different as often claimed. Though Kracauer's *Theory of Film* is vastly dissimilar from his earlier work of the 1920s, the critical, metaphysical, and gnostic aspects of his Weimar thought had not gone entirely underground when Kracauer conceptualized the redemptive qualities of film.[5] And even though Kracauer's postwar writings might rest on different sensibilities than his work preceding his exile,[6] they bring similar questions, anxieties, and hopes to the role of mechanically produced images in the modern world. It is by synthesizing the different phases of Kracauer's intellectual development, rather than by segregating them, that his potential role in contributing to a theory of contemporary photography will become the clearest.

The second assumption is that Kracauer's writings on photography throughout his entire career consider states of alienation as vital playgrounds of human experience, liquefying the reified structures of the bourgeois subject and thus reenabling the possibility of nonintentional behavior and perception.[7] Alienation, in Kracauer, is photography's irreducible, albeit historically inflected, nature. The role of nature throughout Kracauer's writings on photography, in turn, is to envision a new kind of techno-humanism, an enriched and enriching notion of the human subject reflexively aware of its own often quite fluid extensions and sensory interactions.[8]

I

Though critics are quick to talk about the digital image as a radical departure from the analog photograph, we do well to first pause and identify the location of the digital. If in traditional photography images resulted from a physical transcription of light into an analogous spread of tonal differences, digitality signifies the conversion of visual information into computable numbers and discrete sets of data. But where do we locate the work of this conversion? Is it simply enough to point our digital cameras at the world in order to participate in digital photography? Or do we also need to rework their data with various software programs, store them in digital archives, and disseminate them electronically? Do images built from scratch on the computer count as digital photographs? Or do we only want to consider what engages certain optical lenses before visual information is being converted into code?

Whether theorists locate the threshold of digitality in the actual capturing, the electronic manipulation, or the distribution of photographic images, the newness of the digital is normally associated with the way in which the digital image breaks with the logic of indexicality, the physical mark left on the surface of the film negative. Digital photography, it is argued, no longer subscribes to the chain of material in- and transcriptions that are at the core of predigital processes. As a result, digital imaging ostensibly liberates the photographic image from its realist credo and evidential force, from its ability to authenticate rather than represent the world. Whereas analog photography, due to its material bond to the object, cannot but remain ensnared to naturalizing ideologies of the real, digital photography—precisely because it suspends the indexical—not only ushers image making into an age of modularity, unfixity, and simulation, but in doing so also reveals the fundamental untruth of all photography—the fact that technological manipulation is at the center of every act of image making.

While there are no doubt fundamental differences between nondigital and digital modes of photographic image production, there are nevertheless also good reasons to be wary of the critical burden placed on the role of the indexical and, by extension, the material as a watershed between old and new.[9] First of all, the process of capturing images with the help of digital cameras relies as much on the physical impact of light as does the act of taking an image with a conventional camera, with the sole difference that in traditional photography this impact restructures the arrangement of silver halide molecules, whereas in digital photography incoming light makes contact with an electronic sensor. Though the process of electronic encoding might be harder to visualize than the reshuffling of molecules, both forms of photography essentially originate in a material footprint left by incoming light on a receptive surface. Second, due to the ever-shrinking size of digital imaging devices, the instantaneity of image viewing, and the suspension of expensive development costs, digital photography not only fosters modes of picture taking that actively engage the photographer's body in the production of images (think only of all the postures photographers today assume to look at the tiny screens of their cameras) but also fosters a snapshot aesthetic much more open to the contingencies of the profilmic world than the old deliberate family image seeking to stage memorable moments for the future. Third, while critics clearly overestimate the number of users actively employing imaging software to rework their images before they ever achieve material form, they rarely ask themselves what even the minority of users actually do when altering the surface of their images. Pixels might be at the bottom of each digital image, but even the most expert users will hardly ever manipulate the image at the level of the individual pixel or code but instead use software functions as if they were extensions of analog darkroom practices. The metaphors of how technology makes itself available in this case matter: it is our hand physically drawing the mouse that, when using PhotoShop, retouches the image, not our mind instructing the computer to change the numerical value of discrete pixels. There is no need to know anything at all about the makeup of digital code to modify certain aspects of an image on screen. There is no need, therefore, to think we have all turned into Neo-Cartesians,[10] leaving all things physical at the doorstep when we entered the realm of digital photography.

Digital imaging, as this overview suggests, by no means shepherds its users automatically into a dematerialized Cartesian space of postindexicality. To center debates about the newness of the digital around the principle of indexicality, in fact, not only means to subscribe to ill-advised forms of media determinism, it also suggests a monolithic understanding of analog photography that cannot but do grave injustice to everything that doesn't follow the tradition of straight photography. Digital photography potentially engages with materiality and the tactile as much as analog photography has done in all its various manifestations. The question, therefore, is not whether the technological setup of the digital camera inevitably buries traditional forms of photographic image making. The decisive question instead is how the digital in photography causes us to readdress the very notion of medium specificity, and how we should think about the relation between the technological—or if you wish, material—makeup of a medium and its representational registers, its vernacular uses, and its artistic possibilities. How, then, can we theorize the material base of a medium without subscribing to prescriptive notions of medium specificity that leave no room for the possibility of variation, historical transformation, and multiplicity?

II

Kracauer's work offers critical answers to these questions: answers that not only complicate our notion of a medium's materiality but also help realize critical continuities between analog and digital forms of photographic practice. Kracauer, to be sure, at first presents himself as a staunch advocate of a rigidly modernist concept of medium specificity. In particular, *Theory of Film* appears to detail an ontology of photography that seeks to define a template for its appropriate uses and potential aesthetic failures. "This study," Kracauer famously begins *Theory of Film*, "rests upon the assumption that each medium has a specific nature which invites certain kinds of communication while obstructing others."[11] Kracauer's notion of medium specificity immediately invokes a long tradition of aesthetic thought stretching from Lessing's musings about the difference between visual and poetic art forms in his *Laocoon* essay, via Rudolf Arnheim's Weimar attempts to define the distinctiveness of silent filmmaking, to Clement Greenberg's desire to declare self-reflexive explorations of medium specificity in painting—the quality of the brushstroke, the surface of the canvas, the dynamic of color, line, and shape—as modernist painting's autonomous repository of meaning. But Kracauer, rather than aligning himself self-confidently with this prominent line of thought, is quick to admit considerable doubts about how to determine the nature of a medium such as photography in the first place, only to then emphasize that any effort to define the specificity of photography must begin with reconstructing the unfolding of this nature as it manifested itself in what users thought about and did with the medium since its inception in the 1830s.

Contemporary theorists of photography tend to distinguish between *photography* and *the photographic*, the former term designating technological assemblies that enable photographic image making, the latter term describing the discourses, desires, and practices that have guided its historical role in society. The opening of *Theory of Film*, instead of self-confidently identifying the technological essence of photography, significantly approaches the medium's nature by first tracing shifting historical notions of the photographic. Kracauer's stance here is driven by the assumption that our understanding of *photography*, in the above sense of the word, is historical through and through; that we cannot speak about photography, the medium's nature, without mapping the unfolding of this nature in what contemporary discourse calls *the photographic*. The first chapter of *Theory of Film* rigorously follows this assumption as Kracauer, in a brief historical survey, discusses different views about photographic practice since its inception in the early nineteenth century before he proceeds to delineate basic aesthetic principles of the photographic approach to the world. Nothing could be more wrong than to call this approach a naive ontology of medium specificity, one that would regard the technological makeup of the photographic camera as a prescriptive framework to define what Kracauer considers the medium's appropriate—that is, documentary, realist, and redemptive—uses. Though contemporary media theory, in its preoccupation with the indexical, often wants us to believe that photography precedes the photographic, Kracauer proposes something quite different: photography and the photographic are locked into a historical dialectic, a reciprocal dynamic in which one simultaneously needs and helps constitute the other. This dialectic is closely bound up with another, central to Kracauer and to Critical Theory more generally: Nature, in Kracauer, is not history's radical Other; history in fact is what reveals nature in all its contingency and mutability. We therefore would be mistaken to see photography as a transcendental depository of the truth about the photographic. Instead, we must come to realize that this truth exists in history and experience alone; that photography's nature is transitory and far from absolute.

Kracauer's principal understanding of the photographic medium not only as body and form of materialization, but as something whose very nature is involved in a historical dynamic, deserves more attention than it has received from previous scholars. It is not difficult to see, however, that in Kracauer's work this understanding is driven by much more general thoughts about the role and reconfiguration of nature in modern technological culture, by historicophilosophical assumptions about the course of modern disenchantment, and about the role of the aesthetic in encoding or unsettling the path of rationalization—thoughts that Kracauer substantially shared with intellectual companions such as Walter Benjamin and Theodor W. Adorno. Kracauer's ostensibly restrictive notion of medium specificity, of the technological nature of photography, is far less restrictive once we understand its status as a decisive crossroad within Kracauer's general theory of modernization. For Kracauer considers the nature of a medium in all its materiality as a site at once revealing and disputing the repression of sensory immediacy, of inner and outer nature, in the fallen world of modernity. The nature of photography, in Kracauer's view, simultaneously exposes and offsets what has happened to nature in industrial society. Medium and mediated are affected by one and same process of rationalization and alienation; but photography, by putting to work what in its very material setup exceeds human intentionality, can recall lost experiences of sensory contact, dissolve the hardened contours of modern subjectivity, and thus bring users in touch with a world that no longer seems to afford the indeterminacy of the sensory and nonintentional.

Two steps are of critical importance here to unpack how Kracauer situates his notion of medium specificity within a larger dialectic of nature and rationalization. First of all, it is important to recall that Kracauer understands photography as a technology whose rise parallels not only that of modern industrial society, but also those processes of rationalization that have alienated human consciousness from nature and stripped the latter of its previous meanings. "No different from earlier modes of representation," Kracauer writes in 1927, "photography, too, is assigned to a particular developmental stage of practical and material life. It is a secretion of the capitalist mode of production. The same mere nature which appears in photography flourishes in the reality of the society produced by this capitalist mode of production."[12] Capitalist modernity, in Kracauer's at once Weberian and gnostic understanding, leads to a progressive regimentation of sensory experience and how we connect sensorily to the objects of the world. Modernity has empowered the human consciousness to emancipate itself from the originary identity of nature and man. Through technological advances and cognitive schematizations, it has allowed humanity to gain control over what had once controlled the human mind and folded all possible meanings and actions into one mythological cocoon. Liberation and reification have thus gone hand in hand: we have learned how to disentangle consciousness from the authority of nature, but we have done so by muting the world, by subsuming the material and the sensory under organizing concepts, by evacuating subjective intuitions and undoing the kind of meaningful connections premodern ages sensed between the elements of the world, between inner and outer nature.

The photographic image, in Kracauer's view, clearly participates in this emancipation of consciousness from myth and nature and thus contributes to the progressive flattening of meaning and materiality. Yet Kracauer is far from arguing that photography necessarily seals our fate as inhabitants of a world fallen from prelapsarian plenitude. On the contrary, in alienating viewers from an alienated world, in making us see aspects of reality often invisible to the human eye, photography has the ability to transmit the raw and unshaped and thus reopen the case of nature in all its incommensurability. Photographic modes of seeing the world decenter the rationalistic schemas and imperial visions of modern consciousness; they have the potential to humble the viewer's gaze, to estrange us from our own Cartesian alienation, and in so doing to loosen the presumed sovereignty of modern subjectivity and its gestures of strategic control over the world. Photographic seeing, in Kracauer, allows the repressed materiality of the disenchanted world to return its gaze at us and untie the knots of our own repressed inner nature. It reminds us of that which exceeds control and manageability, including the vagaries of our bodies, even if the sheer accumulation of images in the illustrated press seems to promise us fake liberation from the "clutch of death."[13] In Kracauer's early writing on the photographic image, photography's dynamic of alienation has the utopian charge to move us through and beyond the meaningless and senseless topographies of disenchanted modernity, toward a state in which consciousness and nature can coexist in nonhierarchical reciprocity. In his later writing on photography, Kracauer seems to lower photography's transformative bar a little, as he now wants photography simply to compensate for the abstraction and alienation caused by industrial capitalism—to remedy the factual fragmentation of the world by reminding viewers of the material dimensions of all things and relations. In both versions of Kracauer's argument, however, the photographic engages dialectically with the fallen world that defines the very conditions of photography's possibility. It alienates us from the mechanisms of alienation so as to allow us to cling to the idea of a future reconciliation between humanity and nature, between the rational and the material dimensions of the world.

The second step that needs to be taken to illuminate Kracauer's notion of medium specificity is to stress the extent to which this dialectic of nature and disenchantment also unfolds within the heart of what modernist aesthetic theory understands as artistic medium in the first place. "A consciousness caught up in nature," Kracauer writes in his 1927 essay, "is unable to see its own material base. It is the task of photography to disclose this previously unexamined *foundation in nature*. For the first time in history, photography brings to light the entire natural cocoon; for the first time, the inert world presents itself in its independence from human beings."[14] What allows photography to accomplish this task is nothing other than the fact that *as a medium* photography expresses the separation of consciousness from the authority of nature while at the same time serving as a physical stand-in for the former role of nature as a resource of sense-making and meaningful orientation. A medium, in modernist discourse, is often seen as the quasi-transcendental condition for the possibility of artistic practice. At the same time, however, as J. M. Bernstein has argued, mediums[15] in various modernist accounts embody materialized forms of modern disenchanting rationality precisely because no medium can do without some material substrate—the brushstroke, the body of the camera, the hand moving the film camera, the physical imprint of the word on the page. Modern rationalization might result in a progressive dematerialization of nature and human experience. But no matter how much modernist aesthetic practice participates in this process of mechanization and abstraction, it is the very idea of the nature of the medium—understood as an art form's material-specific potential for sense-making—that allows for a certain suspension, negation, or recalibration of what modernity is doing to nature: "The idea of an artistic medium," Bernstein concludes, "is perhaps the last idea of material nature as possessing potentialities for meaning, or, more accurately, . . . as remnants of sense-making, as materials about to lose their potential for sense-making, as the decay of material meaning, as the material a priori of sense collapsing, as the dissolving, fragmenting, folding in on itself of reason materialized in things."[16]

Mediums are part of the world of human consciousness: a set of practices and ideas by which artists structure their material and subsume their expressive visions to larger schemata. But mediums are also part of the world of nature; they are matter themselves, not only providing embodied forms of engaging with inner and outer nature, but also offering counterfactual models of how to reconcile the discursive demands of artistic technique with what is incommensurable and hence nondiscursive about human intuition, spontaneity, and sensory experience. It is in recourse to what we might want to call the natural history of its mediums that modernist art situates artistic works as effigies holding up the claims of subjectivity in spite of their factual dematerialization; it is by reflecting on the materiality of the medium itself, in all its historical constitution, that modernism seeks, again in Bernstein's words, "to rescue from cognitive and rational oblivion our embodied experience and the standing of unique, particular things as the proper objects of such experience, albeit only in the form of a reminder or promise."[17]

The medium of photography, in Kracauer's view, is at the forefront of this process. Though it participates in the rationalization of culture and hence the devaluation of the sensory, it also brings into play material techniques of representation that recall what it might mean to be "in touch" beyond the logic of modern science and rationality. Medium specificity matters to Kracauer because the very matter of the medium retains a material trace of what scientific reason and technological disenchantment have evacuated from modern social life: the capacity of sensory encounters between nonidentical particulars.

Nature, then, in Kracauer's thought, is not only the Other of human consciousness and intentionality, that which precedes the shaping power of mind, will, reason, and goal-oriented subjectivity. It also—and as importantly—describes a historically contingent source of sensory connections, of structures of embodiment, of matter and materiality as they exceed the realm of deliberate conceptualization and instrumental reason. Photography brings consciousness to the material world, and yet because *as a medium* it remains partly bound to the realm of nature itself, and because *as a practice* it has the ability to picture the world without physically shaping what is in front of the camera, photography secretly expresses solidarity with the repressed cause of nature and materiality in modern life. Ironically, however, and contrary to common assumption, what qualifies photographic images as advocates of the material dimension, in Kracauer's view, is not the medium's ability to capture the visible world through an indexical process of inscription, that is, the way in which light may touch upon a receptive surface. Kracauer suggests instead that photography communicates nature's muted voice best whenever photographic practice engages the viewer in a dual process of alienation: alienation from a world that revels in standardizing and hence emptying the meaning of the visible; and alienation from our own sovereign selves so as to open our eyes for the unexpected, unnoticed, aleatory, and spontaneous. Photography, in other words, has the capacity to remind us of the meaning of being in touch with the matter of the world precisely because its images refuse to touch upon what they depict, thereby subjecting the viewer to a productive process of estrangement and self-estrangement. What defines the specificity of photography, in Kracauer's view, is not—as so often claimed—the evidentiary force of the indexical, but how photographic ways of seeing the world, by alienating viewer and viewed and suspending the logics of instrumental reason, evoke solidarity with the material dimension of inner and outer life—with the sensory, the nonintentional, the unshaped and indeterminate.

We thus return to my initial claim, namely, that Kracauer may have much more to say about digital photography than many critics might assume. In an effort to prepare the ground for this claim, I argued above that digital photography relies as much on indexical processes of transcribing light as traditional forms of photography. As it turns out now, however, we do not even need to follow this line of reasoning in order to stress Kracauer's ongoing actuality. For what matters most to Kracauer's theory is not how photography—in a purely technological sense—provides physical imprints of the material world. What matters instead is how photographic processes express our deepest need for an emphatic sense of experience, of sensory contact and material meaning, in the form of a reminder and promise. The task of photography, in Kracauer's view, is by no means simply to shoot straight pictures of life and time passing by. Photography's task instead is to reveal and examine the material dimension as a historically dwindling residue for making meaning and sense. It is to map, with unique methods indeed, the fine and shifting line between the determinate and the indeterminate, between the intentional and the nonintentional, between the spontaneous and the formative. It is to investigate the dialectic of mind and matter, consciousness and embodiment, as a dynamic in which the future of human experience is being negotiated.

Photography's nature, in other words, is to reveal what is or has become natural even about advanced technological configurations and modes of perception, not in order to celebrate the end of human subjectivity and freedom, but in order to probe the natural substrate of things for their capacity to redeem the claims of the sensory against the onslaught of technological rationality and thereby warrant the possibility of meaning and freedom. It would be wrong to identify this position as medium-deterministic, as a position eagerly understanding the hardware of certain mediums as an unalterable base for defining proper uses of their software. The relation of photography to the photographic, of technology and technique, is part of the same dynamic that energizes the relationship of matter and mind, nature and consciousness. One cannot do without the other; one helps define the contours and range of the other; and both together, in their very tension and interaction, provide an open-ended space in which history defines itself, not as a dimension of causally determined patterns, transcendental laws, and scientific certainties, but—as Kracauer puts it in his final metaphysics of history—as a "realm of contingencies, of new beginning."[18]

Photography, in Kracauer's view, becomes photography by evoking the language of nature—inner and outer—against the grain of its historical repression and dematerialization. There is no need at all to think that photographic images based on digital procedures of encoding and transcoding cannot participate in this project. While there are surely good reasons to assume that digital imaging has the capacity to question the evidentiary rhetoric of straight photography, there is ample evidence that even highly manipulated images today hold on to the representational registers of conventional photography such as linear perspective and different zones of focus, not because synthetic image makers lack creative imagination, but because these registers communicate what Kracauer believed to be the unique utopian promise of photographic images.[19] Digital imaging might fake the real (just as conventional photography did), but in faking the real, in inventing alternate natures, and in alienating viewers from preconceived views, even digital images appeal to nothing other than our fundamental hope for indeterminate forms of perceptual and bodily experience, for the material and sensory—and they do so perhaps even more strongly than analog photography ever did.

III

In closing, I would like to turn briefly to the work of German photographer Thomas Ruff to illustrate the extent to which Kracauer's theory of photography remains in conversation with photographic work building on pixels rather than silver halide crystals. Like his colleagues Andreas Gursky, Candida Hoefer, and Thomas Struth, Ruff studied photography with Bernd and Hilla Becher in Düsseldorf, much of his work since the late 1970s—similar to that of his teachers and fellow students—pursuing expansive series and typologies of the present. In contrast to his colleagues, however, Ruff's work has also been driven by considerable analytical impulses, namely his relentless desire to investigate not only the way in which photographic images construct different notions of visual truth, but also how camera, film, and lens relate to the operations of biological vision and may reveal the perceptual procedures of the so-called naked eye. "That the camera," writes Matthias Winzen, "not only captures but projects reality; that it robs what it identically copies of its identity; that it conceals, fictionalizes, and devalues the model in visible reality to which the copy owes its existence by way of that very copy—these are contradictions which Ruff not only recognized, but utilized, developed, and then let go their own way that they might become more truthful when their artificiality is forcefully (though not parodistically) amplified."[20] Throughout the thirty years of his career, Ruff's photography, one might argue, has been photography in reverse: an ongoing effort to examine and uncover the grammar and standardized conventions of the photographic process, yet neither in order to ascertain with some postmodern self-affection that all images may lie, nor to celebrate the putative authenticity of unadulterated biological vision, but first and foremost to make us recognize the mediated character of all reality and sight and precisely thus to probe measures of visual objectivity and allow images to emerge by and speak for themselves.

Since the early 2000s Ruff has gained wide recognition for his *jpeg* series: images that were originally downloaded from the Internet and then blown-up to such proportions that we often, like Kracauer in 1927, struggle to find the image in the image and instead fasten our gaze to the sculptural qualities of the pictures' most rudimentary building blocks—the grid of individual pixels (see figure 1). The dominant focus of Ruff's *jpeg* series is on images of destruction and disaster as proliferated by on-line news servers. The series consists of many distorted depictions capturing the effects of human warfare, of terrorist activities, and of natural and man-made catastrophes. We witness architectural ruins produced by deliberate bomb attacks, improvised graves in some desert area, black smoke clouds ascending into the sky. And yet, aside from all of these images of contemporary devastation, Ruff also includes low-resolution pictures of natural topographies seemingly untouched by human hands or catastrophic civilization: the intricate leaves of palm trees as set against a blue sky; sun light flooding and illuminating a clearing in some dark forest; waves crashing against an unpopulated shoreline. The purpose of including such pictures may simply testify to what Ruff's series at first sight might be all about: to document the catastrophic loss of sensory immediacy, of visual truth and authenticity, in a world in which technological mediation reigns triumphant. Advanced pixilation, one might want to argue, here not only allegorizes our age's fascination with violent outbursts and cataclysmic excesses, but denotes the very violence administered to what we call an image in a world of advanced electronic circulation and consumption. In Ruff's unrelenting perspective, we might thus conclude, nature is as much in ruins as the disastrous sites shown in other pictures, pixilation here encoding nothing other than a world in which ground zero has become the order of the day.

Ruff, no doubt, is a photographer nourished by postmodern sentiments. His world is one always already mediated by and through photographic images, one in which the act of producing images cannot but engage with an endless set of other images. Visual representations, in

Fig. 1. Thomas Ruff, "jpeg rio2" (2007). Courtesy David Zwirner, New York.

Ruff's universe, stand between viewer and physical reality long before the photographer's camera reframes our relation to the real; images are part and parcel of this real. And yet, it is more than tempting to bring Kracauer to the table of how Ruff's work speaks about the muting of physical reality and nature and thus reveal the extent to which Ruff's work with pixels does not end in a cynical exposure of postmodern simulation and virtuality. Consider *Jpeg eao1*, a 2007 image showing a small river surrounded by lavish trees and branches as it rushes toward the viewer, sun light illuminating various sections of the stream, in particular the one in the image's foreground where a tiny cascade causes the water to be in considerable commotion. We all have seen pictures like this: as wallpapers in dreary interior spaces; as part of a friend's photo album displaying the visual trophies of last year's outdoor activities; as visual fodder to an advertising campaign promoting the eternal youth granted by some beauty product. But in lowering its resolution to such a degree that individual pixels become visible, and in at once massively blowing up and softening the visual gestalt of the grid of pixels, Ruff achieves something quite unexpected. As with all of the other *jpeg* images, the viewer here needs to step back in order to look through the image's pixilated structure and recognize its representational content, whereas close range viewing allows us to explore the image as a feast of abstraction, a grid of various blocks of color that do not really seem to add up to much. The viewer's bodily activity, his probing of ever shifting viewing positions, her act of moving toward, away, and along the photograph's rather expansive display, thus becomes key to our relation to and aesthetic experience of the image.

A Kracauerian reading of Ruff's photographs would certainly stress such tactile responses. It would point out the extent to which, in alternatively stepping up close and moving away from the picture, the viewer of Ruff's pixilated image would seek out to establish some sense of physical contact to the material dimension of the image and, in so doing, perceive his or her body itself as the primary medium of experience and perception. More specifically, however, Kracauer teaches us, firstly, to see Ruff's exposure and manipulation of individual pixels as an attempt not only to lay bare his medium's material base, its nature as it were, but also to put this nature to work; to reveal the body of digital image production, but in doing so also show that this material base is not entirely oblivious to the course of time and the traces of human interventions. Secondly, Kracauer urges us to emphasize how Ruff's image opens our eyes for a digital image's "optical unconscious"[21] (in Benjamin's terms), allows us to suspend ordinary regiments of intentional and goal-oriented looking, and thus to probe the possibilities of reciprocal and non-coercive relationships between the subjective and the objective. Third, and finally, Kracauer's understanding of photography would draw our attention to how in Ruff's image the representation and mediation of the river's ongoing movement allegorizes what the medium of photography is all about: to capture images that depict a world fallen from prelapsarian grace, but that by recognizing their own material base recall the sensory dimension as an arena of indeterminate relationships and principally open-ended experiences, of transience and flow.

In our age of ubiquitous digital mediation, the model for taking photographs—as Ruff has repeatedly insisted—may rarely be still physical reality itself, but all kinds of other images we have of that reality. However, as Ruff himself is eager to admit, photography's task today is not only to explore how mediation has become second nature, but also how nature itself has always been and continues to be a mediated process. Digital photography disintegrates the body of reality into grids of pixels, yet pixels aren't just abstract codes or immaterial representations of sets of numbers. They instead have a body too and in this they are linked to the very reality they evoke. What Ruff's *jpeg* series shares with Kracauer's thought on photography is precisely this assumption that photographic images at heart, whether digital or not, carry with them a certain promise of touch and physical contact and secretly protest the total dematerialization of nature and the scientific regimentation of physical reality. "For me," Ruff has explained in an interview, "within all the images, there is something fundamental that I wish to reveal. Thus it is necessary to strip the various stratae from the image until the essence is reached; in other words, I need to 'undress' the image until I can see it naked. I try to remove every level of meaning until I reach its heart. As soon as I have done this, I can start to add new meanings, as though wishing to 'redress' this."[22] Kracauer's theory of photography, in all of its different versions, aims at exactly this: to undress what we perceive as images in such a way that we not only understand their material base and historically shifting nature, but also experience them as an effigy of new meanings and sensory contacts to the world. Whether digital or analogue, photography is and has always been involved in actively removing us from being in physical touch with reality. But, as both Kracauer and Ruff remind us, it is only by alienating us from the physical in the first place that photographic images, in our fallen world, can recall the forgotten qualities of the material dimension of inner and outer life—can serve as an organon *redeeming* the utopian promise of non-coercive sensory relationships to the material world and its ongoing flux and transformation.

NOTES

1. Siegfried Kracauer, "Photography," in *The Mass Ornament: Weimar Essays*, trans., ed., and with an introduction by Thomas Y. Levin (Cambridge: Harvard University Press, 1995), 47–63; *Theory of Film: The Redemption of Physical Reality*, with an introduction by Miriam Bratu Hansen (Princeton: Princeton University Press, 1997).

2. See Theodor W. Adorno, "The Curious Realist: On Siegfried Kracauer," *New German Critique* 54 (Autumn 1991): 159–77; and, as a response, Miriam Hansen, "Decentric Perspectives: Kracauer's Early Writings on Film and Mass Culture," *New German Critique* 54 (Autumn 1991): 47–76.

3. See Janet Harbord, "Contingency at Work: Kracauer's *Theory of Film* and the Trope of the Accidental," *New Formations* (Summer 2007): 90–103.

4. Kracauer, *Theory of Film*, xlix.

5. For more on the continuities between Kracauer's early and later work on film and photography, see Miriam Hansen, "'With Skin and Hair': Kracauer's Theory of Film, Marseilles 1940," *Critical Inquiry* 19, no. 3 (Spring 1993): 437–69.

6. Heide Schlüpmann, "The Subject of Survival: On Kracauer's Theory of Film," *New German Critique* 54 (Autumn 1991): 111–26; Gertrud Koch, "'Not Yet

Accepted Anywhere': Exile, Memory, and Image in Kracauer's Conception of History," *New German Critique* 54 (Autumn 1991): 95–109.

7. Steve Giles, "Making Visible, Making Strange: Photography and Representation in Kracauer, Brecht, and Benjamin," *New Formations* (Summer 2007): 64–75.

8. In this, my effort in this essay echoes the argument of Miriam Hansen's contribution to this volume. Like Hansen, my aim is to argue against the view of Kracauer as a media pessimist and instead highlight the extent to which his notion of the temporality and the historicity of the photographic image situate him at a crucial juncture of modern and modernist culture, one anticipating some of the key issues of our contemporary media culture and practice.

9. For incisive discussions of the indexical in recent image and film theory, see Mary Ann Doane, "The Indexical and the Concept of Medium Specificity," *differences: A Journal of Feminist Cultural Studies* 18, no. 1 (2007): 128–52; D. N. Rodowick, *The Virtual Life of Film* (Cambridge: Harvard University Press, 2007); Tom Gunning, "What's the Point of an Index? or, Faking Photographs," in *Still Moving*, ed. Karen Beckman and Jean Ma (Durham: Duke University Press, 2008), 23–40.

10. For more on the Neo-Cartesian rhetoric of recent writing on the digital, see, among others, Anna Munster, *Materializing New Media: Embodiment in Information Aesthetics* (Hanover, NH: Dartmouth College Press, 2006).

11. Kracauer, *Theory of Film*, 3.

12. Kracauer, "Photography," 61.

13. Kracauer, "Photography," 59.

14. Kracauer, "Photography," 61–62.

15. Though the grammatically correct plural of medium is of course media, "mediums" here is being used to discuss the plural of certain media when, in a rather art-theoretical sense, referring to their material base and ontological specificity. Whereas, for instance, "media" talks about film as a mass cultural phenomenon and tool of mass communication, "medium" speaks about it as a specific set of material technologies and practices capturing, recording, expressing, and displaying elements of the world.

16. J. M. Bernstein, *Against Voluptuous Bodies: Late Modernism and the Meaning of Painting* (Stanford: Stanford University Press, 2006), 75.

17. Bernstein, *Against Voluptuous Bodies*, 7.

18. Siegfried Kracauer, *History: The Last Things Before the Last* (Princeton: Markus Wiener, 1994), 31.

19. On the hyperrealism of synthetic digital images, see Lev Manovich, "The Paradoxes of Digital Photography," http://manovich.net/TEXT/digital_photo.html.

20. Matthias Winzen, "A Credible Invention of Reality: Thomas Ruff's Precise Reproductions of Our Fantasies of Reality," *Thomas Ruff: Photography 1979 to the Present*, ed. Matthias Winzen (New York: Distributed Art Publishers, 2002), 155.

21. Walter Benjamin, "The Work of Art in the Age of Its Technological Reproducibility," *Selected Writings*, eds. Howard Eiland and Michael W. Jennings (Cambridge, MA: Harvard University Press, 2003), 4: 266.

22. *Thomas Ruff: The Grammar of Photography*, ed. Filippo Maggia (Milan: Nepente, 2006), 143.

Siegfried Kracauer's Two Art Histories

Elizabeth Otto

The work of art holds a mirror up to the world that not only reflects it, but makes it see.
> —Siegfried Kracauer, "The Artist in These Times"
> ("Der Künstler in dieser Zeit"), 1925[1]

The wide-ranging and revolutionary nature of Siegfried Kracauer's critique of interwar visual culture has only begun to come to light decades after he was working. His status in the history of critical cultural theory as the "odd uncle" of the Frankfurt School has slowly given way to an understanding of the depth and breadth of his subject matter as his writings have again become increasingly available. Kracauer's engagement with the visual field was lifelong and always multifaceted. He studied with Georg Simmel, a thinker whose importance for art history has also only recently been rediscovered, and Kracauer's education included courses on the decorative arts and in "ornamental drawing."[2] His first book was art historical in nature; it was his doctoral thesis on wrought iron work, which he published in 1925.[3] This interest in decoration and architecture as organizing forces for modern experience never left him, and his subsequent training and work as an architect only furthered his eclectic interest in the visual. Beginning in the early 1920s, his essays published in the *Frankfurter Zeitung* and elsewhere often took up visual themes and contributed to a program of "the readability of the world."[4] In addition to his nearly one thousand film reviews, he wrote on ornament, architecture, and symbols; these essays suggest the power of the visual to come to grips with the trappings, diversions, and classed experience of modernity.[5]

A number of scholars have identified significant ideas that animate Kracauer's approach to the visual. Miriam Hansen points to the shift in his interwar writings from "the great metaphysical questions of the age to the phenomena of daily life, the ephemeral, culturally marginal, and despised spaces, media, and rituals of an emerging mass culture."[6] Frederic Schwartz traces the origin of Kracauer's self-expressed interest in the mass ornament as among "surface-level expressions" that reveal "the position that an epoch occupies in the historical process."[7] Schwartz argues that, through his studies with Simmel, Kracauer absorbed the work of Heinrich Wölfflin and Alois Riegl, both of whom were fundamentally rethinking art history during the late nineteenth and early twentieth centuries and reinventing it as a *Geisteswissenschaft*, or humanities discipline. For both Wölfflin and Riegl, art, decoration, architecture, and fashion are aspects of a culture's particular style or its *Kunstwollen*. As Schwartz shows, Kracauer deepens this approach by not only seeing even the mundane aspects of cultural production as indicative of a period's style but also reading "content, indeed the 'basic content of an era,' in form, not merely its manipulation as a sign."[8] Much of what has been written on Kracauer focuses on his rejection of traditionally valued arts and culture in order to write on film and mass spectacle. Yet there are still many aspects of Kracauer's astute analyses of art, photography, and urban visual spaces to be explored in order to make overt his understanding of representation as a powerful cultural force.

While Kracauer did not complete any longer art-historical texts after the dissertation, in shorter essays he developed a set of premises and ideas about the function of art and the visual in society. These writings are significant both as case studies and as examples of the development of his theoretical methods, methods to which we are only now returning in what has often been referred to as the "Visual Turn" in history or in the rise of academic departments of Visual Culture and Visual Studies. Further, these texts demonstrate Kracauer's critical engagement with Germany's avant-gardes, including Expressionism, Dada, International Constructivism, and the Bauhaus, and they reveal how these movements paralleled Kracauer's own interests and ideas.

In this essay I focus on a selection of Kracauer's interwar texts, many of which have never been translated, in order to bring out the art-historical nature of his work. The "two art histories" of my essay's title point to a strong shift from the early years, when he wrote directly on art, to his subsequent focus in the later 1920s on photography, mass media, and spectacle. My title also traces a shift in Kracauer's art writing from an Expressionist-influenced and impassioned engagement to a dryer, more ironic approach that belonged to the *neue Sachlichkeit*. Despite these shifts, however, there are significant continuities in Kracauer's thought on the role and function of representation in society. In my analyses I provide examples of the artifacts that drew his gaze in order to deepen our understanding of Kracauer's two art histories and the visual world he inhabited.

A cutting-edge debate on the viability of Expressionism as an artistic mode is the backdrop to one of Kracauer's very early articles, "A Change in the Fate of Art" ("Schicksalswende der Kunst"), published in 1920. *Expressionism* was a term that, as Dennis Crockett explains, critics in the interwar context used to describe a wide range of movements including Post-Impressionism, Cubism, Fauvism, and Futurism, as well as German Expressionism as we think of it today.[9] While Expressionism would live on through the next decades, such movements as Dada and Constructivism were also in the process of rejecting it as Kracauer wrote this impassioned call for a renewal of the arts. When the German monarchy fell in 1918, Expressionism came to be seen as both more radical, due to its association with the November Revolution, and less so since it lost its status as an outsider art that had been so hated by the Kaiser.[10] By the June 1920 opening of the exhibition *Deutscher Expressionismus Darmstadt*, the largest Expressionist show to date, a debate was raging as to whether or not the movement was over. The poster for the exhibition, created by Carl Gunschmann, suggests how modern and powerful Expressionism could be, with its explosive fracturing of figure and landscape and its abstractly limited palette of red, black, and beige (fig. 1). The exhibition was based on the premise that Expressionism had long been a misunderstood movement, and Gunschmann's poster manifests its triumph at this time. According to Crockett, the show received wide attention and sparked intense discussion on whether or not the movement should, by that time, be seen as a historical phenomenon that had run its course.[11]

Kracauer's essay appeared in August of that year; it would have been one of the most widely read responses to this exhibition, even though he does not name it directly. In pondering questions of Expressionism's viability, Kracauer also theorizes the historical role and function of art. At the outset he calls Expressionism out as a dead movement: "The experiences embodied in [these works] are already no longer our experiences. There is no helping it; one must have courage and admit that Expressionism has exhausted its possibilities, that, after a brief flowering, it has become a historical phenomenon with sharply delineated outlines."[12] Kracauer situates

Fig. 1. Carl Gunschmann, *Deutscher Expressionismus*, 1920. Exhibition poster. Copyright Nachlass Carl Gunschmann.

the initial impulse behind Expressionism as a response to a particular set of historical circumstances in the decades preceding the First World War, namely, the increasing dominance of science and capitalism that had led to a culture that was overly rational, objective, impersonal, and mechanized. He asserts that, "detached from the roots of society, enslaved by a pitiless economic system, caught in an incalculable network of national and rational-technical relations, the individual can only assert himself as a private self, as a specific identity."[13] Yet not all thinkers or artists reacted in the same way to these circumstances; both the natural scientist and the Impressionist simply took this cold reality as a given. Kracauer says that while the former sucked this reality into himself, the latter attempted to capture its individual moments.[14] By contrast, Expressionism tried to break through this state of things. It turned away from "the world of our senses" in traditional pictorial representation and toward abstraction by embracing an inner reality and a primal self (*Ur-Ich*).[15] For Kracauer, who was steeped in Karl Marx's cultural theory, this formal change was nothing less than revolutionary: "The ruling powers are thus attacked from all sides, time-honored idols fall from their heights, and what remains is a singular heap of rubble from which rises the adverse stink of decay."[16] Expressionism strikes a blow to rationalized reality and gives artists the freedom to dream of a "paradisiacal innocence," a reference to such Post-Impressionists as Paul Gauguin as much as to German Expressionists like Gunschmann or Ernst Ludwig Kirchner.

Kracauer finds that, while Expressionism was once revolutionary, in his own time its original effect has turned against itself.[17] For an example of what Kracauer means, we might look again to the Gunschmann poster. The exploded red landscape speaks not to war, oppression, or alienation but simply shows an Expressionist vision already repeated a thousand times: a female nude in a nature represented with intentionally primitivized forms. The landscape (but not the beige-toned figure) is rendered in the nonsynchronous color of red. This passionate and bloody color seems only to advertise the movement and exhibition that are featured in the poster's prominent text, rather than to image any challenge to convention. Kracauer nearly shouts it: "Truly, it is time to start work on that for which Expressionism has prepared us: *the creation of a new reality in art*."[18] He envisions this new art as both an extension and a rejection of Expressionism, but also as more all-encompassing than any movement that had preceded it. "First and foremost, one thing is clear: a new composition of reality must be tantamount to the coming to terms with *life*."[19]

Compared to the sober and ironic tone that Kracauer would develop later, this early essay is itself Expressionistic in its soulfulness. But already here Kracauer articulates a number of ideas about art's cultural role that would remain constant in his interwar essays. First, art must respond to and be of its own time; to repeat the art of the past is an empty gesture. Second, he advocates a more *Sachlich* or objective approach to representation in his call for an end to abstraction as a style and the advent of an art based in pared-down honesty.[20] And third—prefiguring his own work from nearly a decade later, such as *The Salaried Masses (Die Angestellten)*—he sees the visual realm as both the product and producer of cultural realities. In writing "A Change in the Fate of Art" in 1920, Kracauer did not yet know what the new, post–World War I art would be, but his call to turn away from emotional and expressive art ran parallel to the work of many of his avant-garde contemporaries.

A few years later Kracauer would develop a number of his most significant ideas on art in a longer essay, "The Artist in These Times" ("Der Künstler in diesen Zeit" 1925), published in the Jewish journal *Der Morgen*. The quotation with which I began, on how the work of art not only reflects the world but makes it see, stems from this essay. It is indicative of one of the most important arguments in Kracauer's art writing, specifically that an artist should offer a new vision to his or her audience, but should never be didactic. Instead, this vision should enable the spectator to approach the contemporary situation fresh. Kracauer finds that the artist "doesn't declare what one should believe or how one should lead a proper life; rather, he reveals the world in relation to what is believed and puts each life in its true place."[21] Kracauer's approach is avant-garde in its advancement of a mystical and potentially nonsensical art. He also relieves artists from the burden of conveying their messages in an "aesthetic manner," another gesture that links him to the cutting edge.[22]

In "The Artist in These Times," Kracauer explores the artist's essential role in the modern world. Hansen has shown how, for Kracauer, the avant-garde is "itself a symptom of the growing distance between the sphere of truth and modern existence, and the dilemma resulting from that distance for the contemporary artist."[23] The artist is driven by the need to join or make connections (*Verknüpfung*) in the world based on divine understanding. Yet he is trapped between "the principles of aesthetic creation and the need to confront contemporary reality."[24] Kracauer finds that "only in a world in which this joining [*Verknüpfung*] occurs, in which people accept the terms given to them from above, can art be fulfilled."[25] The artist's role is to relate the material to the spiritual, the earthly to the divine. This process is not merely important for the aesthetic sphere; through it the artist serves humanity.[26]

The intellectual work that *Verknüpfung* performs makes it akin to Benjamin's ideas on allegory in his contemporaneous text, *The Origin of German Tragic Drama* (1925). For Benjamin, allegory communicates through fragments. He writes that "ideas are to objects as constellations are to stars"; the parts that make up the whole are not themselves ideas but become them once they are joined mentally.[27] Therefore both authors allow us to understand the role of the avant-garde in interwar culture and the radical changes in aesthetics that occur at this time, particularly in the turn away from painting and toward a deskilling of art through photography, montage, and assemblage. Whether in an update of the age-old tradition of allegory or in the modern act of *Verknüpfung*, the spectator is required to be active and make connections, or his contemporaries' strange, often-unaesthetic works fail.

In addition to his like-minded approach to art, Benjamin was also one of the very first to see a hallmark of Kracauer's writing in its inherent visuality. In a 1930 review of *The Salaried Masses*, Benjamin argues that Kracauer's literary approach is itself based in representation, in that he replaces wordplay with the visual pun: "Kracauer's pictorial wit is no chance affair, but is related to those composite Surrealist images that not only characterize dreams (as we have learned from Freud) and the sensual world (as we have learned from Paul Klee and Max Ernst), but also define our social reality."[28] In another review of the same volume, Benjamin characterizes Kracauer's cultural criticism as the work of an outsider, malcontent, and spoilsport, but also—most famously—as that of a ragpicker, a term for an anachronistic cultural scavenger that would later be applied to Benjamin himself. Kracauer is "a ragpicker at daybreak, lancing with his stick scraps of language and tatters of speech in order to throw them into his cart, grumblingly, stubbornly, somewhat the worse for drink, and not without now and again letting one or other of these faded calicoes—'humanity,' 'inner nature,' 'enrichment'—flutter ironically in the dawn breeze. A ragpicker at daybreak—in the dawn of the day of revolution."[29]

This work as a half-crazy scavenger who finds deep and inherent meaning in detritus was practiced not only by the ragpicker and the writer of cultural criticism; it was also a fundamentally new and revolutionary practice of Benjamin's and Kracauer's avant-garde contemporaries in the form of photomontage. This visual practice arose in the later nineteenth century in various composite forms such as advertisements. It became an avantgarde medium toward the end of the First World War and rose to international prominence in the late 1910s and early 1920s in the work of Dadaists, Constructivists, and Surrealists. Kracauer was thus doing in language what some of his most interesting contemporaries were doing with pictures.[30] This new tendency, which Benjamin hails in Kracauer's work, brings us to the second of Kracauer's two art histories, namely, his move away from his passionate tone and his focus on painting—especially Expressionist painting—in his art writing in order to turn to examine photography and other modern sights in an approach to writing that was increasingly sober and ironic.

While his essays on film are certainly more numerous, Kracauer wrote several essays on photography during the latter half of the Weimar period. In fact, this interest would continue on; as literary and photographic historian Elena Gualtieri asserts, photography "seems to accompany Kracauer wherever he goes, both intellectually and geographically, lending his *oeuvre* the coherence of a running thread."[31] In his now famous 1927 "Photography" essay, Kracauer emphasizes the medium's power as a cultural agent and points to the large number of illustrated newspapers that existed at the time as evidence of the medium's cultural relevance.[32] Yet his writings also suggest a profound ambivalence about the plethora of photographic reproductions that had come to dominate the visual landscape of the Weimar Republic. "The aim of the illustrated newspapers is the complete reproduction of the world accessible to the photographic apparatus. They record the spatial impressions of people, conditions, and events from every possible perspective. Their method corresponds to that of the weekly newsreel, which is nothing but a collection of photographs, whereas an authentic film employs photography merely as a means."[33] While it would seem logical that a society that saw its world infinitely reproduced would be self-reflexive and extremely self-informed, Kracauer finds that, instead,

> never before has a period known so little about itself. In the hands of the ruling society, the invention of illustrated magazines is one of the most powerful means of organizing a strike against understanding. Even the colorful arrangement of the images provides a not insignificant means for successfully implementing such a strike. The *contiguity* of these images systematically excludes their contextual framework available to consciousness. . . . The blizzard of photographs betrays an indifference toward what the things mean.[34]

For Kracauer, the viewer of illustrated newspapers is barraged with photographic reproductions that do not convey meaning; they serve only to distract. This is not ragpicking; for Kracauer, it is contiguity without context, in images without content.

While Kracauer's "Photography" essay is largely critical of his contemporaries' use of this medium, he also imagined a different and better approach to the photographic archive. Rather than presenting viewers with an onslaught of images that they must attempt to configure logically, Kracauer turns to the writings of Franz Kafka as an alternative model, in which "a liberated consciousness absolves itself of this responsibility by destroying natural reality and scrambling the fragments."[35] Such a mode of visual scrambling already exists for Kracauer in film. Whereas the combinations of images in the illustrated newspapers are in "disarray" and "confusion," he compares the disjuncture of film to that of dreams, in which parts of the day are recalled and jumble themselves to create something new.[36] Rather than trying to make sense of the world through a photographic cataloging of it, Kracauer advocates letting go of order to derive meaning from nonsense, an approach we might call "montage thinking."

Given Kracauer's ragpicker aesthetic, it only makes sense that he wrote directly on photomontage. His review of "Revolutionary Pictorial Montage" ("Revolutionäre Bildmontage") was written in 1932, a time when—with increasing political polarization—the question of whether or not representation could effect change in an increasingly unstable society had become truly pressing. This essay is significant not only for its direct discussion of a relatively new form of art but also for its theorization of the efficacy of political art. The show was made up of politically themed photomontages by members of the activist Union of Revolutionary Artists (Bund revolutionärer Künstler), Ernst Oskar Albrecht, Paul Fuhrmann, Alice Lex-Nerlinger, and Oskar Nerlinger.[37] Throughout this essay, Kracauer seems torn between mocking these artists' earnestness and admiring their attempts to engage the public and to shift art's role in society. The artists' goal for the exhibition to function "as a weapon in class warfare" was realized through its installation in the stairwell and hallway of a building with political offices in it, so that visitors had to pass by the pictures.[38] The artists offered viewers questionnaires that asked, for example, if they liked the exhibition, or if they would change it. Kracauer argues that, while these elements—the location, the questionnaires—appear to be extrinsic to the show, they are actually central to it, in that they integrate these works into daily life, the field they seek to change. Further, since the artists want to work collectively, it only makes sense to include viewers in the discussion.[39]

While this exhibition was small, it was written about by several critics associated with Communism and the Left.[40] Kracauer's response was among the most negative, but even if he did not support their methods, he was still sympathetic to their aims. His twofold critique clarifies his view on how art functions and returns him to his art-historical roots. First, he finds the exhibition's location to be problematic.

Current painting does not meet people on their way to the factory or the office, but invites them to secluded rooms that are far from the main thoroughfares. And then it leaves the audience on its own without providing a platform upon which the viewers' experiences and the artists' intentions can be compared. And that is as it should be. For, firstly, most of what is offered to us as art is still a product of an idealistic point of view; and, secondly, true art naturally cannot elude the laws that regulate the exchange of goods.[41]

Kracauer sees even new media as subject to the structures of traditional art and exhibitions, for these traditions create a space for effective contemplation that cannot exist in the workplace.

Kracauer's second critique is that, while these montages communicate revolutionary political messages, they do not function in a manner that is pictorially revolutionary.

> These works limit themselves to communicating insights that the workers already know through other means; instead, [these pictures'] task should be not only to repeat the intended insights, but to montage them in such a way that the composition [*Gestalt*] of the pictorial montage leaves a logical imprint. Precisely then would these works have their full use value, which they lack in their current form because they convey insights rather than taking these insights as their basis.[42]

Among the specific photomontages that Kracauer mentions is one by Alice Lex-Nerlinger called *Work Work Work* (*Arbeiten Arbeiten Arbeiten*) (fig. 2). In retrospect we might admire Lex-Nerlinger's creation of an interplay of machine parts with an anonymous worker for whom even eating has become mechanized; her spatialization of power relationships; and the aural component of this work—in which the viewer is compelled mechanically to read out the words on its surface and thus finds herself mimicking a machine. Yet in the context of this exhibition, Kracauer says only that it was an image that was fighting against contemporary modes of production.[43] This assessment is true enough but also suggests that these works fell particularly flat when seen amidst hustle and bustle and on the way to something else.

As in his earlier writings on Expressionism, Kracauer charges these political artists with the responsibility of constantly creating art anew so that it responds to its time. In his criticism of "Revolutionary Pictorial Montage," a leftist-communist exhibition held on the eve of the Nazi era, Kracauer calls for art that provides an oasis in which to consider new ideas and that will always reinvent itself through the innovations of its makers. These are powerful arguments for the special role of art, visual representation, and experimental media in culture.

Fig. 2. Alice Lex-Nerlinger, *Arbeiten, Arbeiten, Arbeiten*, 1928.
Photomontage of magazine and gelatin silver prints. Collection of Stiftung
Archiv Akademie der Künste, Berlin.

Photography of the interwar period has most often been seen as a
medium that revealed society to itself as fundamentally modern; by contrast, Kracauer wrote of photography as an instrument of memory. In another exhibition review from 1932, "Photographed Berlin" ("Photographiertes Berlin"), Kracauer discusses the soulful "1000 Views of Berlin"
("1000 Berliner Ansichten"), which were the work of Albert Vennemann, a

photographer associated with the *neue Sachlichkeit*.[44] For Kracauer, Vennemann's haunting images of Berlin's representative and typical sights do just what photography does best: they "speak, above all, to memory."[45] Rather than linking photography to film, here he contrasts the two media and finds that photography is most appropriate for memorializing rather than for documenting.

In the earlier "Photography" essay, Kracauer ponders the paradox of this medium having both an indexical and, over time, a nonindexical connection to the objects represented. For example, people age so that earlier photographs of them become unrecognizable as the person who has lived on. Further, as Gertrud Koch summarizes, "the photograph buries that which it depicts—'covering it with snow,' as it were—because the medium of photography cannot present the 'history' of the object photographed."[46] In "Photographed Berlin," Kracauer nuances this idea to assert that, in some cases, photography does represent its subjects truly. It is most appropriately used as a romantic, almost ghostly medium that, like another technology founded at the same time, the train, is on the "threshold of yesterday."[47] Compared to the fast-moving medium of film, photography already belonged in part to the past, like the Tiergarten as it was pictured in some of the photographs in the show.[48] One of the extant examples of Vennemann's work that may have appeared in this exhibition, a photograph of the Kaiser-Wilhelm-Strasse taken from the tower of the Marienkirche in the direction of the Lustgarten (fig. 3), suggests how Kracauer arrived at the notion that photography was best in the service of memory. In Vennemann's photograph, the city appears magical. It is glowingly illuminated by the dappled sky above; the Kaiser-Wilhelm-Strasse breaks through the dense cityscape of nineteenth-century buildings and spires and seems to reach up to the hazy horizon and majestic sky. In joining heaven and earth with his glowing sepia tones, Vennemann thus renders the heavy architecture of the past as if it were weightless.

Among his investigations of the new kinds of visual experiences that the interwar period offered, Kracauer's interest in architecture reemerged in relation to a medium that preoccupied several of his avant-garde contemporaries: light.[49] In his writings, Kracauer often suggests that light is a powerful force for creating such modern visual effects as the illusions of grandeur essential to contemporary public leisure spaces. In *The Salaried Masses* he describes the new large-scale entertainment complexes as "binding employees by enchantment . . . and diverting them from critical questions—for which they anyway feel little inclination."[50] An essential compo-

Fig. 3. Albert Vennemann, View of the Kaiser-Wilhelm-Straße from the
Marienkirche tower in the direction of the Lustgarten, ca. 1920.
Photograph. Collection Stiftung Stadtmuseum Berlin.

nent of these distracting interiors are "floods of light" that "contribute
everywhere to the ensemble" and that evoke natural effects in a manner
much more spectacular than nature itself.[51]

Outside, light in the Berlin cityscape for Kracauer is a powerful but
rogue element, as if the irrationality that he once ascribed to Expressionism has now been taken up by the mixing of chance elements in the
cityscape. Light is described as an embodiment of capitalism in his 1927
"Lighted Advertisements" ("Lichtreklame"), and yet "colorful letters that
are supposed to advertise white laundry are not completely on task, even
when they cover five stories. . . . Light remains light."[52] It brightens the
city's night, the sky, and ultimately the Milky Way. It "overshoots the economy, and what was meant as advertisement becomes illumination."[53]

The renegade transformative powers of light are, for Kracauer, emblematic of the way in which traditional institutions take on a new meaning in the modern world. In "Picture Postcard" ("Ansichtspostkarte") from
1930, he focuses on one of the dominant structures of Berlin, the Kaiser-

Fig. 4. *Kaiser-Wilhelm-Gedächtniskirche bei Nacht*, postcard, late 1920s or early 1930s.

Wilhelm-Gedächtniskirche, a church "that isn't a church" and that during the day serves primarily as "a giant traffic obstacle."[54] At night, however, it appears to emit an otherworldly and profane red light that is "as calming as it is inexplicable."[55] A particular image of this church in a picture post-card—perhaps like the one that inspired Kracauer's meditation—suggests the glow of this otherworldly light (fig. 4). As Kracauer explains, the light emitted by the church actually comes from the Ufapalast cinema next door.

It is in keeping with the Gedächniskirche's location in a commercial district, yet Kracauer finds that this is "an uninhibited twinkling that does not merely serve advertising, but is, above that, an end in itself."[56] This light produces a strange sort of beauty; the old stone walls absorb the "light spectacle" and serve as an emotional cipher. "Secret tears thus find their place of memory [*Gedächnisort*]. Not in the hidden interior—in the middle of the street the neglected and inconspicuous is gathered and transformed until it begins to radiate, a comfort for everyone."[57]

Banal modern light thus turns a representative building with little purpose into a spectacle for the collective and an emotionally alive component of the Berlin cityscape. The building becomes more than a memorial; it is a repository of emotion. Here a nocturnal image of architecture in a photographic picture postcard echoes Kracauer's art writings from the earliest days. Like Expressionism in its first incarnations, and like his interest in new media exhibitions such as "Revolutionary Pictorial Montage," it is the individual, private experience that is potentially transformative. In the abstraction of reality—here through light—new understandings and even redemption are made possible.

One of Kracauer's most moving essays on the public reception of the mediated cityscape is "Around the Reichstag" ("Rund um den Reichstag"). This was likely written the day after the Reichstag fire on 27 February 1933, an event that the new Nazi government used to dramatically curtail civil liberties and to consolidate its power. Kracauer and his wife left Berlin for good on 28 February, and the essay was published on 2 March. Not light, but smoke rises from the building discussed in this essay, and people from all walks of life gather together, having arrived by streetcar and bus, in order to proceed silently around the site. While children at this scene still laugh and play and seem oblivious to the seriousness of this event, Kracauer conjectures that "when they are grown one day, they will learn from history what the Reichstag fire really meant."[58] By contrast, the adults in the crowd are profoundly affected by what they see; "what is so surprising about them is their insistent silence."[59] A photograph from the time captures the way Berlin's citizens were drawn to stop and ponder the profound in the smoldering remains (fig. 5). They seem to have been shocked into a kind of knowing stupor, as participants in the reception and interpretation of a profoundly disturbing visual spectacle. Looking at the photograph of that day, we can almost see—the connections being made—*Verknüpfung* in their minds. Kracauer posits these viewers as painfully aware of the seri-

Fig. 5. Photographer unknown, "View of the Reichstag building on the morning after the fire, Feb. 28, 1933," Berlin, 1933. Photograph. Courtesy of Bildarchiv Preussischer Kulturbesitz / Art Resource, NY. Image Reference: ART390581.

ousness of this event and yet as silent and seemingly powerless to do anything but observe.

Over the course of the Weimar Republic, Kracauer's approach to visual history shifted profoundly. Yet certain things remained consistent in his approach throughout this period. His ragpicking aesthetic led to eclectic choices of cultural criticism in his approach to art, photography, and spectacle, and to his fellow ragpickers, the avant-garde photomontagists. And Kracauer's engagement with the visual was always informed by a belief that it mattered deeply to society. The show of outmoded painting, the political exhibition seen by chance on the way to somewhere else, or the church with the unholy beautiful light were all elements of a modern and urban visuality that was always potentially transformative. At the close of this period of Kracauer's writings, he came to see his fellow citizens as engaged viewers, subtle prognosticators who, like himself, saw a frightening future writ large in the smoke and ashes of a dead democracy's representative architecture.

Kracauer left Germany for an uncertain future. While he subsequently made his name in the United States as a film historian and theorist, we should remember that it was with the support of an art institution that he wrote much of *From Caligari to Hitler.* This book was supported by a young museum that was already forming the careers of many of the twentieth century's artists, curators, and art historians, and profoundly shaping the discipline of art history as we know it: New York's Museum of Modern Art.

NOTES

My thanks go to Gerd Gemünden and Johannes von Moltke for including me in this project; to Tobias Westermann, my intrepid translation partner; and to Miriam Hansen for her thoughtful comments on my work. This essay is dedicated to her memory. Unless otherwise noted, translations are mine.

1. Siegfried Kracauer, "Der Künstler in dieser Zeit," *Der Morgen* 1, no. 1 (April 1925): 101–9; rpt. in *Aufsätze I, 1915–1926*, vol 5.1 of *Siegfried Kracauer: Schriften* (Frankfurt am Main: Suhrkamp, 1990), 302. "Das Kunstwerk hält der Welt einen Spiegel vor, der sie nicht nur spiegelt, sondern sehend macht."

2. Henrik Reeh, *Ornaments of the Metropolis: Siegfried Kracauer and Modern Urban Culture* (Cambridge: MIT Press, 2004), 63–64.

3. *Die Entwicklung der Schmiedekunst in Berlin, Potsdam und einigen Städten der Mark vom 17. Jahrhundert bis zum Beginn des 19. Jahrhunderts* (Worms am Rhein: Wormser Verlags- und Druckereigesellschaft m.b.H., 1915).

4. The phrase is from Hans Blumenberg, *Die Lesbarkeit der Welt* (Frankfurt am Main: Suhrkamp, 1986), cited in Miriam Hansen, "Mass Culture as Hieroglyphic Writing: Adorno, Derrida, Kracauer," *New German Critique* 56 (1992): 63.

5. The count of films is from Miriam Hansen, "Decentric Perspectives: Kracauer's Early Writings on Film and Mass Culture," *New German Critique* 54 (Autumn 1991): 48.

6. Hansen, "Decentric Perspectives," 51.

7. Frederic Schwartz, *Blind Spots: Critical Theory and the History of Art in Twentieth-Century Germany* (New Haven: Yale University Press, 2005), 138.

8. Schwartz, 140.

9. Dennis Crockett, *German Post-Expressionism: The Art of the Great Disorder, 1918–1924* (University Park: Pennsylvania State University Press, 1999), 8.

10. For more on how the embedded meanings of Expressionism changed through the revolution, see Joan Weinstein, *The End of Expressionism: Art and the November Revolution in Germany, 1918–19* (Chicago: University of Chicago Press, 1990), 1–22.

11. Crockett, 12.

12. Kracauer, "Schicksalswende der Kunst," *FZ*, 18 August 1920, n. 606, rpt. in *Siegfried Kracauer. Schriften*, 5.1, 72. ". . . daß die in ihnen verkörperten Erlebnisse schon nicht mehr unsere Erlebnisse sind. Es hilft nichts, man muß den Mut besitzen und sich eingestehen, daß der Expressionismus seine Möglichkeiten erschöpft hat, daß er nach kurzer Blütezeit zu einer historischen Erscheinung von scharf ausgeprägten Umrissen geworden ist."

13. Kracauer, "Schicksalswende," 73. "Losgelöst von dem Urgrund der Gemeinschaft, versklavt einem unbarmherzigen Wirtschaftssystem, eingespannt in

ein unabsehbares Netz nationaler und sachlich-technischer Beziehungen, vermag sich der Einzelmensch nur noch also privates Ich, als Sonderindividualität zu behaupten."

14. Kracauer, "Schicksalswende," 73.

15. Kracauer, "Schicksalswende," 73–74, 75. Here Kracauer's formulation anticipates discussions of Primitivism as an artistic strategy, which has received significant critical attention in the art history of the past twenty years.

16. Kracauer, "Schicksalswende," 75–76. "Von allen Seiten her werden so die herrschenden Mächte angegriffen, altehrwürdige Götzen stürzen von ihrer Höhe herab, und übrig bleibt ein einziger Schutthaufen, dem widriger Verwesungsgestank entsteigt."

17. Kracauer, "Schicksalswende," 75, 76, 77. "Für jede geistige Bewegung, die gewissen seelischen Bedürfnissen einer Epoche antwortet, kommt aber einmal die Zeit, von der ab sich ihre anfängliche Wirkung in das gerade Gegenteil verkehrt" (76).

18. Kracauer, "Schicksalswende," 77. "Wahrlich, es ist an der Zeit, daß endlich das ins Werk gesetzt wird, wozu erst der Expressionismus uns reif gemacht hat: *der Aufbau einer neuen Wirklichkeit in der Kunst*" (emphasis in the original).

19. Kracauer, "Schicksalswende," 77. "Eines leuchtet vor allem ein: eine Neugestaltung der Wirklichkeit muß gleichbedeutend sein mit der vollen Bewältigung des *Lebens*" (emphasis in the original).

20. Kracauer, "Schicksalswende," 78. "Wir sehnen uns einer Kunst entgegen, die . . . nicht mehr wie der Expressionismus die Angelegenheiten einer abstrakten Menschheit durch ebenso abstrakte Typen verfechten läßt, sondern, das Allgemeine im Besonderen erlebend, menschliches Wesen seiner ganzen schwellenden Fülle nach rundum verkörpert." This approach will become more pronounced in some of his architectural writing of the mid-1920s, such as "Stuttgarter Kunstsommer [Teil II:] Werkbundausstellung: 'Die Form,'" *FZ*, 10 July 1924, n. 508, rpt. in *Siegfried Kracauer: Schriften*, 5.1, 262–67.

21. Kracauer, "Der Künstler in dieser Zeit," 302. "Nicht sagt er aus, was zu glauben sei und wie man ein richtiges Leben zu führen habe; doch er enthüllt die Welt im Hinblick auf das Geglaubte und stellt ein jedes Leben in seine Richtigkeit ein."

22. Kracauer, "Der Künstler in dieser Zeit," 302.

23. Hansen, "Decentric Perspectives," 58.

24. Hansen, "Decentric Perspectives," 58. See also Kracauer, "Der Künstler in dieser Zeit," 300.

25. Kracauer, "Der Künstler in dieser Zeit," 302. "Nur in einem Weltzustand also, in dem die Verknüpfung geschieht, in dem die Menschen die Bestimmungen anerkennen, die ihnen von oben her zukommen, ist der Kunst die Erfüllung gegönnt."

26. Kracauer, "Der Künstler in dieser Zeit," 302, 303. "In einer Welt, in der das Zwielicht der Beziehung herrscht, ist die ästhetische Sphäre nicht nur freigegeben, sondern durch ihre Erfüllung erst wirkt das Menschliche ganz sich aus."

27. Walter Benjamin, *The Origin of German Tragic Drama*, trans. J. Osborne

(London: Verso, 1977 [*Habilitationsschrift* submitted in 1925; first published in 1928]), 34.

28. Walter Benjamin, "Review of Kracauer's *Die Angestellten*," *Die literarische Welt*, 5 May 1930 (6:20), 5. Rpt. in Walter Benjamin, *Selected Writings*, vol. 2, 1927–1934, trans. Rodney Livingstone (Cambridge: Harvard University Press, 1999), 356.

29. Benjamin, "'An Outsider Attracts Attention': on *The Salaried Masses*, by S. Kracauer," reprinted in Kracauer, *The Salaried Masses: Duty and Distraction in Weimar Germany*, trans. Quintin Hoare (London: Verso, 1998), 109, 114. First printed in *Die Gesellschaft* 7 (1930), vol. 1, 473–77.

30. For more on the history of montage see Robert A. Sobieszek, "Composite Imagery and the Origins of Photomontage, Part I: The Naturalistic Strain," *Artforum* (September 1978): 58–65; and "Part II: The Formalist Strain" *Artforum* (October 1978): 40–45. See also Elizabeth Otto, "The Secret History of Photomontage: On the Origins of the Composite Form and the Weimar Photomontages of Marianne Brandt," *Weimar Publics/Weimar Subjects: Rethinking the Political Culture of Germany in the 1920s*, ed. Kerstin Barndt, Kathleen Canning, and Kristin McGuire (Oxford: Berghahn Books, 2010), 66–91.

31. Elena Gualtieri, "The Territory of Photography: Between Modernity and Utopia in Kracauer's Thought," *New Formations* 61 (2007): 76.

32. Kracauer, "Photography" ("Die Photographie," *Frankfurter Zeitung*, 28 October 1927), *The Mass Ornament*, ed. and trans. Thomas Levin (Cambridge: Harvard University Press, 1995), 57.

33. Kracauer, "Photography," 57–58.

34. Kracauer, "Photography," 58.

35. Kracauer, "Photography," 62.

36. Kracauer, "Photography," 63.

37. Kracauer, "Revolutionäre Bildmontage," *Frankfurter Zeitung*, 24 February 1932, rpt. *Siegfried Kracauer: Schriften*, 5.3, 30. Nerlinger is here called "Nilgreen," an Anglicized pseudonym he used for his more political work.

38. Kracauer, "Revolutionäre Bildmontage," 31. ". . . als Waffe im Klassenkampf zu wirken . . ."

39. Kracauer, "Revolutionäre Bildmontage," 31. "Da es ihre Absicht ist, zur Veränderung des Alltages beizutragen, begibt sie sich in den Alltag hinein; da sie den Grundsatz kollektiver Arbeit anerkennt, nötigt sie, durchaus folgerichtig, die Beschauer, an die sie sich wendet, zur Diskussion. Andere Kunstbegriffe, andere Methoden."

40. See, for example, Durus (Alfred Kemeny), "Revolutionäre Bildmontage: Zur 4. Ausstellung des Bundes revolutionärer bildender Künstler," *Die Rote Fahne*, 25 February 1932; and Erich Neumann, "Künstler im Klassenkampf: die Ausstellung 'Revolutionäre Bildmontage,'" *Die Welt am Abend* (Berlin), 27 February 1932.

41. Kracauer, "Revolutionäre Bildmontage," 30. "Die bisherige Malerei kommt den Menschen nicht auf ihrem Weg zur Fabrik oder zum Büro entgegen, sondern lädt sie in abgeschiedene Räume ein, die weitab von der Heerstraße liegen. Und dann überläßt sie das Publikum sich selber, ohne eine Plattform herzustellen, auf der das von ihm Empfundene und das von den Künstlern Gewollte sich wech-

selseitig kontrollierte. So muß es auch sein. Denn einmal ist das meiste, was uns als Kunst dargeboten wird, noch immer ein Produkt idealistischer Weltanschauung, und zum anderen kann sich natürlich die Ware Kunst nicht den Gesetzen entziehen, die den allgemeinen Warenaustausch regeln."

42. Kracauer, "Revolutionäre Bildmontage," 32. "Diese Arbeiten beschränken sich darauf, dem Werktätigen Erkenntnisse zu vermitteln, die ihm auch auf andere Weise zugeführt werden; während es ihre Aufgabe sein sollte, die gemeinten Erkenntnisse nicht nur zu wiederholen, sondern sie so zu montieren, daß die Gestalt der Bildmontage sich sinnfällig einprägt. Dann erst nämlich hätten die Blätter wirklich den vollen Gebrauchswert, den sie in der vorliegenden Form noch nicht haben, weil sie in Erkenntnisse einmünden statt diese zugrunde zu legen."

43. Kracauer, "Revolutionäre Bildmontage," 31. For further analysis of this work see Elizabeth Otto, "Montage and Message: The Photography-Based Works of Alice Lex-Nerlinger in Publications of the Weimar Republic," *Printed Matter: Fotografie im/und Buch*, ed. Barbara Lange (Leipzig: Leipziger Universitätsverlag, 2004), 57–77.

44. Christine Kühn, *Neues Sehen in Berlin: Fotografie der Zwanziger Jahre* (Exhibition Catalogue, Kunstbibliothek, Berlin, 2005), 254–55.

45. Kracauer, "Photographiertes Berlin," *Frankfurter Zeitung*, 15 December 1932, n. 937–39, rpt. in *Siegfried Kracauer: Schriften*, 5.3, Aufsätze, 1932–1965 (Frankfurt am Main: Suhrkamp, 1990), 169.

46. Gertrud Koch, *Siegfried Kracauer: An Introduction* (Princeton: Princeton University Press, 2000), 99.

47. Kracauer, "Photographiertes Berlin," 168–69, 170.

48. Kracauer, "Photographiertes Berlin," 170.

49. See, e.g., Moholy-Nagy, "Light: A Medium of Plastic Expression" (1923), in Krisztina Passuth, *Moholy-Nagy*, trans. Éva Grus, Judy Szöllsy, and László Bаránsky Jób (London: Thames and Hudson, 1982), 292–93; and Ulrike Gärtner, Kai-Uwe Hemken, and Kai Uwe Schierz, eds., *KunstLichtSpiele: Lichtästhetik der klassischen Avantgarde* (Bielefeld: Kerber, 2009).

50. Kracauer, *The Salaried Masses*, 94.

51. Kracauer, *The Salaried Masses*, 93.

52. Kracauer, "Lichtreklame," *Frankfurter Zeitung*, 15 January 1927, 115, n. 38, rpt. in *Siegfried Kracauer: Schriften*, 5.2, Aufsätze, 1927–1931 (Frankfurt: Suhrkamp, 1990), 19. "Bunte Lettern, die weiße Wäsche ankündigen sollen, sind nicht ganz bei der Sache, selbst wenn sie fünf Stockwerke bedecken. . . . Licht bleibt Licht . . . "

53. Kracauer, "Lichtreklame," 19. "Sie schießt über die Wirtschaft hinaus, und was als Reklame gemeint ist, wird zur Illumination."

54. Kracauer, "Ansichtspostkarte," *Frankfurter Zeitung*, 26 May 1930, rpt. in *Straßen in Berlin und Anderswo* (Frankfurt: Suhrkamp, 1964), 46–48. The quotations in the original are: ". . . Kirche, die keine Kirche ist . . ." (48) and "ein riesenhaftes Verkehrshindernis" (46).

55. Kracauer, "Ansichtspostkarte," 46–47. Trans. from Miriam Hansen, "Decentric Perspectives," 69.

56. Kracauer, "Ansichtspostkarte," 47. "Ein hemmungsloses Funkeln, das keineswegs nur der Reklame dient, sondern darüber hinaus sich Selbstzweck ist."

57. Kracauer, "Ansichtspostkarte," 48. Trans. Miriam Hansen, "Decentric Perspectives," 70.

58. Kracauer, "Rund um den Reichstag," [*Frankfurter Zeitung*, 2 March 1933, n. 163–65. *Siegfried Kracauer: Schriften*, 5.3], 212. "Wenn sie einmal groß sind, werden sie aus der Geschichte erfahren, was der Reichstagsbrand in Wirklichkeit zu bedeuten hatte."

59. Kracauer, "Rund um den Reichstag," 211. "Was an ihnen befremdet, ist ihr beharrliches Schweigen."

Siegfried Kracauer's Architectures

Claire Zimmerman

By many accounts Siegfried Kracauer was interested in surface manifestations of consumer capitalism and what they revealed about modern subjects. Whether he encountered them on the stage, in the movie palace, on the film screen, or in the street, Kracauer analyzed the vapors of contemporary culture—superficial pop culture spectacle and mass media appearances—for clues with which to unravel cultural conditions and philosophical realities of his day. Kracauer's interest in surface, however, relates to previous generations of art and architectural historians writing on the same subject. Kracauer's training as an architect, his studies in Darmstadt, Berlin, and Munich under architects Theodor Fischer and Richard Borrmann, and his doctoral dissertation on architectural metalwork were linked to nineteenth-century studies of architectural detail, surface ornament, and theories of perception. These subjects also ramify through his later work on a host of different topics. Kracauer's transition from the study of ornamental architectural surface in his dissertation to the study of other forms of cultural surface reflects the historical shift that took place from the nineteenth to the twentieth centuries, and provides a framework for the present essay. Kracauer began with the physical architecture of the city and its buildings; over time, he became increasingly preoccupied with the very architecture of modern society itself.[1]

In the years around World War I, Kracauer stood at the entry to a path that almost bypassed modern architecture completely. He explored conditions of physical experience and collectivity in modern society across fields, but his prewar diary shows his consistent ambivalence about his own future in professional architecture. He addressed the repositioning of art in relation to everyday life in his dissertation, by emphasizing the simultaneous presence of art and craft in his subject and by implicitly accepting the nineteenth-century notion that craft and applied arts production were accessible, populist arts without class restriction. In so doing, he anticipated one of the prime directives of the 1920s artistic avant-gardes, which articulated the same idea in mass culture and new media. Kracauer's early work, studied here from his dissertation to his essay "Cult of Distraction," connects the history of craft to the new mass culture of an emergent media society, through the historiographical project of late nineteenth-century art history and its emphasis on applied arts, surface, and material.

In recent years, architecture has been heavily oriented toward new surface treatments, thanks to the continuing importance of frame construction. At the same time, new fabrication methods have begun to complicate the separation between structure and surface. These engagements with the architecture of surfaces have made Kracauer newly important to contemporary architects and scholars.[2] Linking nineteenth-century theories of ornament and the decorative arts to contemporary building production through Kracauer's theoretical writing on contemporary surface treatments (whether physical, virtual, or conceptual) opens the past to the present, and the present to the past. This is not historicism but a historical clarification that allows us to better distinguish the new from the old, or the familiar from the unprecedented.[3]

Siegfried Kracauer came to the defense of the much-contested architecture exhibition that took place at Stuttgart in the summer of 1927. This Werkbund-sponsored exhibition, entitled "The Dwelling," displayed the initiatives of "The New Building" (*Neues Bauen*) in the innovative production of buildings, interior fittings, and textual/photographic representations of a contemporary forward-looking architecture.[4] The progressive architect Ludwig Mies van der Rohe directed the complex, tripartite exhibition. Its largest and most ambitious component consisted of full-scale prototype buildings on the Weissenhof hill on the outskirts of the city. Kracauer joined other progressive left-leaning critics in positive assessments of the three component exhibitions, addressing a strong counterreaction from the largely South German Right—both because of its ideological opposition to the Neues Bauen, but also because of the near-total exclusion of Stuttgart architects from this display of contemporary German architecture culture by the Berlin-based Werkbund administration.[5]

Kracauer's writings on "The Dwelling" are interesting to read. They join a limited array of writing on architecture from a remarkably prolific writer, an array that gradually declined in volume from the early 1920s, soon after he gave up architecture to begin his journalistic career in

1919/20, to an all-time low in 1929. He resumed writing on architecture in the early 1930s, perhaps because the politics in which it became enmeshed called for active response. An examination of the architectural writings of the early to mid-1920s corroborates Kracauer's statements about his disappointing practice of architecture before 1919 and provides a plausible explanation for the decline in volume of his architectural writing.[6] Kracauer may have been hampered by his own insider professional knowledge; his building critiques focus on microanalysis and macroanalysis, but they seldom seem to bring his insightful eye into proper focus on individual buildings. He knows too much about buildings and writes too little about their social significance. Truthfully, he was often compelled to write about local Frankfurt events, such as the various expansions of the civic center (*Messe*), or the addition to the main post office. The latter only proved, Kracauer wrote, the urgent necessity of open architectural criticism for the sake of necessary future improvement in constructed buildings.[7]

Such was not the case when he wrote about building programs and functions. When the architecture itself receded from his attention, and the activities that buildings house came to the fore, his writing took on its familiar liveliness. Thus his prescient piece critiquing Berlin's pseudo-neo-Baroque movie palaces, "Cult of Distraction," suggests the near complete vaporization of architectural detail and ornament, as if to leave only the screen still in place within a blank interior in which nothing mediates between viewer and spectacle. In this de-architectured setting, Kracauer wrote, the intensity of the experience of pure opticality might hurtle the viewer into "the abyss" of a fully disembodied yet communal experience of mass entertainment. The architecture of the movie palace hadn't arrived at this point in Kracauer's time (arguably, it has today, but as a dinosaur); it was, however, anticipated as a necessary or logical development of the type.[8] The nature of the optical experience that Kracauer anticipated is obliquely described in "Cult of Distraction," but it circles around the melding of subject and image, interiority and exteriority that has been described as essential in Kracauer's other work.[9] In the movie palace, Kracauer identified the spatial opportunity for a transcendent visual experience of what might be called *mass subjectivity*—a shared experience nevertheless absorbed individually through transitive imagery flitting across a screen.

If Kracauer's relationship to architecture produced some of his least interesting writing, the Stuttgart exhibition piece constitutes an important exception. His analysis of the ghostly Glass Room in the materials exhibition at Stuttgart surely relates to his description of the nonarchitecture of the movie screen in its pallid box, as sketched the previous year in "Cult of Distraction" and discussed below. A more general survey of Kracauer's writing as a whole reveals procedures in which analytic or conceptual methodologies that were closely associated with the recent history of architecture and the decorative arts, but that have nothing to do with buildings per se, were put to use in analyzing material conditions of twentieth-century culture, what Gerwin Zohlen refers to as the "Metaphorisierung der Architektur."[10] Precisely how Kracauer adapted a set of specifically architectural concerns to a nonarchitectural body of matter, how his preoccupation with surface manifestations resembled the engagement of an architect with a set of available materials of construction, and how the results of his constructive efforts were quite defiantly architectural in the way in which they proposed a new framework for contemporary life are worthy questions. The plural term *architectures* provides the requisite expanded concept—as already noted, Kracauer's post–World War I work recalls the term currently in use by computer scientists, politicians, and even businessmen (who use it metaphorically), not the narrow definition that distinguished it from the more wishfully egalitarian "Baukunst" of Weimar debates. Kracauer was, if anything, deciphering the architecture of our current operating system—rather ahead of his day, but not unrelated to the rather more technical efforts of Norbert Wiener and Buckminster Fuller. Before releasing Kracauer to his later self, however, it is worth examining in some detail the nature of the affiliations established by his early education in the practice and theory of architecture. I will briefly consider these affiliations before returning to the Stuttgart exhibition, a site where two of Kracauer's architectures—a literal one and a conceptual one—crossed over one another, if briefly.

Kracauer gave up a professional career in architecture in 1919 to embark on a writing career as a journalist, where he analyzed surface manifestations of contemporary mass culture. The practice of architecture held little attraction for him—nor could he find a steady job after World War I.[11] Indeed, Kracauer's major preoccupations bear little relationship to the construction of a fixed social frame such as that which architecture provides, no matter how obsolescent, how traditional, or how progressive. Trained in *Bauforschung* (building research), in which architects embarked on historical study for a career in applied architectural history (often archaeology), or for practice in the profession, or both, Kracauer studied first with Fischer in Munich, and then with Borrmann at the Technische Hochschule in Berlin.[12]

Kracauer's education as architect and scholar would have revealed the complex engagements between buildings and industrial modernity from the nineteenth century, when historicist architecture was deployed as rhetorical or didactic reflection on modern society.[13] Nineteenth-century architects and theorists addressed how (and whether) history could remain a source for new architectures in spite of new and distinctly nontraditional production and construction methods. The development of frame construction in metal and concrete after the second half of the nineteenth century had irrevocably changed the game, pushing the question of how buildings should *look* to the forefront of architects' concerns by separating external building appearance from internal structural necessity. The eclectic narrative expression by which nineteenth-century buildings told stories in relation to the past had often occurred in buildings with hybrid construction systems that used old and new technologies opportunistically. This ad hoc way of building appeared obsolete by World War I, although it did not completely disappear. Nevertheless, architects began to turn from historical analogy to conceptual analysis in search of "essence," medium specificity, and abstraction, and for ways to assert the architect's artist status on a world stage preoccupied with safeguarding revenue sources through copyright law.[14] Kracauer's doctoral work was suspended between these poles, balancing the theory of Georg Simmel, the historicist engagements of Fischer, and the exacting research methods of Borrmann.

Kracauer's retreat from the concerns of architecture culture began in his dissertation, *The Development of the Art of Forging in Berlin, Potsdam, and Some Cities of the Mark from the Seventeenth Century to the Beginning of the Nineteenth Century*. This work focuses on material that lies quite literally on the periphery of architecture.[15] It is a stylistic and historical analysis of wrought iron architectural detail in Berlin and Brandenburg written under the supervision of Borrmann, with Friedrich Klingholz and Friedrich Laske at the Technische Hochschule.[16] The topic recalls Borrmann's own research on architectural detail and surface ornamentation, and might also be compared to dissertation topics by Kracauer's peers in Berlin, Paul Zucker and Adolf Behne, and Paul Frankl in Munich.[17] Borrmann evidently demanded exacting archaeological study recorded in careful measured drawings duly prepared by Kracauer, whose dissertation reflects a meticulous attention to detail.[18]

Kracauer's subject was wrought iron decoration in architectural appli-

figuren, in welche die Spiralen auslaufen. Die ganze Struktur des Gitters erinnert an das Oberlicht Abb. 19.¹) Der Entstehungszeit nach später scheint uns das zweite Kapellengitter, Abb. 17, zu sein. Die Führung der Spiralen ist hier wesentlich einfacher und grosszügiger. Eigenartig sind die vielen an die Windungen geschweissten Blätter, die zur Füllung der etwas breiten Zwischenräume dienen; sie geben aber der Gitterfläche ein leichtes und lockeres Aussehen. Die naturalistische Behandlung der grossen Blattrosetten, der Engelfiguren²) und der Endigung des Mittelstabes sind durchaus individuell und nicht weiter zurückführbar. Typisch dagegen ist die Ausbildung der kleinen Krone in der Mitte, der wir später noch bei anderen Beispielen begegnen werden. Beide Gitter waren farbig. — Ein sehr reiches Gitter aus dem Jahre 1722³), Abb. 18, findet sich noch zu Brandenburg in der St. Gotthardkirche;

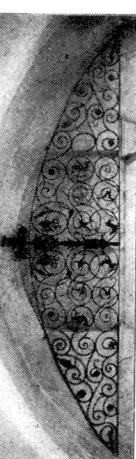

Abb. 14   Fensterfüllung   Berlin, Marienkirche

Abb. 15   Türfüllung   Berlin, Friedrichsgracht 58

¹) Vergl. auch Bemerkung zu Abb. 2.   ²) Vergl. Abb. 8.   ³) Inventar
a. a. O. Bd. II. 3. 16.

es schliesst die mittlere der Chorkapellen ab. In der unteren Hälfte sind schon barocke Einflüsse verarbeitet, während der obere Teil sich noch in der alten Formensprache bewegt, allerdings mit ziemlich willkürlicher Verwendung der einzelnen Stilelemente. Ich sehe

Phot. Kgl. Messbildanstal, Berlin.

Abb. 16   Kapellengitter   Brandenburg, St. Katharinenkirche

Abb. 17   Kapellengitter   Brandenburg. St. Katharinenkirche

mich hier zu einer Bemerkung veranlasst, die sich auch beim Berliner bürgerlichen Rokoko der Spätzeit bestätigt: Erst wenn der Geist eines Stiles völlig in die ausübenden Künstler eingegangen ist, was gewöhnlich gegen das Ende einer ausgeprägten Stilperiode statt hat, vermag dieser seiner eigenen Fantasie und seines handwerklichen Könnens in ihm auszudrücken. Das Typische differenziert sich zu immer individuelleren Gebilden und erscheint häufig als Willkürlichkeit und Ausartung. Es macht den eigentümlichen Reiz des auf Abb. 18 dargestellten Gitters aus, dass

Fig. 1. Page reproductions from Kracauer's dissertation, "Die Entwicklung der Schmiedekunst in Berlin, Potsdam und einigen Städten der Mark vom 17. Jahrhundert bis zum Beginn des 20. Jahrhunderts." Worms, 1915.

cations. Balcony railings, gates, fences, lampposts, grave markers, signage brackets and frames, and window grilles form the subject matter of this early writing. Even the examples drawn from architectural interiors were confined to lobbies or transitional spaces like stairways, as if Kracauer were gradually backing down the stairs, out of the edifice and onto the street—where his real locus of interest lay. This early study reflects nineteenth-century architectural historiography, where focused studies of architectural ornament and building detail were numerous.

Although the dissertation includes smaller-scale architectural elements like lampposts, much of it concerns surfaces with the minimal depth of a wrought iron stick (*Stab*) and maximal length; like fabrics or screens, these surfaces are both sheetlike and see-through at the same time, and they have no conceptual boundary. They are also adjunct or supplementary to architecture; in the case of court boundary fences (*Hofabschlussgitter*) Kracauer notes, "they close off the court and tie the wings of the building together architectonically without hindering the view to the main building."[19] They could be (in theory) infinitely long perforated fences—a little like plate glass during the Weimar period (when Mies once installed a single sheet almost nine meters long in a residential addition in Essen). The notable difference lies in fabrication: plate glass was extruded in regular widths and variable lengths by machine; wrought iron fences were laboriously constructed by hand.

Kracauer's interest in these objects reflects the concerns of late Wilhelmine architects in at least two respects. First, eighteenth-century architecture and design objects had been the subject of revived historical interest at the turn of the nineteenth century, and second, the study of surface ornament had been a major preoccupation of nineteenth-century architects. Paul Mebes's influential *Um 1800* was a possible precedent for Kracauer's study, together with other early twentieth-century returns to neoclassical and vernacular "indigenous" architectural style.[20] Screens and gates similar to those recorded in Kracauer's dissertation can be found in contemporary projects like Erik Gunnar Asplund's tiny Woodland Chapel of 1918–20 outside of Stockholm.[21] In light of post–World War I affiliations between traditional form and right-wing politics (particularly in the late 1920s and 1930s), it is small wonder that this minor work has been so carefully overlooked subsequently.[22]

In turn, two issues fueled interest in architectural surface in the nineteenth century. The first was metallic frame construction, which was rooted in the late eighteenth century but blossomed after the construction of the

Crystal Palace in London in 1851. Its genesis led indirectly to new historical studies of nonsupporting wall surfaces and architectural ornament. The second was archaeological research, particularly the close study and documentation of ancient sites, beginning in Italy and Greece, and the extensive debates on architectural polychromy.[23] Historians worked simultaneously on theoretical or conceptual models by which to historicize metallic frame construction and on the earlier genesis of the ornamental architectural surface, trying to establish genealogies for new construction methods.

Scholars of nonstructural or ornamental architectural surface included Jacques-Ignace Hittorf (1792–1867), Gottfried Semper (1803–79), Karl Bötticher (1806–89), Owen Jones (1809–74), and Alois Riegl (1858–1905). While Kracauer did not cite these authors in his bibliography (brief as it is), the history of their published work suggests that it would have constituted basic reading material for a young researcher in architecture, as well as part of the historical curriculum of any architectural education before World War I.[24] The relationship between structure and surface appearance was understood very differently among these scholars. For Semper, the relationship was direct and instrumental; traces of building manufacture were recorded in ornamental detail that persisted as decoration even after construction techniques changed. For Bötticher, it was direct but imaginative; external form echoed interior structure but could deflect and exaggerate according to an architect's expressive intent. For Riegl, it was indirect, motivated by conceptual intention rather than constructive necessity. Debates among these and other late nineteenth-century historians (such as Eugène-Emmanuel Viollet-le-Duc in France) were vivid and abundant.[25]

Riegl noted that expressive motifs reflected the ongoing cultural concerns of producers and consumers, not merely technical or material restrictions on producers. He redirected art-historical study to so-called minor arts at the end of the century and shifted the emphasis of art history from materialist to historicoformalist.[26] Perhaps most pertinent in the context of Kracauer's training, Riegl framed the history of ornament as the expression of time-dependent cultural preoccupations that he characterized as "artistic desire" (*Kunstwollen*), a term that roughly subtends the idea of a core of artistic ideas of abiding communal interest that coalesce at a given historical conjuncture.[27] Just like Kracauer's, Riegl's interests traversed ornament *and* surface as the site of interpretive analysis—not unlike Kracauer's later notion of the hieroglyphic. And yet, in the pages of his dissertation Kracauer returned repeatedly to material and technical matters and how they left their traces in objects.

The methods of Semper and Riegl were not dissimilar; both required intensive examination and close historical analysis, and both were based on acute observation and deductive method. Rather their conclusion—the nature of the truth they wished to emphasize—differed. Perhaps most important, Riegl and Semper did not address themselves to the qualitative distinction between works of applied art and works of fine art, upon which the foundations of art history were subsequently built. This distinction belongs to the twentieth century—to the followers of Riegl and Semper—Heinrich Wölfflin and Erwin Panofsky, among others. Kracauer bypassed this later development within art history, one that was brandished so loudly by Loos and Le Corbusier, as Henrik Reeh notes. For Kracauer, twentieth-century mass media had a similar audience profile to that of nineteenth-century applied arts, indicating a point of historical noncorrespondence between Kracauer and his time. In the post–World War I years, the notion of revolutionary change between the nineteenth and twentieth centuries was much more appealing than the continuity reflected in Kracauer's scholarly path. Schwartz has pointed to Kracauer's simultaneous dependence on and distance from Riegl in "The Mass Ornament"; other writings (including the dissertation) attest a productive engagement with Riegl's work, suggesting that Kracauer embraced it, engaged it, and moved on.

Semper and Riegl are divided by a line drawn between history as material and technical explication and history as autonomous development of style, or formalism. Neither description quite suffices to describe Kracauer's work. In his dissertation, he conceptualized his material in relation to surface representation. His textual references are narrowly focused on the history of Berlin architecture and of wrought iron architectural detail in Europe. Borrmann's influence is evident in frequent citations of *Die Bau- und Kunstdenkmäler von Berlin* of 1893. In tracing the development of wrought iron ornament, Kracauer noted the importance of the general development of art (*Gesamtentwicklung der Kunst*) within a given period. Yet he also distinguished indigenous developments from imported French and South German decorative motifs, identifying a particular series of artifacts (mostly stair railings) from the 1770s and 1880s. He attributed these to the "conscious artistic will of the individual" (*bewusster künstlerischer Individual-Wille*) within a given historical moment. Throughout the dissertation he thus positioned himself between the overarching *Kunstwollen* and the particularity of his immediate subject matter—logical for a young researcher absorbing the history and historiography of ornament. While the dissertation is heavily indebted to Rieglian analysis, it also draws on Georg Simmel's 1907–8 essays on ornament, which extend Riegl's discussion of subjectivity to show how the decorative arts participated in defining collective experience, thus connecting individual and mass subject in immediately accessible art forms.[28]

In describing the "indigenous" wrought-iron ornament in Berlin and Potsdam that gives his project a central focus, the author notes changes in composition and execution. Centralized motifs such as monograms were replaced over time by a looser and more regular treatment across the ornamental surface. The center of the decorative motif (*Schmuckzentrum*) of earlier work was replaced instead by the decoration of the surface (*Schmückung der Fläche*) of this indigenous craftwork. Conventional motifs are softened and transformed through adaptation from distant originals to new surface fields. In one case, a tomb grille appears with the comment, "The monogram in the middle . . . loses the meaning that it had in the Baroque as a decorative piece. As in this particular example, so generally. It becomes one among many coordinated scrolled embellishments, when earlier it created a decorative center and was the ornamental point of the grille surface. . . . The typical form of the Baroque crown is dissolved into shell-like ornamentation."[29] Kracauer comments repeatedly on the network (*Netzwerk*) of ornamental fields, calling out the moments when these surfaces become repetitive and rhythmic, and lose hierarchical subdivision and the residual references to ornamental stone construction that dominated earlier French imports. The German artisans neglected structural concerns in order to "really fill the surface abundantly."[30]

Kracauer's analysis of metallic surfaces that do no more than carry their own weight evaded the conceptual protocols of Bötticher and Semper, with their emphasis on structure versus cladding, but engaged that of Riegl.[31] As noted, wrought iron is sheetlike, resembling nonstructural wall cladding, but standing up on its own without additional support. It is, in effect, a structural building material used in a nonstructural application, thus confounding existing hierarchies of architectural form. Kracauer's dissertation traced the activities of a group of artisans and a material that would later become associated with industrialization. Furthermore, his description of their ornamental strategy as one that emphasized regularly diffused patterns over large surfaces anticipated the products of industrially produced ornament. Given the importance of Semper's and Bötticher's structural theories, both of which engaged the implicit hierarchy of classical architecture (in which ornament is inevitably nonstructural) in different ways, Kracauer's choice of subject matter was both fortuitously liberating and

dreieckigen Raum, der östlich an die Sakristei der Marienkirche anstösst. Er enthält die Grabsteine der Simonschen Familie und soll früher bedacht gewesen sein. Zwei ovale Fenster mit Schmiedearbeiten liessen das Licht hinein¹). Abb. 11—13 zeigen die Gittertür mit Details. Dass die Arbeit eine späte ist, beweist das fleischige, sehr ausgebildete Blattwerk. Beachtenswert sind die aus Blech gestanzten Schnörkel in der Mitte des Oberlichtes. Man hat hier offenbar einen Uebergang vor sich von den Schreiberschnörkeln des Mittelalters zu den Monogrammen, die als füllender Schmuck mit Beginn des 18. Jahrhunderts überall auftauchen (vgl. Abb. 22 und 23). Die Gravierung und die recht komplizierte Zusammensetzung des Rahmens der Felder erkennt man aus den Details, Abb. 12 und 13. Die Füllung eines ovalen Fensters am dreieckigen Anbau bringt Abb. 14. Auch hier Linienführung, Blattwerk und Zierat typisch für den Stil um die Wende de des 17. Jahrhunderts.

Sehr ähnlich gestaltet ist eine Turfüllung aus dem Haus Friedrichsgracht 58, Abb. 15, vielleicht aus den 90er Jahren des 17. Jahrhunderts²) (vgl Abb. 6). Für die damals hochentwickelte Kunstfertig-

¹ Borrmann a a. O. S. 221. Nach ihm stammt der Anbau aus dem Anfang des 18 Jahrhunderts. ²) Borrmann a a. O. S. 166. Es heisst hier „Zwei vornehme Häuser Friedrichsgracht Nr. 57 und 58, auf dem Schütz'schen Plan (1688) sowie bei Strádbeck abgebildet und vermutlich kurz vorher entstanden, gehören demselben Typus an, den auch das Mattz'sche Haus vertrat....“

Abb. 11   Gittertüre   Berlin, Marienkirche

keit der Berliner Schmiede legen die reichen Blattkelche Zeugnis ab.

Nur spärlich begegnet man im Innern der überwiegend protestantischen Kirchen der Mark grösseren Abschlussgittern, wie solche an Chören und Kapellen des katholischen Kirchenraumes häufig Verwendung gefunden haben.¹)

Einige wenige Kapellengitter habe ich in Brandenburg a. H. angetroffen. Von zweien sind in der dortigen Katharinenkirche die oberen Teile erhalten. Früher standen sie in einem Winkel verborgen; bei der kürzlichen Renovierung der Kirche hat man sie wieder zu Ehren gebracht.²) Das offenbar ältere, auf Abb. 16 dargestellte, ist wohl in die zweite Hälfte des 17. Jahrhunderts zu verweisen. Der senkrechte Stab in der Mitte endigt in reiche Spindelblumen und ist in sich wieder gut gegliedert. Recht anmutig und zierlich sind die aus Blech geschnittenen Wappenlöwen, Tritonen und Zier-

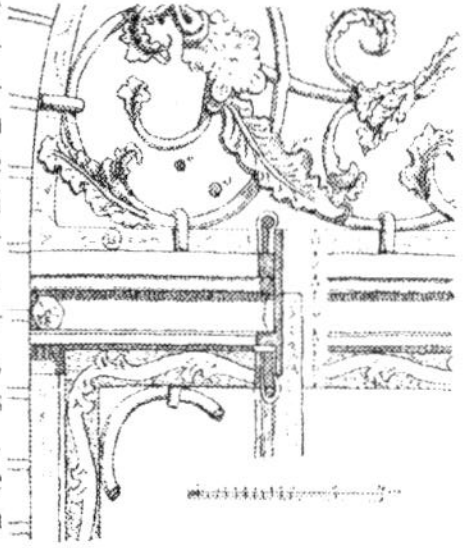

¹) Ueber Chorgitter, besonders perspektivische, in der Schweiz und Süddeutschland: Brüning a.a.O.S. 64 ff. Zetzsche a.a.O.S. 136 über die spanischen Chorgitter. ²) Inventar z.a.O. Bd. I. 3. S 71. „Es sind noch einige schmiedeeiserne Gitter zu erwähnen, die — Bestandteile ehemaliger Grabkapellen — einst die Stirnseiten zwei als Begräbniskapellen zwischen den Strebepfeilern des nördlichen Seitenschiffes schlossen.“

Abb. 12   Detail zu Abb. 11   Berlin, Marienkirche

Abb. 13   Detail zu Abb. 12   Berlin, Marienkirche

Fig. 2. Page reproductions from Kracauer's dissertation, "Die Entwicklung der Schmiedekunst in Berlin, Potsdam und einigen Städten der Mark vom 17. Jahrhundert bis zum Beginn des 20. Jahrhunderts." Worms, 1915.

slightly contrary. But if we examine it in relation to contemporary architectural surfaces of his own day, it becomes far more comprehensible—not a historical cul-de-sac but a major stop on the main highway.

Kracauer's investigative method, relying on surface appearance to provide the clues for its own analysis, took the historical precedents provided by Semper and Riegl as given. He transferred the investigation from one of research into the past (that of his dissertation) to one with a contemporary focus (that of his critical work of the 1920s). At the same time, the raw material of his investigations also shifted from architecture and the decorative arts to more ephemeral surfaces that were beginning to receive the same intense scrutiny as remnant colored marble surfaces had received from nineteenth-century archaeologists—the new surfaces of photograph and film screen. If architecture had not provided enough purchase for his investigations, this was almost certainly connected to the top-down power structures of the profession until the tipping point of 1926, when control of the Werkbund and the Bund Deutscher Architekten (BDA) passed into the hands of younger architects more or less free of the control of the old Wilhelmine power brokers. At this point, and only then, could architects begin to engage contemporary mass culture in ways that might seem relevant to a population (and a journalist) growing increasingly enamored with the movie screen and the illustrated press. Mies van der Rohe became the vice president of the Werkbund in 1926 and was given the task of organizing the Stuttgart exhibition that struck Kracauer so forcibly. For a brief moment, Kracauer's two architectures came together. By the end of the decade, they were splitting apart again, when Kracauer, like Ernst Bloch and Behne, accused the radical project of the *Neues Bauen* as being unknowingly complicit with and obedient to the reductive rationalization of capitalism.[32]

In the opening of his long and interesting article on the exhibition in Stuttgart in 1927, Kracauer's tongue was seemingly in his cheek, as he celebrated the advanced condition of water faucets and bathroom fixtures—harbingers of the new architecture (perhaps nodding to Adolf Loos, long an admirer of the advanced state of American and English plumbing). One of the greatest achievements of the full-scale buildings constructed on the Weissenhofsiedlung above Stuttgart was the fact that "the bathtubs don't have to be ashamed of the dining room anymore" (*die Badewannen brauchen sich der Speisezimmer nicht mehr zu schämen*).[33] No matter how skeptical, Kracauer's written remarks on the individual buildings of the *Siedlung* seem to indicate acceptance of the *Neues Bauen*, for better or worse, and recognition of the need for solidarity on the front of "the new." What attracted him most was the Glass Room at the materials exhibition downtown. This was a small installation commissioned by the German glass industry where plate glass walls subdivided the exhibition space with no other structural support. The walls were partially reflective; like mirrors, they brought filmic experience into real space and time, complicating present space through virtual projection, just as Kracauer had called for in "Cult of Distraction." In this space, architecture appeared and disappeared simultaneously. According to Kracauer, the installation was a marker for an architecture that didn't yet exist, "contemporary constructive foreordinations of elements cleansed of bad superfluities" (*zeitgemäße konstruktive Fügungen der von schlechtem Überfluß gereinigten Elemente*).[34] It marked a point where surface, ornament, and image came together in simultaneous representation on the stage of architecture. At this point we might recall the fields of late Baroque and Rococo wrought iron, where ornamental detail was cleansed of specificity as a field of complex patterning, richly full.

Kracauer's use of the word *Fügungen* recalls Mies's explanations of the Stuttgart exhibition from a slightly different standpoint. Mies described the architecture and design installations as projective examples—prototypes—of an architecture that hadn't yet arrived.[35] The notion of standing in the anticipation of an event also figures in Kracauer's other writings on architectural and nonarchitectural topics, such as "Those Who Wait." At Stuttgart it was both literally and figuratively true: the Weissenhofsiedlung, while it was a display of new (and potentially more economical) construction technologies, was also vastly expensive. It was defeated by its own failure to command the economies of scale on which it was premised. It was itself a fore-ordination—a prototype, or a handmade readymade awaiting factory production. This anticipatory, sketchlike character of a large mass of constructed architecture was the subject of virulent attacks from the Right, for profligate waste of public funds.

Kracauer's refunctioning of nineteenth-century art-historical method to contemporary surface analysis in the first few decades of the twentieth century was immensely fruitful for his cultural theory. But tracing links to the nineteenth century doesn't feature as a large component of Kracauer studies. This may in part be explained by his seeming presentism for late twentieth- and early twenty-first-century audiences. It may in part lie with his own rejection of architecture, his less impressive early journalism on the subject, and the inadvertently nationalistic overtones of a thesis on Berlin's "indigenous" contribution to a history of wrought iron. Later,

Kracauer substituted the unknown future for the unknown past, producing a kind of therapeutic projective historical materialism; the nineteenth century overlaid on the twentieth. In fact, he seems to have existed in a different time zone from that of the "real time" of historical events as they unfolded. He was prescient—ahead of his time—and rather retrograde—rooted in certain old habits of analysis that were not generally admired by his contemporaries. If anything, his lack of correspondence to his own biological moment (the span of years in which he lived) provides an overpass—a superhighway, or even a wormhole—back to the nineteenth century. We might adjust the facts to fit the reality; Kracauer was born at the 1851 exhibition, and, apparently, he hasn't yet died.

Returning to his work offers a guideline for navigating the contemporary surface, where images themselves have proliferated to the point where they produce the visual equivalent of white noise, but where image effects have also long since outstripped textual explanations. Roland Barthes's "rhetoric of the image" has made way for remarkably sophisticated image rhetorics that exploit the versatility and flexibility of images to broadly inconsistent effect—and to increasingly self-selected microaudiences. Adroit combinations of visual imagery and minimal textual adjunct attest how pluralism has become a form of sectarianism. In truth, any sort of visual argument can be made through the current instruments of media society; equally truthfully, no one seems to mind. Our helplessness against such pluralist anomie challenges our ability to address a future where surface effects have no counterweight. Investment in a pluralist society is given; but this historical moment hasn't quite decided how to marry pluralism with the subdivision and factionalization that go with global capitalism. Thus students of image culture look hopefully to Kracauer for some new analytic tools to navigate the present. For architects and designers, the matter appears even clearer. As John Ashbery noted some years ago, "The surface is what's there / And nothing can exist except what's there . . ."[36]

NOTES

1. For literature on Kracauer and architecture, see Henrik Reeh, *Ornaments of the Metropolis: Siegfried Kracauer and Modern Urban Culture* (Cambridge: MIT Press, 2004); Tilmann Heß, "Zur Architektur in Kracauers Stadtbildern" in A. Volk, ed., *Siegfried Kracauer: Zum Werk des Romanciers, Feuilletonisten, Architekten, Filmwissenschaftlers und Soziologen* (Zurich: Seismo, 1996), 111–30; Juliet Koss "Hooked on Kracauer," *Assemblage* 31 (December 1996): 30–39; Anthony Vidler,

"Agoraphobia: Spatial Estrangement in Simmel and Kracauer," *New German Critique* 54 (1991): 31–46; Gerwin Zohlen, "Schmugglerpfad: Siegfried Kracauer, Architekt und Schriftsteller," in *Siegfried Kracauer: Neue Interpretationen* (Tübingen: Stauffenberg, 1990), 324–441.

2. Among many sources that might be cited here are Christy Anderson and Karen Koehler, eds., *The Built Surface* (Burlington: Ashgate, 2002); Janet Ward, *Weimar Surfaces: Urban Visual Culture in 1920s Germany* (Berkeley: University of California Press, 2001); Farshid Moussavi, *The Function of Ornament* (Barcelona: Actar, 2006).

3. I frame this essay in relation to architectural *surface* rather than *ornament* in contrast to Henrik Reeh's book-length study.

4. See Richard Pommer and Christian Otto, *The Weissenhof 1927 and the Modern Movement in Architecture* (Chicago: University of Chicago Press, 1991); Karin Kirsch, *The Weissenhofsiedlung: Experimental Housing Built for the Deutscher Werkbund, Stuttgart, 1927* (New York: Rizzoli, 1989); also see *Bau und Wohnung: Die Bauten der Weissenhofsiedlung in Stuttgart* (Stuttgart: F. Wedekind, 1927); Stephanie Plarre, *Die Kochenhofsiedlung, das Gegenmodell zur Weissenhofsiedlung: Paul Schmitthenners Siedlungsprojekt in Stuttgart von 1927 bis 1933* (Stuttgart: Hohenheim, 2001).

5. Siegfried Kracauer, "Das neue Bauen. Zur Stuttgarter Werkbund-Ausstellung: 'Die Wohnung.'" *Frankfurter Zeitung* (henceforth *FZ*), 31 July 1927, Jg. 72, Nr. 561, 2.

6. See Ingrid Belke and Irina Renz, eds., *Siegfried Kracauer 1889–1966*, special issue, *Marbacher Magazin* 47 (1988): 17–36; and Siegfried Kracauer, *Frankfurter Turmhäuser: Ausgewählte Feuilletons, 1906–30* (Zurich: Epocha, 1997).

7. "Erweiterungsbauten der Hauptpost." *FZ*, 26 May 1921, Jg. 65, Nr. 381, 2. Reprinted in *Frankfurter Turmhäuser,* 143.

8. Siegfried Kracauer, "Cult of Distraction," in *The Mass Ornament: Weimar Essays*, trans. and ed. Thomas Y. Levin (Cambridge: Harvard University Press, 1995), 323–28.

9. Frederic J. Schwartz, *Blind Spots: Critical Theory and the History of Art in Twentieth-Century Germany* (London: Yale University Press, 2005); Reeh, *Ornaments*.

10. Zohlen, "Schmugglerpfad," 340.

11. Kracauer's retroactive description of this transitional moment in *Ginster* should be regarded with appropriate skepticism. See *Ginster, von ihm selbst geschrieben* (Frankfurt: Fischer, 1928, reprinted 1963/1973). See Reeh, *Ornaments*, chapter 2.

12. Richard Borrmann was a student of Friedrich Adler and a member of the archaeological team at ancient Olympia. He specialized in architectural terra-cottas and the architectural history of Berlin. See "Richard Borrmann, 1852–1931," in Reinhard Lullies and Wolfgang Schiering, eds., *Archäologenbildnisse* (Mainz: Philipp von Zabern, 1988), 108–9.

13. For example, see Heinrich Hübsch, *In welchem Stil sollen wir bauen?* (Karlsruhe: C. F. Müller, 1984/1828); trans. W. Hermann, *In What Style Should We Build? The German Debate on Architectural Style* (Santa Monica: Getty Center, 1992). National Socialist architecture returned to this system of linguistic association.

14. See Frederic Schwartz, *The Werkbund: Design Theory and Mass Culture Before the First World War* (New Haven: Yale University Press, 1996).

15. Siegfried Kracauer, *Die Entwicklung der Schmiedekunst in Berlin, Potsdam und einigen Städten der Mark vom 17. Jahrhundert bis zum Beginn des 19. Jahrhunderts* (Berlin: Gebrüder Mann, 1997 [1915]).

16. Belke and Renz, *Siegfried Kracauer 1889–1966*, 17; *Die Entwicklung der Schmiedekunst*, viii.

17. See Borrmann's contribution to Wilhelm Dörpfeld et al., *Über die Verwendung von Terrakotten am Geison und Dache griechischer Bauwerke* (Berlin: G. Reimer, 1881); Richard Borrmann, *Geschnittene Gläser des 17. und 18. Jahrhunderts* (Berlin: E. Wasmuth, 1901); Borrmann, *Aufnahmen mittelalterlicher Wand- und Deckenmalereien in Deutschland*, 2 vols. (Berlin: E. Wasmuth, 1897–1928); Paul Zucker, *Raumdarstellungen und Bildarchitekturen bei den florentiner Malern der ersten Häfte des Quattrocento* (Leipzig: Klinkhardt und Biermann, 1913); Adolf Behne, *Der Inkrustationsstil in der Toskana* (Berlin, 1913). On Behne, see Frederic J. Schwartz, "Form Follows Fetish: Adolf Behne and the Problem of Sachlichkeit," *Oxford Art Journal* 21, no. 2 (1998): 57.

18. See Reeh, *Ornaments*, 64–65, on Kracauer's drawings.

19. ". . . sie schliessen den Hof ab und fassen die Gebäudeflügel architektonisch zusammen, ohne den Durchblick auf den Hauptbau zu hindern." Kracauer, *Die Entwicklung der Schmiedekunst*, 40.

20. Paul Mebes, *Um 1800* (Munich: Bruckmann, 1908; 2 vols.); the book was organized by type of architectural element: staircases, doorways, iron grilles (*Gittern*), and gates. A similar typological organization is found in Paul Schultze-Naumburg's extensive publications. See the various volumes of the *Kulturarbeiten* starting in 1902. Schultze-Naumburg is better known for determining National Socialist culture policy, and for books like *Kunst und Rasse* (Munich: Lehmann, 1928). His books include an early and strategic use of photography.

21. See Caroline Constant, *The Woodland Cemetery: Toward a Spiritual Landscape* (Stockholm: Byggförlaget, 1994); Barbara Miller Lane, *National Romanticism and Modern Architecture in Germany and the Scandinavian Countries* (Cambridge: Cambridge University Press, 2000).

22. See Kerstin Barndt's essay in this volume for further commentary on Kracauer's interest in German identity, and for discussion of Kracauer's commentary on architecture exhibitions, including the Stuttgart exhibition of 1927.

23. In this regard, Borrmann's work in Greece is relevant; Richard Borrmann, *Die Baudenkmäler von Olympia*, vol. 2 of *Olympia: die Ergebnisse der von dem Deutschen Reich veranstalteten Ausgrabung, im Auftrage des Königlich preussischen Ministers der geistlichen, unterrichts- und medicinal-Angelegenheiten*, Ernst Curtius et al. (Berlin: A. Asher, 1890–97). For a general treatment of the polychromy debate, see Barry Bergdoll, *European Architecture, 1750–1900* (New York: Oxford University Press, 2000), chapters 5–7.

24. The work of Riegl, Semper, and Bötticher were published throughout the nineteenth century. For example, Semper's *Kleine Schriften* appeared in 1884 and his major work *Der Stil* in 1878–79. Critical commentaries on Semper's aesthetics were published in 1880, 1904, and 1909.

25. For Bötticher, the structural performance of metal (its *Kernform* or core form) was not isomorphic with the expressive envelope that contained it (its *Kunstform*, or art form). Thus Bötticher allowed for the simultaneous coexistence of rational structure and expressive form. Semper, by contrast, saw frame construction as the skeleton whose presence might be read through exterior cladding, chiefly by the system of attachment between frame and surface. In addition to the clear articulation of connections between surface and structure, Semper also noted that obsolete technologies of attachment or manufacture might nevertheless subsequently leave traces on building surface in the form of stylized ornamental motifs, long after new technologies had come into use. These traces allowed the historian to "read" earlier origins of architecture and applied art objects. Both Semper and Bötticher were concerned with articulating a relationship between load-bearing structure and architectural expression.

26. Outside of Germany, Hittorf in France and Owen Jones in England had also studied surface ornamentation as an index to conditions of its origin; both are well known for theories of ornament, and Hittorf particularly for investigating the highly colored surface painting of ancient Greek temples. See Bergdoll, *European Architecture, 1750–1900.*

27. Riegl's *Stilfragen: Grundlegungen zu einer Geschichte der Ornamentik*, published in Berlin in 1893, was an important source on ornament.

28. Georg Simmel, "Das Problem des Stiles," *Dekorative Kunst* 11 (1908); "Psychologie des Schmuckes," *Der Morgen* 2 (1908): 15, 454–59. Also see Belke and Renz, *Siegfried Kracauer 1889–1966*, 11–12; Schwartz, 139.

29. "Das Monogramm in der Mitte . . . verliert als Schmuckteil die Bedeutung, die ihm im Baroock zukam. Wie bei diesem Gitter im besonderen, so allgemein. Es wird zu einem den vielen Schnörkeln gleichgeordneten Zierat, während es früher, im Barock, ein Schmuckzentrum bildete und gleichsam der ornamentale Punkt der Gitterfläche war. Die typische Form der barocken Krone wird zu naturalistischem Muschelwerk aufgelöst." Kracauer, *Entwicklung der Schmiedekunst*, 54. See the "ornamentation of the surface" on 74.

30. Ibid., 74. Also see Margaret Iversen, *Alois Riegl: Art History and Theory* (Cambridge: MIT Press, 1993), particularly "The Aesthetics of Disintegration" and "The Articulation of Ornament."

31. See Schwartz, *Blind Spots.*

32. On Bloch, see Hilde Heynen, *Architecture and Modernity: A Critique* (Cambridge: MIT Press, 1999), chapter 3; on Kracauer, see Schwartz, "Form Follows Fetish," 65, n. 80.

33. Kracauer, "Das neue Bauen. Zur Stuttgarter Werkbund-Ausstellung: 'Die Wohnung,'" *Frankfurter Zeitung*, 31 July 1927, Jg. 72, Nr. 561, 2; also see Ward, *Weimar Surfaces;* and Daniele Pisani, "Kracauer sul Weissenhof Stoccarda 1927," *Casabella* 67, no. 713 (July–August 2003): 48–59.

34. Kracauer, "Das neue Bauen."

35. See Ludwig Mies van der Rohe's opening statement in *Bau und Wohnung* (Stuttgart: Wedekind, 1927).

36. John Ashbery, "Self-Portrait in a Convex Mirror," *Self Portrait in a Convex Mirror and other Poems* (New York: Viking Press, 1975).

"Dioramas of a New World"

Siegfried Kracauer and Weimar Exhibition Culture

Kerstin Barndt

Siegfried Kracauer is well known to us as a film historian, as a theorist of visual and mass culture, and as a literary author in his own right. But alongside film, photography, and literature, Kracauer fine-tuned his cultural philosophy by attending to exhibition as a medium that profoundly shaped Weimar modernity. Kracauer's lesser-known writings on trade shows, building expositions, and contemporary design invite us to revisit key tropes of his cultural theory such as waiting, ornamentation, or spatial images (*Raumbilder*) that gesture beyond the constraints of the interwar present. While conceptually linked to other intellectual projects that occupied Kracauer in the 1920s—the theorization of film, photography and mass culture, or the writing of "modernist miniatures,"[1]—his exhibition reviews also depart from these writings as they consistently stress the *enlightening* prospects of this particular mass medium.

In a recent article on Kracauer's city miniatures, Andreas Huyssen notes how these texts expose agoraphobia, a fear of empty spaces, and recognize "the disciplining power of a rationalist and abstract regime of visuality that denies agency to the human body as subject of sensual perception."[2] In contrast to, and alongside, this ideology critique, his writings about interwar exhibition culture celebrate the staging of alternative and more livable worlds. The spatial and theatrical aspects of exhibition, Kracauer suggests, hold open the possibility to cut through the "abstract regimes of visuality" and to empower the audience through a form of visual pedagogy. In the displays of futuristic housing models Kracauer detected a more open and democratic society, and he was intrigued by elaborate city models that rendered visible the hidden infrastructure of urban life. None of this, however, meant giving up on the critique of modernism, and Kracauer did not approach Weimar exhibition culture only affirmatively. Pointing out the "dreamy" side of particular Werkbund objects and the elusive ghosts inhabiting the glass architecture of Mies van der Rohe, Kracauer also read the sober surfaces of contemporary display culture as negations: not as full-fledged new, modern forms but as lack; not for what they were in the present but for what they recalled from the past and for what they pointed to in the future.

As a journalist working for the *Frankfurter Zeitung*, Kracauer reviewed local exhibitions as early as 1921. One of his first reviews concerned a memorial show for Ferdinand Luthmer, an architect and former director of Frankfurt's Museum for Arts and Crafts who had recently died. Kracauer celebrates Luthmer as a master of his field whose "indomitable creativity"[3] resulted in an impressive oeuvre ranging from silver metal art to architectural drawings of French, Italian, and German buildings and their ornaments. Searching for works by Luthmer that may "meet our contemporary artistic sensibilities," however, he finds only very few; Kracauer is impressed by the depth and breadth of Luthmer's encyclopedic erudition but considers him representative of a bygone era. Some forty years later, having devoted his attention to exhibitions as a cultural form throughout his time in Germany and into exile in France and the United States, Kracauer would pen his last museum notes after a visit to Henri Langlois's collection of visual technology and film memorabilia, exhibited in Paris's *Cinemathèque*. Kracauer visited Paris in 1960, and Langlois himself guided him through his show. In his notes, Kracauer dwells on the historicity of pre-cinema devices such as the zootrope or praxinoscope, leading up to Lumière's camera: "In looking at these nineteenth century products, it is as if one watched the secret life of this marvelous century which still harbors so many secrets—as if, for the first time, one caught a glimpse of its *entrailles*."[4]

In both his first and his last notes, Kracauer records his thoughts on shows devoted to memory—to a past life and the subterranean (pre)history of a young medium, respectively. Both cases, in other words, conjure up an idea of the museum as linked to rituals of mourning, dream, and death (as Adorno reminds us, museum and mausoleum are connected by more than phonetic association).[5] The main body of Kracauer's exhibition reviews, by contrast, emphasizes a temporality perhaps best characterized as "present future" or "future made present."[6] Quite in distinction from the nostalgia for the nineteenth century that we find in Kracauer's praise of Langlois's eclectic collection, he adopts an antinostalgic stance in the majority of his reviews. Hints at the importance of loss and the integration of processes of mourning into a forward-moving temporality, however, remain.

Throughout his Weimar years, Kracauer would travel to various exhibitions, trade shows, *Bauausstellungen* (building expositions), and finally the Paris World's Fair in 1937, in search of cultural practices that might open up new horizons of expectation.[7] In characteristic fashion, he would find the leads toward these new horizons in even the seemingly minute details of a given exhibit's design. On the occasion of the *Sun, Air, and House* Berlin trade exposition in 1932, for instance, Kracauer reflects upon the power of exhibition to provide "dioramas of a new world" (*Guckkastenbilder einer neuen Welt*).[8] Full-scale garden sheds, workbenches that allow visitors to experiment with woodcarving, and grazing antelopes between airplanes and locomotives may have realized the show's commercial "propaganda for the weekend,"[9] but to Kracauer, these displays also inherited the wondrous quality of the Renaissance curiosity cabinet. While thoroughly anchored in the commercial present of the trade show, some tableaus of the exhibit, he claimed, succeeded in allegorically suspending "space and time,"[10] thereby transcending the here and now and gesturing toward deep-seated yet unrealized collective longings.

Kracauer's view of exhibitions as utopian enterprises echoed Walter Benjamin's reflections on museums as "dream houses of the collective"— spaces that recruit the most advanced scientific research and display techniques, but whose specific spatial utopianism at times also betrays the "dreamy side of bad taste."[11] Benjamin derived this evocative constellation between museum, dream, and kitsch from his reading of surrealism: its aesthetic strategies, Benjamin claimed, amounted to an interrogation of the "outlived world of things." Left over from the long nineteenth century, they still structured the "interior" of contemporary humanity—its psyche—at the time of Benjamin's writing.[12]

Sharing Benjamin's understanding of surrealism, Kracauer also approached the mundane but nevertheless utopian objects on display in contemporary museums and fairs with a surrealist sensibility, thereby stressing the *unconscious* transformative power of particular modes of display. At the same time as Kracauer stressed the pedagogical potential of exhibition as form, his subtle readings also cautioned against an uncritical embrace of the new modern forms of Bauhaus and Werkbund: the future had not yet arrived, and the present persistence of the past had to be reckoned with. It was the hybrid nature of exhibition culture that fascinated both Benjamin and Kracauer: its constant temporal fluctuation between radical pasts and futures. Without downplaying the connection between the fair, exhibition culture, and the marketplace, both authors were inspired by the medium's cultural productivity as it provided a space to mediate between advanced techniques of display, long-lived vernacular fair (and object) traditions, and present-day avant-garde practices.

These interests came to a head for Kracauer as early as 1922, when he reported for the *Frankfurter Zeitung* from the first postwar German trade show in Munich (see Fig. 1). In his essays from Munich, he stressed the national importance of a fair that might decide over *"our* position in the world."[13] Kracauer approvingly summarized the commercial success of the trade show that drew more than three million visitors from within Germany and abroad. Inflation had quadrupled the price of a simple *Kleinhaus* (small home) on display from 600,000 Marks at the beginning of the exhibition to 2.5 million Marks six months later. And yet, three-quarters of all sales went to Germans. According to Kracauer, these numbers amounted to a resounding success story evidencing the "unbowed will to life of the German people."[14]

Besides such patriotic fervor, Kracauer's reports also exhibit a keen eye for the specific aesthetic quality of the show. He notes the playful appropriation of expressionistic color charts in the interior design of the show. Toys, for example, were framed by saturated colors and surrounded by a life-sized wall panorama of a fairground.[15] The room for *Packungen* (packaging), on the other hand was painted in pink, grey, and gold. On the wall, visitors would encounter poster art ironically mimicking the very advertisement strategies that were on display in the room. Designers of the book exhibit, by contrast, used bright lighting to draw attention to the sober display of the latest publications and book art. Kracauer's commentary consistently links these aesthetic observations to their pragmatic functions, culture to commerce. According to Kracauer, the artistic frame of each individual room—including its ironic commentary—lent expression to the "spirit of the goods [*Waren*]."[16] In Kracauer's early postwar thinking, industrial production and trade are essential factors to secure the success of the young and war-torn republic. In his review of the Berlin Trade Exhibition in 1896, Kracauer's teacher Georg Simmel had described the aesthetization of the modern commodity form as highlighting the "shop window quality of things"—an idea that Walter Benjamin would further explore in his *Arcades Project*, where he coined the often-cited phrase that "world exhibitions are places of pilgrimage to the commodity fetish."[17] Short of offering a dialectical critique of capitalism in the spirit of Benjamin's later

Fig. 1. *Deutsche Gewerbe Ausstellung*, poster, Munich, 1922. Courtesy of
Bayerisches Wirtschaftsarchiv.

writings, Kracauer in his early Weimar essays appears to be interested foremost in the restorative power of good contemporary design—which, for
him, meant an approach to design that took the break with Wilhelmine
culture into account. In line with the German *Werkbund*, he asked of the
applied arts that they aim for the "essence" of things, that they avoid os-
tentatiousness, and retreat into life's background.[18] For Kracauer, the Munich trade show, then, represented an important step in overcoming the
postwar Depression by confidently displaying industrial wares, arts, and
crafts; at the same time, it offered an opportunity to aesthetically educate
the younger generation through the encounter with exemplary goods of
everyday life.[19]

The optimistic tone of this review, and Kracauer's clear identification
with efforts at reconstruction, would soon be supplanted by more distanced
and cautious appraisals. When in subsequent exhibition reviews Kracauer
explored ideas of form and aesthetic perception, his writings adopted the
soberly ironic tone (interspersed with occasional passages full of pathos)
characteristic of his better-known cultural criticism of the period. In 1924,
he visited the first Frankfurt fair after monetary stabilization as well as

Stuttgart's *Kunstsommer* and *Bauausstellung* (building exposition). Enthused by the festive atmosphere of the Stuttgart fairgrounds within and around the old train station (embellished by a miniature copy of the Eiffel Tower), Kracauer comments on the fair's characteristic blending of "pleasure and sobriety": "Sites of entertainment reconcile visitors with the seriousness of living, if they don't seduce them to the latter. A dance hall acts more glamorous than by rights it should, and the restaurant does not only serve food but also provides the opportunity to study how to build with wood.[20]

Still overshadowed by inflation and economic crisis, the exhibition gave consumers and citizens practical advice on ways to economize in their everyday lives. Model housing for Bosch workers, designed by Martin Wagner, for instance, proposed an open floor plan and counted on the practical building skills of each inhabitant to finish the building according to individual needs. The necessity for better and more housing also became apparent in an exhibit on the reconstruction and expansion plans of numerous German cities. Kracauer applauded the citizens of Württemberg for their careful reconstruction programs that aimed to protect the "unity of the city structure" with a commitment to "protection of local patrimony and monument preservation [*Heimatschutz und Denkmalpflege*]." On the other hand, Kracauer deemed Ulm's plan to erect *new* buildings in historicist, neo-Romantic style "suicidal": "If we have to build at all, then we should rather use ferroconcrete than [construct] this withered soul kitsch."[21] Confronted with a wide plurality of housing programs and styles, including the "excess of ornamental arts [*Schnörkelkunst*]" in the *Haus des Handwerks*, Kracauer sides with the proponents of *Neues Bauen* and functional, industrial design. It is therefore not surprising that the author spent the second part of his long Stuttgart review exclusively on the Werkbund exhibit *The Form*, the first major postwar show of objects of everyday life that adhered to the sober aesthetic standards of the Werkbund (see Fig. 2). Organized independently from the *Bauaustellung*, this exhibit was on view in downtown Stuttgart. It was linked to the larger event through institutions such as the Weimar Bauhaus, which exhibited at both venues.

But Kracauer would qualify even his praise for Werkbund aesthetics by pointing to the latter's inability to offer constructive alternatives to the defunct design of the Wilhelmine era. In his critique of the Werkbund's attempt to define contemporary design standards through "pure negation" (*bloße Negation*)—that is, by insisting on the absence of ornamentation—Kracauer gestures toward the limits of the aesthetics of sobriety. He thus takes issue with the very foundations on which this first Werkbund travel-

Fig. 2. Richard Herre, *Die Form* (The Form), Werkbund Exhibition, poster, July 1924. Courtesy of Staatsgalerie Stuttgart.

ing exhibit rests: for the Werkbund, form is defined as "that which has no ornamentation"; it offers an aesthetic, in other words, that "sees form where there is no ornament."[22] While recognizing the place of asceticism and restraint as adequate to the economic "bottleneck" and the ongoing "constraints of contemporary reality," he questions whether pure abstinence from artistic ornamentation is itself enough of an artistic statement to transcend the metaphysical emptiness of contemporary life. "Is the retreat into pure sobriety already its redemption," Kracauer asks skeptically, "is the avoidance of insincere extras anything more than the honest confession about what is lacking?"[23]

To readers of the essays Kracauer would later collect in *The Mass Ornament*, this line of thinking will resonate with motifs developed in an earlier programmatic essay entitled "Those Who Wait." However, in contrast to the false retreat from "transcendental homelessness" into a new spirituality, which that essay critiques, Kracauer sees in the negative aesthetics of the Werkbund a positive *transitional* art of everyday objects. Werkbund artifacts function as placeholders, in tune with the open-minded state of waiting for an overcoming of negativity and alienation. "The art that designs the consumer good—and perhaps not just that—should today be compared to a ship that waits in quarantine, and the retreat to form demanded of this art only signifies a period of waiting of the kind that also befits those who stand in the negative at other sites. Whether their muteness will find a future release depends on the turn from real life to reality [*Wirklichkeit*]."[24]

According to Kracauer, the "fearless nihilism" embodied by the functional and starkly rectilinear forms of a Bauhaus chair on display might lead the way here as it already "aims towards the truth."[25] Other objects that Kracauer likewise singles out circumvent the present metaphysical void in more poetic ways than the technical ingenuity of the Bauhaus. Touched by the melancholy of lamps designed by Viennese architect Ernst Lichtblau, Kracauer praises the eccentric liberties through which Lichtblau imbues Werkbund aesthetics with individuality: "The subtle lamp speaks of loneliness and reminds one of a doodle by Klee, and the eccentric elegance of a floor lamp composed of bamboo, silk, metal bars, and straw, resembles the helpless sadness of a gallows song by Morgenstern."[26]

Three years after submitting these reviews, Kracauer returned to Stuttgart to comment on the 1927 Werkbund exhibit "The Dwelling" (*Die Wohnung*). Best known for the Weißenhof settlement, a group of model public-housing units built for the occasion by the international architectural avant-garde, this Werkbund event also included a photography show of new buildings from Europe and the United States, and an exhibit of industrially produced appliances, consumer goods, and design elements intended to furnish a room according to its function. Kracauer praised all of these parts as extraordinary shows but focused more extensively on the latter, with its displays of water faucets, built-in kitchens, dinner- and glassware, linoleum, curtains, wallpaper, and furniture.[27] He noted that in distinction to the earlier show *The Form*, the objects of *The Dwelling* were not unique exhibition copies but rather functional design already in the process of industrial production. As the ranks between the German Werkbund Association and the Bauhaus became more entangled, so did the connection between industry and contemporary interior design grow. Mies, who together with Lilly Reich had spearheaded the realization of *The Dwelling*, had advanced to the second executorship of the Werkbund Association in 1926 and would also assume the directorship of Dessau's Bauhaus in 1930. Pushing modern architecture itself onto the stage of public display, Mies's most remarkable Weimar exhibition projects include the master plan for the Weißenhof settlement as well as the overall conception of *The Dwelling* in Stuttgart, the German Pavilion at the 1929 World's Fair in Barcelona, and the exhibit of model houses in *The Dwelling of Our Time* under the aegis of the German Building Exhibit in Berlin 1931, an event on which Kracauer would also comment.[28]

Kracauer followed Mies's lead as expressed in his opening remarks to *The Dwelling* and searched for the "new ways of life" inherent in the architectural and material displays.[29] Tongue in cheek, his review describes the new building style's dynamization of all stabile elements and the subsequent dissolution of a central perspective as a suitable environment for "savvy little water faucets" and inhabitants dressed in sports gear (see Figs. 3 and 4).[30] In the *Hausgeräte* exhibit, he observes, Lilly Reich's interior exhibition architecture fosters an open, light, and airy floor plan. Underscoring the new proximity between modern design and industry, Reich removed the borders between individual exhibitors. At times, Reich's spatial choreography of building materials evoked a modernist gallery space as in the case of the linoleum hall where large pieces of material in varying shades covered the walls and pedestals.[31] As Kracauer shows in his essay "The Mass Ornament," published during the same year, the excess of ornamentation, successfully suppressed in the realm of contemporary interior and exterior design, reemerges in Weimar's entertainment industry. There, Kracauer reads the orchestrated movements of the Tiller Girls allegorically as a modern-day mass ornament that adequately expresses the rationalization of everyday life; in his essay on *The Dwelling*, he employs the same reading strategy. Congruent with the ambiguity of the mass ornament that anthropomorphizes alienated technical rationality but also conveys, according to Miriam Hansen, the possibility of critical self-recognition for the mass audience, Kracauer reads the breaking-down of architectural partitions on two allegorical levels: even as this shift expresses the

Figs. 3, 4. *The Dwelling of Our Time*, German Building Exhibit, Berlin, 1931, Mies van der Rohe and Lilly Reich, exhibition design and architecture. Courtesy of VG Wort und Kunst.

anonymity of being under capitalism, it functions as the semiotic harbinger of a not-yet-determined (new) structure of society.[32] In keeping with his philosophical turn to Marxism during the later years of the Weimar Republic, Kracauer's writing had shifted from the epistemology of "waiting" to the horizon of a new humanism.

In his final praise of the show's extraordinary Plate-Glass Hall, however, the epistemology of waiting and an echo of his earlier reviews find their way back into his prose. Where partitions still stand in the exhibition hall as in the Plate-Glass Hall, they are made transparent, reflecting objects, lights, and movements "like a kaleidoscope." Struck by the special, ghostlike effects of this installation, Kracauer reverts to his critical stance vis-à-vis the Bauhaus aesthetic of sobriety. By showing nothing but reflections, the installation's *"gläserne Spuk"* (transparent spook) foregrounds what is missing in contemporary material culture: Mies's transparent architecture and Reich's bare-bones interior design exemplify for Kracauer a transitional, functional break with the past, a break defined by the repudiation of anachronistic ornamentation. But the luminous, immaterial shadows on the glass walls speak to a "burlesque grief" over the renunciation required for these ascetic performances. This melancholic reading of *Neues Bauen*, however, remains firmly grounded within the progressive crisis discourses of the time, anchored as they were in temporalities of becoming rather than impending doom: "For these housing skeletons are not an end in themselves, but the necessary bridge to a fullness that will no longer require any concessions, and which today can only be manifested negatively through mourning. They can only be fleshed out once man ascends from the glass."[33] Thus Kracauer ends his review with a call for a "new man" that takes the transparency of modernist glass architecture only as a point of departure into a future humanism.

Thinking through the effects of the Plate-Glass Hall and the show *The Dwelling* more generally, Kracauer stresses the possibility of social self-recognition inherent in the choreographed spaces of the exhibition. With this critical conception of the medium, Kracauer echoes reflections on the history of exhibition culture by his contemporary, the influential architectural critic and historian Sigfried Giedion. Giedion points to the semantics of the French word *exposition* and its association with "survey, juxtaposition, comparison, indeed presentation of our doctrine."[34] He emphasizes the medium's tradition of popular enlightenment (*Volksaufklärung*), most evident in the exhibitions at world's fairs, which aims at disseminating knowledge and pushing the envelope of exhibition methods by drawing on the popular pleasures of the fairground. Walter Benjamin, too, would draw heavily on this understanding of the medium in his own theorization of exhibition culture; Kracauer already gestures toward a similar concept of exhibition as a progressive mass medium in his writings of the 1920s and early 1930s. Discussing the vast array of shows and model housing on view in Berlin during the German Building Exhibit of 1931, Kracauer foregrounds the practical value of the event, its demonstrative *Nutzwert*. A model of the underground structure of Berlin's new Alexanderplatz or a vertical cut through a house, which exposes all intricacies of its installations and wiring, Kracauer claims, functions in terms of an instructive show (*Lehrschau*) that appeals to the specialist as well as to the layman "without succumbing to false popularity."[35] In a similar vein, Kracauer points the interested lay public to the exhibition hall designed by Mies and Reich, where an assembly of modern housing models is "choreographed without force as if it were a picnic."[36]

Like his contemporaries Giedion and Benjamin, Kracauer underlines the epistemological promise implicit in the very fabric of exhibition as a medium: a self-reflexive form relying on advanced illustration methods that evoke, map, and order the complexities of modern life, exhibitions further knowledge about society, modernity, and subjectivity. It is with this model in mind that Kracauer visits the Paris World's Fair in 1937, the year in which his biography of Jacques Offenbach was published. In his reviews from the fair for the Swiss architecture journal *Das Werk*, he neither comments on the monstrosity of the fair's architecture of power, the signature buildings of Speer's Nazi pavilion vis-à-vis the Soviet pavilion, nor does he mention Lilly Reich's exhibition design for National Socialist Germany in the international exhibit.[37] Instead, he focuses on politically more neutral shows such as the science exhibit in the *Palais de la Découverte* and an exposition of French literary classics. For Kracauer, the cabinets that illustrate mathematical maxims and chemical and physical laws by way of interactive models and life experiments trump any popular fair and its "showbooth-attractions."[38] The "white magic" of the show seduces its audience into knowledge and enlists future scientists in the process. The exhibit on French literature, in turn, captures Kracauer's attention for the ways in which it situates literature in its social contexts and addresses a readership beyond the cultural elite. In providing biographical details, images, and historical contexts, the displays on Flaubert's *Education Sentimentale*, for example, spatialize the text and lend immediacy to the writing process: "It is as though the novel acquires a body and leans forward so far that the viewer can immediately grasp a being to which otherwise only genuine readers have access."[39] Through its visual pedagogy, by embedding the artwork within the sociohistorical context from which it derives, the exhibition brings the literary classic back to life. If exhibitions are able to summon an as-yet-unfulfilled future, they are also able to bring past "intellectual works" (*Werke des Geistes*) back into the present.[40]

For all their temporal implications, Kracauer's writings on exhibition give a powerful sense of the medium's particular spatiality, and one is tempted to group them under Kracauer's own notion of *Raumbild*, or spatial image, which recurs throughout these reviews. In retrospect, connections between Kracauer's stance here and his own work on the Offenbach project become clear. Adorno, among others, had criticized the latter for its lack of aesthetic analysis, but as a "social biography," *Offenbach and the Paris of His Time* is rich in historical context.[41] Looking back on the development of his writings on exhibition during the 1930s, we may now read the choices Kracauer made in the Offenbach book as a principled aesthetic decision. There, Kracauer had emulated in his writing the specific *Raumbilder* from which Offenbach's oeuvre drew its inspiration—most obviously the operettas' mise-en-scène, the spaces of the theater, and the cityscapes of Paris; reading the book in light of his theorization of exhibition shows how Kracauer consciously emulated certain techniques of spatial visualization to *exhibit* Offenbach's life for a broad readership.

Kracauer himself, of course, preferred to think of his Offenbach book in cinematic terms as he turned his attention to his book on film aesthetics during the last years of his French exile.[42] The notion of *Raumbild*, however, is as central to Kracauer's thinking about the medium of exhibition as it is to his theory on film perception. Like film, exhibition "makes spaces available to sensuous experience."[43] Attending to Kracauer as a "reader of spaces," Esther Leslie shows the versatility of the concept of *Raumbild* for Kracauer's writing as it moves from the description of Berlin's built environment, its streets, office buildings, and pedestrian underpasses to the spaces of the movie palaces and film itself. If we grant the importance of spatial images for Kracauer's epistemology we should no longer exclude his deep engagement with the exhibition culture of his time as part of this project. Throughout the interwar period, Kracauer's reading of exhibition culture shifts from the aesthetic of the singular Werkbund object toward a more expansive view of exhibition as a social mass medium suited, in its most successful manifestations, to advancing knowledge and expanding the sense of futurity.

NOTES

1. See Miriam Bratu Hansen, introduction to *Theory of Film: The Redemption of Physical Reality*, by Siegfried Kracauer (Princeton: Princeton University Press, 1997), vii–xlv; Andreas Huyssen, "Modernist Miniatures: Literary Snapshots of Urban Spaces," *PMLA* 122, no. 1 (2007): 27–42; Inka Mülder-Bach, introduction to *The Salaried Masses: Duty and Distraction in Weimar Germany*, by Siegfried Kracauer, trans. Quintin Hoare (London: Verso, 1998), 1–22.

2. Huyssen, "Modernist Miniatures," 35. See also Huyssen's contribution to this volume.

3. Siegfried Kracauer, "Frankfurter Angelegenheiten. Gedächtnisausstellung Ferdinand Luthmer im Kunstgewerbemuseum," *Frankfurter Zeitung* (hereafter *FZ*), 6 February 1921. If not otherwise noted, all translations are my own.

4. Siegfried Kracauer, "Reisenotizen 1960. Ideas: About the Museum of Cinematèque, shown us by Langlois & Lotti, Oct. 3," Kracauer Papers, Deutsches Literaturarchiv Marbach.

5. Theodor Adorno, "Valéry Proust Museum," in *Prisms*, trans. Samuel Weber and Sherry Weber (Cambridge: MIT Press, 1996), 175–85.

6. I am here extending Reinhart Koselleck's suggestive metaphor of "futures past" and the exploration of "present pasts" in contemporary memory cultures by Andreas Huyssen. See Reinhart Koselleck, *Futures Past: On the Semantics of Historical Time*, trans. and intro. by Keith Tribe (New York: Columbia University Press, 2004); and Andreas Huyssen, *Present Pasts: Urban Palimpsests and the Politics of Memory* (Stanford: Stanford University Press, 2003). For a more exhaustive reading of Koselleck and Huyssen with respect to contemporary exhibition culture, see my article "Layers of Time: Industrial Ruins and Exhibitionary Temporalities," *PMLA* 125, no. 1 (January 2010): 134–41.

7. The term *horizon of expectation* is drawn from Koselleck's writings where it functions (in tandem with *space of experience*) as a metahistorical category. While space of experience provides a link to a known but continuously shrinking present past, the horizon of expectation calls on an unknown, ever-expanding future. Koselleck, *Futures Past*, 159–62.

8. Siegfried Kracauer, "Guckkasten-Bilder. Besuch einer Wochenend-Ausstellung," *Frankfurter Zeitung*, 8 June 1932. Reprint in *Aufsätze 1927–1931*, vol 5.2 of Siegfried Kracauer, *Schriften*, ed. Inka Mülder-Bach (Frankfurt am Main: Suhrkamp, 1990), 79–81.

9. Ibid., 80.

10. Ibid., 81.

11. Walter Benjamin, *The Arcades Project*, trans. Howard Eiland and Kevin McLaughlin, (Cambridge: Belknap Press of Harvard University Press, 1999), L1a, 2. On the relation between "dream" and "kitsch" (i.e., "bad taste") in Benjamin's writings, see Brigid Doherty, "Learning Things," in *Companion Manifesta 7: The European Biennial of Contemporary Art*, ed. Rana Dascupta, Nina Montmann, and Avi Pitchon (Trentino: Silvana Editoriale, 2008), 239–55.

12. Walter Benjamin, "Dream Kitsch," in *1927–1934*, vol. 2.1 of *Selected Writ-*

ings, ed. Michael Jennings, Howard Eiland, and Gary Smith, trans. Howard Eiland (Cambridge: Harvard University Press, 2005), 3–4.

13. Siegfried Kracauer, "Frankfurter Angelegenheiten. Deutsche Gewerbeschau 1922," *FZ* 31 May 1922, my emphasis and translation if not otherwise noted. Kracauer traveled to Munich before the opening of the show and reported regularly during the four months of its opening. Cf. Kracauer's reviews of the event for the *FZ* dated 16 May, 21 May, 25 May, 4 June, and 8 October 1922.

14. Siegfried Kracauer, "Die Deutsche Gewerbeschau. Schlussbetrachtungen," *FZ*, 8 October 1922.

15. Siegfried Kracauer, "Die Deutsche Gewerbeschau," *FZ*, 25 May 1922.

16. Ibid. In translating the German *Ware* with the neutral good and not with commodity, I emphasize Kracauer's own focus on the awakening of the "spiritual power" of industrial design through the medium of exhibition.

17. Georg Simmel, "The Berlin Trade Show," *Theory, Culture, Society* 8 (1991): 119–23, here 122. Walter Benjamin, *The Arcades Project*, 7.

18. Siegfried Kracauer, "Kunstgewerbe und Handwerk. Begleitgedanken zur Deutschen Gewerbeschau," *FZ*, 4 June 1922. While Kracauer contemplates the loss of metaphysical and religious certainty (in the arts and the realm of society), the trade show provides plenty of evidence for "skeptical optimism" and "trust in the future."

19. "Vergnügungsstätten söhnen mit dem Ernst des Wohnens aus oder verführen zu ihm; eine Tanzdiele geberdet [*sic!*] sich mondäner als ihr zukommt, und in dem Restaurant kann man nicht nur essen, sondern auch die Holzbauweise erforschen." Ibid.

20. Siegfried Kracauer, "Stuttgarter Kunst-Sommer" *FZ*, 10 July 1924. Partly reproduced in *Aufsätze, 1915–1926*, vol 5.1 of *Siegfried Kracauer: Schriften*, ed. Inka Mülder-Bach (Frankfurt am Main: Suhrkamp, 1990), 262–67. When possible, the page number of the reprint is given in parenthesis.

21. "Wenn schon gebaut werden muß, dann lieber Eisenbeton als dieser verblühte Seelenkitsch." Ibid.

22. *Form ohne Ornament*, introduction by W. Pfleiderer, preface by W. Riezler (Stuttgart: Deutsche Verlags-Anstalt, 1925), 5.

23. "Ist der Rückgang zur puren Sachlichkeit schon ihre Rettung, ist Meidung erlogener Zutat mehr als das ehrliche Eingeständnis dessen, was fehlt?" Kracauer, "Stuttgarter Kunst-Sommer," *FZ*, 10 July 1924, 263, 265.

24. "Die Kunst, die das Gebrauchsding gestaltet—und nicht nur sie vielleicht—, darf heute einem Schiff verglichen werden, das in Quarantäne liegt, und der ihr geheißene Rückzug auf die Form hat lediglich die Bedeutung des Wartens, das auch an anderen Orten den im Negativen Stehenden vorläufig ziemt. An die Wendung des realen Lebens zur Wirklichkeit ist geknüpft, ob ihre Stummheit dereinst sich löse." Ibid., 266–67. Levin and Hansen discuss Kracauer's metaphysics in relation to modern, secular Jewish messianism and neo-Kantianism; see Levin, 18–23, and Hansen, 52. Ibid.

25. Ibid., 266.

26. "Einsamkeit spricht aus dem subtilen Leuchter, der an ein Gekritzel von

Klee gemahnt, und die verschrullte Eleganz einer Stehlampe, die sich aus Bambus, Seide, Metallstäben und Stroh zusammensetzt, kommt an hilfloser Traurigkeit einem Galgenlied Morgensterns gleich." Ibid., 267. For Lichtblau's contribution to Viennese modernism and public housing, see *Ernst Lichtblau. Architect 1883–1963*, ed. August Sarnitz (Vienna: Böhlau, 1994).

27. See Claire Zimmerman's contribution to this volume for a more extensive reading of Kracauer's writings pertaining to the *Weissenhofsiedlung*.

28. See Wallis Miller, "Mies and Exhibitions," ed. Terence Riley and Barry Bergdoll, in *Mies in Berlin* (New York: Museum of Modern Art, 2001), 338–49.

29. Siegfried Kracauer, "Das neue Bauen. Zur Stuttgarter Werkbund-Ausstellung: *Die Wohnung*," *FZ*, 31 July 1927. Fully reproduced in *Aufsätze, 1927–1931*, 68–74. A few days earlier, Kracauer had already briefly reported from the opening of the exhibition. Kracauer, "Werkbundausstellung: *Die Wohnung*. Die Eröffnung," *FZ*, 24 July 1927. See also Kracauer, "Werkbundausstellung *Die Wohnung*," *FZ*, 23 July 1927.

30. Ibid.

31. Lilly Reich, who also designed the exhibit *The Form*, has evolved as the most important Werkbund exhibition designer of the Weimar Republic. See Matilda McQuaid, *Lilly Reich: Designer and Architect* (New York: Museum of Modern Art, 1996), and Esther da Costa Meyer, "Cruel Metonomies: Lilly Reich's Design for the 1937 World's Fair," *New German Critique*, no. 76 (Winter 1999): 161–89.

32. Kracauer, "Das neue Bauen," 73.

33. "Denn die Hausgerippe sind sich nicht Selbstzweck, sondern der notwendige Durchgang zu einer Fülle, die keiner Abzüge mehr bedarf und heute nur negativ durch die Trauer bezeugt werden kann. Sie werden erst Fleisch ansetzen, wenn der Mensch aus dem Glas steigt." Ibid., 74. Commenting on the nonauratic quality of glass architecture in 1933, Benjamin challenged Kracauer's redemptive reading of modernist glass architecture. Embracing the negativity of glass as a material that leaves no trace, he envisioned glass as a medium of camouflage (Benjamin himself used the term *survival*) congruent with times of renunciation and danger. See Benjamin, "Experience and Poverty," in *1927–1934*, vol. 2 of *Selected Writings*, ed. Michael Jennings, trans. Rodney Livingstone (Cambridge: Harvard University Press 1933), 732–34.

34. Sigfried Giedion, cited in Gottfried Korff, "Exhibitions as Constructed Mnemonic Worlds," *Hans Dieter Schaal In-Between. Exhibition Architecture. Ausstellungsarchitektur*, ed. by Frank R. Werner (Stuttgart: Edition Axel Menges 1999), 6–11; here 8.

35. Kracauer, "Deutsche Bauausstellung. Vorläufige Bemerkungen," *FZ* Jg. 75, Nr. 348, 12 May 1931.

36. Ibid. See also Kracauer, "Kleine Patrouille durch die Bauausstellung," *FZ* Jg. 75, Nr. 415, 6 June 1931; and Kracauer, "Bauausstellung im Osten," *FZ* Jg. 75, Nr. 457, 22 June 1931. Produced by a group of socialist architects, this antishow to the main building exhibit exposed the housing dilemma from a distinct working-class standpoint. Kracauer sympathetically described the congenial spatial setting

of the exhibit in an abandoned button factory but critiqued the show's polemical political dogma, which framed the presented material in a way that discouraged open dialogue.

37. On Reich's engagement at the World's Fair, see da Costa Meyer, "Cruel Metonomies," 185–87.

38. Siegfried Kracauer, "Kosmos der Wissenschaften—Konglomerat der Künste," *Das Werk*, 25, no. 1 (January 1938): 21–24; Kracauer, "Ein neuer Typus von Ausstellungen," *Das Werk* 25, no. 1 (January 1938): 19–21.

39. "Es ist, als nähme der Roman Körper an und neige sich so weit vor, dass sich der Beschauer unmittelbar von einem Dasein überzeugen kann, das sich sonst nur dem echten Leser erschliesst." Kracauer, "Ein neuer Typus von Ausstellungen," 20.

40. Ibid.

41. Theodor W. Adorno, [Rezension zu Siegfried Kracauer, Jacques Offenbach und das Paris seiner Zeit, Amsterdam 1937], *Zeitschrift für Sozialforschung* 6 (1937): 697–98; on the reception of Kracauer's *Jacques Offenbach* more generally, see Ingrid Belke, "Nachbemerkung und editorische Notiz," in Siegfried Kracauer, *Jacques Offenbach und das Paris seiner Zeit*, vol. 8 of *Werke*, ed. Inka Mülder-Bach and Ingrid Belke (Frankfurt am Main: Suhrkamp, 2005), 537–49.

42. See Graeme Gilloch, "Orpheus in Hollywood. Siegfried Kracauer's Offenbach Film," in *Tracing Modernity: Manifestations of the Modern in Architecture and the City*, ed. Marie Hvattum and Christian Hermansen (New York: Routledge, 2004), 307–24.

43. Esther Leslie, "Kracauer's Weimar Geometry and Geomancy," *New Formations* 61 (Summer 2007): 45.

Kracauer and Sound

Reading with an Anxious Ear

Theodore F. Rippey

If the texts grounded in the perceptual labor of Kracauer's eye convey his success in reading modern urban surfaces, his ear frequently suggests frustration and failure. To provide initial indications of how one might approach Kracauer with an ear toward sound, I will analyze a selection of texts that ranges from Weimar-era feuilletons to *Theory of Film*. My readings test the hypothesis that greater attention to sound can enhance our understanding of Kracauer's work on interconnected problems of perception, reading, and subjectivity. I follow Kracauer away from the sonic environs of the street, into the enclosure of the archive. There, he can docilize the audible, but the disquieting noise of the interwar metropolis lingers on.

The Street

It is a hot summer night in Berlin, late June perhaps, 1930, and a feuilletonist is out and about in the well-manicured West. A scream pierces the night, and he visually scans the area for its source. In pursuit, he comes upon a drunk, who silently stumbles away. The source of the scream remains undetected. A few nights later comes the next scream, which this time hangs in the air over a young couple who have just resolved a spat. Again he scans; again he finds nothing. A couple of nights after that, yet another scream, only hearing this one, Siegfried Kracauer viscerally knows that it marks a murder. Now he dashes into action with several others who, like him, were meandering along only moments before. They round a corner, expecting to be right on top of the crime, only to encounter other passersby, who regard those grinding to a halt with curiosity: Why rush over, just to watch us stroll?

The riddle of the sourceless scream eats at the stroller, the looker, the writer. The feuilletonist earns his pay with sensory refinement and critical acumen, but these enigmatically sourced sonic signs push his perceptual and analytical capacities to their limit. "Today I suspect that it is not the people in these streets who scream, but the streets themselves," Kracauer writes in "Screams in the Street" (*Schreie auf der Straße*), published 19 July 1930. "When they can no longer bear it, they scream their emptiness. But I don't exactly know."[1]

"Screams in the Street" displays the underconfidence, discomfort, even anxiety of its narrator. The strolling observer confesses his case of nerves at the outset. These West Berlin boulevards, so "friendly and clean," so "proper" in their very width, traffic in a brand of panic that can grip those who travel them without warning. Like that of the screams, the origin of this panic remains unknown. Mob anxiety is one possibility: "Sometimes, when I cross these streets that I am so used to, I am overcome by a fear that a crowd will suddenly form and something bad will happen." Then again, the unease may be more spatially than socially based: "Perhaps this fear springs from the way the streets run on, losing themselves in endlessness." Yet another hypothesis combines and transforms the first two: "Perhaps it is that countless hordes of people move in these streets, always new people with unknown destinations, overlapping like the tangle of lines on a sewing pattern."[2] Here the specter of subsumption in the mass as loss of personal domain links with the threat of lost visual command, intensifying unease about what remains, in the moment, imperceptible—even in familiar environs.

The scream is a stark, sudden, ear-filling sign of the emptiness (*Leere*, in the original) that makes the streets so threatening. The account, which draws on structural conventions of suspense familiar from the crime fiction and popular film Kracauer studied so intently, reaches its climax with the succession of three screams—but the case cannot be cracked, leaving impressions of a visually frustrated observer as recipient of aural shock; a distracted stroller who must suddenly achieve the investigative focus of the detective (a challenge he does not meet); and to take a step back, an eminently sophisticated intellectual, who is so shaken by the materiality of the scream that he can offer no nuanced account of it, even days later.

To consider that encounter as concretely as possible, and to begin describing the difference, for Kracauer, between aural and visual experience, one must consider how sound *touches* us in a way that visual impressions do not. Sounds, as Holger Schulze points out, "*seize* us, and their sonic for-mations leave different relations of tenseness in laxness behind in our bod-ies."[3] We are constantly coated by the sound's principal medium of propa-gation—air—and when sound hits us, our bodies become not only receivers but a further medium as well. Sound strikes us, grips us, and (per-haps) passes through, physically altering us in the process. If the compo-sure to which Kracauer is accustomed requires distance and abstraction, then is it the unavoidable physical contact of sound that stands in the way of analyzing aural experience?

The Headphones and the Loudspeaker

At the risk of jarring, let us move back six years from the screams in the street. It is November 1924, and the feuilletonist is taking stock of the so-cial, technological, and philosophical reasons why it is impossible to achieve boredom in the busy world of the postinflation republic. The radio is a major obstacle: "Because many believe they must broadcast," argues Kracauer, "one finds oneself in a continuous state of reception, pregnant with the signals of London, the Eiffel Tower, and Berlin."[4] In the text, "Boredom" (*Langeweile*), Kracauer provides two concrete images of the impregnated radio listener. The first features headphones: "They gleam in the salons, they entwine themselves around the heads—and instead of en-gaging in cultivated conversation, which would surely bore, one becomes a stomping ground for world-noises which, their objectively boring traits notwithstanding, do not permit one to claim the right of personal bore-dom."[5] The second features loudspeakers, which the modern urbanite seeking solitude in the crowd must confront. "Even in the café," writes Kracauer, "where one would like to curl up like a porcupine and *become aware* of one's own nothingness [*Nichtigkeit*], a loudspeaker of consequence eradicates any trace of private existence."[6] Here, the move away from tightly monitored domestic interiors to less controlled, more fluid urban public realms does not bring the hoped-for freedom of anonymity. The tympanic membranes are set upon by emanations from the membranes of the loudspeaker's cone; the calm, clear nothingness of the personal mi-crodomain (highly desirable, in contradistinction to the emptiness of the streets) becomes unattainable.

In conveying his irritation with these sonic disturbances, Kracauer joins the forces behind the European noise abatement campaigns of the 1910s and early 1920s. In that phase, as reconstructed by Karen Bijsterveld, the paradigmatic model was an elite plea to the "uncivilized" masses to control the noise that was ostensibly making the more refined classes increasingly nervous, thus less able to perform the sophisticated intellectual labor that, in the elite view, was so socially valuable. (In Germany, Theodor Lessing's treatise *Din: A Battle-Call against the Noises of Our Lives* and his organization, the German Association for Protection from Noise, were leading examples.)[7] But even as he complains, Kracauer avoids the "Don't bother me, I'm trying to think" line of argument, making instead a more concretely sensual point. The loudspeaker's emanations do not fray listener nerves, making it difficult to concentrate; rather, they *penetrate* and *occupy*, making both the intellectual and the corporal conditions for concentration a practical impossibility.

"Boredom" exposes roots of the aural anxiety that manifests itself so strongly years later, in "Screams in the Street." In each instance, we find a failure to achieve analytical composure. In the later text, this is a function of the sound's source eluding the hearer's cognitive command. In the earlier text, such command is thwarted preemptively when the cognitive apparatus is overrun: consciousness impregnated, consciousness as stomping ground. In both instances, physical impact inhibits intellectual action. Could it be achieved, the titular state of the 1924 text would negate the logic of the frenetic world the writer inhabits, yielding a mode of inactivity that would be the first condition for a critique of ubiquitous overactivity. Boredom would thus be a matrix in which critical readings of modern culture and society might coalesce, readings of the sort that Kracauer models in the Weimar press. For those sonically encapsulated by headphones or awash in the waves of loudspeaker blare, the impetus to such activity is impossible because the matrix itself does not form. The potentially active reader remains a chronically occupied, passive listener.

Achieving this boredom would be contingent, at a minimum, on a state of equilibrium, in which the subject's sensory system could deflect or channel the streams and bursts of modern sonic stimuli effectively enough to foster contemplation. One is reminded of Benjamin's Baudelaire, mentally and physically parrying the shocks of nineteenth-century Paris; or Buck-Morss's Benjamin, implicitly mapping in the Passagen-Werk a "circuit from sense-perception to motor response [that] begins and ends in the world, a system that passes through the person and her or his environment; . . . an aesthetic system of sense-consciousness, de-centered from the classical subject, wherein external sense-perceptions come together with internal images and anticipation, . . . a *synaesthetic system*."[8] Kracauer's coffee-drinking nothingness seeker is synaesthetically impaired: unable to parry the loudspeaker's sonic shocks, the café customer remains occupied by subject-external forces, closer to sensory overload (and its concomitant *anaesthetic* shutdown) than to Baudelairean aesthetic interactivity between subject and city.

Remaining with the overarching conceptual problem of the subject, we note an intriguing tension in "Boredom" that characterizes much of Kracauer's work in the early to mid-1920s. He writes of the nonbored, "Their self has gone missing [*ihr Selbst ist verschollen*]; were it present, it would force them, especially in this fast-paced world, to pause at no place in particular and linger a long time with no purpose." As used here, the term *self* displays significant comfort with the classical subject, even as Kracauer's *aisthesis materialis*—the investigation of fields of perception that remains tightly connected to concrete experience and conscious of that experience's historical contingency—knocks that subject off balance.[9] This tension, which never fully resolves in Kracauer's work, captures a central dilemma: the critique of the classical subject, taken to its logical extreme, threatens to make the kind of critical autonomy Kracauer strives for a theoretical impossibility.

Kracauer's response to this quandary remains generally implicit, legible to us in the way he constitutes a reading subject position in the discourse of his texts. If he was astute enough to recognize that his mourning of the missing self may actually have been the sensation of loss of something that one never really had, then we might ask how he established, perceptual case by perceptual case, the range of subjectivities between the classical (sovereign, integral) subject envisioned by the Enlightenment and the engulfed mass-atom of interwar Berlin, that is, how acts of reading model the modern self's degrees of composure.

The Mass Ornament and the Self

Between the café of 1924 and the streets of 1930 lies the mass ornament, which Kracauer contours while holding open the possibility of a time, after the demystification of the world, when the I of the Enlightenment might be reimagined and realized. In 1927, he argues the following: "Efforts to reconstruct a form of state, a community, or a mode of artistic expression, to the extent that these presuppose a human being that has come into question in today's thought, a human being that by rights no longer exists—such efforts disregard our place in history, and they cannot hold their own against the mass ornament's baseness."[10] Is this human being another instance of the classical subject, slipping further away (or coming into clearer focus as unrealistic fantasy)? Perhaps the difference between the *Selbst* of 1924 and the *Mensch* of 1927 is the difference between two translations of *verschollen*. In "Boredom," the classical subject is missing; in "The Mass Ornament," it is lost.

This loss, or the emerging realization that there was nothing to lose, is mostly the result of Kracauer's own efforts. In his move away from an integral self and toward a more theoretically rigorous and historically conscious positing of a subject that is at once a mass component and an active processor of image flows and textual surfaces, he pounds any number of nails into the Cartesian subject's coffin. But involved pursuit of the question of whether that subject is viable in his historical moment would be an academic exercise, and the feuilletonist must maintain dialogue with the street. The Kracauer of the republic defers foundational inquiries into the ideal subject in favor of experience-based sketches of the subject not as sovereign individual in a world clarified by reason but as alert interpreter of a world flooded by meaning-bearing superfice that obliquely characterizes the place that the present takes in the historical process.

As Miriam Bratu Hansen elegantly summarizes in her introduction to *Theory of Film*, "Kracauer insisted that intellectuals should engage the yet unnamed, untheorized realities of daily life and try to register them in their material density and multiplicity, to read them as indexes of history in the making."[11] *Registering* and *reading* are components of the synaesthetic system physiologically interior to the subject, collaborating to produce meaning from raw sensory input. Given the sheer magnitude of such input in the Weimar-era city, the extent and quality of Kracauer's critical output is breathtaking. His reading assignment was not easy, given that it involved characterizing the impact of modernity on subjectivity even as modern technologies of communication and representation were reshaping the very conceptual and material matrices through which such characterizations could form. In this situation, the logic of Kracauer's attraction to the movie house was perfect, for as Hansen further argues, "the cinema engaged the contradictions of modernity at the level of the senses, the level at which the impact of modern technology on human experience was most palpable and irreversible."[12] Like Buck Morss's discussion of synaesthesia, Hansen's breakdown of Kracauer's approach to cinema draws our attention to an increasingly unstable center: "Kracauer discerned in cinema's decentering mode of reception ('distraction'), . . . a practical critique of the sovereign subject, of outdated notions of . . . self-identity, and of the traditional subject-object dichotomy."[13]

As an experiment, allow me to extrapolate from this decentering an *eccentric* reader, a dual entity composed of a decentered spectator, moving into the blizzard of images, and a shadowing self-observer, if not centered in a Cartesian or Kantian way, and if not concentrically surrounding the decentered spectator, then at least sufficiently composed to track, record, and, later, reconstruct—and thus distill focused, deliberate readings from the impressions of the distracted spectator. This trailing reader is an instantiation that both recalls the classical subject and displays the inability to be identical to the original. For such a reader, going to the movies would not be *like* going to school, it would *be* going to school, each film a training session for a mode of analytical subjectivity that could be content, for the time being, to let the problem of the lost self go unsolved, indeed, to draw critical energy from the tension that existed between the dream of the classical subject and the modern world that would not let the dream become real.

Since the sounds of the city seem indifferent to that critical energy, aural anxiety persists as Kracauer's public-intellectual project evolves. "Screams in the Street" comes in the midst of an intellectual tearing-down of the façade of the self that is still predominantly intact when Kracauer writes "Boredom" in 1924, but there is a striking degree of analogy between the reading problems of the highly structured apparatus and process of broadcast reception and the spontaneous, less mediated hearing of the scream illustrate. In both cases, the ear is ill-equipped to meet a cognitive challenge, and the listening subject fails to collect and focus itself to the degree that effective reading requires. The agitation and anxiety associated with this failure are disproportionally linked to the ear, and they haunt Kracauer, as they haunt any effort to characterize the significance of sensate experience.

The Pendulum

Extending and augmenting Karsten Witte's periodization of Kracauer's thought, Helmut Lethen describes a pendular pattern that further emphasizes continuities across time and philosophical shifts.[14] Witte traces Kracauer's move from idealism to materialism in the interwar era; looking beyond, Lethen sees in the objects and methods of the late work (*Alterswerk* is his term) connections between Kracauer in exile and Kracauer in the early 1920s. Kracauer, argues Lethen, focuses at some points on meaningful constructions that the keen observer can discern within, beneath, or against image flurries, faceless masses, and unassuming surfaces; at others on phenomena so diffuse and opaque that they thwart production of meaning or remain unpenetrated by signification of any kind. But regardless of the pendulum's direction, Kracauer remains attentive to the modern human subject and concrete problems of sensory perception. (This is also a crucial point for Hansen.) *Concrete* here encompasses corporal, and Lethen argues that the late work in particular, in its preoccupation with value-indifferent, asemantic flow, endeavors to ascertain the "corporality of the human being as a 'thing among things.'"[15]

Film sound plays a significant role in Kracauer's work on these problems (as it does Lethen's analysis) because it is both a matrix in which entrenched audio sign-systems (speech in particular) propagate, as well as a set of conditions under which the claustrophobia-inducing semantic closure of such systems can be undone. As Lethen puts it, "If semiotics considers 'noise' (*Geräusch*) a relatively global designation for phenomena that span a highly differentiated scale, then we must recognize that Kracauer's valuation of noise gravitates to that point on the spectrum where sense-making all but ceases, that he directs his listening toward sounds without recognizable meaning."[16] Where there is no meaning, there can be no reading, and as Kracauer draws closer to this point, his well-practiced reading-positions (and the contours of the subject that those positions make perceptible) evanesce. Kracauer undergoes no existential crisis; he simply switches from a hermeneutic to a cartographic mode of reading, looking to map the sensory possibilities generated by the impossibility of making sense. This position may be the trailing reader's final destination, a location beyond the dialectical field marked off on one end by the sovereign subject, on the other by the mass atom. No longer does Kracauer as reader oscillate between the two: as he reads his way out of reading in the late work, he works with a contradiction that he is now content to leave unresolved. And yet, despite this stoic calm at the edge of meaningful reality, Kracauer the film theorist still betrays a need to overcome sound, by visual means if necessary. I want to explore some cases in point from *Theory of Film*, preceded by a moment with Kracauer and René Clair in 1932.

From the Unity of All Things Sonic to the Word Carpet

As the talking picture era dawned, Kracauer rarely found a work that met his standards for truly cinematic use of sound. In the films of René Clair (starting with *Sous les toits de Paris* in 1930), he found exceptions to the rule. In a comment on Clair's 1931 film *The Million* (*Le Million*), we find a bridge between Kracauer's critique of early sound cinema and his exploration of sound in *Theory of Film*. What sets Clair apart, according to Kracauer, is an ability to "produce ideas that can endure nowhere but on screen."[17] Clair impresses especially in his use of cinematic speech, which is used in such a way as to make subtitles superfluous. "The literal sense of the words does not construe the meaning of the situation," argues Kracauer. "Rather, the situation, which develops purely via images, leads to the sense of words. Musical illustrations outweigh dialog; in a way, dialog is released out of the music. Clair's objective is obviously the unity of all things sonic."[18] The article ends abruptly at this point, leaving "the unity of all things sonic" as a tantalizing conceptual hinge between the unruly, overwhelming sound-scapes of the Weimar street and later cinematic configurations that, though they lead the listener beyond meaning, are nonetheless eminently manageable in the order that Kracauer, as film theorist, superimposes on them.

At the outset of chapter 7 of *Theory of Film*, Kracauer explains that in his use, the term *sound* may refer strictly to "sound proper—all kinds of noises, that is" and loosely to "not only sound proper but the spoken word or dialogue as well."[19] He then considers how the boundary between speech and noise might be made porous, that is, how cinematic techniques might shift "emphasis from the meaning of speech to its material qualities" (109). He offers Anthony Asquith and Leslie Howard's 1938 film *Pygmalion* as an example, noting that the sonic contours of Eliza Doolittle's cockney idiom are more significant than the specific content of what she is saying. This shift away from standard semantic convention is cinematic because it "alienates words, thereby exposing their material characteristics" (109). Further variations of such alienation include Groucho Marx, whose verbal cascades shatter standard patterns of speech; Harpo Marx, who thrives in the silent rubble of language that Groucho creates; and the radio chatter of pilots in the B-movie *Jungle Patrol*, which transforms into an "endless sound strip" (108–11).

Disparate as they may be, such examples demonstrate the connections between cinematic treatment of the aural and visual world. Kracauer continues, "Within the world of sound, the effect thus produced parallels that of photography in the visual world. Remember the Proust passage in which the narrator looks at his grandmother with the eyes of a stranger: estranged from her, he sees her, roughly speaking, as she really is, not as he imagines her to be" (109). The Proust example is intriguing: it suggests a general strategy for tackling sound, in which Kracauer shifts to visually centered discourse in order to characterize the significance of aural experience, *and* it furnishes writing about a photographic effect instead of an actual photograph as a basis for theorization of visual, then by extension aural, representation and reality. As the theorist works to make aural experience knowable in visual terms, discursive buffers between theorist and aural experience accumulate. The point about estrangement from habitually applied semantic veneers of aural experience is made, but the Proust reference also distances the theorist from the type of disconcerting, visceral sonic impact recorded in the Weimar feuilletons.

With Doolittle and Proust, Kracauer draws an analogy between aural and visual experience and processing, considering them side by side. Shortly thereafter, things intertwine: "Emphasis on voices as sounds may serve to open up the material regions of the speech world for their own sake. What is thought of here is a sort of word carpet which, woven from scraps of dialogue or other kinds of communications, impresses the audience mainly as a coherent sound pattern. Grierson coins the term 'chorus' to define such patterns" (110). The metaphorical relationship between chorus and carpet is already somewhat strained, but the plot quickly thickens: "These 'choruses' may be inserted in such a way that it is they rather than the synchronized visuals which captivate the spectator—or should one say, listener? Being all ear, he will not care much about what the pictures try to impart" (110–11). Faced with aural usurpation of the visual's central position in the film medium, the theorist remains eminently cool and composed. When word carpets obliterate images in the spectator's (auditor's) field of perception, speech may "seem to go against the grain of the medium by disregarding visual contributions. And yet it is cinematic by extension. The voice patterns brought into focus belong to the physical world about us no less than its visible components; and they are so elusive that they would hardly be noticed were it not for the sound camera which records them faithfully. *Only in photographing them like any visible phenomenon . . .* are we able to lay hold on these transitory verbal conglomerates" (111, emphasis added).

The visual preoccupation of these remarks finds its strongest expression in the use of the verb *to photograph* to describe the process of audio recording, and the basic image of the carpet, an intricate weave that reveals its patterns under visual scrutiny, suggests the difficulty of conceptualizing the ear's experience without involving the eye. Unlike in "Screams in the Street," in which Kracauer is forced to concede perceptual and epistemological limits, the film-theoretical magnum opus is driven to make the aural knowable, by visual means if necessary; surveillable, even when not understandable.

The very writing of the 1930 text suggests a compulsion to revisit the insoluble problems that the screams in the night place before the modern urban auditor. The randomness, the lack of infrastructure underlying the screams, makes them the jarring midrange between the two heavily structured environs of media use represented by "Boredom" and *Theory of Film*. In the early feuilleton, the sonic-textual offerings of the radio invade and conquer; sitting in film archives in New York, London, and Paris, the fruits of the apparatus are at Kracauer's disposal, there for eye and ear to cycle through again and again, as the theorist pleases. The treatise, characterized by retro*spective* distance and arrangements of disparate examples that reveal connecting principles, provides the perfect generic setting in which to graph a visually specifiable sonic unity.

Conclusion: Silent Echoes in the Archive

The move to the controlled environment of the archive may be necessary to keep the practice of *aisthesis materialis* from inadvertently stumbling into synaesthetic overload triggered by sound, to protect against the anaesthesia that is tantamount to analytical paralysis. Kracauer made that move not on a personal whim, of course, but in the midst and the wake of the upheaval of exile, after escaping alive from the catastrophe that shattered the feuilletonist's world. If there was no conceivable return to the streets of Berlin, is the word carpet a select manifestation of a general impulse to meet the perceptual and practical challenge inherent in the sewing pattern that Kracauer read in the pedestrian-trajectories of the late Weimar metropolis, and thus to overcome the threatening emptiness of the streets that underlay those trajectories and confronted the feuilletonist in the scream? Can we read this tapestry as a best possible nonsolution, a fabric, substituted for a garment that could only be projected from the late Weimar pattern? A continuation of a project that could no longer be pursued at street level?

Edward Branigan notes that the sound "processed by the human ear is
... able to bend around corners or come up behind an auditor, reporting
its object more globally as a 'motion-event,' a disturbance within the surrounding space."[20] This spatial dynamism, and the unpredictability it generates in the auditor's physical encounter with sound, are clearly in play in
"Screams in the Street." Just as Kracauer knows the streets but is discon-
certed by the ways that they exceed his sensory command, he can read the
scream as a sign of murder yet become frustrated and anxious at its resistance to his situating impulses. Cinema loudspeakers, Branigan continues,
"literally create a disturbance in the three-dimensional space of the movie
theater."[21] But the cinema is a more controlled listening environment than
the sidewalk. Disturbance and response are more structured, and the secu-
rity of that structure can compensate for a loss of meaning. The scream in
the street, after all, has a meaning that is graspable but not localizable, and
the resulting disorientation verges on trauma. The word carpet has no
meaning, but its cinematic site (a function of its inability to exist anywhere
else) is mercifully stable.

In the scream, a sense shock that is opaque in its invisibility to the look of
the eccentric reader's eye, that reader confronts a limit of what can be ana-
lytically rendered, even were visual command to know no boundaries.
Reflecting on that limit, and thinking about what to do with material that exceeds it, would be worthwhile for those who would both critically assess and
continue to draw on Kracauer's *aisthesis materialis* in theoretically informed,
historically aware investigations of audiovisual media or experience. Probing
dilemmas of sound perception, or at least considering the extent to which visually focused approaches are vulnerable to being caught off-guard by sound,
might well open new critical perspectives. Echoing through the work of the
scholar in the archive, the screams of 1930 remind us of the things that we
know are there but cannot see. How might we read them?

NOTES

1. Siegfried Kracauer, "Schreie auf der Straße," in *Aufsätze I, 1927–1931*, vol.
5.2 of *Siegfried Kracauer: Schriften*, ed. Inka Mülder-Bach (Frankfurt am Main:
Suhrkamp, 1990), 207.
2. Kracauer, "Schreie auf der Straße," 205–6.
3. Holger Schulze, "Bewegung Berührung Übertragung: Einführung in eine
historische Anthropologie des Klangs," in *Sound Studies: Traditionen—Methoden—
Desiderate* (Bielefeld: Transcript Verlag, 2008), 144.

4. Kracauer, "Langeweile," in *Aufsätze I, 1915–1926*, vol. 5.1 of *Siegfried Kracauer: Schriften*, ed. Inka Mülder- Bach (Frankfurt am Main: Suhrkamp, 1990), 279. English translation: Kracauer, "Boredom," in Kracauer, *The Mass Ornament: Weimar Essays*, ed. and trans. Thomas Y. Levin (Cambridge: Harvard University Press, 1995), 331–36.

5. Kracauer, "Langeweile," 279.

6. Kracauer, "Langeweile," 279.

7. Karin Bijsterveld, "The Diabolical Symphony of the Mechanical Age: Technology and Symbolism of Sound in European and North American Noise Abatement Campaigns, 1900–40," in *The Auditory Cultures Reader*, ed. Michael Bull and Les Back (Oxford: Berg, 2003), 166–74.

8. Walter Benjamin, "Über einige Motive bei Baudelaire," in *Abhandlungen*, vol. 1.2 of *Gesammelte Schriften*, ed. Rolf Tiedemann et al. (Frankfurt am Main: Suhrkamp, 1991), 616; Susan Buck-Morss, "Aesthetics and Anaesthetics: Walter Benjamin's Artwork Essay Reconsidered," *October* 62 (1992): 12–13.

9. For more on *aisthesis materialis*, see Bernhard J. Dotzler and Ernst Müller, eds., *Wahrnehmung und Geschichte: Markierungen zur Aisthesis materialis* (Berlin: Akademie Verlag, 1996); and Uta Beiküfner, *Blick, Figuration, Gestalt: Elemente einer aisthesis materialis im Werk von Walter Benjamin, Siegfried Kracauer und Rudolf Arnheim* (Bielefeld: Aisthesis Verlag, 2003).

10. Kracauer, "Das Ornament der Masse," in vol. 5.2 of *Siegfried Kracauer: Schriften*, 67. English translation, "The Mass Ornament," in Kracauer, *The Mass Ornament: Weimar Essays*, 75–86.

11. Miriam Bratu Hansen, introduction to *Theory of Film: The Redemption of Physical Reality*, by Siegfried Kracauer (Princeton: Princeton University Press, 1997), x.

12. Hansen, introduction to *Theory of Film*, xi.

13. Hansen, introduction to *Theory of Film*, xi.

14. See Karsten Witte, "Nachwort" in Siegfried Kracauer, *Das Ornament der Masse* (Frankfurt am Main: Suhrkamp, 1977), 335–47; and Helmut Lethen, "Sichtbarkeit: Kracauers Liebeslehre," in *Siegfried Kracauer: Neue Interpretationen. Akten des internationalen interdisziplinären Kracauer Symposions, Weingarten, 2.–4. März 1989*, ed. Michael Kessler and Thomas Y. Levin (Tübingen: Stauffenburg, 1990), 216–17.

15. Lethen, "Sichtbarkeit: Kracauers Liebeslehre," 209.

16. Lethen, "Sichtbarkeit: Kracauers Liebeslehre," 206.

17. Kracauer, "Tonfilm von heute," 1932, in *Kleine Schriften zum Film*, ed. Inka Mülder-Bach and Ingrid Belke, vol. 6.3 of *Werke* (Frankfurt am Main: Suhrkamp, 2004), 34.

18. Kracauer, "Tonfilm von heute," 34.

19. Kracauer, *Theory of Film*, 102. Subsequent page references in the text.

20. Edward Branigan, "Sound and Epistemology in Film," *Journal of Aesthetics and Art Criticism* 47, no. 4 (1989): 312.

21. Branigan, "Sound and Epistemology in Film," 313.

Literary Genres

"Written by Himself"

Siegfried Kracauer's "Auto-Biographical" Novels

Christian Rogowski

Siegfried Kracauer's first novel, *Ginster* (1928), ends with an enigmatic visual image: the protagonist finds himself in Marseille, near the harbor, amid the hustle and bustle of passersby, street vendors, sailors, prostitutes, and street kids. He buys a peculiar toy, an artificial canary perched on a bar around which a metal ring is attached that, when rotated, encircles the bird in a kind of virtual cage. The image of the protagonist listlessly spinning the ring around a toy canary trapped like a "prisoner" (*Häftling*) evokes Ginster's sense of narcissistic isolation and alienation.[1] Looking through the apparatus in the searing heat, Ginster views the world as a kaleidoscope of disjointed visual stimuli, people, and things turn into refracted flashes of light, blurring into the "scraps of a shimmering language devoid of rules" (7:246).

Kracauer's two novels, *Ginster* (1928) and *Georg* (1934), engage the reader in an elaborate game of hide-and-seek, by taking well-known experiences from Kracauer's life and transforming them into symbolically significant episodes. For the Marseille chapter, Kracauer took a personal experience dating to the fall of 1926, when he first visited the city with his future wife Lili Ehrenreich. On 13 September 1926, Kracauer published a short prose piece, entitled "Die Frau vor dem Café" (The Woman in Front of the Café), in the *Frankfurter Zeitung* that clearly forms the basis for the novel's Marseille episode. Both are set in a café on the city's bustling boulevard, the Canebière. In the prose vignette, Kracauer observes a strange woman in the act of looking: with her back to the "panopticum" of the street, she focuses her gaze on the café itself.[2] Like Kracauer himself, who in his own journalistic, sociological, and philosophical writings directed his attention to surface phenomena, the woman exhibits a peculiar way of looking at the seemingly marginal.

The episode introduces another important theme, that of being looked at. Kracauer observes how a passerby hands the woman a coin, apparently assuming that she is a beggar. The woman responds by lifting her gaze, her eyes displaying a "confused language of images" (*konfuse Bilderschrift*, 297). She refuses the coin, and it ends up rolling down onto the pavement. Kracauer thus joins two concomitant motifs: the woman's gaze that focuses on the apparently marginal and the passerby's gaze that seeks but fails to assign an identity to a person based on visual clues.

I take the reworking of the prose vignette into the Marseille episode at the end of *Ginster* as the key to a reading of Kracauer's novels as truly "auto-biographical," in which the transformation of experience into fiction emerges as a kind of self-fashioning, an authoring of an alternate self. Set in 1923–24, five years after the war (7:246), the chapter disrupts the temporal flow: *Ginster* primarily concerns the war years (1914 to 1918), while the second novel, *Georg*, covers the years 1919 to around 1926–28 (7:603). The chapter thus acts as a kind of hinge in the shift from one persona to another, from "Ginster" to "Georg." The self-critical image of the yellow bird in a virtual cage with which the first novel ends visualizes a transformation that is associated with a dialectic of looking and being looked at—an effort to describe and escape multiple misrecognitions.[3]

Even though *Ginster* was first published anonymously, with the cryptic subtitle, "written by himself" (*Von ihm selbst geschrieben*), the alert reader of the *Frankfurter Zeitung*, along with Kracauer's fellow intellectuals and friends, would have had little difficulty recognizing the numerous auto-biographical elements in the novel, as various related feuilleton pieces had been published there before the novel was serialized in that same newspaper and then published in book form. These prose vignettes concern personal experiences and observations and are written in the first person; in the novel, they are changed into third-person narratives with enhanced significance through symbolic imagery.

Like his protagonist Ginster, Kracauer found himself at the outbreak of the Great War in M. (= Munich) at age twenty-five, working as an architect, with a freshly minted doctoral degree; both had an absentee, emotionally detached father who traveled as a cloth salesman; both were raised primarily by their aunt and uncle, a prominent local historian; both worked for an architectural firm in F. (= Frankfurt) for most of the war, while volunteering as medical helpers on the home front; both had a close friend, Otto, who was killed at Verdun; both participated in an architectural com-

Fig. 1. Cover of Kracauer's first
novel, *Ginster. Written by Himself*,
published anonymously (Berlin:
Samuel Fischer, 1928).

petition for the design of a soldiers' cemetery that was then built in their
hometown; both received multiple deferments before being recruited into
the German army in September 1917; both were discharged for medical
reasons after a few months; and both were employed until the end of the
war in the municipal offices of a small northern German town (Os-
nabrück).

Unlike Ginster, Kracauer had during the war years already begun to
pursue his project of becoming a writer, penning major philosophical and
sociological reflections, conducting extensive correspondence with some
of the leading intellects of the period, such as Georg Simmel and Max
Scheler, and publishing the occasional prose piece. Ginster, on the other
hand, is decidedly un- or even anti-intellectual, displaying no literary am-
bitions. Kracauer rewrites another aspect of his earlier wartime self,
namely, his initial adherence to a staunch German nationalism: in two of
his earliest publications he had displayed considerable patriotic fervor, first
in a chauvinistic poem "Auf der großen Fahrt" (Embarked on a Grand
Journey), then in a gushing article, "Vom Erleben des Kriegs" (On Experiencing War), both published in 1915, that hailed the war as a liberating,
quasi-mystical experience of national unity.[4] By contrast, the Ginster of the
novel is at odds with the chauvinism of his environment that experiences it-

self as a unified *Volk*—finding himself "unable to get his lips to utter the 'we'" (7:12).[5]

Celebrated diarist Victor Klemperer, noting his irritation over Kracauer's "sudden conversion to patriotism," recounts a disturbing episode in which his young friend was involved in August 1914: after being mistaken for a foreigner by an angry crowd in Munich, Kracauer decided to have his black hair shorn off, which—as Klemperer wryly notes—did nothing to change his "exotic" appearance.[6] Kracauer's patriotic fervor is missing in the novel, while the episode reemerges in altered form as Ginster recounts his encounter with xenophobic hostility in a barbershop: "The apprentice asked me if I were a foreigner [*ein Fremder*]. I had to detail my family tree, or else he would perhaps have cut me" (7:16). Something sets Ginster visually apart that puts him under pressure to prove that he is in fact German. Later, Ginster is surprised to find that the people around him don't accept it when he spouts the very same patriotic clichés that he has heard others utter to general acclaim: "Whenever *he* had hardly uttered his opinion—an opinion of which he could assume that it would correspond to the needs of the people—he was met with mistrust. The public looked at him in astonishment" (7:20). Ginster finds himself subjected to a judgmental look that defines him as not belonging to the group in which he tries to claim membership.

Every now and then, Ginster responds by assuming a fake identity in seemingly random fashion: at a masked ball, for instance, he seeks to impress one of the young women by pretending to be friends with a Polish countess (7:30). Later, his awkward sexual initiation with a prostitute is predicated upon him claiming to be Polish himself (7:251). At the beginning of the novel, when, after the outbreak of the war, Ginster is confronted with an outburst of German nationalism, the narrative traces a strange set of associations. In a kind of flashback, Ginster remembers when he lived in Berlin, where he used to watch trains depart from the Friedrichstraße station: poor people would board third-class compartments to exotic-sounding locations such as "Myslowitz" (7:12). Contemporary encyclopedias inform us that Myslowitz/Myslovice was a railway junction on the border of Polish and German Silesia, at what was known as the *Dreikaisereck*, the place where the German, the Russian, and the Austro-Hungarian Empire conjoined after they had carved up Poland in 1795 in the so-called Third Partition. Myslowitz was the last stop on the German side of the railway connection from Berlin via Breslau to Cracow. Among the few notable buildings in the largely nondescript town, which around

1905 had a population of just under 16,000, was a synagogue, opened in 1899.[7] Silesia also happens to be the region from which Kracauer's paternal ancestors originated, with his grandfather, Saul Kracauer, born in Zülz, Upper Silesia, and his father Adolf and uncle Isidor both born in Sagan, Lower Silesia.[8] Ginster's recollections stop, quite literally, on the German side of the border to Poland; his evocation of Myslowitz, of Poland and Silesia, retraces Kracauer's ancestral roots in the Eastern European border region, reversing, as it were, the westward migration of his father's family toward Frankfurt am Main, the shift from an Eastern Jewish to a Western Jewish identity. That road back, however, ends in abrupt disavowal: "Myslowitz didn't exist" (7:12).[9]

The railroad motif is picked up later in the novel, in conjunction with Ginster's only reflection on his name. Ginster is on a walk with Elfriede, his ambivalent quasi love interest, who has a penchant for naming plants and flowers. She focuses on the barren soil: "'Soon the hairy broom [*Ginster*] will be blossoming here,'" Elfriede said and pointed to the embankment. Ginster would have never thought of his own name. It pleased him that broom would accompany the railroad tracks, which set off straight into the distance. He would have loved it most if he too could blossom on both sides of the railway embankment" (7:221).

Ginster (hairy broom; heather) is the scraggly yellow bushlike plant that manages to blossom in inhospitable environments. The color yellow is, of course, associated with Jews, dating back to the yellow identifying rings that Jews in medieval Europe were forced to wear; in Christian symbolism, the color was associated with avarice, treachery (Judas), and heresy.[10] In this light, both the protagonist's name and novel's final image, that of the yellow toy canary sitting in a self-created virtual cage, attain a special significance: their common color hints at Ginster's predicament of entrapment in self-absorption as the result of being viewed as "Jewish"—different and not belonging.

Yet such hints remain on a subtextual (or contextual) level; there are few overt references to the presence of Jews in Ginster's fictional world. Frankfurt, Ginster's hometown, is wryly described as a place where "some Christian and Jewish families trace their origins back to [their] ancestors" (7:22). Later, the narrator describes the location of the architect's office in that city's East End, where people who can visually be identified as Jews congregate: "They wore caftans and flowing beards, they talked in pairs as if they were walking in foursomes—Jews that appeared like imitations, because they looked so real" (7:62). The narrator focuses on the visual appearance that marks Jews as aliens, on a "realness" that appears fake, since it seems to conform so well to the stereotype. The "ghetto Jews" still seem to be present in Frankfurt despite the dissolution of the ghetto in 1796, and these seem to be the only Jews in Frankfurt. By focusing on the visual distinctiveness of Jews that conform to the clichéd image, Kracauer's novel reduces the complexity of the Jewish presence in Frankfurt, effectively erasing the diversity of people of Jewish descent residing in the city, including those who—like his own family—had long left the ghetto behind. Ginster is later shown looking out the window of his office, absentmindedly "observing the Jews in their caftans" (7:77). Ginster, it would appear, has nothing whatsoever to do with the kind of Jews the novel acknowledges. Yet the proximity of his employer's office to the places where such Jews can be observed establishes a subtextual linkage between Ginster and the Jewish presence in Frankfurt that alerts the reader to the absence of any such presence in the narrative.

Herr Valentin and his wife Bertha, Ginster's employers in the novel, are modeled on Kracauer's real employer during the war in Frankfurt, Max Seckbach (1866–1922), and his wife Amalie (1870–1944), both of whom were of Jewish descent. During the war the firm made an unsuccessful bid on the construction of a new synagogue in Zurich.[11] The novel effaces the Jewishness of the biographical models of these characters and others who played major roles in Kracauer's life, most notably his uncle Isidor Kracauer (1852–1923), the prominent historian of Frankfurt's Jewish community, with his massive two-volume *Geschichte der Frankfurter Juden* published posthumously in 1925, who appears in the novel as a fastidious collector of (generic) historical information.

One reason for the omission or erasure of the German-Jewish dynamic from the novel may be that it strives for general significance as an account of the war experience in the German hinterlands, aiming to appeal to all German readers, regardless of religious affiliation. Yet the war had rendered issues of German-Jewish identity particularly acute: the majority of Jews in Germany had, like the young Kracauer himself, welcomed the outbreak of the war as an opportunity to prove to their gentile fellow-countrymen once and for all their commitment to the fatherland. Such hopes were bitterly crushed within a short time: in August 1916, for instance, industrialist Walther Rathenau, who alongside other Germans of Jewish descent, like the shipping magnate Albert Ballin and the banker Max Warburg, organized the supply system for the German military forces, dejectedly commented on German wartime anti-Semitism: "The more

Jews are killed in combat in this war, the more their opponents will prove that they all sat behind the front lines, engaged in war profiteering."[12] Two months later, in October 1916, the German Military High Command conducted a "Jewish census" to establish reliable statistical figures, which revealed that Jews contributed and suffered either on a par with or at higher rates than their gentile counterparts, yet the findings of this *Judenzählung* were kept secret, in effect bolstering anti-Semitic resentment.[13]

Kracauer's novel contains an episode that can be read as a grotesque version of the *Judenzählung* of 1916: during a leave of absence from military training, Ginster meets some friends in a café, where Ginster reports about the military practice of inspecting the recruits' genitals for signs of venereal disease, which, as he wryly notes, "take the same ineffectual course as customs inspections at the border" (7:178). The futile inspection of the recruits' genitals would, of course, reveal whether they are circumcised or not, that is, whether they are Jewish. Ginster remains silent on the subject; yet the motif of smuggling contraband across borders subtly hints that, during the war, new lines of demarcation were being drawn among German citizens.

While Kracauer was working on his first novel, he found a sympathetic reader and interlocutor in the young Marxist philosopher Ernst Bloch. In his correspondence with Bloch, Kracauer noted the novel's theme of Ginster's *Drückebergerei* (shirking, evasion of responsibility).[14] Joseph Roth, who helped place the novel with the Samuel Fischer publishing house, picked up on this aspect in his enthusiastic review of *Ginster:* "For the first time in German 'war literature,' the 'shirker' (*Drückeberger*) is being depicted."[15] To Roth, the novel breaks new ground by exposing war to ridicule, as the logical continuation of a false peace, and by taking sides with the common man trying to muddle through an impossible situation. Had Kracauer highlighted his own Jewishness and that of his protagonist, he would have played into the hands of the anti-Semites who had launched the *Judenzählung*, potentially confirming the prejudice that German Jews were dodging their responsibilities in defending the fatherland.

Traditionally, a name is the guarantor of identity. Yet, in its very first lines, Kracauer's novel disassociates its protagonist from any such equation.

> When the war broke out, Ginster—a young man of twenty-five—found himself in the state capital M. A week before, he had started a job, after having passed his doctoral exam. The academic title would have been

superfluous, but Ginster loved the tension associated with an exam, and he wanted—in the awareness of having rightfully acquired the title—later to live, incognito, as it were. The city M. had become to Ginster a sort of habit; he had spent more than four years there. Actually, he wasn't called Ginster—the name had stuck with him from school. (7:11)

In an odd act of simultaneous naming and disavowal, the narrator undercuts any notion of a fixed, stable identity: almost everything is provisional, corresponding to the protagonist's desire to live "incognito, as it were." His ostensible name, we read, is something imposed upon him from outside.

In his famous 1964 homage to Kracauer, Theodor W. Adorno calls his childhood friend "a man without skin," to highlight Kracauer's extreme vulnerability: "He had had a difficult time in his childhood, in more than one regard; as a pupil in the Klinger Upper School he had also suffered anti-Semitism, something quite unusual in the commercial city of Frankfurt, and a sort of joylessness hovered over his milieu, despite its humane scholarly tradition."[16] The nickname "Ginster," which Kracauer adopted for the protagonist of his first novel, and which he would use as a pseudonym for some subsequent publications, seems to be linked with the experience of being taunted by his fellow students, with the experience of anti-Semitic prejudice Adorno mentions.

From this perspective, the novel's subtitle, "written by himself," attains a particular significance: the entire novel can be read as an effort on the part of the subject, Ginster (i.e., Kracauer), to control the narrative of his own life, to "write" the story "himself," rather than having a story and an identity ascribed to him by others. Both of Kracauer's novels, then, are "auto-biographical" in a literal sense: they represent an effort to rewrite the story of his life from his own perspective, to combat misnaming and misrecognition.

In early 1928, Kracauer's friendship with Bloch solidified to a point where Bloch suggested shifting from last- to first-name terms (although the two would continue to use the formal *Sie* well into the 1930s). In their correspondence, Kracauer hesitated: "The official 'Siegfried' has to be ruled out altogether and the private 'Friedel' is charged with a series of such unpleasant associations from the past—I have to tell that to you orally sometime—that I cannot see myself attached to that name. . . . By the way, in my pedantry, out of antipathy for my first name I developed for the hero of my novel the Ginster formula."[17] Kracauer here presents himself as someone for whom no name fits: it is a foregone conclusion that the Teutonic *Siegfried* is inappropriate. He has equal trouble with *Friedel,* a nickname derived from *Siegfried.* In his account of Jewish names in Frankfurt during the Middle Ages, Kracauer's uncle Isidor had noted that *Friedel* is the Germanized synonym for *Salomo,* and this is how the name was used by Kracauer's family and close friends.[18] Even so, Kracauer rejects this Jewish name as well. With Bloch, Kracauer settles for an odd substitute, the harsh sounding *Krac*—one of the many bylines he used in his work as a journalist.

Lacking a suitable name, the protagonist of Kracauer's first novel can be viewed as addressing the "modes of being which still lack a name and hence are overlooked or misjudged" in which Kracauer would remain interested throughout his life.[19] The "Ginster formula" subtextually addresses the impossible subject position of a young man who is judged by a gaze that continually misses the mark: the protagonist seeks to identify himself as German but finds his environment imposing on him the identity as Jew, resulting in the concept of a subject devoid of substance, yet caught up in solipsist isolation.

By contrast, Kracauer's second novel, *Georg,* represents a defiant reconfiguration: it contains no discussion, oblique or direct, of the problem of naming, and the act of viewing is now firmly under the protagonist's control. He simply goes by the name of Georg—a version of Siegfried, the dragon slayer, stripped of the nationalistic charge (and, perhaps, an homage to Kracauer's philosophical mentor, Georg Simmel). It would appear, then, that Kracauer's second auto-biographical incarnation has indeed managed to create a story "written by himself" as a regular German: if Jewish aspects had been relegated to a subtext in the first novel, in the second they seem to have disappeared altogether.

In his quest for a job, and for existential orientation, Georg drifts through a panorama of postwar ideologies, encountering adherents of the *Jugendbewegung* (youth movement), a Catholic reformer, and communist activists. The novel traces the development of Georg's disengaged political consciousness that will eventually get him into trouble at the newspaper for which he works. Georg does not seem to have to confront the many burning German-Jewish issues and tensions that Kracauer faced during the postwar period. For instance, in 1926, Kracauer became embroiled in a bitter controversy over the efforts by Martin Buber and Franz Rosenzweig, the leaders of the Jewish Revival in Germany, to translate the Bible into German, when he launched a sharp polemic against their *Die Bibel auf*

Deutsch, which cost him his friendship with Margarete Susman and turned Rosenzweig into his enemy.[20] Kracauer's personal and philosophical activities took place in a decidedly German-Jewish, primarily left-liberal, milieu, and much of his intellectual work is determined by his association with, and his position within, the German-Jewish intelligentsia of the time. None of this makes its way into Kracauer's second novel.

Like his predecessor Ginster, Georg at first clearly lacks the political awareness of his author, an astute critic of sociopolitical developments during the 1920s and early 1930s. Georg's solipsist struggle for orientation in the crisis-ridden Weimar Republic makes him notice significant political events only peripherally. The only acknowledgment of emerging National Socialism, for instance, is the passing reference—while Georg is preoccupied with his awkward quasi romance with Beate Walter—that far away in Munich, Hitler attempts a *Putsch*, which "fails miserably" (7:404). The society Kracauer portrays seems to be devoid of Jews—and of anti-Semitism, the very force which drove the author, who described himself in 1933 as "the Jew and leftist," into exile.[21] It is almost as if Kracauer is trying to excise Jewishness from the fictional world of his novel at the very time that political forces insist on reinscribing Jewishness-as-difference into the reality of the day. Political circumstances would turn Georg's quest for a job and a place for himself in an inhospitable environment into Kracauer's all-too-real struggle for sheer survival.

At the end of the novel, Georg walks alone down Kurfürstendamm in Berlin West, the heartland of what Hitler, writing in *Mein Kampf*, denounced as the center of "luxury, perversion, iniquity, wanton display, and the Jewish materialism" of Weimar Germany.[22] The character disappears from the narrative as Georg, jobless and disillusioned, dissolves into the "ant army" of the white-collar employees that pour out of office buildings onto the busy street (7:516).[23] Approaching Gedächtniskirche (Memorial Church), a series of seemingly dissociated visual images evoke the sense of an impending apocalyptic storm: "The wind was blowing harder and harder. On the unprotected square [or place], in whose midst the church arose, it bellowed along a front of glittering pillars and pipes, mirror panes and gigantic billboards. The light that the front [or facade] sent forth dispersed the nocturnal terror and was more terrifying than the night. Its relentless clamor blended with the howling of the storm" (7:516). The apocalyptic vision resonates with imagery derived from Joseph Goebbels'

Fig. 2. Title page of Salomon
Maimon's *Life Story. Written by Himself.*
Edited by Karl Philipp Moritz (1792).

notorious anti-Semitic polemic "Rund um die Gedächtniskirche" (Around
Memorial Church) of January 1928.[24]

Less than a hundred and fifty years before Georg, rabbinical scholar Salomon Ben Josua from Polish Lithuania arrived on the outskirts of Berlin
as a "beggar Jew" (*Betteljude*), seeking access to the land of Immanuel Kant
and Moses Mendelssohn, the center of the German Enlightenment.[25] It
was in Berlin that the eastern Jew Salomon took a new name out of rever-
ence for the controversial medieval Jewish theologian Moses Maimonides
(1130–1204), refashioning himself into Salomon Maimon, the enlightened
secular intellectual who refuses to give up his Jewish heritage. Salomon
documented his story in a two-part book: in 1792, Karl-Philip Moritz
edited and published Salomon's *Lebensgeschichte* with the subtitle "von ihm
selbst geschrieben"—"written by himself."[26]

Kracauer would use the same phrase as the subtitle of his first book,
suggesting a direct link between his own life story and that of Salomon,
whose *Lebensgeschichte* was republished in Munich in 1911—at a time when
Kracauer lived in that city.[27] In Kracauer's second novel, Berlin has become
an "unprotected place," the eye of an apocalyptic storm; the rationalistic

enlightened secularism that had attracted Salomon has turned into a "terrible" light that emanates from the "front" and ricochets from the buildings in an unsettling experience of "nocturnal terror."

In the synesthetic vision, full of warlike imagery, there emerges a lone voice of a blind beggar selling matches: "It belonged, as it finally turned out, to a blind man, who wore an old soldier's hat and who was standing in such a detached manner, as if he were mute as well and could only listen. Sent out by him wandering [auf Wanderschaft], the voice followed its own path like a messenger" (7:515).

Writing in 1934, in his precarious exile in Paris, Kracauer constructs an image of the unheeded voice sent out on a *Wanderschaft* that evokes both the motif of the homeless old woman in the Marseille episode at the end of *Ginster* and the tradition of the Wandering Jew. The beggar's cries of "'matches, matches—please, help me'" (7:515), are later shorn of quotation marks and merge with the overall cacophony of sounds, in a stark plea for help: "please, help me" (7:516). The *Betteljude* seeking enlightenment has been reduced to a blind beggar, a war veteran calling out into an unresponsive void.

Kracauer's first novel, *Ginster,* closed on an image that suggested a partial retreat into a self-imposed narcissistic isolation as a response to the paradoxical subject position imposed upon the young Jewish male by an indifferent or hostile gentile environment: while he may experience himself to be without substantive identity, it is the gaze of others that imposes an identity on him. The second novel, *Georg*, radicalizes this dialectic of looking and being looked at: its protagonist, who has shed any identifiable association with Jewishness, finds himself confronted with ominous forces that place him on the verge of annihilation. Kracauer's two novels thus mark what Martin Buber would later famously call the "end of the German-Jewish symbiosis" and the ultimate failure of the project of the German Enlightenment.[28]

The life story Kracauer set out to write "by himself," the story of a self devoid of substance and open to infinite rewritings, is overwritten in the late 1920s by an ideology that demonizes those defined as different and that inscribes Jews into a grand narrative of world history as the story of racial warfare. Following Maimon, Kracauer and countless others of Jewish descent attempted to write an auto-biographical (hi)story on their own terms within German culture; the task of the reader is to look for (and after) the pieces they left behind, in an effort—as futile as it is necessary—to reassemble the vital and indispensable German-Jewish mosaic.

NOTES

I would like to thank Cynthia Walk and Liliane Weissberg for their feedback on an earlier version of this essay. Thanks are also due, as always, to my wife, Nona Monáhin, for her help in editing the final version.

1. All references to Kracauer's fictional writings are to *Romane und Erzählungen*, vol. 7 of Kracauer, *Werke*, ed. Inka Mülder-Bach and Sabine Biebl (Frankfurt am Main: Suhrkamp, 2004); here 245. Unless otherwise noted, translations from German are my own.

2. Reprinted in Andreas Volk, *Siegfried Kracauer. Zum Werk des Romanciers, Feuilletonisten, Architekten, Filmwissenschaftlers und Soziologen* (Zurich: Seismo, 1996), 295–97. Interestingly, Kracauer leaves out his encounter with his friend Walter Benjamin, whom he met in Marseille at that time, from both accounts. See Walter Benjamin, *Briefe an Siegfried Kracauer* (Marbach: Deutsche Schillergesellschaft, 1987), 30.

3. To date, there is only one detailed reading in English of the novel, by Henrik Reeh, who focuses on the nexus between Kracauer's architectural thinking and the novel, as a "biographically and historically precise analysis of the opposition between the individual and totality" (*Ornaments of the Metropolis: Siegfried Kracauer and Modern Urban Culture* [Cambridge: MIT Press, 2004], 37). My reading renders this somewhat abstract "opposition" more concrete and, it is hoped, more "biographically and historically precise."

4. The poem is reproduced in Ingrid Belke, and Irina Renz, eds., *Siegfried Kracauer, 1889–1966. Marbacher Magazin* 47 (Marbach: Deutsches Literaturarchiv, 1988), 26. The essay appears in *Aufsätze 1915–1926*, vol. 5.1 of Kracauer, *Schriften*, ed. Inka Mülder-Bach (Frankfurt am Main: Suhrkamp, 1990), 11–22.

5. The passage may also be read as an oblique reference to Kracauer's stammer, which significantly affected his social interaction since childhood; see Belke and Renz, 5.

6. Victor Klemperer, *Curriculum vitae. Erinnerungen 1881–1918*, ed. Walter Nowojski, 2 vols., (Berlin: Aufbau, 1996), 2:184.

7. *Meyers Großes Konversations-Lexikon*, vol. 14 (Leipzig: Meyer, 1909), 345–46.

8. Belke and Renz, 1.

9. It would appear that Kracauer's novel and their 1926 encounter in Marseille function as associative subtexts in Walter Benjamin's famous prose piece, "Myslovice—Braunschweig—Marseille" of 1930; in *On Hashish*, ed. Howard Eiland (Cambridge: Harvard University Press, 2006), 105–16.

10. Elena Romero Castelló and Uriel Macías Kapón, *The Jews and Europe: 2,000 Years of History* (New York: Henry Holt, 1994), 32–39.

11. Belke and Renz, 29.

12. Quoted in Clemens Picht, "'Er will der Messias der Juden werden.' Walther Rathenau zwischen Assimilation und jüdischer Prophetie," in *Die Extreme berühren sich. Walther Rathenau 1867–1922*, ed. Hans Wilderotter (Berlin: Argon/Deutsches Historisches Museum, 1993), 117–29, here 124.

13. Werner T. Angress, "The German Army's *Judenzählung* of 1916: Genesis—Consequences—Significance," *Leo Baeck Yearbook* 23 (1978): 117–38; Volker Ullrich, "Dazu hält man für sein Land den Schädel hin!" *Die Zeit*, October 11, 1996, 42.

14. Kracauer, letter to Ernst Bloch, 5 January 1928. Letter number 10 of "Briefwechsel Siegfried Kracauer—Ernst Bloch 1921–1966," ed. Inka Mülder, in Ernst Bloch, *Briefe I. 1903–1975* (Frankfurt am Main: Suhrkamp, 1985), 289.

15. Joseph Roth, "Wer ist Ginster?" *Frankfurter Zeitung*, 25 November 1928; see also Momme Brodersen, *Siegfried Kracauer* (Reinbek: Rowohlt, 2001), 68.

16. Theodor W. Adorno, "Der wunderliche Realist" (1964), translated as "The Curious Realist: On Siegfried Kracauer," trans. Shierry Weber Nicholsen, *New German Critique* 54 (Autumn 1991), 159–77, here 161.

17. Letter number 9 to Bloch, early January 1928, in Bloch, *Briefe*, 288–89.

18. Isidor Kracauer, "Die Namen der Frankfurter Juden bis zum Jahre 1400," *Monatsschrift für Geschichte und Wissenschaft des Judentums* 55, no. 4 (1911): 447–63, here 449.

19. *History: The Last Things Before the Last* (New York: Oxford University Press, 1996), 4.

20. Martin Jay, "Politics of Translation. Siegfried Kracauer and Walter Benjamin on the Buber-Rosenzweig Bible," *Leo Baeck Yearbook* 21 (1976): 3–24.

21. Belke and Renz, 76.

22. George Victor, *Hitler: The Pathology of Evil* (Washington, DC: Brassey's, 1998), 21.

23. The mention of "Angestellten" (white-collar workers) is of course a reference to Kracauer's seminal sociological study, *Die Angestellten* (The Salaried Masses) of 1929, the time when this episode is set.

24. Joseph Goebbels, "Around the *Gedächtniskirche*," *Der Angriff*, 23 January 1928, reprinted in *The Weimar Republic Sourcebook*, ed. Anton Kaes, Martin Jay, and Edward Dimendberg (Berkeley: University of California Press, 1994), 560–62.

25. Liliane Weissberg, "Salomon Maimon Writes His *Lebensgeschichte*," in *The Yale Companion to Jewish Writing and Thought in German Culture, 1096–1996*, ed. Sander L. Gilman and Jack Zipes (New Haven: Yale University Press, 1997), 108–15.

26. *Salomon Maimon's Lebensgeschichte. Von ihm selbst geschrieben und herausgegeben von K. P. Moritz*, 2 vols. (Berlin: Friedrich Vieweg, 1792–93).

27. *Salomon Maimons Lebensgeschichte*, ed. Dr. Jakob Fromer (Munich: Georg Müller, 1911).

28. Wolfgang Benz, "The Legend of a German-Jewish Symbiosis," *Leo Baeck Yearbook* 37 (1992): 95–102. Benz is referring to Buber's essay "Das Ende der deutsch-jüdischen Symbiose," *Jüdische Weltrundschau* (10 March 1939).

The Urban Miniature and the Feuilleton in Kracauer and Benjamin

Andreas Huyssen

In the wake of Adorno, Kracauer's urban miniatures and street texts, first published in the *Frankfurter Zeitung*'s feuilleton, have often been labeled *Denkbilder*, suggesting close proximity, if not identity with Benjamin's writing about urban spaces. In this essay I want to suggest that such claims of proximity are highly exaggerated, if not false. The same goes for the scholarly tendency to relate Kracauer's miniatures too exclusively to film and *flânerie*, the moving pictures and the urban subject in motion, thereby neglecting their equally important relation to photography, manifest in a certain stasis of a cold allegorical gaze in and at urban space. A close reading of Benjamin's *Einbahnstraße* (1928) together with Kracauer's urban miniatures of the 1920s and early 1930s, many though by no means the majority of which were collected only much later by Kracauer himself in *Straßen in Berlin und anderswo* (1964), may help us make clearer distinctions between Kracauer's and Benjamin's writing practices and their different approaches to urban perception in the context of the European avant-gardes of the 1920s. It should give us pause that Benjamin himself did not speak of *Denkbilder* until years after publishing *Einbahnstraße*. Instead he kept calling these texts aphorisms, though clearly at times with significant hesitation. Kracauer, on the other hand, called his texts quite appropriately *Raumbilder*, always maintaining a close relationship between built urban space, its varied social uses, and the human imaginary. The miniatures of *Einbahnstraße*, I want to argue, are precisely not *Raumbilder* à la Kracauer. To the extent that they offer *Bildlichkeit* at all, they are *Schrift-Bilder*. And it is in this distinction between *Schrift-Bild* and *Raum-Bild* and their different media dimensions, I will argue, that Kracauer and Benjamin part ways in their literary reactions to the city.

Of course, I do not want to deny that both authors partake in the writing of a very specific form of short prose the literary genealogy of which goes back to Baudelaire's *Petits poèmes en prose*, itself a significant transformation of an even older type of urban sketch that had flourished in the newspapers of European cities since the eighteenth century[1] and remains prominent even today. Given Benjamin's literary philological versus Kracauer's architectural sociological imagination, the link to Baudelaire is clearly much more direct in Benjamin than in Kracauer. But of course there is a strong biographical and intellectual closeness in the fact that the two authors, who spent time together in Marseille and by and large wrote about the same cities (Marseille, Paris, and Berlin), also read and commented on each other's prose, as it was first published in the feuilleton of the *Frankfurter Zeitung* where Kracauer also published one of the very first incisive reviews of *Einbahnstraße*.[2]

How, then, did the *Frankfurter Zeitung* envision the function of the urban miniature? Specific editorial comments are hard to come by, but the following 1929 gloss by Benno Reifenberg, editor in chief of the paper's feuilleton, articulates his and Kracauer's new understanding of the cultural section: "Hier wird ins allgemeine Bewusstsein gebracht, wie die Substanzen unserer Gegenwart gelagert sind, nach welchen Absichten sie sich ändern. Die Berichte zeigen den Raum an, in dem überhaupt Politik gemacht werden kann."[3] Although Reifenberg speaks about *Berichte*, reportage, his comment also maps onto the urban miniature, even if in a more mediated way. Certainly his conclusion would have been embraced by both Kracauer and Benjamin: "Das Feuilleton ist der fortlaufende Kommentar zur Politik" (the feuilleton is the ongoing commentary on politics).[4] And yet, proximity to social and urban reportage is precisely what distinguishes Kracauer's *Raum-Bilder* such as "Unemployment Office," "Hotel Lobby," "Underpass," and "Farewell to the Linden Arcade" from the texts of Benjamin's *Einbahnstraße* such as "Filling Station," "Stamp Shop," or "Imperial Panorama." Reading the titles only, one might be lulled into that false sense of similarity. But while both Kracauer's and Benjamin's texts embody a kind of hybrid urban writing that crosses the boundaries between the written, the seen, and the sociopolitical realm, they do so in significantly different ways.

Before defining this difference further, let me add a few contextualizing comments on the trajectory of this new mode of writing that, as Robert Musil suggested in a review of Kafka's *Betrachtung*, is not suitable to preside over a literary genre.[5] In German and Austrian literature, modernist miniatures flourished in the first three decades of the twentieth century, with contributors ranging from Hofmannsthal and Rilke, Kafka, Walser, and Musil, Benn, Brecht, and Jünger, Kracauer and Bloch, Benjamin and Adorno, to lesser known authors such as Altenberg and Polgar, Hessel and Mynona, Serner and many others. Among Germanists, many of these texts are fairly well known. All the more puzzling is the absence of any broader critical analysis that would attempt to read this whole body of very diverse writing practices as a central phenomenon of metropolitan modernism rather than denigrating it with a far too generic term as short prose, *Kurzprosa*, leaving it to hover in some decontextualized and dehistoricized limbo. In a small way, this essay hopes to contribute to such a project, which to me represents the other, micrological side of Franco Moretti's macrological revaluation of the modern epic in distinction from the novel. If, for Moretti, the modern epic represents something like national encyclopedias in the form of macroscopic fictional maps, then the modernist miniature in all its incredible variety represents the microscopic condensation of a metropolitan imaginary that never gels into any encyclopedic totality.

Much has been written, of course, about the alleged crises of perceptions of space and time around 1900, phenomena that had as much to do with the rise of new media technologies as with the rapid, both disturbing and exhilarating urbanization of new metropolitan centers such as Berlin and Vienna that grew much faster in the later nineteenth century than older cities such as London or Paris. The place of the restructuring of temporal and spatial perception, for which the modernist miniature is an important field of experimentation, is the metropolis during the period of European high modernism and an emerging avant-gardism—a time when the city was still an island of modernization, and country and small-town life were still dominant but losing ground. In this historically very specific context the urban miniature emerged as a mode of writing that, like reportage and the documentary, may be more central to the "new" in literary modernism than the novel, drama, or poetry. In this context, the fact that Kracauer, Benjamin, and so many other authors of the time focused on *Bilder*, thus describing their texts and writing projects in terms not of reality but its visual representation, must itself be read as an effect of the increasing presence of technological image media in public and everyday life.

In my comparison of Benjamin's and Kracauer's street texts, I want to focus on a specific media aspect that has been largely overlooked due to the far too facile designation of these texts as *Denkbilder*. In an earlier essay, I proposed to read Kracauer's miniatures as snapshots of urban space and to see them as a field of experimentation that tests the validity of what Kracauer described in the 1920s as "das neue Raumgefühl" (the new sense of space). Architectural historian Sigfried Giedion at the same time described the new feeling of space as spatial *Durchdringung* (interpenetration, overlapping) in modern architecture.[6]

Since Kracauer was trained as an architect and had studied with the author of the *Sociology of Space*, Georg Simmel, he had a very astute sense of urban space. Space in Kracauer's miniatures, however, is typically layered in different registers. There is concretely described architectural and urban space such as the hotel lobby, the renovated arcade, a street in a Paris neighborhood, the Ku'damm in Berlin, the roller coaster, the unemployment office. Urban space is coded here, long before Henri Lefebvre's seminal work, as social space, which is then textually transfigured into a spatial imaginary or even into dream space. In the miniature on the unemployment office we read, "The images of space are the dreams of society."[7] Deeply influenced by Lukács's notion of the transcendental homelessness of the modern subject, Kracauer deploys this layering to allegorize the fallen state of the world, at first in rather metaphysical, later, from the mid-1920s on, in sociological and Marxist ways. "Das neue Raumgefühl" that energizes his urban miniatures recodes Giedion's *Durchdringung* as an interweaving of objective and subjective culture within built urban space. This spatial fabric, in turn, generates psychic reactions that are not simply private and internal to the subject but enunciated and performed.

Photography of urban spaces was of course widespread in the Weimar Republic as elsewhere. But how legitimate can it be for us to think of Kracauer's literary texts as snapshots? *Snapshot* at first sight suggests superficiality, reification of time, arbitrariness of the image, as Kracauer himself argues in his famous essay on photography.[8] It may also seem poorly chosen as a guiding concept to discuss the new modernist regime of space with its disturbances of vision: for does not photography remain tied to the very perspectival organization of space challenged and transformed in the urban miniature as well as in modernist painting, paradigmatically in cubism and constructivism? But it is the temporal rather than spatial dimension of the snapshot that justifies its usage here. After all, snapshots can be fundamentally opaque and resist rendering a mystery they harbor. Any snapshot, as Roland Barthes has taught us, may have its *punctum*, the dimension of the photograph that eludes transparence, "that accident which pricks me (but also bruises me, is poignant to me)."[9] The easy legibility of the snapshot clearly is a myth. Similarly, the modernist miniature seems easily legible, but more often than not it resists facile understanding. Snapshots also require careful reading because, as Merleau-Ponty has argued, any photograph holds open a specific moment that the rush of (lived) time would otherwise have immediately closed.[10] In other words: it resists quick forgetting. The snapshot marks the space where a present moment turns into memory, but simultaneously it preserves the appearance of a presence. What interests me in the miniature is precisely this unexpected eruption onto the scene of vision that Barthes called the *punctum* and Merleau-Ponty described in its temporal dimension as the "holding open" of the moment in space toward its present, its past, and its future. When transposed into writing, this holding open, as it were, allows for a palimpsestic writing of space, one that transcends the seen/scene and acknowledges the present and past imaginary any snapshot of space carries with it. Deciphering the *punctum* in Barthes perhaps corresponds to what Kracauer has in mind when he speaks of "deciphering the dream-like spoken images of cities."[11] Any deeper knowledge of cities depends on the making visible of such unconscious images, which are not subject to rational urban planning. This job of deciphering cannot be done by urban photography alone; it needs the literary articulation in the miniature that supplements the photographic representation of the seen urban space. Kracauer's street texts must thus be read in conjunction with his theoretical reflections on the promises and deficiencies of photography. In that context, they become part of his famous "go-for-broke game of history."

As literary snapshots of space open up to the passing of time, urban miniatures articulate that new dynamic experience of space that Giedion describes positively as *Durchdringung*. Kracauer's street texts complicate the commonsense understanding of the snapshot just as they reveal the threatening aspect of the new experience of space, which is absent in Giedion's rather triumphalist account of the programmatic, even utopian dimensions of building in glass, iron, and concrete. They articulate a negative side of *Durchdringung*, its threatening, even horrifying dimension as experienced by the subject lost in urban space, paradigmatically in miniatures like "The Quadrangle," "Screams in the Street," or "Underpass." This fundamental difference between Kracauer and Giedion in assessing the phenomenon of *Durchdringung* as central to the experience of urban space could be further explored, but it is no coincidence that the two opposing utopian and dystopian senses of the concept mesh most interestingly in Kracauer's writing.

Let me take "The Bay," one of the two Marseille miniatures from the first section of *The Mass Ornament* that carries the Cartesian title "natural geometry." Here Kracauer gives us a snapshot of the old harbor of Marseille, in a bird's-eye view, with the city of Marseille rising like a "dazzling amphitheater . . . around the rectangle of the now largely abandoned and empty old harbor," a "square paved with sea" (*MO*, 37). It's like a mix of a Google map with architectural and social detail, but the language immediately introduces a temporal dimension: "The splendor has lost its luster, and the bay has degenerated from the street of all streets into a rectangle." The harbor has become "desolate," an "emptiness," a "cavity." Kracauer was one of the first critics to analyze photography in relationship to transitoriness, lost temporalities, and death. But rather than reading a photograph only in terms of reification and forgetting, as Adorno would, he insists on the dimension of the past, however specterlike and spooky it might appear. It is the miniature that is able, through its verbal strategies, to hold the snapshot of the old Marseille harbor open to its teeming past and thus to its future, even when the pessimistic tones of *Kulturkritik* and dystopian modernity prevail in the end of the text. If life has been drained from the old harbor, its memory still holds a residue of another life to be imagined and counterposed to a modernity that has become a void, an empty shell.

The miniatures of Benjamin's *Einbahnstraße* are neither *Denkbilder*, nor *Raumbilder*, nor are they, as critics have claimed, snapshots in any rigorous intermedial sense. Ernst Bloch got it right but failed to pursue his insight when he said that Benjamin perceived reality "as if the world were script, . . . as if he were simultaneously writing a book entirely made up of emblems."[12] Emblems instead of snapshots then: how can this be read? Any number of critics, of course, have referred to the emblematic nature of *Einbahnstraße* that is nowadays read in close proximity to *Origin of Tragic German Drama*, published in the very same year of 1928. But they have failed to pay attention to the medium-specific nature of the emblem that, for Benjamin, is primarily the emblem of the baroque. My argument here is in brief: what photography and the snapshot were for Kracauer's writing practice, the baroque emblem is for Benjamin. Both the differences and the affinities of their writing practices as well as their respective conceptualizations of the literary in relation to the visual result from these different intermedialities subtly inscribed into their texts.

Now the art-historical, literary, and philosophical debate about emblems can be as befuddling as that about allegory. I would start here with a simple observation. The baroque emblem, especially in the seventeenth century, was a multimedial mode of representing and interpreting a world out of joint. The coupling of words and pictures was of course not all that remarkable in a period that still upheld the Horatian view of *ut pictura poesis*. More important for my argument is the fact that the baroque emblem books were enormously popular, widely distributed all over Europe and used as educational and pedagogic tools in the period of the Counter-Reformation. Most famous was the emblem book of 1531 by the Italian lawyer and humanist Andrea Alciati, which soon made it from its original Latin into vernacular languages in more than 150 editions. Images and words combined in the emblem to re-create and to secure or even enforce a kind of harmony of the cosmic, religious, and secular universe that had become historically elusive and threatened in an age of religious wars. The critical view that the emblem articulates a fundamental crisis in the world is of course also Benjamin's own take when he says, "Allegories are, in the realm of thoughts what ruins are in the realm of things."[13] I suggest a paraphrase: Emblems are in the realm of media what ruins are in the realm of architecture. The notion of the emblem as ruin of course suggests a tension or conflict rather than harmony between its constitutive elements: words and pictures. This very tension, I would argue, is mobilized and translated in the miniatures of *Einbahnstraße*. Central to this translation of the baroque emblem smack into twentieth-century modernity, however, is a structure of absence: the absence of the emblematic picture in *Einbahnstraße*. This is a significant absence in the context of the historical avant-garde's, and especially the constructivists', privileged juxtaposition of word and image in the visual arts—developments for which Benjamin had great affinity.

When critics have read *Einbahnstraße* as emblematic prose they have not taken the specific media constellation of the emblem seriously enough. Time and again, they have reduced the fundamental tripartite structure of the emblem to the binary of word and image; in this account, the image quickly lost its meaning as *picture* in the concrete sense and was seen as literary or thought image. As literary-visual form, however, the emblem has not two but three parts: the *inscriptio* (title), the *pictura* (the image as picture), and the *subscriptio* (the interpretation of or commentary on the image). In his influential reading of Benjamin's *Denkbilder*, however, Heinz Schlaffer speaks of *Zweiteilung* (dichotomy) between report and reflection, *Erfahrung* and *Erkenntnis* (experience and knowledge), and of the doubling of *Gedanke* and *Anschauung* (thought and intuition).[14] The notion of *Zweiteilung* is of course not incorrect, but it is oblivious to the fact that the visual even as ekphrastic description in language (not to speak of real pictures such as fotos) is largely absent in *Einbahnstraße* as opposed to Kracauer's *Straßen*. The duality of report and reflection pertains more accurately to Benjamin's *Denkbilder* proper, that is, to the texts about Naples, Marseille, Moscow, and other concrete cities, texts that indeed do mix ekphrastic description with reflection, a mix that can then be seen as the equivalent in language of the alternation between *pictura* and *subscriptio* in the emblem. Only these *Städtebilder* contain extensive description of architectural space and urban context.[15] Neither *Einbahnstraße* nor *Denkbilder* include pictures, but the linguistic dimension of *res picta* is overwhelmingly present in the latter and largely absent from the former. It is thus simply not adequate to short-circuit the *Denkbilder* of 1933, which are thick with description, with the texts of *Einbahnstraße*.

Once we note this difference from the *Denkbilder* collection, *Einbahnstraße* appears as a very special case of urban writing. It does not, as is so often claimed, read the city in a broad metaphoric way—the city as a book, as it were, in Victor Hugo's sense. It rather reads script and only script in the city: the store signs, names of buildings, graffiti, advertising, public announcements. It focuses on where the city street is literally, not metaphorically, legible. As Bloch suggested: the city as script.[16]

Here it becomes telling that the *pictura*, central to the baroque emblem, is missing. There are only title and text, *inscriptio* and *subscriptio*. The baroque emblem, signature of a ruinous world, has become a ruin twice over. The only images conjured up are the internal images generated by the miniatures' titles, all of which refer to something seen in urban space

I have already noted that most of the miniatures themselves avoid any explicit ekphrastic or indexical dimension. So *pictura* is missing not only literally as real picture, but even in its linguistic transformation, except, that is, in the titles. But then the titles are closer to naming than to any recognizable ekphrasis. Names of sites of course do conjure up images, but these images remain rather generic in the text just as the names themselves are. Here they refer to specific urban sites such as Filling Station, Imperial Panorama, Construction Site; or to specific stores such as Chinese Curios, Stationers, Stamp Shop; or to public buildings like Mexican Embassy, Ministry of the Interior, First Aid; or to advertisements like *Germans, Drink German Beer, This Space for Rent*, and so forth. The sequence of the miniatures then resembles a street of shops and public buildings, but only insofar as they are visibly named in letters in their urban environment.

By forgoing the emblematic picture in the text, Benjamin marks his position vis-à-vis the avant-gardist montage experiments with word/image constellations, practices toward which he felt drawn theoretically and philosophically. It is therefore puzzling that Benjamin, who along with Kracauer did so much to validate the new media of technical reproducibility, never used images in his own literary experiments. Benjamin does not defend *Schrifttum* in a traditional sense, as Hofmannsthal and others fearful of the new media would have done at the same time. But he does go all out for script in his focus on the radical change of literary culture, which he calls for in the first miniature, "Filling Station." Phrases there like "the construction of life" or "the power of facts" as well as the privileging of "leaflets, brochures, articles, and placards" come directly out of constructivist manifestoes and magazines of the early 1920s to which he himself contributed occasionally.

The key programmatic text here is "Attested Auditor of Books" with its claim that "the book in its traditional form is nearing its end."[17] It elaborates the theme already struck in "Filling Station," which argues that "true literary activity cannot aspire to take place within a literary framework." "Attested Auditor of Books" provides the rationale. After a reference to Mallarmé, the Dadaists, and new typographic experiments, the exposition continues.

> Script—having found, in the book, a refuge in which it can lead an autonomous existence—is pitilessly dragged out into the street by advertisements and subjected to the brutal heteronomies of economic chaos. This is the hard schooling of its new form. If centuries ago it began gradually to lie down, passing from the upright inscription to the manuscript resting on sloping desks before finally taking itself to bed in the printed book, it now begins just as slowly to rise again from the ground. The newspaper is read more in the vertical than in the horizontal plane, while film and advertisement force the printed word entirely into the dictatorial perpendicular. And before a contemporary finds his way clear to opening a book, his eyes have been exposed to such a blizzard [*dichtes Gestöber*] of changing, colorful, conflicting letters that the chances of his penetrating the archaic stillness of the book are slight. Locust swarms of print [*Heuschreckenschwärme von Schrift*], which already eclipse the sun of what city dwellers take for intellect, will grow thicker with each succeeding year.[18]

What Benjamin describes here as the new forms of script creating both an urban imaginary and a new form of mediated subjectivity is noticeably close in language to how Kracauer, in his 1927 essay "On Photography," writes of the "blizzard of photographs." Kracauer's urban miniatures are indeed as suggestive of the photograph as Benjamin's are close to the emblem. But photography as (arguably) the modern media equivalent of the baroque emblem's etching/woodcuts is precisely denied in *Einbahnstraße* and replaced by the focus on script in its new urban transformation. Indeed, even when writing about photography, Benjamin saw script as indispensable. Thus in his essay on photography, he referred to Moholy-Nagy's famous statement "The illiteracy of the future will be ignorance not of reading or writing, but of photography" and then followed up with a rather rhetorical question: "But shouldn't a photographer who cannot read his own pictures be no less accounted an illiterate? Won't inscription become the most important part of the photograph?"[19] And five years later in his "Second Letter from Paris" on painting and photography he criticized the surrealists' failure "to recognize the social impact of photography, and therefore the importance of inscription—the fuse guiding the critical spark to the image mass (as is best seen in Heartfield)."[20] If in Kracauer the "image mass" or "blizzard of image" needed to be *umfunktioniert* (repurposed) by critical consciousness, that is, philosophical and sociological intervention, to develop the medium's emancipatory potential, Benjamin ascribes the same task to inscription—*Schrift*. Thus Benjamin, in "Attested Auditor of Books," imagines a radically new "eccentric figurativeness" (*exzentrische Bildlichkeit*), a kind of "picture-writing" in which "poets . . . will be able to participate only by mastering the fields in which (quite unobtrusively) it is being constructed: statistical and technical diagrams."[21] This, of course, is over the top. For the lover of letters like Walter Benjamin, it is an almost masochistic embrace of constructivist and Soviet-style factography and its (entropic) minimalism of both language and vision.

Given his insistence on captions for images—captions that are more than captions—one wonders to what extent Benjamin shared a then widespread view of photography itself as merely an indexical reproduction of the seen. In this regard, adding photographs to the texts of *Einbahnstraße* might have completed the tripartite structure of the emblem, but at the price of sacrificing the truly allegorical nature of the baroque visual emblem—images that were not immediately accessible to understanding without the *subscriptio*. If the baroque emblem already was a sign of a ruinous world, then the structure of absence in Benjamin's prose miniatures mutilates the emblem even further; but it also endows the remaining script with the hope for some new awakening and for the imagined new social order toward which the one-way street is pointed. Throughout *Einbahnstraße* Benjamin imagines another *Schrifttum* destined to join the phantasm of an alternative technology that would reestablish a mythical union of man and nature, the world and the cosmos, as it is laid out in "To the Planetarium," the final text at the end of the one-way street.

What then can we conclude from this comparison of Benjamin's and Kracauer's *Städtebilder*? Emblem and photograph are different media of reproducibility in print. Both rely on a combination of the visual with the verbal, with *subscriptio* corresponding to the caption. Both are part of popular or mass culture. But this is as far as the affinity between Kracauer and Benjamin goes. For while Kracauer always conjures up the sheer visible materiality of built space and constructs it as social space, Benjamin focuses on script and legibility only, leaving observed architectural and urban realities out of the picture. If I am right in suggesting that Benjamin consciously tried to articulate a conflict between the visual and the verbal, emblemlike, in his texts, then the absence of images (except of course on the famous cover picture designed by Sasha Stone) is indeed stunning. What else could these images have been in the twentieth century but photographs of urban scenes about which Benjamin wrote eloquently in his comments on Atget? And yet: Benjamin who has done so much to validate image media such as photography and film betrayed a deep mistrust in pictures alone, a mistrust he shared with Kracauer. Reading Kracauer's street texts back from Benjamin, then, it becomes clear that Kracauer, too, could not have placed real snapshots of urban spaces into his texts. Any such illustration would have simply undone the complexity of *Durchdringung* he had achieved in the writing of his urban texts.

Which street texts are finally more successful in getting at urban imaginaries—*Einbahnstraße* or *Straßen in Berlin und anderswo*? Benjamin's book has often been read as a literary failure. The rigor of his focus on the literal legibility of urban space has indeed limited the range of his insight into built urban space and its social and political dimensions. But if it is a failure, it is a conceptually highly interesting one resulting from the need to rethink the relationship between the visual and the verbal in urban modernity in novel ways. Josef Roth makes no bones about his preference for Kracauer: "Krac is clear, grounded, sharp, bitter. Krac pulls abstractions from the air and makes them come alive, Krac is a philosophical poet and therefore valuable to journalism."[22] About Benjamin, by contrast, Roth had little better to say—unfairly—than that he was getting lost in *Luftgeschäfte*. But Roth is right on one thing: Kracauer's urban miniatures are quite different from Benjamin's in that they are saturated with concrete perceptions of urban space. They reveal the nightmarish dimensions of built space, thus getting at the political unconscious of a metropolitan transformation in the clutch of capitalist modernization.

NOTES

1. Louis Sébastien Mercier, *Tableau de Paris* (Paris: Mercure de France, 1994).

2. Siegfried Kracauer, "Zu den Schriften Walter Benjamins," *Frankfurter Zeitung*, 15 July 1928, 72. English trans. in Siegfried Kracauer, *The Mass Ornament* (Cambridge: Harvard University Press, 1995), 259–66.

3. "Here we bring to general consciousness how the matter of our present is arranged, and according to which intentions it shifts. The reports point up the very space for politics." Benno Reifenberg, "Gewissenshaft" *Frankfurter Zeitung*, 1 July 1929.

4. Ibid.

5. Robert Musil, *Kritik. Literatur-Theater-Kunst 1912–1930*, vol. 9 of *Gesammelte Werke*, ed. Adolf Frisé (Reinbek: Rowohlt, 1978), 1468.

6. Siegfried Kracauer, "Exposé zur Reorganisation der Neuen Rundschau," 18 July 1928. Kracauer Nachlass, Deutsches Literaturarchiv, Marbach. Sigfried Giedion, *Bauen in Frankreich, Bauen in Eisen, Bauen in Eisenbeton* (Leipzig: Klinckhardt, 1928). Cf. Andreas Huyssen, "Modernist Miniatures: Literary Snapshots of Urban Space," *PMLA* 122, no. 1 (January 2007): 27–42, esp. 38. This earlier essay's argument about Kracauer returns here in order to develop the comparison with Benjamin.

7. Siegfried Kracauer, "Über Arbeitsnachweise," *Schriften* 5.2 (Frankfurt am Main: Suhrkamp, 1990), 186. Translation mine.

8. Siegfried Kracauer, "Photography," in *Mass Ornament*, 75–88.

9. Roland Barthes, *Camera Lucida* (New York: Farrar, 1981), 27.

10. Maurice Merleau-Ponty, *Das Auge und der Geist* (Reinbek: Rowohlt, 1967), 39.

11. Siegfried Kracauer, "Aus dem Fenster gesehen," in *Straßen in Berlin und anderswo* (Berlin: Arsenal, 1987), 41.

12. Ernst Bloch, "Erinnerungen," in *Über Walter Benjamin* (Frankfurt am Main: Suhrkamp, 1968), 17.

13. Walter Benjamin, *The Origin of Tragic German Drama* (London: NLB, 1977), 178.

14. Heinz Schlaffer, "Denkbilder: Eine kleine Prosaform zwischen Dichtung und Gesellschaftstheorie," in *Poesie und Politik*, ed. Wolfgang Kuttenkeuler (Stuttgart: Kohlhammer, 1973), 137–54.

15. On *Städtebilder*, see Peter Szondi, "Benjamins Städtebilder," in *Schriften* II, ed. Wolfgang Fietkau (Frankfurt am Main: Suhrkamp, 1978), 295–309.

16. Ernst Bloch, "Revueform in der Philosophie," in *Erbschaft dieser Zeit* (Frankfurt am Main: Suhrkamp, 1973), 368–71.

17. Walter Benjamin, "One-Way Street," in *1913–1926*, vol. 1 of *Selected Writings* (Cambridge: Harvard University Press, 1996), 456.

18. Ibid.

19. Walter Benjamin, *1927–1934*, vol. 2 of *Selected Writings* (Cambridge: Harvard University Press, 1999), 527.

20. Walter Benjamin, *1935–1938*, vol. 3 of *Selected Writings* (Cambridge: Harvard University Press, 2002), 241.

21. Benjamin, "One-Way Street," 457.

22. Joseph Roth, letter to Reifenberg, 13 May 1926. Quoted in Helmut Stalder, *Siegfried Kracauer: Das journalistische Werk in der 'Frankfurter Zeitung' 1921–1933* (Würzburg: Königshausen und Neumann, 2003), 97.

*Last Things Before the Last:
History, Anthropology,
Ethnography, Ethics*

On Natural History

Concepts of History in Adorno and Kracauer

Christina Gerhardt

In "Adorno and Kracauer: Notes on a Troubled Friendship," Martin Jay reveals the tensions between Theodor W. Adorno and Siegfried Kracauer during the last years of Kracauer's life as evidenced in memoranda Kracauer wrote about two particular meetings they had in August 1960 and July 1964.[1] At the time of the meetings, Adorno was working on *Negative Dialectics* (1966)[2] and Kracauer was working on *History: The Last Things Before the Last* (1969).[3] To a large extent, their discussions, documented and responded to in the memoranda, outline the critiques Adorno and Kracauer have of one another's projects, in particular, but more broadly, these discussions also pinpoint systemic critiques that reach beyond the focus of these two specific works.

In the memoranda of 1960, Kracauer lays out disagreements between his and Adorno's understandings of concepts such as utopia, dialectics, ontology, ideology and sociology. The memorandum written after a meeting in 1964 focuses renewed attention on what Kracauer deems to be the pitfalls of Adorno's *Negative Dialectics*.[4] As Jay argues, "Many of the points he made against *Negative Dialectics* and Adorno's approach in general must be acknowledged as serious obstacles for anyone anxious to defend the Frankfurt School's legacy."[5] Inversely, Adorno's critiques of the shortcomings of Kracauer's methodology surface in "The Curious Realist," an article he wrote in 1964 on the occasion of Kracauer's seventy-fifth birthday.[6] Little subsequent research has taken up these memos and studied their implications for their differing philosophical, political, and historical models.

Weaving together an analysis of these memos and of the models of nature and history in Kracauer's *History* and Adorno's *Negative Dialectics* reveals their varying notions of history.[7] In their early exchanges about natural history, found in the memos, their diverging beliefs are nascent but not yet fully fledged. The differences emerge starkly in their later work. Specifically, in Adorno's *Negative Dialectics* the term *natural history* appears in order to revise Hegel's model of history, and in Kracauer's *History*, *natural history* articulates the border between the disciplines of the natural sciences and the social sciences. Thus, a careful study and comparison of these latter two texts reveals an asymmetry in their uses of the term: for Adorno *natural history* appears as a *philosophical concept*, while Kracauer reads it as a *disciplinary object*. The divergences yield a deeper understanding of variegated uses of the term in Frankfurt School writing. With renewed interest in the concept of nature and of natural history in the Frankfurt School,[8] it is my wager that this analysis will add a useful chapter to our knowledge not only of Adorno's and Kracauer's friendship but also of their thinking and writings, particularly vis-à-vis models of history and of the Frankfurt School.

I. Early Disagreements: Memos on "Dialectics and Ontology" (1960)

Adorno met Kracauer, a family friend who was fourteen years his senior, in 1918 when he was only fifteen years old. In this final year of World War I, Adorno was still a Gymnasiast and Kracauer already an architect. A friendship quickly ensued. "Over a period of years, regularly on Saturday afternoons, Kracauer read the *Critique of Pure Reason* with me," Adorno recalls in 1964.[9] The meetings planted the seeds of a lifelong friendship and, looking backward, had a lifelong impact, as Adorno acknowledges: "I am not exaggerating in the slightest when I say that I owe more to this reading than to my academic teachers."[10] Their correspondence reflects this enduring friendship.

The epistolary exchange spans from letters written a few years after they met to ones exchanged a month before Kracauer's passing, thus revealing the history of Adorno and Kracauer's friendship. The letters are interspersed with the two memoranda or notes Kracauer made after Adorno and he met on 12 August 1960 at Hotel Sonnenheim in Bergün, Switzerland, in order to discuss their respective projects: Adorno's *Negative Dialectics*, published in 1966, and Kracauer's *History*, published posthumously in 1969. While Kracauer mentions in a subsequent letter that he thinks often about the meeting and their conversations, the substantive nature of the debate between the two remains for the most part unmentioned in their correspondence.[11] According to Kracauer's first memorandum, the debates hinge on three main topics: (1) the concept of utopia; (2) dialectics vs. ontology; and (3) ideology and sociology.

Kracauer's and Adorno's differing views on "dialectics vs. ontology" constitute the substantive part of their disagreements with serious implications for their varying systems of history as exemplified in Adorno's *Negative Dialectics* and Kracauer's *History*. To some extent, the differing viewpoints expressed in Kracauer's notes can already be traced in earlier writings, but they took on a new form in the explicit discussions they had about them, both at Bergün in 1960 and in their correspondence around the time. While the period starting around 1960 was a challenging one for the friendship between Adorno and Kracauer, these years were also the ones in which some of their deepest and most enduring works were written and published. In the last two decades of Adorno's life volumes of his late musical and literary criticism appeared one after the other. During the same decade, Kracauer's *Theory of Film: The Redemption of Physical Reality* (1960), *Ornament der Masse* (1963), *Ginster* (1964), *Straßen in Berlin und anderswo* (1964), and *Theorie des Films. Die Errettung der äußeren Wirklichkeit* (1964) were published. Meanwhile, Kracauer focused on conceptualizing *History: The Last Things Before the Last*, which he first mentions in a letter to Leo Löwenthal in October 1960 and to Adorno in December 1960,[12] and Adorno focused on *Negative Dialectics*, which he first mentions in a letter to Kracauer in November 1960.

II. Natural History in Adorno's *Negative Dialectics*

Fundamental to Adorno's *Negative Dialectics* are the concepts of dialectics and of ontology; they anchor the initial two parts of the book and are followed by three chapters, laying out the implications of Adorno's revised models of dialectics and of ontology for Kant's concept of freedom, Hegel's model of history, and metaphysics after Auschwitz. In preparation for the volume, Adorno wrote a series of lectures on dialectics and ontology, which he gave at the Collège de France and in Frankfurt in 1961.[13] At the time of their meeting in 1960, as Kracauer puts forth in his notes on their conversation, Adorno was "making notes for a course on this theme [Dialectics vs. Ontology]."[14] According to Adorno, these lectures together with notes on Hegel's *Logic* were to form the basis of a new introduction to dialectics. At the time, the volume had the working title "Dialectical Meditations"; it eventually became *Negative Dialectics*.[15] In essence, Adorno proposes a concept of history in order to undertake a philosophical revision.

At the heart of Kracauer's critique rests his accusation that Adorno rejects "any ontological stipulations in favor of an infinite dialectics."[16] Kracauer argues that there had to be some relationship between the two. Ontology and dialectics are not—in Kracauer's estimation—related in Adorno's model, as illustrated by a drawing he included with the memo and also by Kracauer's characterization of the issue in his notes as one of "dialectics *vs*. ontology" (emphasis added). The model that Adorno proposes, Kracauer counters, resulted in "a process which has no goal outside of movement itself" and which "made me just dizzy."[17]

Adorno responds to this allegation with a section of *Negative Dialectics* entitled "Vertiginousness": "A dialectics no longer glued to identity will provoke either the charge that it is bottomless . . . or the objection that it is dizzying. . . . The anachronistic suggestion often made to philosophy is that it must have no part in any such thing."[18] He also takes up the issue in his 1965–66 *Lectures on Negative Dialectic*, which begins with the note, "The charge against negative dialectics that it is vertigo arousing (Kracauer)" and continues further on to state, "The vertigo, which the thought that cannot be reconstructed afterwards arouses, is index veri."[19] In other words, Adorno does not deny that his model of dialectics, "no longer glued to identity," will provoke a feeling of dizziness or vertigo. Instead, Adorno argues that this very movement is an index of truth or of the *actual* properties of identity: it is ever-changing.

On this point, Kracauer is right: Adorno's model of dialectics is predicated on continual movement, or, rather, it pinpoints what Adorno deems to be a blind spot in Hegel's model of dialectics and of ontology, that is, a structure of stasis that fallaciously presupposes stable relations. In a section of *Negative Dialectics* entitled "Dialectics Cut Short by Hegel" in the English edition (for the German original had no such section headings),[20] Adorno quotes Hegel, who says, "Substantial unity is an absolute and motionless end in itself."[21] Adorno believes neither in the unity proclaimed by Hegel nor in its absolute and motionless nature. He retorts, Hegel "does not put his trust in dialectics, does not look upon it as the force to cure itself, and disavows his own assurance that identity will produce itself in dialectics."[22] For Adorno, an actual dialectics—and hence his emphasis on the negative, the Other, the thing that undoes or keeps in motion—consists of movement. That is, in Adorno's estimation, the opposite of what

Hegel argues holds true: dialectics, precisely by dint of its motion, produces the end, which is never an end. Furthermore, according to Adorno, the motion of dialectics produces a form of identity that is always in renegotiation and contestation.

Adorno revises Hegel's account of identity, grappling with it from the very first pages of *Negative Dialectics* on, in a section entitled "Dialectics at a Standstill." Hegel's account of identity involves the immediacy between subject and predicate.

> To say "this rose is red" (in virtue of the copula "is") involves the coincidence of subject and predicate. The rose however is a concrete thing and so not red only: it also has an odor, a specific form, and many other features not implied in the predicate red. . . . There are other flowers and objects which are red, too. The subject and predicate . . . touch, as it were, only in a single point, but do not cover each other.[23]

Hegel was aware of the problem inherent to identity, of trying to adequate predicate and object. Adorno takes up this quandary, that is, they are not equal. In fact "objects do not go into concepts without leaving a remainder, . . . they contradict the traditional norm of adequation."[24] He lingers on this blind spot and tries to construct a theory around it, one that would accommodate the remainder. Again, Adorno's solution does not shy away from recognizing the limits to providing an account of identity.

Altering the concept of identity, and, by dint of it, of ontology, Adorno suggests a theory of nonidentity. He takes his cue from Hegel, who says that "identity is undoubtedly negative . . . at the same time self-relation, and what is more, negative self-relation."[25] This is the nonidentity of identity in Adorno: identifying something will never quite match up with the thing. As Adorno states, "the thing is not identical with the concept. . . . This is how the sense of nonidentity contains identity."[26] Thus, for Adorno ontology is always already tied not only to what is but also to what is not (included in the definition). When Adorno examines being, he does not seek to purge it of misidentification, rather he is merely demonstrating the *insufficiency* of identification. Ontology or identification always needs nonidentification, the negative. In this sense, Adorno's account of being, of what *is* is, indeed, constantly in motion, seeking the Other, to which it must defer for its meaning.

Adorno's account of ontology or of being as the nonidentification of identification is closely tied to his concept of dialectics, specifically negative dialectics. For Adorno this revised model does not stand in opposition

to ontology, as Kracauer charges: rather the two concepts inform one another but in a manner that is best negotiated by an awareness of the pre-
supposed but unspoken, the unstated and negative aspect of the dialectics,
and this, in his estimation, is ever-changing.

In Adorno's estimation, natural history, which forms the focal point of
the last pages of his second model "World Spirit and Natural History: An
Excursion to Hegel," instantiates not only his revised concept of ontology
and of dialectics but also of history. Contrasting the way that Hegel and
Marx deal with nature in their accounts of history, Adorno argues that
Hegel acknowledged nature in his model of history: "Hegel cites nature
and natural forces as models of history."[27] But in Hegel's model, nature is
absorbed by human history, in Hegel's world spirit of history. Marx, by
contrast, argues that history and nature mutually inform one another:
"History can be considered from two sides, divided into the history of nature and the history of mankind. Yet there is no separating the two sides; as
long as men exist, natural and human history will qualify each other."[28]
The ostensible antithesis or opposition of nature and history is, according
to Adorno, at once conceptual and real. That is, the antithesis expresses
that—conceptually—natural history has typically been absorbed, as in
Hegel's model, into human history, in other words, erased, covered up.
Adorno deems this to be a philosophical and conceptual shortcoming of
Hegel and tries to resolve it via a philosophical or conceptual revision,
however, with real implications. That is, Adorno seeks to underscore the
consequences of his (conceptual) revision for (re-)reading history, as human history *and* natural history, hence his reference to Marx. He seeks to
bring a material base back into the revision.

And in this way, the ostensible antithesis of nature and history is not
real, in that it does not express how vital nature is for human history.[29]
Adorno argues for reading nature and history together with his revised
model of dialectics: he seeks to bring the erased or suppressed element
back into the conversation. And his argument about the relationship between nature and history informs his understanding of ontology. As he puts
it, "The ontological claim to be beyond the divergence of nature and history is surreptitious."[30] Instead, he continues, "it would be up to thought to
see all nature . . . as history, and all history as nature."[31] In these ways,
Adorno's category of nature as *Natur-Geschichte* or *natural history*, whereby
nature stands next to history, exemplifies his revisions, drawing on Benjamin, to models of ontology and of dialectics, with implications for how
we read nature into history and history into nature.[32]

Adorno links his concerns about ontology, negative dialectics, and history with natural history. For while History always carries the same singular message, Adorno's natural history pinpoints the suppression of antagonisms within dialectics, the sort of antagonisms on whose suppression History is founded. The political "lessons" of natural history are ones about contradictions, about the nonidentity of identity, about alterity. What rests at the heart of Adorno's conceptualization of ontology is precisely an identity that is always in the process of becoming, and this process is (to be) negotiated through dialectics. This dialectical process, as Kracauer notices, produces a sense of vertigo as a by-product. And in Adorno's estimation, natural history as a philosophical concept exemplifies such a revised model not only of ontology and of dialectics but also of history.

III. Kracauer's *History: The Last Things Before the Last* (1969)

Kracauer proposes a very different model of history in his *History: The Last Things Before the Last*, but one also predicated on nature. In fact, Kracauer opens his *History* with a chapter entitled "Nature."[33] In it, he grapples with the study of historiography and its "relations to the sciences."[34] He begins by referring to the relationship between the *Geisteswissenschaften* (humanities) and *Naturwissenschaft* (natural sciences) in the German academic tradition, drawing on Wilhelm Dilthey. At the heart of Kracauer's inquiry rests the question whether or not the laws governing nature or the natural sciences can be said to apply to history or the social sciences. Kracauer is concerned both with questions involving discipline and methodology and with the relationship between human and natural history.

Kracauer, like Adorno, discusses history in light of its relationship to nature. Kracauer argues that "human affairs must be assumed to fall largely into the realm of nature or to be an extension of it. On principle, such a fusion may also materialize the other way round; nature may be imagined to partake of man's historicity. This possibility has found a powerful supporter in Marx."[35] And, like Adorno, Kracauer underscores Marx's arguments along these lines.

Kracauer's and Adorno's attention had been brought to the subject of nature in Marx by Alfred Schmidt, a doctoral student of Adorno's, who completed his dissertation on *The Concept of Nature in Marx*, in 1960.[36] References to Schmidt abound in their correspondence, and his study made a deep impression on both Adorno's *Negative Dialectics* and Kracauer's *History*. In a letter to Adorno from 12 October 1962, Kracauer writes, "In the meantime, I have read Alfred Schmidt's study about the concept of nature in Marx, which was enormously profitable for me and also my work. It is an excellent study of source material. . . . The exposure of the utopian findings in Marx was extraordinarily interesting—at least for me."[37] Kracauer references Schmidt's study numerous times in *History*.[38]

Kracauer's reading, however, of the relationship between nature and history differs from Adorno's. As mentioned above, Adorno is keenly aware and appreciative of the imbrication of nature and history in Marx's thinking. Adorno puts it this way in *Negative Dialectics:* "The objectivity of historic life is that of natural history [*Natur-Geschichte*]. Marx, as opposed to Hegel, knew this and knew it strictly in the context of the universal that is realized over the subject's heads."[39] Adorno continues by quoting Marx who said, "Even if a society has found its natural law of motion . . . natural evolutionary phases can be neither skipped nor decreed out of existence . . . I comprehend the development of society's economic formation of society as a process of natural history."[40] For Marx, then, natural history and society's history are bound together.

Furthermore, Marx's history does not form a whole with a universalizing meaning as in Hegel. As Susan Buck-Morss points out, "This total rejection of the Hegelian concept of history as the identity of subject and object . . . was a fundamental point of agreement between Adorno and his closest intellectual colleagues. It defined the limits of their willingness to see Marx through Hegelian glasses."[41] Marxism attempts to grasp a historical process in accordance with the world without resorting to metaphysical dogmas that it places on the world. As Engels said, materialist philosophy consists in explaining "the world from the world itself."[42] In this alternative model, then, the world or nature is anterior to man's ability to reason. It is not, however, "a thing given direct from all eternity, remaining ever the same, but the product of industry and of the state of society."[43] So, even if the Marxist model begins with the world and materiality, it immediately stipulates that it must be recognized that this material reality is, from the beginning, socially mediated. In addition, Marx and Engels stipulate that neither history nor nature remains ever the same. Or, as Marx and Engels put it, "as long as men exist the history of nature and the history of men are mutually conditioned."[44] In this way, nature is mediated by society, and, inversely, society, or human history, is mediated by nature. In Marx, nature and history are tied together.

In contrast to Adorno, Kracauer argues that Marx does not read the relationship between natural history and human history as dialectical. Kracauer states, "While [Marx] is confident that nature, as manifest in man, is subject to historical change, he seems to assign to external nature, nature about us, a nondialectical, independent status and, in consequence, (relative) unchangeability."[45] Furthermore, Kracauer reads nature as fairly immutable: "And since [Carl Friedrich] von Weizsaecker estimates the life expectancy of the historicized cosmos at over a hundred billion years, we may rest assured that natural causes will continue to produce their predicted effects for an indeterminate time."[46] Throughout the first chapter of *History*, Kracauer underscores that he reads nature as unchanging.

Kracauer also reads human history as distinct from nature. "The historian," he states, "must tell a story . . . And why must the historian tell a story? Because he invariably comes across irreducible entities—units which . . . mark the emergence of something new, something beyond the jurisdiction of nature."[47] Human history, Kracauer argues, exists in a jurisdiction or realm separate from nature.

Kracauer's larger project in *History* is to discern what distinguishes the natural sciences and the social sciences, or history and other disciplines. Picking up on Dilthey's observations, Kracauer argues that the application of the laws of the natural sciences to a reading of the social sciences, including history, proves to be reductive for history. In Kracauer's estimation, the attempt to read human history and nature together is problematic, since he believes science reduces the study of forces to mathematical laws and then seeks to apply them to human history, as Kracauer's presentation of "Charles Tilly's attempt to interpret the 1793 Vendée revolt from a social scientist's point of view" makes clear: "Tilly thus implements his interpretative intentions by summoning, and arraying, certain regularities of behavior."[48] Yet "human affairs," Kracauer says elsewhere, "transcend the dimension of natural forces and causally determined patterns."[49] Herein lies the reason for Kracauer's reading of history and nature as divided, as he continues: "In consequence, any approach to history which claims to be scientific in a stricter sense of the word will sooner or later come across unsurmountable [*sic*] obstacles."[50] An attempt to read historical events in accordance with mathematic or scientific laws will inevitably bump into the conceptual limits.

The concern that rests at the heart of Kracauer's disavowal of reading human history together with nature is that it would prevent freedom. As he puts it, "The identification of history with nature . . . yields laws . . . which not only unduly minimize the role of contingencies in history but, more important, preclude man's freedom of his choice."[51] He adds, "A natural law . . . , more rigid than all previous ones, not only obliterates human freedom at the outset but ruthlessly smothers the dream of it."[52] In closing, he states, "To draw the balance, human history irrevocably differs from natural history. . . . Unlike natural history, whose narrative components may, on principle, be superseded by such laws, the history of human affairs must retain an epic quality. Its irreducible share of freedom ultimately defies any treatment in natural science fashion which shuts out that freedom."[53] According to Kracauer, to read human history as natural history means applying the laws of science, and therefore reading history as fairly immutable: it must accord with the model and thus cannot acknowledge realizations that arise from a study of the events themselves.

To some extent, Kracauer's and Adorno's models of history do not diverge as much in their ultimate aspiration even if their points of departure and sites of engagement are radically different. That is, while Adorno's revisions stem from preoccupations within philosophical models, and Kracauer's arguments are based on concerns about disciplinary boundaries, both seem to challenge the same fundamental structure: Adorno is concerned that a model of dialectics at a standstill does not capture the suppressed or negative element, leading him to propose an alternative account that is perpetually in motion, always shifting in order to account for what is neglected or left over as a remainder. Kracauer, meanwhile, frustrated by the immutable laws of science and how—if applied to history—they do not take into account man's freedom, argues for a radical distinction between the disciplines. It seems, however, that both are grappling with the selfsame issue, albeit in differing areas of inquiry: immutable models—be they of philosophy or of the sciences—and their inability to adequate history. Leaving aside whether or not their claims are accurate, it seems that both Adorno and Kracauer seek a model that deals with the changes in history, expressed in Adorno through the negative dialectics or a dialectics perpetually in motion and in Kracauer through man's freedom. While—structurally—they are seeking the same thing, it leads them to a radically different conclusion vis-à-vis nature: Adorno deems it to be an instantiation of negative dialectics, in that it is a form of history that has been suppressed from the master narrative, while Kracauer deems it to be precisely the antithesis: that which places upon history immutable laws.

What Kracauer proposes instead are historical narratives that emerge out of a study of the relationships among events of a historical period. As he puts it in his 1960 memo, "I pointed out that it would be an urgent task for research to find out how the intellectual and social life of a given period are actually connected with each other. What are the channels, if any, that lead from a work of art to the social circumstances under which it was created? What counts now, is to prove or disprove the widespread tacid [*sic*, tacit] assumption of the unity of any historical period."[54] Kracauer's proposed model invokes Adorno's structure of the constellation, in which concepts are clarified out of their relationship to one another.

To be sure, Kracauer's concerns about history and his invocation of nature are motivated by questions about disciplinary differences. That is, he is keen to present a model of history as part of the social sciences with its own attendant methodology in contradistinction to the model of nature as part of the natural sciences governed by its mathematical laws and causality. To some extent, he seeks to separate the disciplines in order to restore an awareness and a sense of man's freedom, and also in order to inspire a reading of history out of its constituent events.

IV. Conclusion—Natural Science, Natural History

Interestingly, both Adorno and Kracauer grapple with the concept of nature in their late works and use the concept of natural history in order to discuss models of history. The conclusions they reach, however, differ radically. For Adorno, natural history evidences not only a dialectical model but also the need to recognize the suppressed aspect of the dialectical model, the negative component of the dialectics, also manifest in the nonidentity of identity. In his estimation, natural history gestures toward the need to read identity and history as ever-changing. Furthermore, history—in Adorno's view—does not always progress teleologically toward some higher ground, as it does in Hegel and in Lukács. He argues against this notion already in his 1932 lecture "On the Idea of Natural History," which he revisits when discussing natural history and human history in *Negative Dialectics*. Bringing in Benjamin's *Origin of the German Tragic Drama*, Adorno argues for a reading of history that would consider the possibility of history as transient rather than progressive.

In Kracauer, by contrast, *nature* refers to the natural sciences and their immutable laws, which—when applied to human history—confine a reading of it to mathematical formulas. Kracauer is concerned that events are read not in light of the context out of which they emerge but rather as a result of causal connections. Furthermore, Kracauer believes that such a reading of historical events curtails human freedom. It stymies the ability to read and formulate historical narratives out of the events of a historical era.

The variations in their models of history, illustrated by their accounts of nature, are already evident in the memos related to their 1960 and 1964 meetings, which focus on utopia, dialectics and ontology, and ideology and sociology. While Kracauer calls for a concrete utopia, Adorno states "that the concept of utopia is a *vanishing* concept. . . . it vanishes if you want to spell it out."[55] Similarly, vis-à-vis ontology, Kracauer argues that events should be read out of what is, something concrete, "terms of substance" as he puts it.[56] (To some extent his argument here echoes his argument for a concrete utopia.) In Kracauer's estimation, Adorno's model of dialectics, whereby things are constantly changing, feels no such compunction to the real or concrete. Lastly, Kracauer argues in the section about ideology and sociology that Adorno never discusses "the material nature of society."[57]

To some extent, the differing notions of nature that appeared in Kracauer's and Adorno's late writings stem from their differing aims: Adorno, as mentioned, uses nature as natural history, as a philosophical concept in order to revise what he deems to be problematic limitations of Hegel's philosophy; Kracauer, by contrast, draws upon nature as an object of inquiry while exploring the border between disciplinary boundaries. And yet, however Adorno and Kraucauer diverge, reading their late writings in which they discuss natural history, nature, and human history together proves edifying for developing new models of history. For while human history rests on or is contingent on nature, as Marx points out, it also exists—to some extent—separately, as Kracauer argues. That is, there are events in human history that are not entirely contingent on natural history, and there are ones that cannot be understood by drawing on scientific laws or mathematical formulae. These events explode or rupture causal accounts. But human history can affect natural history, and, inversely, natural history can inform and influence human history, as Adorno argues. As Pensky puts it, "What Adorno emphatically has in mind here . . . is the singular 'methodological proposal' . . . that such pathologies will remain closed off to critical investigation until the critic is able to bring about a *change of perspective*, and it is this changed perspective that Adorno ultimately means by the concept of natural history."[58] In other words: an account of history that is attendant on natural history would read differently than most current models of history qua history.

NOTES

This article dovetails with my book manuscript, *The Idea of Nature in Theodor W. Adorno's Writings*, currently under review for publication. I thank Gerd Gemünden for his invitation to participate in the 2008 "Looking After Siegfried Kracauer" conference at Dartmouth College and John Abromeit, Robert S. Eshelman, Gerd Gemünden, Martin Jay, Max Pensky, and Johannes von Moltke for their useful feedback on earlier versions of this article.

1. Martin Jay, "Adorno and Kracauer: Notes on a Troubled Friendship," in *Permanent Exiles: Essays on the Intellectual Migration from Germany to America* (New York: Columbia Press, 1985), 216–36. When Jay published his article, the memoranda were unpublished. While the 1960 memorandum was published in 2008 as part of Adorno and Kracauer's correspondence, the 1964 memorandum remains unpublished.

2. Theodor W. Adorno, *Negative Dialektik*, vol. 6 of *Gesammelte Schriften*, ed. Rolf Tiedemann (Frankfurt am Main: Suhrkamp, 1997). Hereafter cited as *ND*. *Negative Dialectics*, trans. E. B. Ashton (New York: Seabury, 1973). Hereafter cited as *NDe*.

3. Siegfried Kracauer, *History: The Last Things Before the Last* (New York: Oxford University Press, 1969). Hereafter cited as *H*.

4. Theodor W. Adorno, *Siegfried Kracauer, Briefwechsel, 1923–1966*, vol. 7 of *Theodor W. Adorno, Briefe und Briefwechsel*, ed. Wolfgang Schopf (Frankfurt am Main: Suhrkamp, 2008). Hereafter cited as *B*. Here, 514–17. The correspondence is unpublished in English; all translations provided are my own. Kracauer's memo was written in English.

5. Jay, 235.

6. Theodor W. Adorno, "Der wunderliche Realist: Über Siegfried Kracauer," *Noten zur Literatur 3*, vol. 11 of *Gesammelte Schriften*, ed. Rolf Tiedemann (Frankfurt am Main: Suhrkamp, 1997), 388–408. Hereafter cited as "WR." In English, "The Curious Realist: On Siegfried Kracauer," trans. Shierry Weber Nicholsen, *Notes on Literature*, vol. 2 (New York: Columbia University Press, 1992). Hereafter cited as "CR."

7. For prior analyses of Kracauer's *History*, see also Gertrud Koch, trans. Jeremy Gaines, "'Not Yet Accepted Anywhere': Exile, Memory, and Image in Kracauer's Conception of History," Special Issue on Siegfried, *New German Critique* 54 (Autumn 1991): 95–109. Inka Mülder-Bach, trans. Gail Finney, "History as Autobiography: The Last Things Before the Last," Special Issue on Siegfried Kracauer, *New German Critique* 54 (Autumn 1991): 139–57.

8. See, e.g., Max Pensky, "Natural History: The Life and Afterlife of a Concept in Adorno," *Critical Horizons* 5, no. 1 (2004): 227–58.

9. Adorno, "CR," 58 / "WR," 388.

10. Adorno, "CR," 58 / "WR," 388.

11. One notable exception is Kracauer's letter to Adorno, dated 11 December 1960, in which he states, "About this matrix—your main ideas *with their radical anti-ontological dialectics*—we talked at length in Bergün, in a conversation that is unforgettable for me. So with regards to your basic position, I will leave it at a simple reference to Bergün" (emphasis added). See Adorno and Kracauer, *B*, 522.

12. See Leo Löwenthal, *In steter Freundschaft. Briefwechsel. Leo Löwenthal / Siegfried Kracauer. 1921–1966*, ed. Peter-Erwin Jansen and Christian Schmidt (Röse: Zu Klampen Verlag 2003), 231. See also Leo Löwenthal, "As I Remember Friedel," *New German Critique* 54 (Autumn 1991): 5–17. Löwenthal quotes a letter Kracauer wrote to him on 29 October 1960, stating, "On the trip I [Kracauer] meditated extensively on history, but nothing has yet been put on paper. My new ideas need time and I have to read a great deal as well. I feel very passionate about my attempt to break into this field. What might come of it, I don't yet know; perhaps a series of interconnected essays." 15. Shortly thereafter, on 11 December 1960, Kracauer writes to Adorno, "I myself am very busy with . . . the preparations for the formulation of numerous thoughts about history." Adorno and Kracauer, *B*, 523.

13. These lectures were held on 15, 18, and 21 March 1961, at the Collège de France and subsequently in Frankfurt. Adorno and Kracauer, *B*, 520. They were first published in 1960. Adorno, *Ontologie und Dialektik 1960/61*, vol. 7 of *Nachgelassene Schriften*, ed. Rolf Tiedemann (Frankfurt am Main: Suhrkamp, 2008).

14. Adorno and Kracauer, *B*, 514.

15. Adorno and Kracauer, *B*, 518. In his correspondence, Adorno last used "Dialectical Meditations" as a working title on 15 November 1962. Adorno and Kracauer, *B*, 560.

16. Adorno and Kracauer, *B*, 514.

17. Adorno and Kracauer, *B*, 518.

18. Adorno, "Das Schwindelerregende," in *ND*, 42. *ND*, trans. E. B. Ashton (New York: Seabury, 1973), 31–33.

19. Adorno, *Vorlesung über Negative Dialektik*, vol. 16 of *Nachgelassene Schriften*, ed. Rolf Tiedemann (Frankfurt am Main: Suhrkamp, 2003), 189. *Lectures on Negative Dialectics: Fragments of a Lecture Course, 1965/1966* (New York: Polity Press, 2008).

20. The German original text of *Negative Dialectics* does not include chapters—unlike its misleading appearance in the English translation, which includes chapters and sections—nor is the work broken down into paragraphs as the English version is.

21. Adorno, *NDe*, 337.

22. Adorno, *NDe*, 337.

23. Hegel, *Logic*, 237.

24. Adorno, *NDe*, 5 / *ND*, 17. Translation modified.

25. Hegel, *Logic*, 169. For Hegel's discussion of Identity, see particularly § 115–20, 168–75.

26. Adorno, *NDe* 149 / *ND* 146.

27. Adorno, *NDe*, 357.

28. Adorno, *NDe*, 358. Adorno quoting Marx and Engels.

29. Adorno, *NDe*, 358.

30. Adorno, *NDe*, 358.

31. Adorno, *NDe*, 359.

32. On the difference between nature and natural history, or how the latter as *Natur-Geschichte* instantiates the dialectical tension between the two concepts, see

Adorno's "Die Idee der Naturgeschichte," in *Philosophische Frühschriften*, vol. 1 of *Gesammelte Schriften*, ed. Rolf Tiedemann (Frankfurt am Main: Suhrkamp, 1997), 345–65. In English, "The Idea of Natural-History," *Telos* 60 (1984): 111–24; Robert Hullot-Kentor, "The Problem of Natural History in the Philosophy of Theodor W. Adorno" (PhD diss., University of Massachusetts–Amherst, 1985; *DAI-A* 46/06 [1985]); and Max Pensky, "Natural History," 6.

33. Siegfried Kracauer, "Nature," in *H*, 17–44.
34. Kracauer, *H*, 17.
35. Kracauer, *H*, 20–21.
36. Alfred Schmidt, *Der Begriff der Natur in der Lehre von Marx* (Frankfurt am Main: Europäische Verlagsanstalt, 1962). Published in English as *The Concept of Nature in Marx*, trans. Ben Fowkes (New York: NLB, 1971). Schmidt's dissertation was written under the guidance of Horkheimer and Adorno.
37. Adorno and Kracauer, *B*, 549.
38. Kracauer, *H*, 21, fn 13.
39. Adorno, *NDe*, 354 / *ND*, 347.
40. Adorno, *NDe*, 354 / *ND*, 347, citing Marx, *Das Kapital*, 7.
41. Susan Buck-Morss, "Dialectics Without Identity: The Idea of Natural History," *The Origins of Negative Dialectics* (New York: Free Press, 1977), 43–62. Here, 47.
42. Friedrich Engels, *Dialectics of Nature*, trans. Clemens Dutt (New York: International Publishers, 1940), 7.
43. Karl Marx and Friedrich Engels, *German Ideology*, trans. William Lough (Amherst, NY: Prometheus, 1998). Here, 57.
44. Karl Marx and Friedrich Engels, *Deutsche Ideologie, Marx-Engels Gesamtausgabe*, vol. 5:1 (Berlin: Dietz, 1932), 567. This textual variant was not included in the final version of *The German Ideology*, printed in the Berlin 1953 edition, on which the English translation is based, and therefore is not included in the English translation.
45. Kracauer, *H*, 21.
46. Kracauer, *H*, 21.
47. Kracauer, *H*, 32.
48. Kracauer, *H*, 30.
49. Kracauer, *H*, 29.
50. Kracauer, *H*, 29.
51. Kracauer, *H*, 37.
52. Kracauer, *H*, 39.
53. Kracauer, *H*, 43.
54. Adorno and Kracauer, *B*, 517.
55. Adorno and Kracauer, *B*, 514.
56. Adorno and Kracauer, *B*, 516.
57. Adorno and Kracauer, *B*, 516.
58. Pensky, "Natural History," 6.

The "Passage" and the "Mission of Film"

Kracauer's Investigations into Modern Realms of Experience

Sabine Biebl

Thanks to Siegfried Kracauer's very painstakingly practiced self-documentation and self-archiving, we know of only two, perhaps three "text ghosts" that have a "discursive existence" in his correspondence but remain unlocatable as a realized text. About one of these ghosts we learn from a letter of June 1926 to the philosopher Ernst Bloch: Having continued a discussion of Marx's idea of materialism over several letters, he mentions near the end that he himself "intends . . . to write a little treatise on Marx' concept of man."[1]

The project remained unfinished, if it was started at all. There is no record of it among his papers, though it is mentioned again in Adorno's portrait of Kracauer as a "curious realist."[2] However, in the context of this essay it is just the idea of this project that matters. Not only does it put across Kracauer's understanding of Marx's concept of materialism as "real humanism,"[3] but it also refers to a question that in my view dominated Kracauer's thinking from the second half of the twenties on, beginning with the programmatic texts "The Bible in German" (1926), "The Mass Ornament" (1927), and "Photography" (1927): the question of the place of man in modernity. How can one think of human existence in an empathizing way under the conditions of a "thoroughly rationalized, civilized society"[4]? How can one realize this, despite the fact that the idealistic idea of an autonomous subject appears untenable in view of the overpowering reality of the current economic, social, and political circumstances?

This essay will sketch out how Kracauer approached the problem of human existence between 1927 and 1941. In its first part I will go briefly into the two essays "The Mass Ornament" and "Photography" as well as the study *The Salaried Masses* (*Die Angestellten*, 1929–30) to highlight the different points of view from which Kracauer looks at the place of man in the modern world. While his texts into the late 1920s were carried by a more or less clearly stated positive definition of human existence, Kracauer starts to withdraw from it beginning in 1930. I follow the hypothesis that the question of feasibility of human existence is being replaced by the question whether it is possible to think it at all under the conditions of the modern world. Thus in this essay's second part I will show with "Farewell to the Linden Arcade" ("Abschied von der Lindenpassage," 1930) on the one hand and the *Marseille Notebooks* on a theory of film (1940–41) on the other how Kracauer interprets the passageway of the nineteenth and the movies of the twentieth centuries as realms of an alienating experience by which modern subjectivity can be constituted anew.

Influenced by idealism and *Lebensphilosophie* Kracauer's early works[5] still revolve around the idea of an autonomous subject and the concept of personality. In the early twenties this idea gives way to a view of human existence for which the disjunction between transcendence and the world matters most: "As one who exists, man is really a citizen of two worlds, or, more correctly, he exists between the two worlds. . . . Caught in the Here and in need of the Beyond, he leads, in the literal sense of the expression, a *double existence*."[6] Two years later Kracauer already secularizes this conflict in "The Mass Ornament"[7] and transfers it onto the dualism of nature and reason that becomes realized in the historical process. At its end stands "the man of reason" (*MO*, 83) who has completely thrown off the shackles of nature.

This abstract idea that passes over man in his individual and historical existence is almost contemporaneously corrected by Kracauer in his essay "Photography."[8] There the human existence of the individual takes center stage. Kracauer reconnects the abstract concept of truth, which is supposed to break through in the course of history,[9] to the truth about man as the truth about his life. He specifically illustrates the defining characteristic of the new medium of photography with the genre of portrait photography and thereby links this distinctive symbol of the current epoch back to man. Even photographic portraits fail, however, in the attempt to depict humans adequately, because they say nothing about the human essence. All they can do is to vaguely allude to the "original" as long as it is in existence. According to Kracauer, the photograph of a dead person cannot preserve the memory of him because it can record nothing but his external shell, his *Raumerscheinung* (spatial appearance; *MO*, 52).[10]

In *Photography* Kracauer turns away from a normative definition of human nature as being entirely reasonable toward a more existentialist interpretation. Throughout the course of each singular life the human essence acquires an individual shape. However, this life requires a witness to become essential. Photographic images are opposed to the "memory images" (*Gedächtnisbilder; MO,* 50) that one person keeps of the other. The quintessential memory image is "the last image of a person" (*das letzte Bild eines Menschen; MO,* 51) that includes "his actual history" (*seine eigentliche Geschichte; MO,* 51), for only in the "last image" does his essence appear, now liberated from his empirically demonstrable existence. The "transcendental excess" of man finds its projection screen in another human as the human essence finds its expression only in interpersonal contact.

Kracauer probes the current society for this anthropological condition by way of its medium of depiction, photography, as a "secretion of the capitalist mode of production" (*MO,* 61). According to Kracauer's diagnosis, this society is doomed to death, because it does not have a "memory image" of itself.

> That it [the camera] devours the world is a sign of the *fear of death.* What the photographs by their sheer accumulation attempt to banish is the recollection of death, which is part and parcel of every memory image. In the illustrated magazines the world has become a photographable present, and the photographed present has been entirely eternalized. Seemingly ripped from the clutch of death, in reality it has succumbed to it. (*MO,* 59, trans. amended)

The functionalization of man in capitalist society is reflected in the imaging process of photography, by which the object undergoes externalization and decomposition.[11] It is only with his study *The Salaried Masses*[12] that Kracauer arrives at the very production site of this alienation. For him the white-collar workers' realm of work and life is the realm of reality in which the "course of history" is determined, because it is here that the truth of man comes under threat. In this study Kracauer claims the space of human existence within the present society as something like a "negative anthropology" since he finds man distorted. The new economic developments toward rationalization and mechanization become ontic in the salaried employees. As opposed to the ideologically literate workers, their alienation by modern work processes concerns their whole human being.

Whereas the life of the worker "as a class-conscious proletarian is roofed over with vulgar-Marxist concepts that do at least tell him what his intended role is," the "mass of salaried employees . . . are spiritually homeless" (*SM*, 88). Thus Kracauer wrote about salaried employees as types whose life "only in a restricted sense can be called a life" (*SM*, 88), and the central chapter of this study, in which Kracauer showcases some specimens from Berlin's new world of white-collar workers, is entitled "Kleines Herbarium," which means a collection of dried plants.[13] He constructs a mosaic of "human shortcomings" (*menschliche Unzulänglichkeiten; SM*, 25) and makes places in social and economic structures visible where man and his relationships have become lost.

Kracauer viewed the bulk of white-collar workers as a group of uniform types under whose standardized surface no individual life story can be found. Thus these "standard types of salesgirl, draper's assistant, shorthand typist, and so on" (*SM*, 68) *are* internally nothing but their shiny surface, their "pleasant appearance, which with the help of photographs can be widely reproduced" (*SM*, 39). In the context of Kracauer's theory of media, they are even adequately captured by their pure "spatial appearance."

Kracauer's study of the salaried employees can be understood as an emphatic "enlightenment project"[14] on the fundamental flaws of German society at the end of the twenties—a capitalist society that, in Kracauer's estimation, had subjected the individual and lost sight of man as its central systemic category. At the same time, the actuality of the salaried employees anticipates, according to Kracauer, the end stage of the capitalist-bourgeois society, because the main ideas of idealism ultimately supply nothing but a set of euphemisms for an inhuman ideology. With the institutions of the "Angestellten-Kultur" (*SM*, 32), such as cinemas, revue theaters, and dance parlors, the old bourgeois society had generated an illusory world in which it survived merely as undead and as its own distortion. This being said, both capitalism and vulgar Marxism are unable to generate the dimension of meaning missing in the secular and rational world, since neither of these is based in man, to whom all meaning must refer.

> The human individual, who confronts death alone, is not submerged in the collectivity striving to elevate itself into a final purpose. He is formed not by community as such but by knowledge, from which community too may arise . . . What matters is not that institutions are changed, what matters is that human individuals change institutions. (*SM*, 106)

In Kracauer's writings from the thirties on, the "redemption of physical reality" increasingly replaces the attempt to enable the liberation of man within society. Since the path to that liberation appears obstructed, *objects* become the medium toward the realization of a true human utopia. Though Kracauer continues his critical enlightenment project as a journalist, he nevertheless shifts his attention to the nonsocial spaces and their physical inhabitants: The "odds and ends" (*Krimskrams*),[15] "the cast-off and the disavowed" (*MO*, 338)—in short, society's "waste products" (*SM*, 66).

Man has not yet found his home in such spaces. Consequently Kracauer describes him as a traveler and passerby. The feuilleton article "Farewell to the Linden Arcade" of December 1930 captures this turning point in Kracauer's thinking: The angle from which the text looks at its object is one of melancholic remembrance. Shocked by the modernist 1930 reconstruction of the eponymous arcade in the heart of Berlin, which aligns it with the cold architecture of the *Neue Sachlichkeit*, Kracauer certainly laments the ongoing decline of this urban nineteenth-century institution; but at the same time, in his memory the arcade rises again in its old form and function.

This piece is another example for Kracauer's method of analysis "of inconspicuous surface-level expressions" (*MO*, 75). Here, the arcade as an actual space in Berlin's urban environment is transformed into a realized metaphor. Metonymically the building represents its own social and political space. The arcade appears as a place of criticism, self reflection, and renewal of nineteenth-century bourgeois society. It is a space that unites those elements that disturbed this society's outer surface and conflicted with its moral, political, and aesthetic order. While bourgeois society defined itself primarily by way of abstract and idealistic concepts, the world of objects was seen merely as a set of tools and devices.

The bookstores and souvenir shops, however, the specimen of the Anatomical Museum, and the curiosity shop's fantastic pictures presented, on the one hand, man in his naked corporeality, his sensuality, and instincts. On the other hand, the arcade exhibits the insignificant little things that had value to the bourgeois world only as long as they could contribute to its shiny surface. "Nail clippers, scissors, powder boxes, cigarette lighters, hand-stitched Hungarian doilies" (*MO*, 339), the inconsiderable companions of daily life find asylum in the arcades: "Here . . . these transient objects attained a kind of right of residence, like gypsies who are allowed to camp only along the highway and not in town" (*MO*, 338).

The arcades appear as nonplaces and exiled areas of the old bourgeois society. They were, however, components of its own construction and interacted with society. They put it in a dialectic relationship to itself by confronting its ideational construction with its material basis. Here its world of concepts become "rattled and shaken" (*MO*, 341) and the result is a "disintegration of all illusory permanence" (*MO*, 341). The concealing darkness of the arcades, where the world of things literally closed in on society, was threatening to the bourgeois world.

> Here, however, they took revenge on the bourgeois idealism that oppressed them by playing off their own defiled existence against the arrogated existence of the bourgeoisie. Degraded as they were, they were able to congregate in the half-light of the passageway and to organize an effective protest against the facade culture outside. They exposed idealism for what it was and revealed its products to be kitsch (*MO*, 341).

In the underworld of the arcades nothing remains of the idealistic facade that hides the pure corporeality all people share equally. Not only do indicators of status get destroyed and disavowed, but also ontological hierarchies break down as man, now just a physical being, becomes part of the world of things down there. The exhibition of everyday objects in the dark of the arcade takes them out of their functional context in the lived-in world and out of man's authority. At the same time it draws attention to the fragility of this bourgeois world that imagines itself as permanent.

In the arcade the historical process passes almost as if in fast-forward—it becomes, literally, a passage. Kracauer consciously plays with the double meaning of the German *Passage* as the piece of architecture and the act of traversing. He describes an epistemological process that occurs within the passerby via the altered perception of the outer world. *Passage* is a place, a physical movement, and a figurative concept for this process. The exhibition of objects for their own sake in the arcades induces a process of alienation, since they are shown outside the realm of their functional purpose. The arcade stroller exposes himself to this experience of alienation and applies it to himself in the movement of passing, the kind of "movement appropriate to us alone" (*MO*, 342). Kracauer equates this movement with the "journey from the near to the far and the linkage of body and image" (*MO*, 338). The movement of *passage* is a form of world perception that does not occur primarily in the realm of reflection but in the preconscious domain of the psyche and the body, for the passage of the arcade "satisfies primarily bodily needs and the craving for images of the sort that appear in daydreams" (*MO*, 338). It is adequate for man, because it depicts his existence as a process. The facade culture of the bourgeois world, in contrast, focuses on a delusive permanence of the present so that "the very near and the very far" (*MO*, 338) are equally out of reach.

> In the arcades, and precisely because they were arcades, the most recently created things separated themselves from living beings earlier than elsewhere, and died still warm . . . What we had inherited and unhesitatingly called our own lay in the passageway as if in a morgue, exposing its extinguished grimace. In this arcade, we ourselves encountered ourselves as deceased. But we also wrested from it what belongs to us today and forever, that which glimmered there unrecognized and distorted. (*MO*, 342)

The experience of alienation, which the passerby is exposed to, is like a confrontation with his own death and impermanence. This is because the pieces that make up the identity of a person present themselves in the exhibits of the passage as isolated and separate from this ostensibly timeless, true, and unique context. In the passage, the life of an individual is not honored with its unique history, but just as a mold of insignificant things that surrounded it in the past. Like photography, as whose architectural equivalent the passage appears—though Kracauer does not make this reference explicitly—the passage captures "the residuum that history has discharged" (*MO*, 55). At the same time the experience of alienation allows the passerby to become aware of his own existence. Thus in "Farewell to the Linden Arcade" Kracauer advances the positive reevaluation of the experience of alienation further that was pronounced as an outlook at the end of his "Photography" essay. By making an inventory of "mute nature" (*MO*, 61) photography enables man's consciousness to confront it by and for itself for the first time in history. "It is therefore incumbent on consciousness to establish the *provisional status* of all given configurations, and perhaps even to awaken an inkling of the right order of the inventory of nature" (*MO*, 62). This subject/object relationship between recognizing consciousness and presented "silent nature" becomes equalized in the passage as the passerby experiences himself as a part of the world of objects.

Kracauer counts the "right passerby" (*Passant*) among those vagabond characters who wander his texts since *Ginster* and his Chaplin reviews.[16] "The passerby, who roams like a vagabond, will someday be united with the person of the changed society" (*MO*, 342). But Kracauer's text brackets this utopia as soon as it has alluded to it. For the present has abolished the passages. Their productive darkness has been extinguished by glass roofs.

In this new lightness objects are reduced to "mute nature" (*MO*, 61) to which capitalist rationality reduced the world and that Kracauer had already seen depicted as such in photography.

> All the objects have been struck dumb. They huddle timidly behind the empty architecture, which, for the time being, acts completely neutral but may later spawn who knows what—perhaps fascism, or perhaps nothing at all. What would be the point of an arcade in a society that is itself only a passageway? (*MO*, 342)

In "Farewell to the Linden Arcade," Kracauer wishes for "magic glasses" (*MO*, 340) that make visible the "illustrations of passing impulses" (*MO*, 340) even beyond the curiosity collection and the space of the passage. Ten years later he finds this magic device in film. In the three *Marseille Notebooks*[17] Kracauer outlined the structure of a theory of Film in feverish concentration while desperately awaiting his own and his wife's lifesaving departure to the United States. Down to the linguistic details, the notebooks appear to tap into the same reservoir of ideas as the 1930 piece—with the crucial difference that film now inherits the destroyed arcade by cleaving a passage through the bourgeois world. However, the scenario has changed: The bourgeois society as a historical formation, to which the arcade relates, has almost completely disappeared from the world that film is relating to, for the "dimension which defines the phenomenon of film at its core lies below the dimension in which political and social events take place" (*MN*, 529).[18] Like a ghost, this dimension inhabits the *Marseille Notebooks* as a reference to a never written chapter. What remains of the bourgeois society is its system of ideas, specifically the principles of its perception of the world, which Kracauer considers represented in classical theater and the bourgeois "subject" as its protagonist and recipient. Film refers to the world as a quasi-ontological order: Starting from the basic layer of the physical, Kracauer's imagery suggests that further layers are piled on top of each other up to the most abstract ideas. It is this construct through which Film "cleaves a passage."

> Film brings the whole material world into play; reaching beyond theatre and painting, it for the first time sets that which exists into motion. It does not aim upward, toward intention, but pushes toward the bottom, to gather and carry along even the dregs. It is interested in the

refuse, in what is just there—both in and outside the human being. The face counts for nothing in film unless it includes the death's-head beneath. "Danse macabre." To which end? That remains to be seen.[19]

Just as the passage offered asylum to "society's waste products" and gave them visibility in its exhibition spaces, "the mission of film" (MN, 529) is to serve the material world. Its goal is to free things from the cage of meaning in order to make them visible for their own sake. Kracauer illustrates this mission by comparing film and theater as competing media, investigating the role of the material world in both.[20] The stage is structurally inimical to "that which just exists" (dem Bloß-Seienden; MN, 551). For theater is externally bound to the auditorium and to the long shot of the acting. Internally this limitation corresponds to a plot that has to be reasonable and leaves the spectator with a sense of closure. Theater can grasp neither the very small nor the very big, whether formally or semantically. On the stage, the world of things congeals into sets and props, rather than being visualized for its own sake. Theater is anthropocentric, and this single-minded emphasis violates the material world, as written in the Marseille Notebooks.

> Tragedy is relentless towards factors of that which exists, which could divert the imagined fate from its course. Actually, tragedy violates that which exists, so that the prevailing of fate is just not hampered, but even supported and advanced. In Tragedy, coincidence is eliminated or even enslaved. (MN, 502)

In film, however, the "unleashed camera" can take up any angle on the world. Thus film can display all those aspects of the world that theater excludes: The very big and the very small and unimposing, the masses, natural disasters and wars. It is such phenomena that, according to the Marseille Notebooks, "break up consciousness" (das Bewußtsein zertrümmern; MN, 597/603).

> All material phenomena or processes that cause man a physical sensation [materielle Sensation] and give him a shock: vertiginous movement, the harrowing, terrifying, catastrophes of the physical kind [materieller Art]. These phenomena are at home in the dark depth of the material dimension, where pressure and impact reign and no meaning can penetrate any longer. (MN, 603–5)

Though the genuine subject matter of film is to be found within the realm of violence, destruction, and war, the only issue Kracauer depicts as ethically objectionable is the conceptual control and monopoly of the bourgeois system of ideas. In the same sense, his concept of "die Totale" (long shot) does not refer to film but to theater and bourgeois society.[21] It is this term that inevitably relates the historical context of a catastrophic modernity in which the *Notebooks* were written.[22] At the same time, in an article for the Basel *National Zeitung* of April 1940 entitled "Terror in Film," Kracauer wrote, "Film illuminates the appearance of the horrifying, which we otherwise encounter in the dark, and makes an exhibition object out of something unimaginable in reality."[23] It is a perception aid to take away the semantic-affective charge from the horrifying, bringing it out of the unsettling darkness and making it accessible to processing in the light of reason and reflection. "Every depiction also is a play with the depicted and perhaps the play with the terrible aims at coming to grips with things at whose mercy people still find themselves" (313).

Concerning the problem of the affinity of film to terrifying phenomena, which Kracauer counts among the primary features of the medium, he offers two solutions that are in contradiction to each other: In the *Marseille Notebooks* these phenomena are semantically neutralized by being grouped among other phenomena of the "basic layer" (*Grundschicht*) while the horrifying itself is attributed to the realm of reasoning that is undermined by film.

In the short newspaper article, however, Kracauer suggests a different understanding of this affinity of film: By presenting phenomena of horror from a "safe" distance, it makes these phenomena accessible to conscious reflection. It is this "pedagogical" interpretation of film in the sense of his "enlightenment project" that found its way into the final version of *Theory of Film*.[24]

What Film seems to carry out here is devaluation in its literal sense, as an elimination of intentional evaluations: Metaphorically it eliminates the filter of differentiating consciousness from perception to make visible that which exists in all of its manifestations.

However, the perceiving subject is required here, too, in order to enter the realm of the visible. That means that the viewer replaces the *Passant*. Yet just as this devaluation occurs in the passerby while transiting, so the mission of film includes the viewer as a subject to be liberated. Film seizes the spectator "with skin and hair" (*MN*, 575) as "corporeal-material being"

(*MN*, 575).[25] What happens to the film viewer is "no different from [what happens to] a human being actually in motion, who stumbles against and becomes irritated by things, materials, fragments—human and non-human": "*His senses are attacked by [these things] directly* and not via the detour of consciousness. The material elements that present themselves in film directly stimulate the *material layers* of the human being: his nerves, his senses, and his entire *physiological substance*" (*MN*, 575/577).

The prison of self as a construction of consciousness "is subject to permanent dissolution" in the film theater (*MN*, 577). Man experiences himself as a physical being via the body's boundaries that collide with external stimuli. As drives and emotions get the upper hand in the darkness of the passage, the elimination of the layer of consciousness allows man to perceive the physical world—including self-perception as a "corporeal-material being"—in a way that was forbidden by the categorical filters that consciousness imposes on things. This new mode of perception facilitates the experience of being part of the physical world, instead of being opposed to it as a self-aware subject. Through the film experience, the human being is no longer metaphysically homeless, but becomes at home in the world. It is no coincidence that Kracauer cites a comment by a French translator friend in the *Marseille Notebooks* and *Theory of Film*: "In the theater I am always I, but in the cinema I dissolve into all things and beings."[26]

Film actually subverts the current circumstances, because it is a "revolutionary fact" (*MN*, 589) not serving any abstract ideology. "The mission of film" is radical, because it is opposed to any construction of meaning that would want to limit or dominate the immenseness, involuntariness, and conceptual inconceivability of what exists. By doing this, it robs man of his consciousness as a production site of meaning and, at the same time, frees him for an existence that has part in the diversity of what exists.

The disturbing radicalism and concurrent fascination of Kracauer's *Marseille Notebooks* finds its starkest expression in the skull as a cinematic paradigm, as which the final statement of the introductory chapter cited above installs: "The face counts for nothing in film unless it includes the death's-head beneath. 'Danse macabre.' To which end? That remains to be seen." The meaning of this passage is not directly comprehensible, remains opaque and appears, exactly because of that, unsettling with its connotations. And yet the function Kracauer attributes to the symbol of death gets illuminated by the context in which it is placed: It is notable that the source from which Kracauer draws the death's-head as a paradigmatic symbol for film is Eisenstein's project on Mexico (1931–32). Kracauer had planned to develop "certain ultimate conclusions"[27] of his theory in later sketches for *Theory of Film* through analysis of one of the edited versions of the film. Although there are no drafts of this final chapter, from Kracauer's notes and sketches on the movie it becomes evident what he found so intriguing: It was the specific staging and celebration of death by the Mexican people. Not only does it honor death as the beginning of life, thereby breaking its destructive powers, but—as Kracauer's sketches of the skeletons of a soldier and a bishop indicate[28]—it also seems to celebrate death as a quasi-revolutionary victory over the ideational constructions of the powerful. In the closer context of the "mission of film" that Kracauer develops in the *Marseille Notebooks,* this aspect is of central importance: It involves the death of the idea of the Subject, because it is this bourgeois idea that is, according to Kracauer, tied to domination and oppression in the two meanings of hermeneutic and political domination. Therefore, the death's-head puts the film into a context Kracauer alluded to already when he wrote about photography and the passage: the experience of extreme alienation in the subject's confrontation with his own death, with the impermanence of the ideational and meaning-carrying shell of his existence. But in 1941, the perspective has changed: The consciousness that becomes aware of his own death is "broken up" and, like a rigid and cold shell, falls off the subject, which is liberated for the experience of his existence. In film as a realm of experience, that is, in the process of its reception, the subject is put into the position to experience itself unconsciously, "without the disturbing interference of consciousness,"[29] as a part of the material world and to fit in.

The essay "Farewell to the Linden Arcade" described the passage as such a realm of experience that was integrated into the bourgeois society of the nineteenth century as a place of its critical self-reflection. It did it in the mode of melancholic remembrance, because, like its passage, it was also that society that emerged out of its modernization disfigured almost to meaninglessness. According to Kracauer in 1941, the "mission of film" has to go back, it seems, behind all historical and social formations to start at the "medial" experience as the condition of the possibility of thinking human existence anew under the circumstances of modernity.

NOTES

1. Siegfried Kracauer, Letter to Ernst Bloch, 29 June 1926, in Ernst Bloch, *Briefe. 1903–1975,* ed. Karola Bloch and Uwe Opolka (Frankfurt am Main: Suhrkamp, 1985), no. 6, 1: 280–84, here 284.

2. Cf. Theodor W. Adorno, "The Curious Realist: On Siegfried Kracauer" (1965), *New German Critique* 54 (1991): 159–79.

3. Kracauer, Letter to Ernst Bloch, 283.

4. Kracauer, *Der Detektiv-Roman. Eine Deutung* (1924), in *Soziologie als Wissenschaft. Der Detektiv-Roman. Die Angestellten*, vol. 1 of Kracauer, *Werke*, ed. Inka Mülder-Bach, in collaboration with Mirjam Wenzel (Frankfurt am Main: Suhrkamp, 2006), 103–209, here 107.

5. Cf. Kracauer, "Über das Wesen der Persönlichkeit" (1916–17) in *Frühe Schriften aus dem Nachlaß*, vol. 9.1 of *Werke* (Frankfurt am Main: Suhrkamp, 2004), 7–120; "Von der Erkenntnismöglichkeit seelischen Lebens. Eine Abhandlung" (1916), in ibid., 121–69; "Das Leiden unter dem Wissen und die Sehnsucht nach der Tat. Eine Abhandlung aus dem Jahr 1917," in ibid., 169–397.

6. Kracauer, "Travel and Dance" ("Die Reise und der Tanz," 1925), in Kracauer, *The Mass Ornament: Weimar Essays*, trans., ed., intro. Thomas Y. Levin (Cambridge: Harvard University Press, 1995), 65–73, here 68–69. Henceforth cited as *MO* in the text. Cf. also "Those Who Wait" ("Die Wartenden," 1922), in ibid., 129–40; *Der Detektiv-Roman*, in *Soziologie als Wissenschaft*, 103–209.

7. "The Mass Ornament" (1927/1963), in *The Mass Ornament*, 75–86.

8. Kracauer, "Photography" (1927/1963), in *The Mass Ornament*, 47–63.

9. Cf. *MO*, 80.

10. For a further interpretation of Kracauer's essay see Miriam Bratu Hansen, "Kracauer's Photography Essay: Dot Matrix—General (An-)Archive—Film," in this volume.

11. Cf. ibid.

12. Kracauer, *The Salaried Masses: Duty and Distraction in the Weimar Germany*, trans. Quintin Hoare, ed. Inka Mülder-Bach (London: Verso, 1998). Henceforth *SM*.

13. The English edition chooses "A Few Choice Specimens" as title for this chapter; see *Salaried Masses*, 68.

14. For this phrase see Kracauer's letter to Ernst Bloch, 4 June 1932, in Ernst Bloch, *Briefe*, no. 59, 1: 365–68, here 367.

15. Kracauer, "Weihnachtlicher Budenzauber" (1932), in *Aufsätze: 1932–1965*, vol. 5.3 of Kracauer, *Schriften*, ed. Inka Mülder-Bach (Frankfurt am Main: Suhrkamp, 1990), 174–76, here 174.

16. Cf. Kracauer, "Chaplin" (1926), in *Kleine Schriften zum Film: 1932–1961*, vol. 6.1 of *Werke*, 269–70, "Chaplin" (1928), in *Kleine Schriften zum Film: 1982–1931*, vol. 6.2 of *Werke* (Frankfurt am Main: Suhrkamp, 2004), 32–35; "Chaplin als Prediger" (1929), in ibid., 312–14; "Lichter der Großstadt. Zur deutschen Uraufführung des Chaplinfilms" (1931), in ibid., 472–74; "Chaplins Triumph" (1931), in ibid., 492–95.

17. Kracauer, *Marseille Notebooks* (*Marseiller Entwurf zu einer Theorie des Films*, 1940–41), in *Theorie des Films. Die Errettung der äußeren Wirklichkeit, Mit einem Anhang "Marseiller Entwurf" zu einer Theorie des Films*, vol. 3 of *Werke* (Frankfurt am Main: Suhrkamp, 2005), 521–803. Henceforth *MN*. The existence of Kracauer's Marseille draft has been made known in Miriam Hansen's seminal essay "'With Skin and Hair': Kracauer's Theory of Film, Marseille 1940," *Critical Inquiry* 19, no.

3 (1993): 437–69, and her introduction to the current English edition of *Theory of Film: The Redemption of Physical Reality* (Princeton: Princeton University Press, 1997), vii–xlv.

18. Translation by Hansen in "'With Skin and Hair,'" 446.

19. Translation by Hansen in "'With Skin and Hair,'" 447.

20. For the following cf. Hansen, Introduction to *Theory of Film*, xvii–xxi.

21. Cf. *MN*, 530, 549, 575, etc.

22. Cf. Inka Mülder-Bach, "Nachbemerkung und editorische Notiz," in *Theorie des Films*, 853.

23. "Terror in Film" ("Das Grauen im Film," 1940), in *Kleine Schriften zum Film: 1932–1961*, vol. 6.3 of *Werke*, 312–13, here 313.

24. Cf. the section "Haupt der Medusa" in the "Epilogue" of *Theory of Film*, 305–6.

25. Translation by Hansen in "'With Skin and Hair,'" 458; also the following quotations 458 (trans. partly cited), 459.

26. *Theory of Film*, 159.

27. Cf. "Tentative Outline of a Book of Film Aesthetics," in *Siegfried Kracauer—Erwin Panofsky. Briefwechsel 1941–1966*, Mit einem Anhang: Siegfried Kracauer "under the spell of the living Warburg tradition," ed. Volker Breidecker (Berlin: Akademie Verlag 1996), 83–92, here 92.

28. Pictured in *Theorie des Films*, 515–16.

29. Kracauer: "Über Arbeitsnachweise" (1930), in *Aufsätze: 1927–1931*, vol. 5.2 of *Schriften*, 186.

Among Other Things—a Miraculous Realist

Political Perspectives on the Theoretical Entanglement of Cinema and History in Siegfried Kracauer

Drehli Robnik

With Siegfried Kracauer, the relationship of cinema to philosophy is peculiar. Much of Kracauer's writing is quite remote from philosophy: for the best part of his career, roughly 1920 to 1950, he was a film critic for newspapers and magazines in Frankfurt and Berlin, then, after Hitler's coming to power and his forced emigration as a Jewish left-wing intellectual in 1933 in Paris and from 1941 in New York. But in Kracauer's theory—from his reviews and essays on modern culture to his books written in America—cinema is not primarily about movies, filmmakers, cultures, or media technologies. Rather, cinema is itself something comparable to philosophy: "an approach to the world, a mode of human existence,"[1] as Kracauer puts it; a never entirely normal mode of perception, sensation, thought—and sometimes enlightenment. "All that remains of the 'art with a difference' in late Kracauer is the subjectivity which constitutes it."[2] In the end, Kracauer sees in (or through) cinema a mode of experience in rivalry with philosophy and art; he calls it "history."

Long before cinema is history, Kracauer equates it to capitalist economy: "The form of free-time busy-ness necessarily corresponds to the form of business."[3] In his 1926 essay "Cult of Distraction," busy-ness/busi-ness—the same word, *Betrieb*, in the original—designates the fragmented mobility experienced both in film and in factory or office work. This view anticipates Benjamin's "Artwork" essay, which reuses Kracauer's notion of distraction, and Adorno's condemnation of "Culture Industry." To Kracauer, however, cinema also offers solutions to the problem it is part of: "One has to hand this to the Americans: with slapstick films they have created a form that offers a counterweight to their reality. If in that reality they subject the world to an often unbearable discipline, the film in turn dismantles this self-imposed order quite forcefully."[4] This passage from a 1926 review of Kracauer's is quoted (and translated) by Miriam Bratu Hansen; Hansen understands Kracauer's concept of cinema as an "alternative public sphere" that "engages the contradictions of modernity at the level of the senses."[5]

Slapstick films especially not only contain an antidote to industrial rationalization but also intimate a different order of things. In his 1928 review of *Steamboat Bill, Jr.*, Kracauer reads Keaton's machinelike "grace" as a "promise": "Buster could at last move freely and laugh" only "when the ban is lifted from the world."[6] The grace of mechanized movement as antidote and promise: This logic also guides Kracauer's interpretation in 1927 of the abstract patterns of movement displayed by girl dance troupes and gymnastic crowd spectacles. With reference to the fragmentation of human behavior by psychotechnical aptitude tests and Taylorist assembly lines, Kracauer writes: "The mass ornament is the aesthetic reflex of the rationality to which the prevailing economic system aspires."[7] Again, Kracauer equates culture to industry, but there is a hopeful ambiguity, because in mass culture's reassembly of life, the rationalization process, which capitalism aborts at the stage of disciplined abstraction, still hints at enlightenment. According to Thomas Y. Levin, translator and editor of *The Mass Ornament*, Kracauer's own compilation of his 1920s essays, Kracauer endorses disintegration as a necessary precondition to a breakthrough of reason.[8] This appears most clearly in cinema: "Here, in pure externality, the audience encounters itself; its own reality is revealed in the fragmented sequence of splendid sense impressions," Kracauer writes; their very lack of deep and stable meaning enables films to expose "the *disorder* of society."[9]

Cinema's experiential potentials also become manifest when compared to photography. Like the mass ornament, photographic images are ambivalent: On one hand, for late 1920s Kracauer "the flight of images is a flight from revolution and from death."[10] There is a high probability that photography's penetration of the world just endlessly reproduces its appearance and mythically naturalizes its presence. (In later decades, such criticism was often directed at television.) And yet, there is a chance that all those photos that make people laugh, even shudder, at the exposure of their own awkward embodiedness and, ultimately, mortality might provide a self-perception in the image of transience. "It is therefore incumbent on consciousness to establish the *provisional status* of all given configurations, and perhaps even to awaken an inkling of the right order of the inventory

of nature." Although Kracauer always thinks of cinema as based on photography, his 1927 essay "Photography" distinguishes between the simply
confusing "disarray of the illustrated newspapers" and film's "capacity to
stir up" and "play with the pieces of disjointed nature."[11] Film has the possibility to literally dis- and re-member the world: "Europe is ready to be
seen through, decomposed in its elements and reassembled in montage by
him,"[12] Kracauer writes with reference to Vsevolod Pudovkin in 1928.
Around 1930, however, the messianic, redemptive orientation running
through Kracauer's theory starts to shift: from revolutionary/messianic intervention into false organizations of reality (which mass culture helps to
disorganize) to redemption as the preservation of what is left of reality to
experience. His criticism increasingly attacks the "blindness to reality" and
"emptiness" especially of German films, from Ruttmann's *Berlin* (1927) to
The Blue Angel (1930); only in dispersed cinematic moments of realism and
disobedience—Jean Renoir's *La chienne* (1931) or Leontine Sagan's *Mäd-
chen in Uniform* (1931)—is an antidote to the "vacuum" provided.

After Hitler's coming to power in 1933, Kracauer's *horror vacui* motif
changes its object: Instead of bourgeois rationalization, he now sees Nazi
rule as hollowing out reality. His study "Propaganda and the Nazi War
Film," undertaken in New York in 1942 and published as a supplement to
his *From Caligari to Hitler* (1947), shows how Nazi documentary films celebrating German conquests in Europe treat reality as material to be ran-
domly formed: The invaders' "blitz" flashes "through an artificial vacuum," a "never-never land where the Germans rule over time and space."[13]
But again, cinema provides an almost homeopathic antidote to the loss of
world, by betraying and exposing a totalitarian media-machinery's grip on
reality. Kracauer reads a newsreel of Hitler's 1940 *blitz* visit to occupied
Paris allegorically so that a resistance of reality to its mistreatment becomes visible: "Paris itself shuts its eyes and withdraws. The touching sight
of this deserted ghost city that once pulsed with feverish life mirrors the
vacuum at the core of the Nazi system."[14]

The ghost city becomes paradigmatic in Kracauer's 1947 book *From
Caligari to Hitler.* It is infamous for its central thesis: The frequency of hyp-
notic tyrants like Dr. Mabuse and fanaticized crowds in the films of Germany's Weimar Republic anticipated the Nazis' seizure of power. The con-
cluding paragraph is typical: "Since Germany thus carried out what had
been anticipated by her cinema from its very beginning, conspicuous
screen characters now came true in life itself."[15] We could read this idea of
reality reenacting images as anticipating postmodernist "simulation" theo-

ries; or we could, as is often done,[16] dismiss it as outright ahistorical—provided that we understand history as being determined by linear causality (which, following Kracauer, we shouldn't do). Thomas Elsaesser suggests a different reading: In an attempt to restore the potentials of Kracauer's critical insight beyond the narrow scope of Nazi cinema, Elsaesser takes Kracauer's *Caligari* argument that had shifted the blame for the subjugation of perception from bourgeois rationality to a (proto-)Nazi media-machinery, and then he turns this argument around, again, as it were. In this perspective, the *Caligari* book is not a teleology of cinema leading to Hitler, but an "incisive analysis of bourgeois conceptions of narrative and subject-positions. . . . Kracauer's antipathy to Weimar films was ultimately due more to their gentrification of cinema than to any anticipation of the course of history."[17] Since the German comedies and action melodramas once cherished by Kracauer the film critic have disappeared from his 1947 retrospection, Weimar cinema now seems to consist of prestige productions and the Expressionist canon. This makes *Caligari* look like a dark mirror-image of Kracauer's subsequent book: Also begun in the 1940s, *Theory of Film* is a celebration of cinema's potential to redeem reality that excludes large parts of international film production as "uncinematic"; *Caligari* is a condemnation of an uncinematic type of film, yet there is a redeeming subcurrent.

Referring to the "Men at Work" road sign, Kracauer writes that films that, like *Das Cabinet des Dr. Caligari* (1920), project vexed psyches into a distorted outside world should be labeled "Soul at Work."[18] But he warns against seeing in his *Psychological History of the German Film* (the subtitle of the *Caligari* book) "the concept of a fixed national character."[19] What *Caligari* offers, rather than a nation's "mentality," may be cinema as a new epistemology, a way of understanding the social alternative to sociology, economics, or politics. In a way, Kracauer suggests that we should have asked the movies in order to find out sooner—about the "secret history"[20] and "emotional fixations"[21] of white-collar workers living in a "vacuum"[22] outside traditional class definitions or about authoritarian dispositions that leftist voters, hateful of liberalism, shared with the Nazis.[23] One could say, using terminology of today's radically democratic political theory or of Deleuze, that the cinema is able, more so than the traditional sciences of politics, to get at and image the affective dimension of politics, its passions as well as its interruptions. For Kracauer, cinema's insights into mass subjectivities are almost psychoanalytic, because film is "particularly concerned with the unobtrusive, the normally neglected."[24] Here, Kracauer is halfway between Benjamin's "optical-unconscious" and his own later realism of the ephemeral; his notion of films as "visible hieroglyphs" recalls his Weimar essays deciphering (cinematic) "daydreams of society."

"Effects may at any time turn into spontaneous causes,"[25] Kracauer writes in the introduction to *Caligari*. "Psychological tendencies often assume independent life, and, instead of automatically changing with ever-changing circumstances, become themselves essential springs of historical evolution."[26] Are German horror films right after all in showing souls coming to life in the outside world? The important thing is the shift introduced here: from a critique of despotic intentions subsuming reality to a philosophy of history highlighting irregularity and heterogeneity. Elsaesser[27] sees a break with traditional logics of causation here: To Kracauer, cinema is irreducible to determining fact(or)s; it is both effect and cause, and effect without cause; its images manifest an event- or phantom-like ontology. Elsaesser traces this back to Lukács's 1913 aesthetics of cinema, where we confront "life without soul, mere surface," and "'virtuality' no longer functions as opposed to 'reality.'"

In 1960, Kracauer's *Theory of Film* appeared. Reading it, we should neither focus on its moments of systematic grandeur nor follow those who condemn its "naive" realism. "Reality is a construction,"[28] Kracauer had asserted already in 1929, and at one point in *Theory of Film*, he qualifies realism in this way: "What accounts for the cinematic quality of films . . . is not so much their truth to our experience of reality or even to reality in a general sense as their absorption in camera reality—visible physical existence."[29] So, what is "visible physical existence"? According to Kracauer's "material aesthetic," films have "an affinity . . . for the continuum of life or the 'flow of life,'" for "open-ended life."[30] This emphasis on "life as a powerful entity," with passing references to Nietzsche and Bergson,[31] echoes in his posthumous *History: The Last Things Before the Last*. Published in 1969, this book uses cinema as a model for defining the experiential specificity of history and often repeats or explicitly quotes passages from *Theory of Film*. As a philosopher of history who sets history apart from philosophy's certainties about "last things," Kracauer equates "historical reality" with "camera-reality" and "life-world": Historical reality is "full of intrinsic contingencies," "virtually endless" and "indeterminate as to meaning."[32] Camera-reality, which structurally parallels historical reality, "has all the earmarks of the *Lebenswelt*. It comprises inanimate objects, faces, crowds, people who intermingle, suffer and hope; its grand theme is life in its fullness."[33]

Is it all about life? Does Kracauer's realism turn into vitalism? Two recent approaches to his work by scholars indebted to feminism and Critical

Theory rather emphasize the role of death in *Theory of Film*. Miriam Bratu Hansen's introduction reconstructs the book's palimpsestic character, beginning with notes Kracauer had taken in Marseille while fleeing from the Nazis in 1940. "The desire for film to 'include the death's head beneath the face' . . . had presided over the Marseille project as an epigraph and a never realized final chapter, to be called, variably, 'Kermesse funèbre,' 'Danse macabre,' or 'The death's head.'"[34] After many revisions this chapter, renamed "The Redemption of Physical Reality," becomes part of the epilogue to *Theory of Film*, which contains passages like this: "We literally redeem the world from its dormant state, its state of virtual nonexistence, by endeavoring to experience it through the camera. And we are free to experience it because we are fragmentized."[35] So, instead of a continuum, fragmentation now appears to be a precondition for experience. Kracauer's deviation from his "life-flow" pathos appears less sudden if one reads it in connection with "The Mass Ornament": There, Kracauer saw the "abstractness" of life under capitalism as "ambivalent," harboring threats of rationalization becoming mythical, but also chances for emancipated experience.[36] The anticommunist climate in 1950s America probably contributed to Kracauer's replacing of the terms *mass, material,* and *capitalism* with *life, physical,* and *science:* In *Theory of Film,* science appears as ambivalent, "double-edged": "it alerts us to the world" but also "tends to remove that world from the field of vision."[37]

Kracauer's emphasis on being fragmentized also recalls the aesthetics of destruction in his Marseille notes from 1940: "The material elements that present themselves in film directly stimulate the *material layers* of the human being: his nerves, his senses, his entire *physiological* substance." The spectator's "'ego' . . . is subject to *permanent dissolution,* is incessantly exploded by material phenomena."[38] Some of this violent aesthetics of reception survives in *Theory of Film,* in passages on how films "cause a stir in deep bodily layers," provoke "organic tensions, nameless excitements"— and turn audiences into "dope addicts," "habitués who frequent [cinemas] out of an all but physiological urge."[39]

Gertrud Koch's analysis of Kracauer's work offers a taxonomy of strains of thought in *Theory of Film:* "a *sensualist* aesthetics," "an *existential ontology,*" "a redemptive figure based on an *aesthetics of reconciliation.*"[40] Kracauer's sensualism seems to turn existentialist in praising cinematic epiphanies experienced by the self-unconscious spectator: "Images begin to sound, and the sounds are again images. When this indeterminate murmur—the murmur of existence—reaches him, he may be nearest to the unattainable goal"[41] of exhausting what the film presents. Koch[42] quotes this passage and rightly calls it "misplaced enthusing" reminiscent of Heidegger. To her, it is important that the pathway to sheer existence, which Kracauer's sensualist "ethics of enjoyment" might open up to us, is blocked by the "crypto-theological core" of *Theory of Film*. In Koch's view, Kracauer's flow of life sweeps away "things and the dead"; film "arrests" that flow to redeem them in a kind of messianic intervention. In her reconstruction of Kracauer's redemptive realism, Koch emphasizes its aspects of Jewish messianic theology, especially the invocation of "redemption through memory" and "solidarity with the dead." This idea, reminiscent of Walter Benjamin's theses on the philosophy of history, echoes in Kracauer's comment on "fact-oriented" historiographies that insist that "nothing should go lost" as if they "breathed pity with the dead."[43] But here, Koch sees Kracauer's insistence on the "primacy of the visual" and on sensory concreteness confronting intrinsic theoretical limits: *Theory of Film* mentions the Nazi Holocaust only in passing (in the "Head of Medusa" section), because that book generally neglects the crisis of representation posed by a mass annihilation that is beyond images and imagination.[44]

A different recent approach is proposed by Heide Schlüpmann. She also (and more explicitly than Koch does in her remark on ethics of enjoyment thwarted by theology) opposes Kracauer's theory to ethics, but focuses on a proto-political notion of life rather than death and theology. Like Koch a German, critical, feminist cinema theorist, Schlüpmann has also written a book on Kracauer (of which chapters are available in translation). Kracauer's concepts appear frequently in her three-part cinema aesthetics. In the third part Schlüpmann sketches a reversal in the relationship of cinema and philosophy:[45] for decades, philosophy time and again gave conceptual shelter, sometimes condescendingly so, to cinema in its cultural worthlessness. Today it is more and more cinema that houses a question peculiar to, but abandoned by philosophy. The question is how to live, especially how to live inactively. The context for this problem is that today's neoliberal economy subsumes inactive life; capital's regime of valorization extends into spheres of life not yet subsumed by the former disciplines of factory and office. Schlüpmann uses Kracauer to point out cinema's separation from the success (hi)story of digital mediatization, in which the screens of labor and leisure are now the same. What is lost in this process is a utopian experience: cinema as an "impossible" site for a "morality" of life, alternative to bourgeois ethics of self-preservation and to neoliberal ethics of universal deregulated productivity (what Post-Operaist discourse calls the "social factory," the place of work now extending over the biopolitical entirety of social life in its whateverness). As early as 1987, Schlüpmann wrote about Kracauer's concept of cinematic self-encounters: "The moral task of the medium is no longer the symbolization of the ethical, but rather the mirroring of the enslaved, damaged quality of life."[46]

But maybe there is something ethical in Kracauer's theory—and also in philosophies close to or indebted to his work. The notion of ethics relevant here is, however, quite different from the ethics of individual self-preservation; we find its definition in Giorgio Agamben whose metapolitical philosophy, as we will see, relates to Kracauer, sometimes explicitly so.[47] Agamben calls "ethos" a manner of proper being that does not forget about the improper that engenders it: "The only ethical experience . . . is the experience of being (one's own) potentiality, of being (one's own) possibility—exposing, that is, in every form one's own amorphousness and in every act one's own inactuality."[48]

Embodying what makes us shapeless, inactual, inactive: There are similarities between this concept of Agamben's and Kracauer's realism, which is realism with a difference. While the realism of classical Hollywood film (and the theory celebrating its normalcy) uses reality as the playground of goal-oriented individuals, Kracauer's realism is about losing one's grip on the world. *Theory of Film* is an ethics of acknowledged powerlessness, which—in a manner comparable to contemporary writings of Bazin—praises Italian neorealism for its "found" rather than constructed stories. In Kracauer's *History*, we reencounter an ethos close to Agamben's idea of every act exposing the nonact: The subject of historical experience is marked by "active passivity" and "self-effacement." What this entails becomes clear in one of Kracauer's comparisons of realist history to filmmaking: Documentary realists like Joris Ivens practice "deliberate suspension of their . . . creative powers" to "produce the effect of impersonal authenticity."[49] Central to history and cinema is a surrender to unexpected life forms and improbable incidents encountered in the past and in physical reality. As Schlüpmann writes about *Theory of Film*: "The priority of physical reality has above all a negative meaning, that is, to negate the principle of self-assertion in the subject."[50]

It is instructive to turn to a review of *Theory of Film* by a German film and art theorist who, like Kracauer, had also emigrated to America, seeking refuge from National-Socialist persecution. In 1963, Rudolf Arnheim saw in Kracauer an aesthetic of "unshaped matter" and "melancholy surrender" to "concrete reality." This aesthetic, Arnheim argued, could point the way to new beginnings of thought—after taking us to the "nadir" of "the world before Creation, the attractive infinity and variety of chaos. It is the escape from the duty of man, the final refuge and the final refreshment."[51] In this perspective on Kracauer's work, reality is redeemed—from humanity: We (whoever that is) regain the world only by letting cinema help the world to get rid of us. To say it with Kracauer, "the world that is ours" is only found as "something we did not look for";[52] history and the cinema are both "means of alienation,"[53] but in their affinity to unshaped life, they "virtually make the world our home."[54]

Such a version of Kracauer matches well with Cavell's ontology of cinema's projecting the world to us and screening us out of it,[55] or with Sobchack's neophenomenology of "being-in-the-world" sensed through the medium of our "lived-bodies" in cinema. Most of all, *Theory of Film* (or let's say: a *Theory of Film* read along the lines of Arnheim's review) appears as a precursor to motifs in Deleuze's philosophy of film, especially the idea of film's reconstitution of the world as prehuman chaos and posthuman outside. To Deleuze, "the luminous plane of immanence, the plane of matter and its cosmic eddying of movement-images"[56] is the matrix, ever-present virtually, to classical film's rhythmicized sensations. In this way, cinema poses (and partly answers) the "question of attaining once more the world before man, before our own dawn."[57] Prehuman movement-in-itself echoes in the posthumanism of modern film's *time-image*: "The point is to discover and restore belief in the world, before or beyond words."[58] Nothing less than the building of "an ethic or a faith"[59] becomes the vocation of cinema, for which, without referring to Kracauer, Deleuze uses the latter's key term: "Redemption, art beyond knowledge, is also creation beyond information." This is reminiscent of Kracauer's invocations of film as a pathway to the murmur of existence and as a means to find the world through its alienation from us.

I suggest Jacques Rancière's politically inflected film aesthetics and the interpretation of Deleuze's film philosophy it contains as an approach, because much in it is valid also for Kracauer's film theory. To Rancière, Deleuze's dualism of classical and modern cinema amounts to a "restitution of world-images to themselves. It is a history of redemption."[60] It is as if the time-image came to the rescue and undid the appropriation of the movement-image by knowledge, human intention, authorial consciousness. Alternative to this, Rancière conceives of cinema dialectically, as an endless spiral: "Artistic activity must always be turned into passivity, find itself in that passivity, and be thwarted anew."[61] This corresponds to the core formula of Rancière's *Film Fables:* "To thwart its servitude, cinema must first thwart its mastery."[62] Are we close to an ethical Kracauer here? Are we close to passivity within activity; to cinema's openness to reality thwarting its formative mastery, thus granting us an ethical relationship to the world, mindful of our tenuous link with it? In fact, Rancièrian "self-thwarting" does *not* restore any cinematic affinities to a Bergsonian immanence of matter, to murmuring existence, to the world before words, redeemed and restituted. It is not the purity, but the impurity of cinema that counts. Rancière locates cinema's strength in a kind of self-abuse (which so many cinephiles deplore as a weakness): Cinema submits its unique potential, the material, sensorial, rhythmic chaos of images, to film industries with their representational orders of genre and storytelling; this submission, however, can in its turn be canceled at any time—and actually is at so many times in film history. This permanent self-thwarting, rather than any Romantic or vitalist utopia of perfect disorder, holds the key to cinema's political dimension. I propose to use Rancière's philosophy, in which the political is inherently aesthetic, as one guideline for tracing political—rather than ethical—aspects of Kracauer's theory of cinema, history, and mass culture. The other guideline is Adorno's 1965 intellectual portrait of his long-term friend Kracauer.

"The state of innocence would be the condition of needy objects, shabby, despised objects alienated from their purposes. For Kracauer they alone embody something that would be other than the universal functional complex, and his idea of philosophy would be to lure their indiscernible life from them."[63] Adorno sees Kracauer's realism, which focuses the *res*, the *thing*, and lacks "indignation about reification," as "curious";[64] the German word for this, *wunderlich*, also intimates "wonder" and "miracle." Kracauer's realism shows how we are among other things; it emphasizes how cinema makes actors appear as "object among objects,"[65] and how film resembles history in that they both "help us to think *through* things, not above them."[66] Starting out from this, Kracauer probes the degree to which the life of things can generate a politics of dissensus. In his 1930 essay on an outdated Berlin shopping arcade, Kracauer bids "Farewell to the Linden Arcade": "What would be the point of an arcade [*Passage*] in a society that is itself only a passageway?" Kracauer reads the "Lindenpassage" as an allegorical space-image of social exclusion: All kinds of shabby commodified objects exiled from respectable life "like gypsies," "banished to the inner Siberia of the arcade, . . . took revenge on the bourgeois idealism that oppressed them by playing off their defiled existence against" it. "By disavowing a form of existence to which it still belonged" the "passageway through the bourgeois world articulated a critique that every true passerby understood."[67]

Rather than Adorno's "state of innocence," what becomes paradigmatic is reified life's capacity to disavow the order it belongs to. Where do things belong? In *History: The Last Things Before the Last*, Kracauer criticizes philosophies of teleology or "present interest" because they treat "history as a success story [and] closed system" that "shuts out the lost causes, the unrealized possibilities."[68] To this he opposes his image of the historian (the subject of historical experience) as someone who is not "the son of his time. Actually he is the son of at least two times—his own and the time he is investigating."[69] Double belonging is a ruptured belonging to the present: This makes Kracauer's historian a critic of the present order, an archaeologist of possibilities marginalized in the past: "His present concerns are identical with a compassionate urge to uncover lost causes in history. He not only views the past in the light of the present but turns to the present from a primary involvement in the past."[70] Schlüpmann subscribes to Kracauer's notion of historicity as "being exterritorial in relation to the present,"[71] because it directs the attention of feminist archaeologies to lost histories of early cinema: a cinema that sheltered the "counter-publicizing" of private existences of women in patriarchy. Philosophical to the extent that it is a morality of nontriumphant life, cinema can preserve lost causes and becomes itself a cause lost to progress of digitization (the latter's ontology understood not in a cognitivist direction of experiential truth-claims but as a matter of capitalist subsumption of any-life-whatever in the formation of neoliberal, "control-societal" [Deleuze] media cultures).

A second objection raised by Adorno concerns Kracauer's "antisystematic tendency":[72] His thinking "binds itself to something contingent and glorifies it simply in order to avoid glorifying the great universal"[73]—"The utopian trait, afraid of its own name and concept, sneaks into the figure of the man who does not quite fit in."[74] One should not argue against such a charge of cowardliness not going all the way; Kracauer[75] freely admits to it: His 1922 essay "Those Who Wait" proposed an attitude of "hesitant openness"[76] toward modernity's ephemera; and in history, a conceptual "anteroom" or "waiting-room" crowded with "last things before the last"; "stopping midway may be ultimate wisdom."[77] To David Rodowick "this acknowledgment constitutes not the problem but the solution,"[78] because history and cinema as modes of "knowing" are to be valued exactly for "their resistance to closure and their elusiveness with respect to systematic thought."[79]

In Kracauer's notion of a "Utopia of the in-between," utopia is not an idea, but rather an aesthetic of what does not quite fit (in); cinema is its model.[80] Explaining the "nonhomogeneous structure"[81] of historical experience, Kracauer compares the problematic "traffic conditions" between the "micro" level of particular events and the "macro" level of explanatory narratives and generalizations to the relationship of close-up and long-shot in cinema.[82] Here, *History* quotes from and refers to passages on Griffith in *Theory of Film*. Where most film theories would see a paradigmatic case of the normalization of cinematic movement through continuity editing, invented, as it were, by filmmakers such as Griffith, Kracauer remarkably (and quite stubbornly) observes a "paradoxical relation" and "fissures."[83] To him, even conventional transitions between part and whole are not smooth; the close-ups Griffith inserts are at the same time part of the narrative flow and independent of it, even arrest it, not unlike Deleuze's "affection-images." The admirable nonsolution, which Kracauer attributes to Griffith, could be another name for his own refusal of conceptual integrity: Griffith "keeps apart what does not belong together."[84] Following a similar logic, Kracauer's intermediary area of history places things "side-by-side,"[85] rather than in subordinations or "either-or"[86] relations, by keeping them apart: Particulars are side by side with generalities, and Kracauer's anteroom filled with penultimate things is a zone of separation, between the "immediacy" of experience and the "timelessness" of philosophy.[87] Instead of film unalienated by story form, plunging us into a wild microphysics of particulars or an idyll of details, Kracauer ultimately votes for cinematic stories that are found or emergent; he favors togetherness in paratactical separation and provisional configurations to utopian purity.

Another criticism of Adorno's accuses Kracauer's antisystematics of opportunism: "The enthronement of a form of individual experience, however eccentric, that is comfortable with itself remains socially acceptable. However much it feels itself to be in opposition to society, the *principium individuationis* is society's own."[88] In this context, Adorno highlights the theoretical importance of Charlie Chaplin: "Kracauer projected his self-understanding of the individual onto Chaplin: Chaplin, he said, is a hole." The phrase is from Kracauer's 1926 review of *The Gold Rush* which under the simple title "Chaplin" contains what is probably Kracauer's shortest sentence: The tramp character "has lost his Ego": "In pathology, this would be called split of ego, schizophrenia. A hole [*Ein Loch*]. But out of the hole, the purely human radiates in disconnection."[89] In *Theory of Film*, Kracauer compares "the life force which [Chaplin] embodies" to "films on plant-growth."[90] Is this the self-assured individualism that Adorno sees in Kracauer? Or isn't there in Kracauer a "dividual" ontology in the sense of Deleuze and Guattari, complete with "schizo" and "becoming-plant"? Even stronger, however, is Kracauer's connection with Agamben's messianic ontology.

In *The Coming Community*, Agamben mentions "Siegfried Kracauer's observations on the 'girls'" as one of those texts that in the 1920s read in cinema's commodifications of bodies a prophecy. "The dances of the 'girls,'" anonymous and coordinated in abstraction, announce a "perfectly communicable" body, free from any foundations in identity or theology: "Neither generic nor individual . . . the body now became something truly *whatever*."[91] Agamben's reference is to Kracauer's "Mass Ornament" essay, which invokes a disorganized, dividual body: "The human figure enlisted in the mass ornament has begun the *exodus* from lush organic splendor and the constitution of individuality toward the realm of anonymity."[92] The mass ornament's promise might be to make Chaplins of all of us: "When the knowledge radiating from the basis of man dissolves the contours of visible natural form," that is also the moment, as Kracauer writes in another essay on Chaplin, "when those features which usually turn humans into individual humans are dropped."[93] In that moment "there remains in Chaplin the human being as such."[94]

Is there a political aspect to being neither generic nor individual? In Agamben, the politics of "whatever being" and belonging without preconditions is always yet to come, pointing toward utopias of perfect peace.[95] Life is categorically powerless: Agamben's ethics of humility displays "bare life" in every life-form, inactivity in every act. With Kracauer, it is also the other way around: he emphasizes moments of unexpected empowerment of the impotent: "Chaplin rules the world from below, as one who represents nothing at all."[96] Carrying on from Kracauer, Schlüpmann criticizes Agamben for leaving no room in his metaphysics of socially excluded life for a perspective in which the excluded might imagine themselves as something other than "bare life."[97] And she proposes a theory focusing the interruption.[98] For Schlüpmann, cinema is a multiple self-interruption or split, an outside externalized, an inside permeated by the excluded.[99] In cinema, we can perceive our belonging to society as something external, while that which capital excludes as superfluous, unproductive life is subjectivized in its images, spaces, durations. Yes, we hear the "murmur of existence" in cinema: it is the stranger next to us in the theater whose talking during the film recalls the contingency of our mass existence.

Using Rancière as a perspective, we can frame Kracauer's hole-thinking politically: "There are always holes in the wall for us to evade and the improbable to slip in."[100] Rather than last things—Utopia to achieve, a world to regain—politics presupposes only the fact that every social order is contingent, every power relation can be changed: subordination can at any time dissolve into the "side-by-side" relation that gives it no secure foundation. The holy is a hole: miracles can always happen. Political acts in this "dissensual" sense are local, provisional, improbable—but always possible; it is an unmotivated subjectivization of the anonymous and speechless, an interruption in the ethos of identity and belonging. Political being-together is a "being in-between," a "belonging twice over": belonging simultaneously to the world of well-defined social parts and to a world of nonparts that disrupt its order.[101] Kracauer gives many examples for the logic of "belonging twice over": the subject of historicity as a child of two times; the passageway—society as the hole in itself—which belongs only by disavowing what it belongs to; the song and dance numbers of film musicals that "form part of the intrigue and at the same time enhance with their glitter its decomposition."[102]

Adorno is wrong in calling Kracauer's thinking "successful adjustment," but he certainly picks the right quotations. Kracauer, he writes, "smuggled a manifesto for himself into his theory of film: 'All these characters seem to yield to powers that be and yet manage to outlast them.' "[103] The sentence is from one of Kracauer's comparisons of neorealist cinema to Chaplin.[104] On neorealism—and its inherent slapstick—Rancière and Kracauer perfectly agree: for the former, Rossellini's "falling bodies" manifest "the incomprehensible power that is the strength of the weak";[105] for the latter, "behind many nonsolutions" of neorealist films and old Chaplin comedies lies "a desire to exalt the power of resistance of the seeming weak."[106] Read politically rather than ethically, Kracauer's philosophy of nonsolution offers a concept of cinema as a mode of theorizing through self-thwarting and waiting that diagnoses how power emerges where no one expected it.

NOTES

This article is a revised and expanded version of Drehli Robnik, "Siegfried Kracauer," in *Film Theory and Philosophy: The Key Thinkers*, edited by Felicity Colman (London: Acumen, 2009).

1. Siegfried Kracauer, *Theory of Film: The Redemption of Physical Reality* (Princeton: Princeton University Press, 1960), li.

2. Heide Schlüpmann, "Phenomenology of Film: On Siegfried Kracauer's Writings of the 1920s," trans. Thomas Y. Levin, *New German Critique* 40 (1987): 97–114; here 107.

3. Kracauer, *The Mass Ornament: Weimar Essays*, trans. and ed. Thomas Y. Levin (Cambridge: Harvard University Press, 1995), 325.

4. Miriam Bratu Hansen, "The Mass Production of the Senses: Classical Cinema as Vernacular Modernism," in *Reinventing Film Studies*, ed. Christine Gledhill and Linda Williams (New York: Arnold, 2000), 332–50; here 342–43.

5. Ibid.

6. Kracauer, "Buster Keaton," review of *Steamboat Bill, Jr.*, by Charles Reisner, in *Kleine Schriften zum Film 1928–1931*, vol. 6.2 of *Werke*, ed. Inka Mülder-Bach (Frankfurt am Main: Suhrkamp, 2004), 148. My translation.

7. *The Mass Ornament*, 79.

8. Thomas Y. Levin, "Introduction," in *The Mass Ornament*, 17.

9. *The Mass Ornament*, 326–27.

10. Kracauer, *The Salaried Masses: Duty and Distraction in Weimar Germany*, trans. Q. Hoare (London: Verso, 1998), 94.

11. Kracauer, "On Photography," *The Mass Ornament*, 62–63.

12. Kracauer, *Kleine Schriften zum Film 1928–1931*, 195. My translation.

13. Kracauer, *From Caligari to Hitler: A Psychological History of the German Film* (Princeton: Princeton University Press, 2004), 279–80.

14. Ibid., 307.

15. Ibid., 272.

16. Cf. L. Quaresima, "Introduction," *From Caligari to Hitler*, xv–xlx.

17. Thomas Elsaesser, "Cinema—The Irresponsible Signifier or 'The Gamble with History': Film Theory or Cinema Theory," *New German Critique* 40 (1987): 65–89; here 84.

18. *From Caligari to Hitler*, 71–72.

19. Ibid., 8.

20. Ibid., 11.

21. *The Salaried Masses*, 81.

22. Ibid., 88.

23. Gertrud Koch, *Siegfried Kracauer: An Introduction*, trans. J. Gaines (Princeton: Princeton University Press, 2000), 79.

24. Kracauer, *From Caligari to Hitler*, 7.

25. Ibid., 9.

26. Ibid.

27. Cf. Elsaesser, "Cinema—The Irresponsible Signifier," 88; and "Zwischen Filmtheorie und Cultural Studies. Mit Kracauer (noch einmal) ins Kino," in *Idole des deutschen Films. Eine Galerie von Schlüsselfiguren*, ed. Thomas Koebner (Munich: text + kritik, 1997), 22–40; here 33–34.

28. *The Salaried Masses*, 32.

29. *Theory of Film*, 116.

30. Ibid., 71.

31. Ibid., 169.

32. Kracauer, *History: The Last Things Before the Last* (New York: Oxford University Press, 1969), 45.

33. Ibid., 58.

34. Miriam Bratu Hansen, "Introduction," *Theory of Film*, vii–xlv; here xxiv.

35. *Theory of Film*, 300.

36. "The Mass Ornament," 83.

37. *Theory of Film*, 299.

38. Quoted in Hansen, "Introduction," xxi.

39. *Theory of Film*, 158–59.

40. Koch, *Siegfried Kracauer*, 106.

41. *Theory of Film*, 165.

42. Koch, *Siegfried Kracauer*, 103, 106.

43. *History*, 136.

44. Koch, *Siegfried Kracauer*, 108–13.

45. Heide Schlüpmann, *Ungeheure Einbildungskraft: Die dunkle Moralität des Kinos* (Frankfurt am Main: Stroemfeld, 2007), 15–16, 291–93, 213.

46. Schlüpmann, "Phenomenology of Film: On Siegfried Kracauer's Writings of the 1920s," trans. T. Y. Levin, *New German Critique* 40 (1987): 97–114; here 102.

47. On the following points on the film aesthetics in contemporary political philosophies, see more extensively: Drehli Robnik, *Film ohne Grund: Filmtheorie, Postpolitik und Dissens bei Jacques Rancière* (Vienna: Turia+Kant, 2010).

48. Giorgio Agamben, *The Coming Community*, trans. M. Hardt (Minneapolis: University of Minnesota Press, 1993), 29–44.

49. *History*, 84, 90.

50. Schlüpmann, "The Subject of Survival: On Kracauer's *Theory of Film*," trans. J. Gaines, *New German Critique* 54 (1991): 111–26; here 123.

51. Rudolf Arnheim, "Melancholy Unshaped," *Journal of Aesthetics and Art Criticism* 21, no. 3 (1963): 291–97; here 296–97.

52. *Theory of Film*, 296.

53. *History*, 5.

54. *Theory of Film*, 304.

55. Stanley Cavell, *The World Viewed: Reflections on the Ontology of Film* (Cambridge: Harvard University Press, 1979).

56. Gilles Deleuze, *The Movement-Image. Cinema 1*, trans. H. Tomlinson and B. Habberjam (Minneapolis: University of Minnesota Press, 1986), 66.

57. Ibid., 68.

58. Deleuze, *The Time-Image. Cinema 2*, trans. H. Tomlinson and R. Galeta (Minneapolis: University of Minnesota Press, 1989), 172.

59. Ibid., 173.

60. Jacques Rancière, *Film Fables*, trans. E. Battista (Oxford: Berg, 2006), 111.

61. Ibid., 119.

62. Ibid., 11.

63. Theodor W. Adorno, "The Curious Realist," trans. Shierry Weber Nicholson, *New German Critique* 54 (1991): 159–77; here 177.

64. Ibid., 177.

65. *Theory of Film*, 45.

66. *History*, 192.

67. *The Mass Ornament*, 341–42.

68. *History*, 199.

69. Ibid., 93.

70. Ibid., 209.

71. Schlüpmann, "Re-reading Nietzsche through Kracauer: Towards a Feminist Perspective on Film History," trans. I. Flett, *Film History* 6 (1994): 80–93; here 84–85.

72. Adorno, "The Curious Realist: On Siegfried Kracauer," trans. Shierry Weber and T. Nicholsen, *New German Critique* 54 (1991): 159–77; here 161.

73. Ibid., 165.

74. Ibid., 176.

75. Cf. *The Mass Ornament*, 138; *History*, 213.

76. Kracauer, "Those Who Wait," in *The Mass Ornament*, 129–40; here 138.

77. *History*, 213.

78. D. N. Rodowick, *Reading the Figural, or, Philosophy after the New Media* (Durham: Duke University Press, 2001), 167.

79. Ibid.

80. *History*, 217, 125.

81. Ibid., 217.

82. Ibid., 125–27.

83. Ibid., 126.

84. *Theory of Film*, 231.

85. *History*, 200–206.

86. Ibid.

87. Rodowick, 169.

88. Adorno, "The Curious Realist," 164–65.

89. Kracauer, "Chaplin," review of *The Gold Rush*, by Charles Chaplin, in *Kleine Schriften zum Film 1921–1927*, vol. 6.1 of *Werke*, 269. My translation.

90. *Theory of Film*, 281.

91. Agamben, *The Coming Community*, 47–48.

92. "The Mass Ornament," 83.

93. Kracauer, *Kleine Schriften zum Film 1928–1931*, 493. My translation.

94. Ibid.

95. Agamben, *The Coming Community*, 83–87; *Homo Sacer: Sovereign Power and Bare Life*, trans. D. Heller-Roazen (Stanford: Stanford University Press, 1998), 180, 188.

96. Kracauer, *Kleine Schriften zum Film 1928–1931*, 493. My translation.

97. Cf. *Ungeheure Einbildungskraft*, 219.

98. Cf. Robnik, "Zur Unterbrechung. Politische Aspekte von Leben im Bruch der Ethik in Heide Schlüpmanns Kinotheorie," in *Unerhörte Erfahrung. Texte zum Kino. Festschrift für Heide Schlüpmann*, ed. Doris Kern and Sabine Nessel (Frankfurt am Main: Stroemfeld, 2008), 71–96.

99. Ibid., 253, 271–74.

100. *History*, 8.

101. Rancière, *Disagreement: Politics and Philosophy*, trans. J. Rose (Minneapolis: University of Minnesota Press, 1999), 137–39.

102. *Theory of Film*, 213.

103. "The Curious Realist," 173.

104. *Theory of Film*, 281.

105. *Film Fables*, 127.

106. *Theory of Film*, 270.

The Exile of Modernity

Kracauer's Figurations of the Stranger

Inka Mülder-Bach

In May 1942, one year after arriving in New York, Siegfried Kracauer published his first essay on film for an American audience under the title "Why France Liked Our Films." Finally having reached a more or less safe haven, Kracauer recalled the American films he had watched in France between 1933 and 1941 and answered the question posed in the title with two observations. On the one hand, while French movies notoriously focused on dialogue to the detriment of action, he noted that American films, keenly aware of the visual essence of the medium, zoomed in on all those material details of the visible world that Kracauer called "camera reality": moving vehicles, passersby, staircases, streets, as well as the speed, ephemerality, and contingency of traffic flows. On the other hand, American movies fascinated the French public because of the way they depicted different milieus, characters, plots, and, not least of all, by their satirical streak. In Kracauer's opinion, foreign viewers, at least those in France, perceived these moments as realistic representations of the American way of life. But would the impressions gathered in Europe by watching American films prove tenable in the United States? This question stands at the center of Kracauer's essay, and his answer is so peculiar that it merits extended quotation:

> There is only one short moment in which the European observer can judge the validity of the images of American life he had received in European theatres: the moment of his arrival in this country. As a newcomer, he is still entirely connected with the Old World and thus can compare his fresh impressions on American soil with the pictures in his mind. These first impressions are rather superficial; but unfortunately, the more he succeeds in deepening them, the more is he unable to ver-

ify those brought over from Europe. It is not so much that they become transformed into pale reminiscences as for quite another reason: the newcomer establishes himself in America, and soon his contacts with the customs of this country are too intimate to permit dispassioned reflections about American life. The whole perspective changes. He is involved in that life, and his reactions are no longer those of a spectator but of a participant. Their views can have no common denominator. Hence, a paradox arises: as soon as the former European acquires an opinion of American reality, he loses the possibility of using it to confirm or reject his old impressions. Probably many of them cannot be maintained here; but that says nothing against their validity in Europe.

To come back to that decisive moment—the marvelous first meeting with life in America. As we entered New York harbor, the strange feeling of having already seen all this began to grow upon me. Each new sight was an act of recognition. We passed such old acquaintances as the Statue of Liberty, Ellis Island and the skyline, which, however, in the vast sky looked smaller than I had imagined it from the pictures. Then the detective-inspectors came aboard, shouting "Take it easy!" and "Go ahead!", and afterwards the dock swarmed with reporters. To the passionate movie-goer it was like a dream: either he had been suddenly transplanted onto the screen or the screen itself had come into three-dimensional existence. Nor did the dream cease in New York, where other familiar types began to emerge from the crowd: the ice-cream man, the shoe-shine boy, the Salvation Army. All the things that had filled in the background of hundreds of American films proved to be true to life. The steps before the brown-stone houses were as real as the furnished rooms, the miraculous drug stores and the splendid lobbies of the apartment houses one had suspected in Europe as mere studio settings.

This was the start—a convincing proof of the realistic power with which Hollywood pictures transmit everyday American life to people abroad. Then followed the slow process of personal adjustment, and with it that change of perspective mentioned above. In due course, things came out which obviously had been overlooked in these films. In New York, for instance, films neither take notice of Broadway in the morning, nor do they picture the hundreds of cross-town streets that end in the empty sky. So far as I remember, there have been no shots either that bring out the various effects produced by high houses and skyscrapers to break up the monotony of the long avenues. Evidentially the same is true of the whole style of life. But it is no longer a European observer who is making these observations."[1]

This is the only passage in Kracauer's work in which the author publicly refers to his arrival in New York. In doing so, he links the answer to the question of whether the impressions gleaned by a European spectator from watching American movies are actually "realistic" to a unique situation: the moment of the first glance, the liminal moment of arrival. Before that moment, viewers lack the possibility of comparison because they have not yet obtained any images of the American reality; later, when that moment has passed, reality is no longer an image but turns into a lived experience—the person who is comparing is no longer a spectator or bystander but a participant. It is only in the initial moment, when an image previously seen on film first comes into view, that observers are able to compare—a comparison which in this case seems to confirm Kracauer's hypothesis of "realism." Not only approaching the city but also entering it provides the newcomer with a continuous déjà vu experience.

The déjà vu is based on images that every moviegoer knows. Again and again, films have depicted New York as a destination for immigrants and from the viewpoint of the newcomer. Kracauer was aware of this prototypical perspective as early as the 1920s. Thus, he introduced William K. Howard's *A Ship Comes In* (1928), a film about émigrés, with the headline "Neue Heimat" (New Home) in allusion to the movie's German distribution title. He praised Harold Lloyd's comedy *Speedy* (1928) for its "excellent shots of New York street life" and frequently referred to King Vidor's classic silent movie *The Crowd* (1928). In both of the latter two films the camera simulates the gaze and the movements of the newcomer as if it were immigrating itself. From afar, the skyline appears on the horizon. After gradually plunging into the city and its streets, camera distances decrease until a closeup focuses on a single point in an interior space. In the passage quoted above, Kracauer constructs his description in a similar vein: After starting out with a panoramic view of the Statue of Liberty, Ellis Island, and the New York skyline, he briefly visits the docks and then immerses himself into the city. By way of street figures, drugstores, and stairwells, he ends up inside apartment buildings. The reason for this parallel approach seems obvious: rather than comparing images, as Kracauer suggests, the newcomers experience their actual arrival in New York on the basis of media-generated reference points of camera views whose images they automatically re-project.

But Kracauer is aware of this pitfall. His report therefore also includes the perception of a divergence—concerning the size of the skyline—which marks the leeway of the comparison and keeps it open. By means of this

Fig. 1. *The Crowd* (USA 1928, dir. King Vidor).

comparison, Kracauer does not aim to test the realism of American movies vis-à-vis any actual reality. He is not interested in the relation between image and reality; rather, he sizes up two versions of, or two perspectives on, reality. On the one hand, there is the perspective that European viewers have gleaned from watching American movies. On the other hand, Kracauer presents the perspective of a European who arrives in the United States as an exile. The fact that these two perspectives are congruent does not mean that movies convey a view of reality that is independent of the observer and subsequently "realistic" in *that* sense. For reality looks different from the perspective of the participant than from that of the observer. Rather, Kracauer argues that movies convey to viewers abroad an image of reality that coincides with the image gleaned by the stranger *in* this reality. In other words, films assign viewers the position of the stranger.

In circuitous ways, Kracauer's report about his arrival in New York leads us to familiar territory. Long before he entered the country, America had become a *topos* for "the foreign land" (*Fremde*) par excellence—a foreign land to which, as Kracauer noted in his review of Kafka's novel *America* in 1927, one "had already emigrated" when one "moved into a hotel room or talked on the phone."[2] The arrival of the exile in New York marks a position that Kracauer had outlined since the 1920s and which informs his early writing both as a concept and a textual perspective.

Kracauer owed the title for the first description of this position to the philosopher Franz Rosenzweig who, criticizing Kracauer's increasing distance from movements of religious renewal in the aftermath of World War I, described Kracauer's atttitude as "waiting with folded arms, folded behind one's *back*."[3] Outlined by Kracauer in his programmatic essay "Those Who Wait" (*Die Wartenden*) in response to Rosenzweig's criticism, the figure of the "person who waits" is rooted in Jewish thought. Its branches, however, lead us to an intricate web of philosophical and sociological theories. While reviewing these theories, Kracauer laboriously modernized his own intellectual existence, thus bringing it on a par with contemporary ideas. The essay begins with the assertion that "those who wait" suffer from "their *exile* from the religious sphere."[4] Whereas the notion of exile echoes Georg Lukács' metaphor of "transcendental homelessness," the concept of the sphere alludes to Søren Kierkegaard's construction of "stages." In Kracauer's topological reading these "stages" encompass interspaces and liminal zones that could be used to situate "those who wait." His description of their position draws on Kierkegaard's understanding of man as a "middle being" between transcendence and immanence, between the unconditional and the conditional.[5] But the "tension" by which this position is marked does not extend from above to below, but from inside to outside, from the familiar to the foreign. "Expelled" from the religios sphere, "those who wait " resist the temptation of a seemingly safe haven of paled bliss and instead take refuge in the exile of disenchanted modernity as one would in a waiting room.

As a result, Kracauer's "person who waits" comes into view as successor to a figure that Georg Simmel in his *Sociology* defined as the "stranger." In contrast to the "wanderer," who "comes today and leaves tomorrow," Simmel's stranger is characterized as coming today and staying tomorrow without ever completely losing the "freedom of coming and going."[6] Kracauer's "person who waits" not only occupies the same structural position as Simmel's stranger—a position that Simmel defines as a paradoxical "synthesis of nearness and distance."[7] He also inherits, or is meant to inherit, the cognitive privilege that stems from this position. As a "fundamentally mobile person," the stranger comes into contact with every individual of the social group without being "organically connected" to anybody. According to Simmel, he can therefore view everything with a "specific attitude of 'objectivity.'"[8] This attitude is not synonymous with mere indifference or detachment. It is a positive behavior, which Kracauer describes rather vaguely as a "*hesitant openness.*"[9] But it is objective in that the stranger has eliminated "accidental dislocations and emphases whose individual and subjective differences would produce different images of the same object."[10]

Simmel's concept of "elimination" (*Ausschaltung*) anticipates the phenomenological *epoché*, which was another theoretical impulse for Kracauer's essay. As a process of reduction that deactivates "natural attitudes" (*natürliche Einstellungen*) in which subjects refer to an existent reality that they know as their environment, *epoché* has two aspects, which Husserl defines as the "disconnexion" (*Ausschaltung*) of the "positing act" of consciousness and the "bracketing" (*Einklammerung*) of the "modality of being" of objects.[11] Even in common parlance the concept of waiting implies a moment of suspension or pausing, an *epoché* as it were. In Kracauer's essay this epoché aims at suspending the affections and concepts that constitute—and thus limit and distort—the subject's attitude. In contrast to the phenomenologist, however, who turns into a disinterested spectator of his own conscious processes by eliminating natural attitudes, *epoché* constitutes "the person who waits" as an observer who tries to familiarize himself with the foreign world of modernity into which he has been thrown, even though it may never become a home.

By objecting to the culture of *lamento*, by hesitantly confirming modernity, and by speaking about distances in the affirmative, Kracauer's essay seems related to interwar attempts at living and orienting oneself that Helmut Lethen described as a behavioral training in the art of *Cool Conduct*. Just as the figures of the armored subject and the cold persona, around which this behavorial training revolves, Kracauer's essay centers on estrangement and the possibility of leading "a life in alienation."[12] Like Lethen's key witnesses—Helmut Plessner, Bertolt Brecht, Carl Schmitt, Ernst Jünger, Walter Benjamin—Kracauer responds to this strangeness by conceiving of a figure that is not rooted in anthropology, but rather is characterized by its habitus. We could even say that, in a stricter sense, Kracauer encourages a kind of *behavior:* for in contrast to the radical avant-garde that armors its subjects as agents in a hostile environment—"the armored human being wants to fight" (Plessner)—Kracauer refrains from equipping his "person who waits" with imaginary options for action. However, is not only this refusal—and the complementary absence of the phantasma of a permanent *agon*—that markedly differentiates Kracauer's stance from avant-garde programs, but also the doubling of the aspect of strangeness. In spite of the obvious counter-examples of Benjamin and Plessner, I know no other explanation for this difference than the Jewish trauma of "problematic membership."[13] After all, what is strange in Kracauer's essay is not only or even primarily the modern world. Rather, the notion of strangeness is linked to the exilic subject. The "person who waits" mirrors the drama of assimilation and it is precisely this aspect, I believe, where Kracauer's path diverges from the radical avant-garde. On the one hand, Kracauer seems to subscribe to an old-fashioned hermeneutic project. Instead of persisting as an armored subject in a foreign environment, he wants to make this environment his own as a stranger, familiarize himself with it, and, ultimately, adapt to it. This leads to the second point that sets him off from the radical avant-garde. What Kracauer did not foresee, and maybe even tried to exclude by generalizing the assimilation paradigm, is the translation, or rather, the perversion, inscribed in the radical avant-garde *agon-phantasma* as a latent danger or conscious/unconscious *telos*. It is the perverse transformation of a hermeneutic opposition of the foreign and familiar into a political opposition of enemy and friend and a racist opposition of one's own kind and another. A third difference to the radical avant-garde concerns the temporal relations involved in Kracauer's key metaphor of expulsion (*Vertriebensein*). Whoever imagines him- or herself as an exile cannot reach a place in the front lines. Unless this person lands on an uninhabited island, the exile always arrives after all the others, with a delay. Others who arrived before are there already. Kracauer did not try to catch up with or compensate for this delay, but instead attempted to take advantage of it. A final point may be added: As Lethen has shown, radical avant-garde concepts of cool conduct resorted to courtly forms of behavior. Kracauer also is an exception in regard to this historical orientation, not only because he wrote a treatise on the detective novel instead of the baroque tragedy, but also because he found his most powerful ally for aligning modernization and assimilation not in a prebourgeois code, but in the leading media of a postbourgeois public sphere, namely photography and film.

The question to what degree the phenomenological concepts of "attitude" (*Einstellung*), "disconnexion" (*Ausschaltung*), and "bracketing" (*Einklammerung*) are part of a contemporary media discourse cannot be discussed in this context. As far as Kracauer is concerned, there is no doubt that technological media were a catalyst for activating both his gaze and his writing. According to Kracauer, photography and film achieve an *epoché* by technological means. They bracket the positing of being and eliminate subjective attitudes that constitute the gaze. They therefore expose the subject to something that he or she would never be able to see on his or her own: a world in which he or she has not yet arrived. From the early essay on "Photography" (1927) to the late *Theory of Film* (1960) Marcel Proust serves as a key witness for these basic tenets of Kracauer's media theory. In a famous scene of his novel *Remembrance of Things Past*, Proust describes how the first-person narrator Marcel enters his grandmother's salon unannounced. For the short time span during which his presence goes unnoticed, Marcel registers his grandmother with an eye in which his own gaze is still absent. "The process that mechanically occurred in my eyes when I caught sight of my grandmother was indeed a photograph." This photograph shows Marcel his grandmother as he has never seen her before, as a "part of a new world," the foreign world of time." The photographic eye, an organ of pure receptivity which for the fraction of a second anticipates the regulative action of subjectivity, sees "sitting on a sofa [. . .] red-faced, heavy and common, sick, lost in thought, following the lines of a book with eyes that seemed hardly sane, a dejected old woman whom I did not know."[14] The stigmas of old age brought to light by Marcel's snapshot represent a time that Kracauer, following Proust and Bergson, defined as an "empty" and "flowing" time, a time that "passes without return."[15] No earlier storage technique and no earlier mode of representation was able to record this time and render it visible. It eludes memory that distills the meaning—the "history"—of an individual or collective life from the contingency or ephemerality of the physical in an unconscious, gradual process of condensation; and it eludes the semiotic systems of symbol and allegory in which physical reality—"nature," as Kracauer defined it in his early essays— serves to represent consciousness. Only photography brings to light the "unexamined foundation of nature."[16] For the first time in history, it gathers the "detritus" (*Abfall*) eliminated in the cultural process, the refuse of an empty time. It records an "inert world,"[17] a world of the dead (*Totenwelt*), which, once captured on film, can no longer pass way. From this moment onward, cultural work must integrate a ghostly world of the nondead into collective memory. This is the process that, for Kracauer, constitutes the mission of film. Both photography and film relate to a physical world devoid of meaning. But it is film alone that, by dislocating and condensing this refuse, can create a new, dreamlike language of things.

Kracauer was keenly aware that factories such as Ufa and Hollywood were interested in creating dreams of a different kind. That is why he engaged tirelessly and ever more acerbically in film criticism as social critique. Kracauer never really managed to clarify the relation between his phenomenological approach to film, which focused on the media's redemptive potentials and his social-psychological criticism based on culture industry's mass production. But it is obvious that for him the mass production of ideology does not vitiate the possibilities inherent in the medium. As the camera intervenes between consciousness and perception, forcing the eye to identify with its mechanical lens, the gaze of the spectator becomes dislocated and disembodied. For this specific effect, Kracauer coined the term "*Zerstreuung*,"[18] which in English is translated as "distraction." But the German term gains its full meaning only if we understand it as a literal translation of the word "diaspora." Films have diasporic effects: They disperse the attention, expel the spectators from the ruins of privacy and interiority, and drive them to a foreign land that Kracauer, under the impression of silent movies of the mid-1920s, recodes as a sphere of mere appearances, a meaningless spatial "side by side,"[19] a "mute outside of the world."[20]

That fact that film can conjure up this "mute exterior of the world" is for Kracauer no accident of the history of technology. Not every era could have been filmed, and not every reality lends itself to being photographed. Modernity, however, has acquired a physiognomy that can be technically reproduced, a "photographic face."[21] This not only means that film has produced icons such as the film diva who smiles from advertising pillars, neon signs, and magazines. Rather, the social and cultural processes of rationalization—the dissolution of social bonds, the disenchantment of traditional horizons of meaning, the fragmentization of space and time, deindividualization and massification—which, according to Kracauer's early essays, inform modernity, almost unnoticeably have helped produce a sphere specifically related to technical means of reproduction. Kracauer's calls this sphere "surface." As a public, visible, two-dimensional, marginal, discontinuous, and permeable sphere the surface is the natural ally of film. It offers an image to the eye, but it does not hold a mirror up to consciousness. Just as the movie image is created by a mechanical eye, the surface is constituted "without the disrupting interference of consciousness."[22]

In the famous opening paragraph of his 1927 essay "The Mass Ornament," Kracauer defines his own method of cultural critique as the analysis of "inconspicuous surface expressions"[23]. The analyst of the surface is exposed to effects similar to those of a spectator in the movies. He, too, is confronted with unconscious, nonsubjective, and disrupting views that position him as a stranger. It is, however, not in the programmatic essays of 1926–27 that Kracauer tests the possibilities of observation inherent in this position. Though his interpretation of the mass ornament as a rational, empty form of the cult is steeped in a certain ethnological vocabulary that questions the narrative of disenchantment, the historical-philosophical construction on which this interpretation is based mitigates the *chocs* of the surface. The *grand récit* of an incomplete and endangered Enlightenment situates the "inconspicuous [. . .] expressions" that the process of rationalizaton has brought to a surface in a history whose outcome may remain open, but whose driving forces are known.

Beyond the major essays, however, the *grand récit* begins to disintegrate as soon as it has been formulated. The texts that testify to this disintegration are as marginal and heterogeneous as the phenomena to which they are dedicated. In contrast to the historical-philosophical essays that would have been the pride of every literary journal and cultural-theoretical anthology of the 1920s, these dispersed *feuilleton*s are indelibly linked to the institution of the *Frankfurter Zeitung*. It is difficult to categorize their "themes" or "subjects." They zoom in on events, things, spaces, gestures, customs, encounters, and personalities. Irrespective of the "themes," Kracauers *feuilletons* share features that all refer to film as a medium.

Thus, all these texts address ephemeral phenomena such as a cigarette filter ("Das Papiermundstück"[24]), traffic lights ("Kleine Signale"[25]), the way a taxi driver greets members of the police force ("Chauffeure grüßen"[26]), or the fate of bathing suits ("Kampf gegen die Badehose"[27]), which, as Kracauer remarks, should be stripped for better reasons than antinudist ideology. These phenomena and events are sometimes visible in themselves; in other cases they are made visible either by enlargement until they peel off from their background or by a panoramic view that zooms in on the spatial or temporal periphery of an event on which all attention is focused. A few examples: With an ironic subtitle Kracauer makes sure to warn all the horse racing experts who are browsing through the pages of the *feuilleton* that his article "Trabrennen in Mariendorf" (Trotting Race in Mariendorf) is not about sports ("Kein Sportbericht").[28] And indeed, the observer does not observe the race, but rather its observers. The article "Zertrümmerte Fensterscheiben" (Broken Window Panes)[29] describes how the observer once again missed being at the historic frontlines, in this case a Nazi riot against Jewish storeowners in Leipziger Strasse. "The same happened as in earlier riots: I had come too late, I was not part of the scene. Riots never occur in the same place. I don't see the stones, but the shards. And nothing else remains for me to do than cover the event retrospectively, as a peace time reporter." From the shards, Kracauer assembles a *feuilleton* that resembles the smashed window panes. Just as the panes have turned into "negative cobwebs,"—"there is a small hole where the spider used to sit. Its threads have turned into gaps"—his impressions revolve around a vacuum. Seemingly at random, he picks up on a sign with the inscription "Beware," on glaziers who are busily fixing the windows, on policemen who are fiddling with telephones, and on police patrols that urge passersby who "want to stand around to stare at shards and splinters" to "go on, just as life does" and who, in doing so, just attract new pedestrians. In the end, the peace time reporter bids his farewell with the words, "I then went to Alexanderplatz, but nothing else happened. Unfortunately, a mishap can happen as soon as I am absent. I cannot be everywhere at the same time." What Kracauer brings into view through the different images of his *feuilletons* is the anonymous and scattered public sphere that, contradicting its very name, has become invisible under the magic cap of mass society. In the withheld report about the horse race, the public comes into focus through the sweeping view that zooms in on the spatial periphery of the event. In the peace reportage, the focus on the temporal margin of "afterwards" captures the public's reflection in the smashed window panes. And sometimes, like in a *feuilleton* in which Kracauer disguises himself as a sports reporter, even a marginal syntactic deviation brings the public to light. Instead of describing the mass phenomenon of sports, he devotes himself to the anonymous mass by making it move sportingly. "They sport" (*Sie sporten*) is the title of this text.[30]

Under the impression of the contemporary (silent) film medium Kracauer depicts the public sphere as a sphere of muteness. Once in a while, this sphere intensifies into a scream ("Schreie auf der Straße"[31]), and sometimes somebody says something or calls out loud ("Worte von der Straße," "Berliner Figuren"[32]). But these words and calls are only of interest insofar as they free themselves from their original communicative situation in order to coagulate as things. The fate of these things remains uncertain, since they are unable to generate a narrative. With the exception of a few articles, Kracauer's *feuilletons* do not have a narrative structure, not even when they explicitly foreground a chronological event ("1. Mai in Berlin"[33]) or a journey ("Ein paar Tage in Paris").[34] The inconspicuous phenomena that they decipher as visual signs and "surface statements" testify not to a historical process but to tremors in the public state of affairs, and the observer leaves it at that. Though he always gets close, he keeps an unbridgeable distance that enables him to see what is in front of everybody's eyes.

This attitude is laconically defined in the German subtitle to *The Salaried Masses:* "Aus dem neuesten Deutschland" (From the Latest Germany). Making his voice heard as if through airwaves, the observer takes on the role of the ethnologist who has set out on an "expedition," "which may be more of an adventure than any film trip to Africa:"[35] It is an expedition to an unknown interior territory, from where he reports as if he had discovered one of those "primitive tribes" at "whose habits [the] employees marvel in films."[36] The superlative of the adjective "latest" stokes the public's hunger for sensation that the raging reporters of the era were committed to increase. Yet the sensation that Kracauer has to offer is nothing but the daily life of a social class that, in the latest Germany of Berlin, has become the defining force of public life without being noticed. Kracauer compares this life to the purloined letter in Edgar Allen Poe's eponymous short story, which is protected from discovery by its very publicity. For one moment, the persona of the ethnologist merges with the figure of the detective who is a remote cousin of the stranger. In contrast to the classical detective figure, however, Kracauer is not concerned with solving the case. Rather, he exposes it as the case of a secret public that has remained a public secret because both the intellectual class and the authorities in charge have failed to acknowledge it. The concepts of contemporary sociology are too schematic and lag behind new socioeconomic realities. Politicians offer solutions even before they have made a diagnosis, and the avant-garde is notoriously blind to the putative *hinterland* in which frontlines and demarcations become blurred and tangled up.

If contemporary film production had been as Kracauer repeatedly urged it to be, it would have intervened at this very point. Yet instead of reporting from unknown interior territories, filmmakers produced movies set in exotic locales such as Africa, if not on the moon. Movies such as *Am Rande der Sahara* (1930), *Simba, der König der Tiere* (1928), or Fritz Lang's *The Woman in the Moon* (1929) are a few cases in point.[37] Kracauer's initial focus on the salaried masses as an audience for exotic films is therefore more than an ironic arabesque. Instead of simply reversing the gaze, he looks at both the audience and the film, thus not only making the public visible, but also revealing what they do not see—themselves. It is not only the simulation of the position of the stranger that turns Kracauer's sociological expedition into a cinematographic enterprise, but also the mimesis of a cinematographic process of dissolves and montage. While the programmatic essays of the mid-1920s announced the author's intention to decipher surface phenomena as a reflection of the historical-philosophical fundamental substance of an epoch,"[38] in his study on *The Salaried Masses* (1930) he comes to question both the notion of a "fundamental substance" and the idea of a unified "epoch." Abstract concepts und preconceived theories lose their hierarchically privileged position. They migrate to the surface, as it were, to become manifest in a construction that Kracauer, alluding to the technique of montage, defined as a "mosaic."[39] This mosaic assembles the shards from which the *feuilleton* writer gleaned his information and mounts them into an "image"[40] that exhibits its own cuts and sutures. In contrast to the mechanical shot of the photo camera, this image holds a mirror up to consciousness. Yet the reflection is obscured and fragmented because the mirror has burst.

In *The Salaried Masses* and the *feuilletons* written in the last years of the Weimar republic, during Kracauer's tenure in Berlin, the ethnologist of unknown territories of the interior returned from his expeditions with an increasing skepticism regarding the radical leftist intelligentsia whose protest is "roused only by extreme cases [. . .] without appreciating the imperceptible dreadfulness of normal existence. It is driven to the gesture of revolt not by the construction of this existence itself, but solely by its visible emissions. Thus it does not really impinge on the core of given conditions, but confines itself to the symptoms."[41] The fact that after 1930 Kracauer was clearer and more farsighted in his analyses than his politically more radical and theoretically more ambitioned friends is closely related to the social distance and the temporal gap inscribed in his position as an observer. This spatio-temporal displacement enabled him to move from a macro to a micro level and register transformations and tremors that did not even show on their seismographs. Other European countries also experienced increasing class conflicts, unemployment, anti-Semitism, and street riots. But in Kracauer's assessment, these countries did not experience a similarly disastrous weakening of what he—with regard to France—occasionally called "society": a sphere of civility whose traditional web of behavioral patterns, values, and communication forms asserted itself relatively independently of politics and economics and acted as a protective buffer. This buffer prevented political antagonisms, economic crises, and cultural turnarounds from penetrating daily life unfiltered. One example for the breakdown of the sphere of civility that Kracauer cites in *The*

Salaried Masses is a letter, preserved in shorthand and stamped "sent," by a 19-year-old female office worker. In this letter, the woman tries to communicate with a pen pal ("Dear Young Colleague") "in reference to" premarital sex. She ends the letter by saying, in officialese, "Deinen weiteren Zeilen sehe ich gern entgegen" ("I look forward to your next communication").[42] Neither the leftist avant-garde nor contemporary sociology were able to conceptualize the level on which this letter becomes a statement. Kracauer, however, is able to construct this level without a concept by not interpreting the letter as a sign for something else, but letting it speak for itself.

As playful and ironic as the identification with the stranger may seem in *The Salaried Masses*—as an affirmation of features ascribed to the Jewish community by anti-Judaists and anti-Semites since time immemorial—it was not without perils. Kracauer must have developed an almost somatic sense for threat very early on in his life. In 1918 he noted in his diary, "I recently dreamt that I had to emigrate. I was expelled to a far away, foreign land." Kracauer's city and street texts from the 1920s are marked by panic-stricken scenarios that disrupt the imaginative digressions and escapes of the *flaneur* and signal a return of the repressed. They feature closed geometric spraces, an exactly outlined square, or a cul-de-sac straight as an arrow, in which the "captured person" knows himself to be exposed to mute observers, and encounters an *imago* of his own future: a man in a cheap hotel who sits motionlessly on a chair, his head resting in his hands, an open, half-packed suitcase at his feet.[43] The future index of this *imago* is uncanny, but is has nothing to do with clairvoyance. The *feuilleton* that includes this scene was published in 1930. A few months previously, the *Deutsche Handelswacht*, the mouthpiece of the biggest association of salaried employees, had published a review of *The Salaried Masses* in which Ernst Niekisch threatened Kracauer publicly. He called for the Jewish "stranger" to be "expelled, chased away, exterminated"[44] if he dared step beyond the limits assigned to him.

When Nazi Germany started to put these threats into practice word for word, Kracauer escaped from Berlin to Paris, and subsequently to Marseille. In the end, he arrived in New York on one of the last boats leaving Lisbon in April 1941. Against the background of his earlier notion of the exilic subject, his description of his arrival in New York, quoted at the beginning of this article, reads like a homecoming. Yet the stories written by the twentieth century seldom had a happy ending. Even after 1933 Kracauer tried to save the cognitive space opened by the threshold between inside and outside, interior and exterior, belonging and not-belonging. But the trauma of exile and genocide turned the exterior into an unsettling entity. According to the surface phenomenology of the 1920s, two aspects of this exterior placed the observer in the position of a stranger: its detached and porous texture and the unconscious, nonsubjective mode of visibility. This porous texture returns both in Kracauer's late *Theory of Film* (1960) and in his posthumously published *History: The Last Things before The Last* (1969). According to Kracauer, it creates a structural analogy between the world of film and the world of the historiographer. Both camera reality and historical reality are governed by the mode of randomness, both are instable, incoherent, nonhomogenous, discontinuous, and potentially endless worlds in which things are "surrounded by a fringe of indistinct, multiple meanings."[45] Kracauer emphasizes the analogy, yet he does not succeed in making the two realities converge. As a final figuration of the stranger, the historian is situated in the "no-man's-land" of "exterritoriality":[46] "His mind is in a measure unlocalizable; it perambulates without a fixed abode."[47] But even though the historian is constantly on the move, he does not capture a single image. The dimension of visibility has vanished, and there is a reason for that. "There are always holes in the wall for us to evade and the improbable to slip in,"[48] Kracauer writes in the introduction, and this statement can be read as a motto. What returns in his last, purely imaginative expedition to a *terra incognita* of modernity is his own survival. The absence—or repression—of the image, however, points to his *Theory of Film*, in which Kracauer indelibly linked the image to an extermination that turns even survival into a trauma.

According to the central argument of this book, film redeems physical reality and the "flow of life" that indiscriminately washes away living things, lifeless matter, and the dead by capturing this reality in images that subjects would never be able to see on their own because the subjective gaze has always already shaped physical reality. In the 1920s, Kracauer had designed his own position as a stranger as just such a camera-eye, training himself to observe the foreign world according to its laws. In the book on *History*, this observer no longer finds a counterpart, but only encounters himself. For in his *Theory of Film* the elaboration of the stranger's view had reached a limit which Kracauer confronted in the epilogue to this book as "The Head of Medusa": the physical reality of murdered European Jews would petrify us if we encountered it in real life. It is only in the mirror of Athena's shield, in the mirror of images captured by the camera eye, that we can see the head of the Medusa, the "litter of tortured human bodies."[49] Kracauer must have been aware of the objections to such a stance. He must have known that the redemption of the dead reaches its limits where mass extermination leaves behind only ashes. Yet, Kracauer insists: not in spite of, but precisely because of the fact that the camera records images of horror by technological means, because it catches the reflection of the world in the nonsubjective mirror of its media-generated protective screen, it becomes the only eyewitness. In contrast to the mythical mirror images, which are a means to an end—confronting the head of Medusa in Athena's shield enables Perseus to decapitate it—the "mirror reflections of horror" on film are "an end in themselves." They do not offer evidence for anything else nor do they call for action. Physical reality can be redeemed only when collective memory absorbs the images for their own sake.

NOTES

Translated by Karin Hanta and Gerd Gemünden

1. "Why France Liked Our Films," *National Board of Review Magazine* 17, no. 5 (May 1942): 15–19.

2. Kracauer, "Amerika," in Kracauer, *Werke*, ed. Inka Mülder-Bach and Ingrid Belke, vol. 5. 2, ed. Inka Mülder-Bach (Frankfurt am Main: Suhrkamp, 2011), 104. Unless indicated otherwise, all translations are my own, KH.

3. Franz Rosenzweig, Letter to Kracauer dated 12 December 1921 (Kracauer Estate, Deutsches Literaturarchiv). Quoted in: *Marbacher Magazin* 47/1988: *Siegfried Kracauer 1889–1966*, ed. Ingrid Belke and Irina Renz (Marbach: Deutsche Schillergesellschaft 1989), 36.

4. Kracauer, "Those Who Wait," in *The Mass Ornament: Weimar Essays*, trans. and ed. Thomas Y. Levin (Cambridge: Harvard University Press, 1995), 129–40; here 130.

5. Kracauer, *Der Detektiv-Roman*, in *Werke*, vol. 1, ed. Inka Mülder-Bach (Frankfurt am Main: Suhrkamp, 2006), 109.

6. Georg Simmel, *The Sociology of Georg Simmel*, trans. and ed. Kurt H. Wolff (Glencoe, IL: Free Press, 1950), 402ff.

7. Simmel, 403.

8. Simmel, 403.

9. Kracauer, "Those Who Wait," 138

10. Simmel, 403.

11. Edmund Husserl, *Ideas: General Introduction to Pure Phenomenology*, first book, trans. W.R. Boyce Gibson (New York: Macmillan, 1931), 107–8.

12. Helmut Lethen, *Cool Conduct: The Culture of Distance in Weimar Germany*, trans. Don Reneau (Berkeley: University of California Press, 2002), XI.

13. Theodor W. Adorno, "The Curious Realist: On Siegfried Kracauer," in

Notes on Literature, vol. 2, ed. Rolf Tiedemann, trans. Shierry Weber Nicholsen (New York: Columbia University Press, 1991), 58–75; here 67.

14. Kracauer, *Theory of Film: The Redemption of Physical Reality* (New York: Oxford University Press, 1960), 14.

15. Kracauer, "On Photography," in *The Mass Ornament*, 47–63; here 49.

16. Kracauer, "On Photography," in *The Mass Ornament*, 63.

17. Kracauer, "On Photography," in *The Mass Ornament*, 62.

18. See Kracauer, "Cult of Distraction," in *The Mass Ornament*, 323–28.

19. Kracauer, "Ein Film," in *Werke*, vol. 6.1, ed. Inka Mülder-Bach, 57.

20. Kracauer, "Der Mythos im Großfilm," in *Werke*, vol. 6.1, 72.

21. Kracauer, "On Photography," in *The Mass Ornament*, 59.

22. Kracauer, "Über Arbeitsnachweise," in *Werke*, vol. 5.3, 250.

23. Kracauer, "The Mass Ornament," in *The Mass Ornament*, 75–86; here 75.

24. Kracauer, *Werke*, vol. 5.3, 392–93.

25. Kracauer, *Werke*, vol. 5.3, 346–48.

26. Kracauer, *Werke*, vol. 5.2, 462–64.

27. Kracauer, *Werke*, vol. 5.3, 473–77.

28. Kracauer, *Werke*, vol. 5.3, 275–78.

29. Kracauer, *Werke*, vol. 5.3, 348–50; all following quotes ibid.

30. Kracauer, *Werke*, vol. 5.2, 524–29.

31. Kracauer, *Werke*, vol. 5.3, 279–81.

32. Kracauer, *Werke*, vol. 5.3, 271–74 and 582–85.

33. Kracauer, *Werke*, vol. 5.3, 222–26.

34. Kracauer, *Werke*, vol. 5.3, 477–83.

35. Kracauer, *The Salaried Masses: Duty and Distraction in Weimar Germany*, trans. Quintin Hoare (New York: Verso, 1989), 32.

36. Kracauer, *The Salaried Masses*, 29.

37. See Kracauer, *Werke*, vol. 6.2, 236–39 ("Lonesome") and 251–54 ("Exotische Filme").

38. Kracauer, "The Mass Ornament," 75.

39. Kracauer, *The Salaried Masses*, 32.

40. Kracauer, *The Salaried Masses*, 32.

41. Kracauer, *The Salaried Masses*, 101.

42. Kracauer, *The Salaried Masses*, 72.

43. See Kracauer, "Erinnerung an eine Pariser Straße," in: *Werke*, vol. 5.3, 358–64.

44. Ernst Niekisch, "Ein Kracauer auf Entdeckungsreisen," *Deutsche Handelswacht* 37 (1930), nos. 2, 27f.

45. Kracauer, *History: The Last Things Before the Last* (New York: Oxford University Press, 1969), 59.

46. Kracauer, *History*, 83.

47. Kracauer, *History*, 93.

48. Kracauer, *History*, 8.

49. See Kracauer, *Theory of Film*, 306. All following quotes ibid.

Contributors

Kerstin Barndt is Associate Professor for German Studies and affiliated faculty member of the Museum Studies Program at the University of Michigan. She is the author of *Sentiment and Sobriety: The Novel of the New Woman in the Weimar Republic* (2004) and the coeditor of *Weimar Subjects/Weimar Publics: Rethinking the Political Culture of Germany in the 1920s* (2010). Currently, she is completing a book-length study on the representation of temporality in conteomporary museum culture, entitled *Non/Synchronicities. Exhibiting Time and History in Contemporary Germany.*

Sabine Biebl received her MA and PhD from the Ludwig Maximilians University at Munich, Germany, where she currently holds a position as Lecturer in German Literature. She has been a research associate for the new edition of Siegfried Kracauer's *Werke* and will be the editor of its forthcoming volume *Von Caligari zu Hitler.* With Verena Mund and Heide Volkening she edited *Working Girls: Zur Ökonomie von Liebe und Arbeit* (2007). Her PhD thesis on the white-collar workers as a cultural phenomenon in Weimar Germany is entitled "Betriebsgeräusch Normalität: Angestelltendiskurs und Gesellschaft um 1930" and will be published by Kulturverlag Kadmos (Berlin) in 2012.

Gerd Gemünden is the Sherman Fairchild Professor in the Humanities at Dartmouth College, where he teaches in the Department of German Studies, Film and Media Studies, and Comparative Literature. He is the author of *Framed Visions: Popular Culture, Americanization, and the Contemporary German and Austrian Imagination* (1998) and *A Foreign Affair: Billy Wilder's American Films* (2008). His volumes as editor include *Wim Wenders: Einstellungen* (1993); *The Cinema of Wim Wenders* (1997); *Germans and Indians: Fantasies, Encounters, Projections* (2002); and *Dietrich Icon* (2007); as well as special issues of *New German Critique* on the director Rainer Werner Fassbinder and on "Film and Exile." He is currently completing a study of German exile cinema in Hollywood, 1933–50.

Christina Gerhardt is Assistant Professor of German at the Universitiy of Hawai'i at Manoa. She is editor of "Adorno and Ethics," a special issue of *New German Critique* (2006), which was nominated by the Council of Editors of Literary Journals (CELJ) for the "2006 Best Special Issue" award. In addition to the introduction to and an article on "The Ethics of Animals in Adorno and Kafka" in this volume, her publications on critical theory include "Thinking With: Animals in Schopenhauer, Horkheimer and Adorno," in *Critical Theory and Animal Liberation* (2010), and the entries in Adorno in the *Johns Hopkins Guide to Literary Theory and Criticism* (2004) and on the Frankfurt School, on Adorno, and on Lukács in *The International Encyclopedia of Revolution and Protest, 1500 to the Present* (2009).

Miriam Bratu Hansen (1949–2011) was Ferdinand Schevill Distinguished Service Professor in the Humanities at the University of Chicago, where she taught in the Department of English and the Committee on Cinema and Media Studies (of which she was founding chair). She was a coeditor of *New German Critique*. Her publications include a book on Ezra Pound's early poetics (1979) and *Babel and Babylon: Spectatorship in American Silent Film* (1991), as well as numerous articles in film history and film theory, focusing on questions of film aesthetics, cinema experience, media culture, and the public sphere. Her final book is *Cinema and Experience: Siegfried Kracauer, Walter Benjamin, and Theodor W. Adorno* (Berkeley: University of California Press, 2011).

Andreas Huyssen is the Villard Professor of German and Comparative Literature at Columbia University. He was founding director of Columbia's Institute for Comparative Literature and Society (1998–2003) and one of the founding editors of *New German Critique* (since 1974). His books include *Drama des Sturm und Drang* (1980), *After the Great Divide: Modernism, Mass Culture, Postmodernism* (1986), *Postmoderne: Zeichen eines kulturellen Wandels* (coeditor with Klaus Scherpe, 1986), *Modernity and the Text: Revisions of German Modernism* (coeditor with David Bathrick, 1989), *Twilight Memories: Marking Time in a Culture of Amnesia* (1995), and *Present Pasts: Urban Palimpsests and the Politics of Memory* (2003). Most recently, he is editor of *Other Cities, Other Worlds: Urban Imaginaries in a Globalizing Age* (2008). His work has been translated into many languages worldwide.

Noah Isenberg is Director of Screen Studies at Eugene Lang College, where he teaches literature, film, and intellectual history, and holds a joint appointment at the New School for Social Research. He is the author, most recently, of *Detour* (2008) and the editor of *Weimar Cinema: An Essential Guide to Classic Films of the Era* (2009). His full-scale critical biography of Austrian émigré filmmaker Edgar G. Ulmer is forthcoming from the University of California Press. The recipient of grants and fellowship support from the National Endowment for the Humanities, Fulbright, the International Research Center for Cultural Studies in Vienna, and the Alexander von Humboldt Foundation, his writing has appeared in such periodicals as *Vertigo, Film Quarterly, Cinema Journal, New German Critique, Raritan, Threepenny Review, Bookforum, The Nation*, the *Times Literary Supplement*, and the *New York Times*.

Lutz Koepnick is Professor of German, Film, and Media Studies at Washington University in St. Louis. He has written widely on German film, visual culture, and literature, on media arts and aesthetics, and on critical theory and cultural politics. Book publications include *Framing Attention: Windows on Modern German Culture* (2007); *The Dark Mirror: German Cinema between Hitler and Hollywood* (2002); *Walter Benjamin and the Aesthetics of Power* (1999); *Nothungs Modernität: Wagners Ring und die Poesie der Politik im neunzehnten Jahrhundert* (1994). Coedited or coauthored volumes include *Window | Interface* (2007); *The Cosmopolitan Screen: German Cinema and the Global Imaginary, 1945 to the Present* (2007); *Caught by Politics: Hitler Exiles and American Visual Culture* (2007); and *Sound Matters: Essays on the Acoustics of German Culture* (2004).

Inka Mülder-Bach is Professor of German and Comparative Literature at the University of Munich. She is the author of *Im Zeichen Pygmalions: Das Modell der Statue und die Entdeckung der "Darstellung" im 18. Jahrhundert* (1998) and *Siegfried Kracauer: Grenzgänger zwischen Theorie und Literatur. Seine frühen Schriften 1913–1933* (1985), and she is editor of *Am Anfang war. . . .* (2008); *Räume der Romantik* (2007); *Wiederholen: Literarische Funktionen und Verfahren* (2005); *Modernität und Trauma: Beiträge zum Zeitenbruch des Ersten Weltkrieges* (2000). She is also coeditor of the journal *Poetica*. With Ingrid Belke she is currently editing the complete writings of Siegfried Kracauer for Suhrkamp Verlag, to be completed in 2012.

Elizabeth Otto is Assistant Professor of modern and contemporary art in the Department of Visual Studies at the University at Buffalo, State University of New York. She is the author of *Tempo, Tempo! The Bauhaus Photomontages of Marianne Brandt* (2005), which accompanied the exhibition of the same name shown at the Bauhaus-Archiv Berlin, Harvard's Busch-

Reisinger Museum, and the International Center for Photography in New York. She is coeditor with Vanessa Rocco of *The New Woman International: Representations in Photography and Film from the 1870s through the 1960s* (2011). The recipient of fellowships from the Alexander von Humboldt Foundation, the American Association of University Women, the Deutscher Akademischer Austausch Dienst, and the University of Pittsburgh's Humanities Center, she is currently working on a book on gender, the body, and occult spirituality at the Bauhaus.

Eric Rentschler is the Arthur Kingsley Porter Professor of Germanic Languages and Literatures at Harvard University where he chairs the German Department and is a member of the Committee on Film and Visual Studies. His books include *West German Film in the Course of Time* (1984) and *The Ministry of Illusion* (1996). He is also the editor of *German Film and Literature* (1986), *West German Filmmakers on Film* (1988), *Augenzeugen* (1988; second updated edition 2001, with Hans Helmut Prinzler), and *The Films of G. W. Pabst* (1990). Presently he is completing a book project, "Haunted by Hitler: The Return of the Nazi Undead" (to be published by Harvard University Press), and working on a manuscript entitled "Courses in Time: Film in the Federal Republic of Germany, 1962–1989" (to be published by Columbia University Press).

Theodore F. Rippey is Associate Professor of German at Bowling Green State University. He has published on Weimar and exile film, literature, and culture in such venues as *Cinema Journal, Monatshefte,* and *German Studies Review.* His work on Kracauer and hearing reflects a broader interest in corporality and the senses in the interwar era. The problem of reading sound is a central concern in his book (in progress), which carries the working title "The Anxious Ear: Aural Experience and German Modernity."

Drehli Robnik is a Vienna-based film scholar. He received his PhD from the University of Amsterdam and has taught at the University of Vienna; Masaryk University in Brno; and the Johann Wolfgang Goethe University in Frankfurt am Main. He has researched and published on the theory and aesthetics of cinema, especially on film/politics/history, National Socialism and World War II in the cinema, horror film, and Siegfried Kracauer. He occasionally works as disc jockey and edutainer. He is the author of *Film ohne Grund: Filmtheorie, Postpolitik und Dissens bei Jacques Rancière* (2010) and *Geschichtsästhetik und Affektpolitik: Stauffenberg und der 20. Juli im Film 1948–2008* (2009), and editor (together with Thomas Hübel and Siegfried

Mattl) of *Das Streit-Bild: Film, Geschichte und Politik bei Jacques Rancière* (2010).

Christian Rogowski is Professor of German and Chair of the German Department at Amherst College. He is the author of two books and several articles on Austrian author Robert Musil, as well as a multimedia CD-ROM for teaching German Cultural Studies. He has published articles on, among others, Hugo von Hofmannsthal, Ingeborg Bachmann, Heiner Müller, Wim Wenders, Thomas Brasch, Siegfried Kracauer, popular genre films in Weimar Cinema, the Medea myth, German Studies in the United States, and colonial propaganda in the Weimar Republic. His current research interests include German film history, the legacy of German colonialism, and issues of racial difference in the culture of the Weimar Republic. He is the editor of a volume on lesser-known films of the Weimar period, entitled *The Many Faces of Weimar Cinema* (2010).

Heide Schlüpmann is Professor Emerita of Film Studies at Frankfurt University. During the 1980s, she was a pivotal member of the group that edited the magazine *Frauen und Film* and continues on its editorial board. Together with Karola Gramann, she founded the "Kinothek Asta Nielsen" in 2000, a living archive especially engaged in curating film history. Books include *Friedrich Nietzsches ästhetische Opposition* (1976); *Unheimlichkeit des Blicks: Das Drama des frühen deutschen Kinos* (1990; English translation: *The Uncanny Gaze: The Drama of Early German Cinema*, trans. Inga Pollmann, foreword Miriam Hansen (Illinois University Press, 2010); *Ein Detektiv des Kinos: Studien zu Siegfried Kracauers Filmtheorie* (1998); and *Ungeheure Einbildungskraft: Die dunkle Moralität des Kinos* (2007).

Johannes von Moltke is an Associate Professor of German Studies and Screen Arts & Cultures at the University of Michigan. He is the author of *No Place Like Home: Locations of Heimat in German Cinema* (2005), serves as editor of the *Germanic Review: Literature, Culture, Theory*, and coedits the *Screen Cultures: German Film and the Visual* series at Camden House with Gerd Gemünden. He has written extensively on German film, popular culture, and critical theory; his work has appeared in *Screen, Cinema Journal, New German Critique*, and *German Studies Review*, among others. He is the editor (with Kristy Rauson) of *Siegfried Kracauer's American Writings: Essays on Film and Popular Culture* (University of California Press, forthcoming 2012), and is completing a manuscript entitled *Manhattan Transfer: Siegfried Kracauer, Critical Theory, and the New York Intellectuals*.

Claire Zimmerman is a member of the faculty in the Department of the History of Art and in the Architecture Program at the University of Michigan. Her coedited essay collection, *Neo-avant-garde and Postmodern: Postwar Architecture in Britain and Beyond* (with Mark Crinson) appeared as volume 21 in the Yale Studies in British Art (Yale University Press) in Fall 2010; an earlier monograph, *Ludwig Mies van der Rohe*, was published by Taschen in 2006. Zimmerman's recent work has appeared in *OASE, AA Files, Perspecta*, the *Journal of Architecture*, and *Harvard Design Magazine*.

Index